ENTERPRISE AND HUMAN RESOURCE DEVELOPMENT

Robert J. Bennett After taking his BA and PhD at the University of Cambridge, he has held appointments at University College, London and the University of Cambridge. Since 1985 he has been Professor of Geography at the London School of Economics. He has been a visiting professor at the Universities of California, Berkeley, Vienna, and Macquarie (Australia), and has been a frequent Guest Scholar at the Brookings Institution, Washington DC.

He has written extensively on the public finance of local government, statistics and labour market institutions. He has also developed a strong concern with reform of local government in Europe, including Eastern and Central Europe. This interest has been developed through his Chairmanship of of the International Geographical Union (IGU) Commission on Geography and Public Administration.

He is currently working on local economic development, labour training policies, and business investment strategies, including Training and Enterprise Councils (TECs).

Andrew McCoshan After studying geography at the University of Cambridge, he took a doctorate at the London School of Economics in the field of education management. The research for this book was undertaken whilst on the research staff of the London School of Economics where he also acted as a consultant to a number of private and public sector bodies. He now works in strategic management in local government.

ENTERPRISE AND HUMAN RESOURCE DEVELOPMENT

Local capacity building

Robert J. Bennett and Andrew McCoshan

Paul Chapman Publishing Ltd
144 Liverpool Road
London
N1 1LA

British Library Cataloguing in Publication Data

Bennett, R. J.
Enterprise and Human Resource Development
I. Title II. McCoshan, Andrew
331.11

ISBN 1-85396-212-0

Typeset by Inforum, Rowlands Castle, Hants
Printed by The Cromwell Press,
Broughton Gifford, Melksham, Wiltshire SN12 8PH

A B C D E F G H 9 8 7 6 5 4 3

CONTENTS

PART III: THE LOCAL DIMENSION: HORIZONTAL INTEGRATION

PART IV: AN AGENDA FOR THE 1990s

PREFACE

This book examines local capacity building initiatives in enterprise and human resource development of the last 20 years, with particular emphasis on the way in which the experience of the 1980s will affect decisions in the 1990s in order to lay the foundations for the 21st century. But the book also seeks to set these changes in the context of the wider developments in Britain's economic culture and to comment on how further change can be encouraged to increase future economic prosperity.

To balance objective analysis with policy advice is difficult and not without its hazards. Certainly we make one assumption transparent, that we believe that the foundation for social achievements is economic success; hence, that economic prosperity for the country as a whole is a *sine qua non* for the other endeavours that we all seek. But the argument is not partisan to a particular political position beyond this.

The conclusions are tough: the road to be followed will not be easy for anyone; the learning required is considerable; success can be achieved only by thinking long-term and giving a sustained commitment; and this can be achieved only through enhanced local institutions. But, in the words of at least one commentator, *"if we don't aim for the stars, we won't reach the hills"*.

The book is based chiefly on the results of a study financed by the Leverhulme Trust under the title 'Business, economic development, education and training'. We are most grateful to the Trust for its support without which this book would never have been written, and to John Sellgren, a co-researcher on that project, who has contributed important inputs at many stages of the work. In addition the book has gained significantly from considerable subsequent research as well as the involvement of the authors in a number of the key policy studies that have been developed over its time of preparation and writing. The most relevant reports are cited in the text, but we would like to take this opportunity to acknowledge the benefits to our learning gained through participation as advisors, authors or consultants to: the House of Commons Employment Committee, particularly the report on *The Employment Effect of UDCs* (HoC, 1989); the Audit Commission (1989) Report on *Urban Regeneration and Economic Development*; Bennett and Business in the Cities (1990) *Leadership in the Community: a Blueprint for Business Involvement in the 1990s*; the EC Local Employment Development Action Programme (Martinos, 1989; Bennett, 1989, 1990); the *British Chambers of Commerce Development Study* (1990); the *Confederation of British Industry Education-Business Partnerships Stocktake Study* (1990 – 92), and a number of local consultancy studies, of which the most significant for our learning have been for Newham (McCoshan, 1989), Kent (Bennett, 1992) and Richmond-upon-Thames (Bennett, McCoshan and Wicks, 1990). We have also gained benefit from overlap of the Leverhulme study with other studies at LSE and would particularly wish to acknowledge the benefits of discussions with Günter Krebs and Peter Wicks as well as the excellent secretarial support of Christine Gazely and cartographic support of Jane Pugh and Mike Scorer.

The approach taken in this book combines a coverage of national programmes with detailed local studies which seek to examine how national actions relate to each other (or not) in different local circumstances. This work has been based on analysis of original surveys collected specifically for this book as well as use of many data not previously studied, and in some cases, confidential to the organisations providing them. In addition a large number of formal and informal interviews at national and local level have been undertaken. Where possible we have sought to support comments and conclusions by attribution to data sources, reports or quotations. This has not always been possible, however, for reasons of confidentiality or sensitivity, but every effort has been made to check our judgements with experts in the relevant fields who have read and commented on various parts of the text. We have also gained significantly from the comments of participants at the LSE's regular Management Training Course on *Management and Leadership of Local Economies* at which many elements of this book have been piloted.

This has led to our need to acknowledge an immense debt to many organisations and individuals. We would particularly like to express our thanks to: Department of Employment, Training Agency (now TEED), the Department of Education and Science, the DTI, the CBI, Association of British Chambers of Commerce, Business in the Community, Business in the Cities, the Phoenix Initiative; and to all the other individuals and organisations in our study areas who, unfortunately, are too numerous individually to mention. Figure 5.14 is reproduced by the kind permission of David Stanley, Local Employer Network Manager, North Oxfordshire. Despite our debt to these bodies this book is independent of any organisation and we remain responsible for its conclusions and any errors or omissions.

London School of Economics

LIST OF ABBREVIATIONS

ABCC	Association of British Chambers of Commerce
AONB	Area of Outstanding Natural Beauty
BIM	British Institute of Management
BiTC	Business in the Community
BOTB	British Overseas Trade Board
BS	British Standards
BSC	British Steel Corporation
BTEC	Business and Technician Education Council
CAT	City Action Team
CBI	Confederation of British Industry
CDA	Cooperative Development Agency
CMED	Charter for Management Education
CoSIRA	Council for Small Industries in Rural Areas
CSE	Certificate of Secondary Education
CTC	City Technology College
CVS	Council for Voluntary Service
DBRW	Development Board for Rural Wales
DE	Department of Employment
DES	Department of Education and Science
DLG	Derelict Land Grant
DoE	Department of the Environment
DSS	Department of Social Security
DTI	Department of Trade and Industry
EAS	Enterprise Allowance Scheme
EBP	Education-Business Partnership
EC	European Community
EDG	Employment Department Group
EDU	Economic Development Unit
EEA	Enterprise and Education Adviser
ERA	Education Reform Act (1988)
ERDF	European Regional Development Fund
ESF	European Social Fund
ET	Employment Training Programme
EZ	Enterprise Zone
FE	Further Education
FME	Foundation for Management Education
GATT	General Agreement on Tariffs and Trade
GCSE	General Certificate of Secondary Education

GLC	Greater London Council
GNVQ	General National Vocational Qualification
HE	Higher Education
HIDB	Highlands and Islands Development Board
HIE	Highlands and Islands Enterprise
HMI	Her Majesty's Inspectorate
HO	Home Office
IIP	Investors in People
ILEA	Inner London Education Authority
IM	Industry Matters
IPM	Institute of Personnel Managers
ITB	Industry Training Board
ITeC	Information Technology Centre
JIT	Just-in-Time
JTS	Job Training Scheme
LA	Local Authority
LAMB	Local Area Manpower Board
LDDC	London Docklands Development Corporation
LEA	Local Education Authority
LEAG	Local Enterprise Agency Grant
LEAP	Local Enterprise Agency Project
LEBP	London Education-Business Partnership
LEC	Local Enterprise Company
LEN	Local Employer Network
LEntA	London Enterprise Agency
MCI	Management Charter Initiative
MSC	Manpower Services Commission
NAFE	Non-Advanced Further Education
NCVO	National Council for Voluntary Organisations
NCVQ	National Council for Vocational Qualifications
NIC	Newly Industralised Country
NRDC	National Research and Development Corporation
NROVA	National Record of Vocational Achievement
NVQ	National Vocational Qualification
OECD	Organisation for Economic Cooperation and Development
PICKUP	Professional Industrial and Commercial Updating
ROA	Record of Achievement
RSA	Royal Society of Arts
SCIP	Schools Council Industry Project / School Curriculum Industry Partnership
SDA	Scottish Development Agency
SE	Scottish Enterprise
SEAC	School Examination and Assessment Council
SFS	Small Firms Service
SSSI	Site of Special Scientific Interest
TA	Training Agency
TAP	Training Access Point
TC	Training Commission

TEC	Training and Enterprise Council
TEED	Training, Education and Enterprise Directorate
TF	Task Force
TNPU	TECs and National Providers Unit
TPO	Teacher Placement Organiser
TQM	Total Quality Management
TTWA	Travel to Work Area
TVEE	Technical and Vocational Education Extension
TVEI	Technical and Vocational Education Initiative
UBI	Understanding British Industry
UDC	Urban Development Corporation
UPA	Urban Programme Area
VET	Vocational Education and Training
WDA	Welsh Development Agency
WO	Welsh Office
WRFE	Work Related Further Education
YOP	Youth Opportunities Programme
YT	Youth Training
YTS	Youth Training Scheme

1. *LEARNING TO MEET THE GLOBAL CHALLENGE*

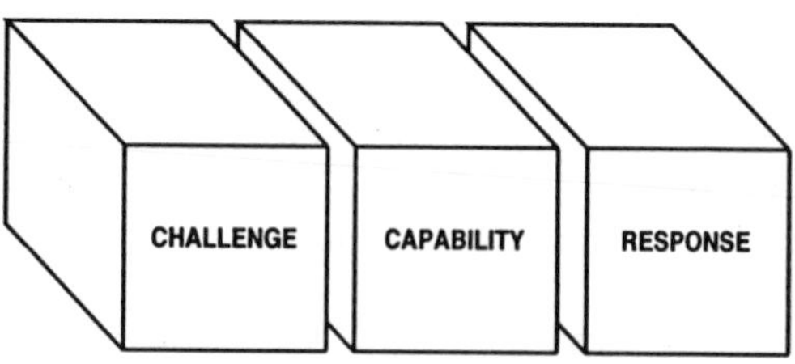

Challenge and response

This book is concerned with how Britain should respond to global economic changes. The challenge to be faced is how far Britain can earn the economic resources to pay for the standard of living that people desire. This will depend on its capacity to compete. Britain's competitiveness in turn depends on the productivity of its human and capital resources. This at root depends on the capacity of its businesses and the people who manage and work in them. That capacity is primarily a local requirement. Hence the focus of this book on *enterprise, education and training as a process of local capacity building.*

Changes in the global economy represent a brutal challenge for Britain in the 21st century. Britain is a country, we argue, which has allowed itself to remain too long equipped with too many of the capacities either of its imperial past or of its response to the challenge to its survival during the Second World War. It has not, until recently, developed the economic and institutional capacity, or exhibited the commitment to a strength of economic purpose, that other major competitor nations have either long possessed, or are now fast developing.

But recent years have seen a major improvement in Britain's response. The new learning required has been hard and the "learning curve" has been steep. Because the problems that remain to be tackled are tougher and the competition harder, the future learning curve required will be even steeper. This book examines what capacity has been developed so far. Detailed studies of selected national programmes and local areas illustrate the local detail of a broader national picture. The central argument is that a major learning process is required to develop more *powerful business-led local institutions,* if Britain is successfully to answer the challenges of the 21st century.

The conclusion of the book is "good marks for effort, but will have to try even harder in future". The developments required in Britain attack deep-rooted traditions and relatively impervious institutions. *System-wide changes* are required. Only long-sustained action and a *shift in national economic commitment* will suffice. As might be expected, it is not clear that all of the learning so far has been useful, nor that all the dazzling and bewildering array of initiatives being developed will succeed. But much has been achieved, and it is from these achievements that it has become possible to look at how success can be sought in the future. Hence this book represents not only an examination of past and present policy; it also suggests means to help achieve the sustained shifts required in the future.

One concept, more than any other, captures the kernel of what has to be achieved. This is the attainment of a *capacity* to respond to change in the economic process. If Britain has experienced a "systems failure" it is because the quality of its economic response has not measured up to that achieved in its major competitors. The concept of global competition, introduced in Chapter 2, is a fierce challenge for Britain. It requires that we seek to do as well as or better than the best, rather than being content merely to do better than the past.

The key to understanding the need to develop capacity comes from three directions. *First*, is recognition that capacity is *relative*. But relative appraisal against the past will lead only to inadequate change when the past has provided significantly less than what we aspire to. In the words of more than one commentator:

If we do what we always do, we'll get what we've always got.

This is a particular problem for Britain.

Second, is recognition that what we aspire to is certainly equivalent to the best in the world – we all want the economic living standards of the USA or Germany or Japan. But we have not all yet recognised that this needs at least an equivalent commitment to achieving *as good or better* productivity and other conditions for economic success from which derive the living standards we desire. In the words of Sir John Banham (Director General, Confederation of British Industry) in a speech at the CBI national conference, Harrogate, 1989:

Britons have tended to want the incomes of Germans or Japanese, but to remain with the skills of coolies.

Third, is recognition that Britain will have to tackle some of the country's most difficult problems. To overcome the characteristics of "systems failure" requires system-wide changes which are often in areas which are least amenable to easy and rapid solutions. Often they are in fields where deep seated barriers have stimulated strategies of avoidance and of damage-limitation. This means refocusing attention on problems which the economic system has developed a capacity to remain apart from. In the assessment of one commentator[1].

Recovery lies in places we would normally prefer to avoid!

Clearly, to develop quality, the resources must be released that are presently tied up in maintaining barriers to change, or avoiding change.

Thus, although the global challenge is an economic one, the response required goes far wider than mere economics. The book focuses chiefly on the dimensions of enterprise development, education and training. However, beyond these fields many other institutions and leaders must be involved – employers, central and local government, political parties, the community and voluntary sector; ultimately, every economic development, management and individual decision is affected.

Method of approach

Economic growth, like economic decline, is not inevitable. It depends on the consequences of a multitude of individual, corporate and institutional decisions. Hence, to achieve economic growth, indeed even to maintain the level of economic prosperity of the present, requires the development of an appropriate capacity to make these decisions. Capacity itself further depends upon developing a means of responding to challenges and changes. Economies do not stand still. The conditions affecting decisions need continually to be kept under review. The best capacity will not only be responding, but also leading that change. Thus economic success is based on putting in place a sequence:

CHALLENGE CAPABILITY RESPONSE

This will determine a nation's capacity to change and adapt. Success is built on assessing challenges and making the most appropriate economic response. Response requires an appropriate system to assess challenges.

The structure of this book takes the framework of challenge ! capability ! response as a means to achieve four objectives:

- To assess the British position;
- To analyse the extent of recent changes;
- To suggest the organisational development required in the future, and thus;
- To identify the "learning" that must be undertaken.

Each of these objectives and the framework of challenge - capability - response is enlarged on at each stage of the discussion.

Global challenge (discussed in Chapter 2) is understood as a function of five dimensions:

- Internationalisation of markets;
- Technological and product development;
- Demands for growing specialisation and flexibility;
- Changing labour supply as a result of global demographic change;
- Changing emphasis towards high quality and environmentally friendly activities.

National and local capability (discussed in Chapter 3) is understood as a function of the six dimensions of:

- The "real" and financial economy: the total level of output;
- Employment and its utilisation;
- Workforce supply (through demographic and technological change) and quality (as an outcome mainly of education and training);
- Innovation, Research and Development;
- The local conditions.
- The institutional environment.

The last dimension, the institutional environment, is singled out for further special attention in Chapter 4. It is given this extensive treatment because of its key role in determining the British economy's capability for economic development. In Chapter 4 we assess the institutional environment through five sub-dimensions, each of which determines the shape of Britain's "systemic goals" in the fields of: business strategy, employment and the labour market, education and training, economic policy and the welfare compromise, central-local government relations and the impact of Europe.

The analysis of the goals of the British institutional system follows from the fundamental tenet of this book: that national economic performance can only be understood through its manifestation in different places. It is chiefly in local contexts that the battle to develop improved capability to respond to the global challenge will be lost or won. But understanding the local variability of economic development is not only necessary to give a feeling for the complexity of the problem. It is also the fundamental link of macroeconomic and microeconomic concerns. System capability is the outcome of the cumulative capacity of every individual, organisation and institution in the economy to contribute to economic progress. System capability, then, focuses on the relation of micro and local decisions to macro and system targets and performance criteria.

Building the capacity for *national and local response* (discussed in Chapter 5) is understood as the result of two interacting structures that derive from systemic goals: (i) programme and process, and (ii) local management and organisation. Capacity building must fit together these two structures in an effective and coordinated structure in each place. The conclusion is that at present vertical fragmentation of programmes leads to separated and fragmented local agents ! a "patchwork quilt" results in each locality.

Programme and process concern "vertical fields" of action. These fields are national, as well as local, programmes and are the detailed concern of Part 2 of the book. The chief concerns of the book cover three fields:

- Enterprise development (Chapter 6);
- Education (Chapter 7);
- Training (Chapter 8).

Management and organisation concern "horizontal fields" of action. These fields are also national as well as local. But the local level is often the most important; and it is the point at which actions have to be put together. If there is no coordination at the local point of delivery, then there is no real coordination at all that is meaningful to local customers, clients or beneficiaries of the development process. Because the form of this horizontal networking (or its absence) will vary very considerably from place to place, it is not possible to cover every possible local outcome. Its form and variability is analysed in Part 3 of the book. The *structure* of local capability is analysed in Chapter 9 and the *major dimensions* which shape the nature of local outcomes are discussed in Chapter 10. Major examples of some of the common and important forms of local organisational responses in different types of places are then assessed in large cities (Chapter 11); metropolitan fringe areas (Chapter 12); dispersed industrial areas (Chapter 13); and central places and rural areas (Chapter 14).

It should be noted that the discussion in this book does not examine in any depth the outcomes of policy (such as the quality of trainees, quality of management, etc.). These have been the subject of a considerable number of studies using traditional evaluation methods. There is no need to repeat their findings here. Rather, it is the purpose of the analysis to go beyond outcomes to analyse the effectiveness of management and local structures in response to global challenge. If the organisational networks have the capability to respond then we can assume that quality outcomes are capable of achievement. If the guns are pointing in the right direction it becomes an empirical question of what adjustments must be made to achieve targets of performance. However, if the guns are pointing in the wrong direction there is little hope of achieving anything. There is not a predetermined organisational solution. Rather, improved capacity lies in developing flexible systems finely tuned to each locality's potential. From this conclusion the policy developments required are outlined in Chapter 15.

Summary of main conclusions

The main conclusions of the book are itemised at the end of each chapter. These lead in Chapter 15 to the overall conclusion that a new national strategic approach is required. The requirement for a national strategy is based on recognising seven key steps:

- *Doing nothing is not an option,* if Britain's economy is to continue to develop or even maintain its present level;
- *Development lies in places we would often prefer to avoid:* many of the most important developments relate to areas that are difficult to tackle;
- *Institutional development* is the key requirement;
- Many of the most important developments concern *governmental institutions,* particularly relating to enterprise, but they also permeate business culture itself; ,
- Many of the key developments required are at *local level,* but these must be bound into a *common strategy;*
- Many developments can be achieved by *developing a learning process;*
- This requires a *sustained and supportive environment,* particularly from government.

The conclusions range over four chief areas: developing local experiences, training, education and enterprise.

The *development of local experiences* is one of the most important foundations upon which a national strategy can be built. This recognises the importance of "bottom-up" processes in the attack on the supply-side problem of the British economy. The conclusions are:

- *Local environments* have a large effect on enterprise and can be modified to encourage it;
- To succeed, local agents have to develop their vision and obtain a sufficient initial *critical mass* in terms of a capacity to respond to external challenges;
- No agents, public or private, have enough resources or vision to "go it alone" in development; *collaboration* is therefore a key ingredient in order to increase the resources that can be applied to any problem;
- Most places have a baffling array of different programmes; the accessibility of the system can be enhanced if all agents are drawn together into a locally flexible *common system;*
- Considerable enhancement of economic performance could be achieved if a stronger *coherence,* or partnership, particularly of links between education and training to the country's economic needs, is developed;
- Development must be built into local communities and their elites and leaders; since local business leaders are often isolated from other local decision makers, this requires major development of *community economic leadership;*

- Many complexities and difficulties at local level have derived from poorly-specified central government initiatives; what is required is a *sustained commitment to a national economic development purpose.*

The analysis concludes that a significant part of the process of learning at local level has to be built around sustained local partnerships that bring agents together into an effective economic development organisation. This learning process will differ considerably between areas. Some areas will have the advantage that local conditions reinforce one another so that the resulting momentum can be a partnership that is greater than the sum of its parts. The examples of "successful" partnerships that we have examined are characterised by these mutually reinforcing local actions.

For *business* the key problem is dispersion across small companies and small business communities. A key part of any solution must entail the development of an effective local business support organisation with sufficient critical mass to make a major impact on filling the gap in the need for business services among micro- and meso-businesses.

For the *government and public sector* greatly enhanced collaboration between local authorities, and between local authorities and private bodies such as Chambers of Commerce and Training and Enterprise Councils (TECs) is required. Central and local government organisation must play a more stable and effective role in partnerships.

Voluntary/community organisations face the greatest challenges since spontaneous demands for inclusion in local partnerships are usually small; key tasks will be finding the most suitable roles for voluntary organisations and demonstrating to them and to the communities they serve the substantive benefits from their involvement.

The analysis gives a detailed assessment of the many developments that have developed, or are being developed, in the fields of training, education and enterprise. The major conclusion is the need to go further and deeper with the developments that have been made.

Many important achievements have been made in each of the fields of enterprise, education and training. But in the field of enterprise, in particular, a major gap exists in national strategy. This reflects a tension in government policy. On the one hand, enhancing factor conditions requires mainly a hands-off policy that seeks to remove barriers to competition and factor mobility. On the other hand, many improvements in factor inputs and the development of business support organisations require either government participation, championship or regulation. This has been more than amply evidenced by the contrast between the Department of Trade and Industry's (DTI) championship of the free market, encouragement of the private sector development of professional services and cutbacks in almost all fields of business support, and the Department of Employment's (DE) use of public money to lever change through TECs. The problem is not one of different departmental approaches, it is a question of the perception of what the problem is and hence how best to address it. The book concludes that what is required is a fuller integration of enterprise with education and training, through government action, as champion and partner, and in a wider range of major business developments, particularly in the development of a more powerful, broad-based, business-led local organisation. The DTI new One Stop Shop initiative may provide the catalyst for this development.

Footnotes: Chapter 1

1. Ted Linzey, former procurement manager of IBM UK, contribution to London School of Economics Programme: 'Management and Leadership of Local Economies', September 1990.

PART I

Challenge – Capability – Response

2. *THE GLOBAL CHALLENGE*

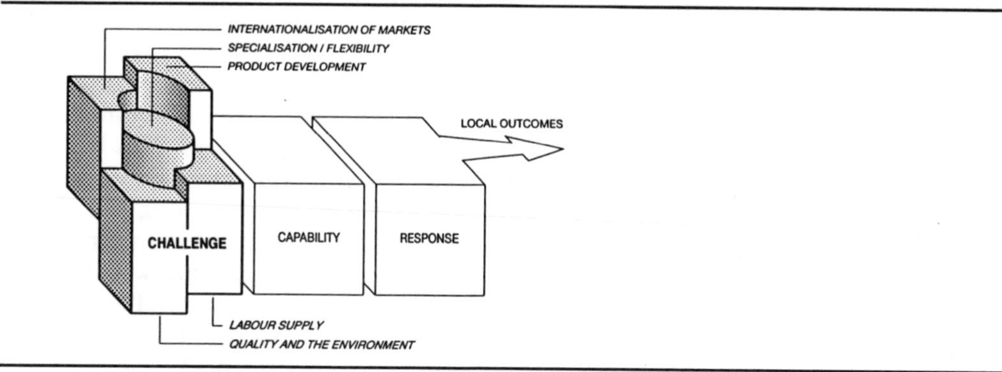

Accelerating interdependence

The economic development and progress of any country, region or local community is not determined solely by its own decisions, but also by its position within a set of trading and investment relationships within the global economic system. Although a central argument of this book is that communities can do a great deal to help themselves realise economic progress and prosperity, local action is set within the constraints of a system of global economic relationships. This interdependence between places is not new, but the level of interdependence is now higher than ever between the economies across the world, and its extent is accelerating rapidly. This means that decisions on how to help national or local economies develop cannot be made in isolation from the influences of that global economic system. "Going it alone" is no longer an option for a locality or even for a large economy the size of Britain or the USA. Economic development is now a global challenge.

The challenge of accelerating global interdependence is analysed here in four dimensions:

- The internationalisation of markets;
- Trends in the global market;
- Changing production structures;
- Global changes of population, resources, environment and the peace dividend.

Our analysis concludes with the lessons to be drawn from this global challenge. These lessons set the context for assessing the response required, and the British capacity to deliver it, which is the subject of the rest of the book.

Internationalisation of markets

The 20th century has seen a growth in competition and decline in the scope to protect markets among the main industrial nations. The pace of this change accelerated, in general, in the 1970s and 1980s. Competition is likely to further increase through the 1990s and beyond. There is a complex "chicken and egg" relationship between past protection and present competition. Extensive protection of national markets often allows "complacent" practices to be developed so that *in the long term*, rather than improving their capacity to hold home markets, whole industries became vulnerable to the superior products, costs, or quality of goods produced elsewhere. This has been exemplified by Britain in its imperial past and by Eastern Europe, but tends to occur in all countries where cherished "national" industries have been protected for long periods.

The erosion of protected markets tended first to come from those international businesses who were not so protected, and had technological, market or other advantages. Protectionism has also been eroded by political pressures. The failure of protectionism in the 1920s and 1930s convinced most Western countries that it had contributed to economic depression. As a result, since the Second World War, the major industrial nations have sought progressive liberalisation of markets. This has resulted in General Agreement on Tariffs and Trade (GATT), the European Community (EC) drive for a single internal market, and the desires of Eastern Europe and the former USSR to access Western markets. The dismantling of protections for national industries is never easy, as the negotiations on the renewal of GATT in 1990–92 and the reduction of EC agricultural subsidies demonstrate. Indeed, there has been a significant increase in non-tariff world trade barriers since the 1960s. Nevertheless the liberalisation of world trade has steadily continued and has become increasingly linked, in many cases, to the deregulation of national industrial policies (especially the US and UK), financial market deregulation and integration, and the opening of former markets of nationalised or state industries to international competitive processes through privatisation (especially in Britain and Eastern Europe).

With the integration of markets the level and complexity of the world economic system has radically increased. With this has been associated growing unpredictability and instability. No single country, large company, or even larger trade bloc such as the EC or USA, so dominates the international system that long-term economic outcomes are fully predictable. This has led some commentators to suggest that the global economy is becoming "unmanageable" (see e.g. Drucker, 1989). This, in major part, reflects the reduced power of national governments to affect their economies. The outcome is that any business decision maker has to cope with a much higher degree of uncertainty and potential instability. Planning for uncertainty has, therefore, became an important part of both business and government economic strategy.

The growth in significance of the international corporation has been both a major cause and outcome of these developments. In economic theory international corporations are seen as a way of internalising the need to cope with complex multinational differences that lead to uncertainty. This means that companies can simultaneously expand markets and reduce uncertainty by international operations. A prime benefit is usually seen as the information and knowledge advantage available to an international company over one based in a single country (Buckley and Casson,

1976; Buckley, 1989; Casson, 1990).

However, Kindleberger (1969) observed, international corporations owe no more loyalty to one country than to any other. They have been a major force for by-passing national barriers, whether these be trade protection, to protect restrictive practices or to safeguard "national" interests. Failure of a nation, or a locality, to conform to the needs of the international corporation have frequently resulted in loss of investment, employment, markets and potential economic growth.

The international corporation has been a vehicle for the progressive "uncoupling" of production from employment. This has meant that products have taken on a global character: design in one country, production of components in many countries, assembly in another country, and marketing in yet other countries. The main employment is likely to go to the production stage which is most labour-intensive, with its location chosen on grounds of relative cheapness. Following the earlier example of Japan, the development of the newly industrialised countries (NICs) particularly illustrates these changes. The four countries of Hong Kong, Singapore, Taiwan and South Korea were initially able to use cheap labour and high productivity to provide intense competition to many labour-intensive older industries in the advanced economies. That advantage is being repeated by Thailand, and can be repeated in other developing countries. Meanwhile, the first NICs have been able to move on to innovate by adding research, design and marketing elements to their previous cheap labour advantages in production. They will become even more formidable competitors in the future.

The degree of economic power concentrated in international corporations was often seen in the past as a problem to be tackled by national governments. In the 1960s the growing importance of US companies in Europe worried many governments (see e.g. Servan-Schreiber, 1967). In Britain, the international corporation was seen as a "bogeyman" by the Wilson government 1964–70. Even as late as Stuart Holland's (1976) book, there was still considerable debate about how to control the influence of international corporations, and how to tax them, in order to protect the "national interest". This tended to encourage the erroneous view that British firms could be protected from international competition, and that the government could provide itself with the scope to pursue its own industrial and regional policies independently of international business interests.

However, the international corporation has now to be regarded in a different light. First, by-passing national barriers and other restrictive practices has made possible many beneficial economic developments, particularly the development of a closer relation between producers and the consumer, and hence between workers and customers. This change has now become one of the fundamental driving forces in future product development and technological change. Secondly, however, the international corporation is now recognised as providing much of the general dynamic for growth, new technological innovation and R&D. Although the important role, too, of smaller firms is recognised in innovation and R&D, it is often only the large international corporations that have the organisational capability to develop genuinely long-term strategies for large-scale continuing investment in manufacturing, marketing and innovation (see e.g. OECD, 1989).

Adjustment of attitudes to the international corporation has also been borne of a new sense of reality. Such companies are powerful and provide major resources for the development and growth of economies. Nations and localities tend to succeed economically if they work with these corporations and integrate into the world economy, rather than resist them. Thus it has become recognised that a bargaining relationship exists between international corporations and the countries and localities in which they are seeking to invest. It has also become recognised that international corporations do not operate in a pure competitive market; rather, they are an oligopoly. Hence, for national or local economies to succeed they have to develop cooperative relationships with international corporations. This is the more true in that international corporations are not yet governed by an homogenous global "corporate culture", but have home bases which require national cooperation (Hamilton, 1976). Similarly, small firms often require the support of contracts from the larger corporations in order to expand or to develop their technical innovations (see Chapter 6). Thus internationalisation and development of markets is inevitably leading to a closer interdependency between firms, and between firms and governments.

Britain is in a particularly vulnerable position because it has a very high degree of international economic interdependence. Always historically strongly interlinked with foreign investors and investments, in the 1980s these links grew very rapidly. Britain became in the late 1980s the second largest recipient in the world of foreign direct investment (FDI) by volume, and the largest recipient as a percentage of GNP. FDI was running at £3.5 billion per year in the late 1970s, but rose to £22 billion per year in 1990, equivalent to 4.5% of GDP. Figures 2.1 and 2.2 show that both inward and outward flows of FDI are very important in Britain, but relative to the other major industrial nations these flows have a far greater significance. It has led to some of the most significant changes in manufacturing output. For example, the change to Britain becoming a net exporter of televisions and refrigerators, and the anticipation of soon becoming a net exporter of cars, is in very large measure a result of FDI, particularly from the USA and Holland, but also from Switzerland, Canada, France, Australia and Japan. This leads to the conclusion that Britain, more than any other country, has to conform to global standards and to the needs of the international corporation.

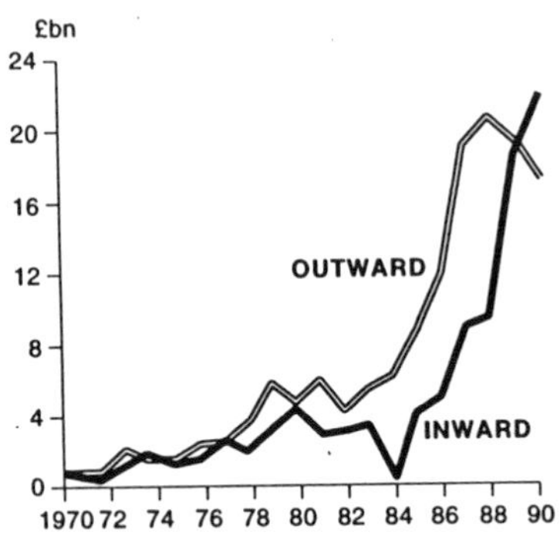

Figure 2.1 Foreign direct investment in Britain 1970–1990
Source: CSO

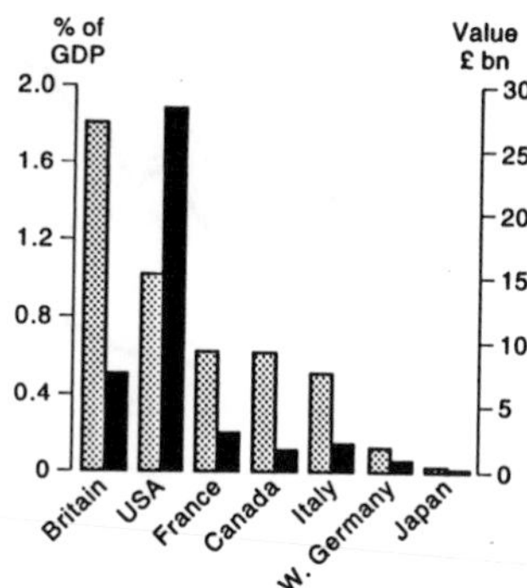

Figure 2.2 Inflows of foreign direct investment £billion (solid) and as a percentage of GDP (shaded); annual average rates for 1986–1989
Source: CSO and OECD

These developments have led to a growing recognition that successful long-term economic growth cannot be achieved by "going it alone": this is simply not an option for a locality, a national economy, or a firm. Although there is still a deep division in the EC over the extent to which an EC-wide policy of industrial intervention is possible, there is little doubt that for Britain, because of its very high international economic interdependence, it is particularly important to work with the needs of the global market. As a result, increasingly complex "partnering" arrangements are necessary: between corporations and local or national institutions, and between companies. These partnerships seek to assure market access, in return for employment and investment.

Trends in the global market

The internationalisation of markets puts important constraints on attempts to stimulate economic development. The 1990s appear to be a period where there will be even more intense competition for shrinking growth in world output and trade. Hence those policies that contribute most to improving competitive performance will have to be followed even more assiduously in the future than the past. This leaves little room for policy luxuries, political licence, mistakes or for diversions that offer second best.

As globalisation of markets and the intensity of competition have increased, the 1970s and 1980s have seen a slowdown in the level of economic growth measured by both output and trade, as shown in Figure 2.3. Up to 1973, world annual income growth (GDP) averaged 5% and trade growth averaged nearly 10%. The 1973 - 1980 period saw output grow at 3.5% and trade grow at 6%, on average. The period after the 1980–1982 recession has seen annual output growth drop to 3% and trade growth drop to 5%. The prospects for the early 1990s are expected to be a further decline to under 3% and 4.5% respectively.

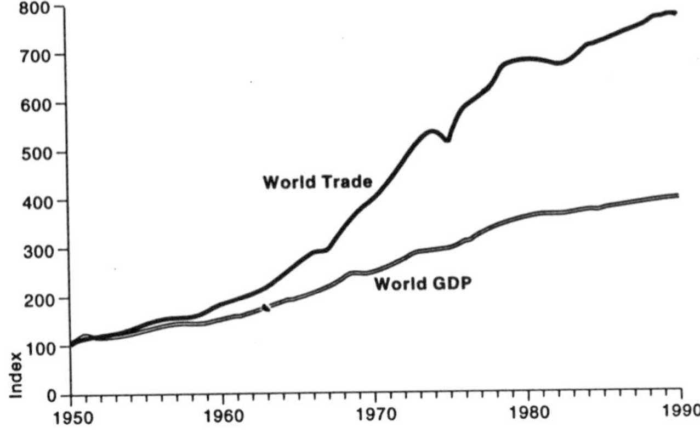

Figure 2.3 World Trade and GDP
Source: United Nations – Statistical Yearbook

These changes in output and trade have been related by an increasing number of commentators to "long waves" of economic development. First identified by Kondratieff (1926) and Schumpeter (1939), these waves have an hypothesised length of approximately 50 years. They arise from an association of innovation, product development and product life cycles. The period of approximately 1948–2000 is argued to be that of the fourth Kondratieff and has been based mainly on the technologies of information technology and electronics. The earlier waves were 1785–1842 based on coal, iron and steam; 1843–1897 based on steel, railways, steamships and machine tools; 1898–1948 based on cars, electrical goods and chemicals. By extension, the fifth Kondratieff wave is forecast to become evident and dominant by 2004, although its foundations are already being laid. It is likely to be based on communications systems, information, the further development of computer aided design (CAD), computer integrated manufacture (CIM) and new materials. The emphasis on communications has led to it being termed *"the carrier wave"* by Peter Hall (Hall and Preston, 1988).

The existence and explanation of long waves is controversial and need not long detain us here (for good reviews see Hall and Preston, 1988; van Duijn, 1983). The key aspects of concern to our argument are that clusters of individual innovations and developments of R&D stimulate phases of product development. It appears that it is not clusters of innovations per se, but chains of related innovations which stem from one or two major technological developments that stimulate upsurges of global development – the development of so-called new "technology systems" (Freeman *et al.*, 1991). A key lesson to be drawn from the analyses by Hall and Freeman is that it is organisational and institutional capacity which is often the most important element in promoting, or preventing, these developments. Hence a major factor in explaining why different countries perform differently at different stages in the different waves is the capacity of those countries' institutions to respond quickly and decisively. But Hall goes further, for the 20th century waves, by identifying as part of that institutional fabric the crucial role of the state and wider society. These, he argues, determine the ability in a country *"to generate the entrepreneurial figures, in the training and aptitudes of its workforce, in its capacity to develop patterns of consumption, in the ability of the state to provide the necessary infrastructural and regulatory framework"* (Hall and Preston, p. 266). These are the elements of support, or synergy, essential for translating an invention into an innovation.

There is nothing inevitable about economic change or development. But there is a danger in many writings on long waves that they are seen as unalterable. The danger is that, if enough important opinion leaders believe that something is inevitable, then it will become so. Economic growth can be "talked down" and forecasts can become "self-fulfilling prophecies". There are a number of arguments to suggest that the end of the fourth and beginning of the fifth wave have different forms to the waves of the past.

The reasons for this may lie in the pace and form of economic change from the fourth to the fifth waves. First, the transition from electronics to communications as the core innovation stimulus is not as radical a change in industrial base as previous changes. Second, there is considerable evidence that rapid commercialisation of the products of the fifth wave is already underway. Third, the role of manufacturing as a driver of economic waves may now have shifted to a position in which development in other fields (such as services, etc.) allows economies to sustain a stable economic base to some extent independently of the manufacturing cycle (this is the controversial argument that we are experiencing a transition to a "post - industrial society"). Fourth, the occasion of the slowdown of the rate of world economic growth and trade in the 1970s is undoubtedly linked to the OPEC oil shocks of 1973/74 and 1979/80 – whatever the form of "long waves", these shocks alone would have led to major adjustments as the vastly changed earnings ("petrodollars") to oil-rich states were recycled around the world economy. This has been argued by some to have accelerated the shift from the fourth to the fifth wave. Fifth, the very advent of the fifth wave suggests a form of technological dependence which, by the rapid flow of information, will eliminate or speed up many of the mechanisms in the cycle of innovation and product development which are the core of most explanations of long waves. If these features are even partially true, then the transition between the dominant technologies of the fourth wave and dominant technology of the fifth wave may be more rapid than in previous waves so that the down cycle of slowdowns in the 1990s will not be deep; and, in many countries, it may not be recognisable at all. Certainly there is no a priori reason to believe that there will be an inevitable economic downturn in the 1990s before the onset of rapid economic growth in the early 21st century.

If this argument is true, then it further supports the suggestions by Hall and others that there will be major variations in the *geography* of world economic development. Transition to the fifth wave is likely to take place most easily, and on the largest scale, only in those areas offering both the best creative milieux and the most supportive economic and institutional environment.

These milieux will contribute by offering a cluster of industries and products that improve each other, and each business, through mutually supporting demand-supply relationships. In speculating on how the race will be won in the future of the fifth wave Hall concurs with Mackintosh (1987), that it will be those areas that support maximum flexibility in production, design, coordination, distribution and marketing – but combine these conditions with the highest value added in terms of human resource inputs (at all levels) and have the most supportive general environment. In this, Japan and the Far East look increasingly impressive in their capacity. Europe as a whole will have problems in keeping up. Britain is likely to experience more difficulties than most countries, for the reasons we outline in the following chapters, and therefore has more difficulties to overcome if it is to maintain its present relative levels of prosperity.

Changing production structures

Globalisation, competition and technological development have driven a series of wider changes in product demand and production structures. Because these changes interrelate with product development and its organisation, they also contribute to the expectations for the long waves of economic development discussed above.

The key aspects are (see e.g. Peters and Waterman, 1982; DTI, 1990a,b; PA, 1989; CE, 1991; Porter, 1990; Stahl and Bounds, 1991; Webb, 1991):

- Since 1970 world trade in basic and low value-added products has relatively declined, whereas trade and high value-added products have consistently increased (especially for telecommunications and data processing equipment, office machinery, electronics and fashion consumer goods);
- High value-added products make demands for high quality, prompt delivery, reliability, high technological, and high design inputs;
- There is increasing demand for "quality of life" products such as high order consumer goods, leisure, travel, health care, and environmentally friendly goods;
- There has been major product proliferation catering for specialised markets and customisation to consumer choices. This results in smaller product runs, shorter production times, and the need for much greater competence and flexibility in production;
- Specialised markets are not necessarily small; size can be gained by globalisation and clever design to cope with easy and rapid variation;
- The speed of change has greatly increased. The ability to respond rapidly is itself a major competitive weapon – so-called "time competition" or the "survival of the fastest" (see Toffler, 1985). This entails radical shortening of the time periods in the product design, development, production, and marketing processes. Just-in-time (JIT) techniques are part of what is now seen as the development of more general "low-inertia" manufacture and distribution[1];
- Products and markets are global so that performance objectives of "doing better than before" are not enough: "doing as well or better than the best" is the only long-term competitive option;
- An emphasis on quality is a preeminent concern;
- All these factors are compelling a drive towards lower overall manufacturing unit costs;
- Technological development is facilitating major reductions in human resource inputs at the manufacturing stage, but increasing labour and skills requirements at the design organisation and marketing stages;
- There is increased emphasis on service, both pre-sales and after-sales.

These changes have stimulated a number of interrelated developments in the structure of industry. Particularly important has been a strong trend towards smaller scale manufacturing units and more flexible arrangements between producers and suppliers at each stage in the production process – termed "flexible specialisation" by

Piore and Sabel (1984). This has changed the whole nature of customer – supplier relationships and is an important part of bringing workers closer to consumers. This has led to a range of developments.

First, large existing vertically integrated companies have tended to be broken up into separate divisions, and sub-companies may be sold off. This has resulted in a general *down-sizing* of large companies. Associated with this trend has been the development of a much larger role played by small firms, both in terms of their total level of economic output and employment, and in terms of their relations to larger firms. This has tended to slim down the size of large firms considerably, as noted in Figure 2.4, replacing their staff by new divisions (transferred functions), spun-off subcontracting (*outsourcing*) to other firms or former parts of the larger firms, and part-time workers[2]. The result is a slimmer core, which is more closely integrated and requires enhanced innovation, entrepreneurial and managerial skills.

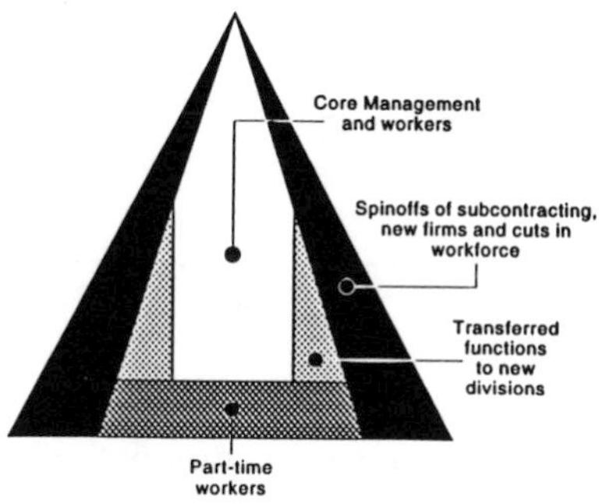

Figure 2.4 Evolution of large companies towards downsizing and subcontracting (adapted from Storey and Johnson, 1987, p.52)

Second, with the abandonment of vertical integration, companies are becoming more organisational structures. At its most extreme this leads to the "hollow corporation" that concentrates on product design and marketing and buys in all components and assembly from low-cost suppliers (often overseas in the NICs). Amstrad has had many of these characteristics.

Figure 2.5 contrasts the traditional line management with flexible structures. The pyramidal structures of management within firms and in their contracting were characteristic of the period up to the 1970s. This structure created a dependency both up and down the size spectrum of firms. There was little independence, opportunity to innovate, or to overcome the rigidities of supply relationships and to adapt to change. Within firms there was an extensive network of hierarchical relations between managers and sub-managers. Flexible structures, by contrast, do not have rigid relations within firms or between small and large firms, but a changing and evolving network of contracting and subcontracting. As a result births and deaths of enterprises, products or processes is easier, allowing more rapid innovation and adaptation to change. It also removes many of the hierarchical distinctions between managers and workers and is beginning to change the nature of work itself[3]. One view is that increasingly people will work in a portfolio of life: sometimes boss, sometimes employee, changing careers several times, and often simultaneously combining several occupations and income sources. Already in 1990 there are 600,000 people in the UK who have two jobs where the main job is as an employee subject to PAYE (Grayson, 1990, p. 7). Flexible working also seems to satisfy most people's aims. For example, the British Social Attitudes Survey in 1989 found interesting work and convenient working hours the first and third ranked attributes sought in a job, with job security and good pay the second and fourth ranked attributes[4].

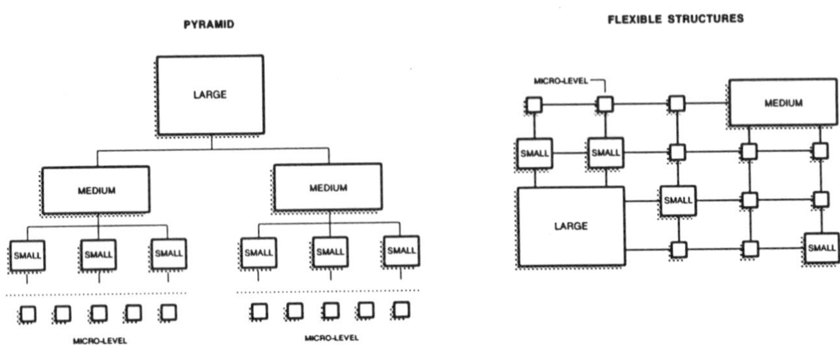

Figure 2.5 Contrasts of traditional pyramid and emerging flexible forms of relationships between and within firms

Third, the development of more flexible structures has given rise to a rapid growth in business services, in part deriving from down-sizing and externalisation of large company activities (Daniels, 1986; Beyers, 1989), and in part deriving from the emergence of new businesses satisfying new needs (Howells, 1987, 1989; Wood, 1991; Keeble *et al.*, 1990; O'Farrell and Hitchens, 1990). Such contracts external to the core firms offer the multiple advantages of savings in management time, cost control, reduced financial risk, reducing capital requirements and removing costs associated with continuous renewal of assets offering state-of-the-art equipment and some labour flexibility. Potential savings typically reach 20–30% of turnover (*Financial Times, Supplement*, "Contracted Business Services", 11 March 1991). This process is stimulative of small firms, complex patterns of firm-to-firm links, and internal management restructuring within large firms to ensure that contracting and purchasing itself becomes part of the corporate capacity to change, adapt and develop quality.

Fourth, the nature of products will change. Increasingly the core products must be low price, zero defect, assured in supply, easy to assemble, and adaptable to as many applications as possible. The computer industry's DRAM chips are examples of this type of core product. Fifth, this process radically affects company organisation. A company must have a clear strategy, with different strategies tailored for its different products and markets. It must be able to respond rapidly to changes, provide excellent quality, and it must have close links to customers and suppliers at every stage of production of the good or service.

Sixth, the level of uncertainty for managers has greatly increased as a result of shortened product life times, more direct customer links, and the more ready ability to switch customers/suppliers. This has placed much greater emphasis on high quality management whilst, at the same time, radically curtailing the scope for relying on government action. Government has been radically reduced in its scope to intervene effectively. Instead managers need government mainly to provide a long-term national stability of policy and a maximum support to the general business environment.

Seventh, the continuing technological innovation likely in the 21st century will be based on accelerating the replacement of labour by machinery and the development of intelligent systems in manufacturing, with a resulting massive cheapening of the production process. For a mature industrial economy this is likely to stimulate a shift in the workforce requirements towards high value-added fields, and from production to design, marketing and innovation.

These developments all have profound implications for economic development. For an advanced industrial country like Britain they suggest that there will be:

- Increased emphasis on design and marketing;
- High value-added products;
- High quality and reliability;
- Rapid adaptability;
- Increasing labour skills;
- Changed industrial organisation;
- A need for closer collaboration between firms (particularly larger and smaller ones);
- Greater emphasis on effective and adaptable management systems;
- Reduced scope for government action.

A controversial argument has developed on the details beyond this. Particularly important is the extent to which a country should aim to be a supplier of core technological developments, or can be satisfied with external sourcing and "hollow corporations". Cohen and Zysman's (1987) analysis confirms the view of Harvey-Jones (former Chairman of ICI) that, *in the long term*, companies and countries that rely solely on external sourcing will lose their long-term capacity to compete. They argue that if a country does not have a capacity in some of the core technologies of manufacture it is likely that it will not for long be able to keep up in their design and use. If this argument is accepted then an emphasis on innovation and R&D of core new technologies must be added to the list of requirements above.

Again, however, there is considerable controversy about how to achieve this technological and innovative capacity. PA (1989), for example, argue that a heavy investment in new technology could prove a handicap because it could lock companies into systems that become rapidly outmoded. Instead, they argue, companies should aim for a flexible and adaptable approach by developing a system of operations that allows retooling at low cost in premises whose layout can be modified quickly. This strategy is the best path to allow producers and designers to compete for the markets of newly emerging national or world products. This approach has been followed by many European and US companies that have rationalised output by reducing capacity or have shifted, through innovation, to high value-added production.

But adaptation of manufacturing systems only partly tackles the problem of increasing the innovative and technological base to create new products. It is an adaptation, not a leadership of change. To lead change requires a much stronger linkage to be developed between market setters, manufacturers, the scientific and technological community, and usually government. To achieve such a potential requires a wide set of collaborative links to be developed of a sustained and longer term character. Many Japanese firms have been the exemplars of this process: promoting change and innovation, "spinning-off" low cost production processes to NICs in the Pacific Rim and continually innovating to aim at a world dominance in given markets (see e.g. Dicken, 1986; 1988). Many European and US companies have been left "*in an uncomfortable middle position, being outdistanced both in process and product innovation, as well as doing little, compared to the Japanese, to seek export production bases*" (Franko and Stephenson, 1982, p. 196). Although the relative role of free markets and government intervention in Japanese success is controversial[5], it is clear that the major lesson to be drawn for the present book is that effective business-to-business links and a strongly supportive government environment have been the crucial ingredients.

Much attention has also been directed to the nature and effects of new forms of flexibility. In the cases of both Britain and the USA it now seems clear that increased labour-relations flexibility[6] is less important than improved organisation, management, adoption of new technology and the capacity to carry through a strategy. As concluded by Rubery *et al.* (1987)[7]:

> *Success depends much more on securing markets, developing new competitive strategies, designing and redesigning new products to meet changing demand and supply requirements, increasing responsiveness to market changes, and adjusting to the organisation of production.*

Skinner (1986), for example argues that there is a 40:40:20 rule describing the competitive advantage of firms: with 40% contributed by long-run changes in strategic position; 40% from technological developments; and only 20% from changes in labour productivity. Although labour flexibility is clearly important (see also later chapters), corporate organisation seems most crucial.

Global development of population, resources and environment

As the global market has become increasingly interdependent, so the distribution of the world's population and resources has become a more important influence on how any one place or country can develop its economy.

Population

There will be a significant influence on the economic potential of different countries arising from a major shift in the relative proportions of the world's population. The rate of growth of population in the industrialised countries is relatively slow (about 1% per year and stagnating), compared to that in developing countries (about 5% per year). Over the 100 years 1950–2050 the relative share of the world population in the industrialised countries will reduce from 29 to 8% and that in the developing countries will increase from 67 to 80% (see Figure 2.6). South Asia's share will increase from 28 to 38% and Africa's from 9 to 23%. The result will be a massive shift of the potential labour force towards the developing countries. Their labour force will grow at approximately 2.4% per year up to 2000 and for sometime beyond. Many countries close to Europe will have the highest growth rates: 17 of the 19 countries in North

Africa and the Middle East have more than half their population under 25 (*The Economist*, 1 September 1990, p. 5). In comparison the industrialised countries have average rates of labour force growth at approximately 0.5% per year, and Britain will have an essentially static labour force until at least the early 21st century (all statistics based on UN and World Bank data).

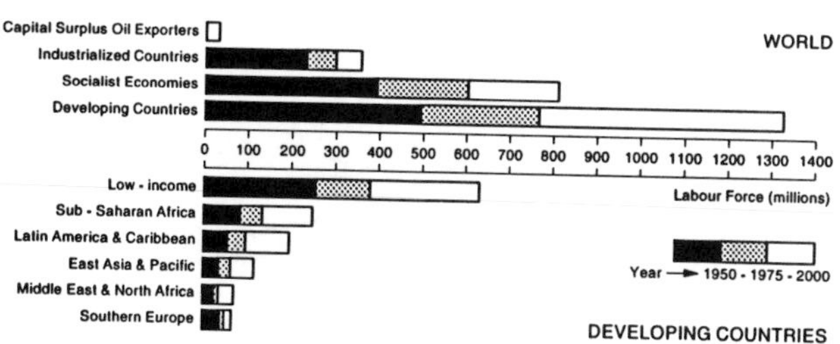

Figure 2.6 Labour force estimates and projections, 1950—2000
Source: after World Bank 1979 *World development report 1979*, and Wallace, 1990

The chief implications of these changes are threefold. First, the main resource of cheap labour in the future will be in the developing countries; hence, it will be very difficult for industrialised countries to compete in any fields with high labour inputs. Second, the Third World's population represents a huge potential market if its income and education can be raised. Third, if Third World income and education can be raised, which will not be easy and will take much time, the industrialised countries will have even greater problems in competing since their control of world markets will reduce.

To give an indication of the potential implications Korea is often used as an example. It has moved from being a developing country to one of the rapidly developing NICs with a larger proportion of its population in universities than any other major industrial country. The example of Korea, and countries like it, has sent a shockwave through the industrialised countries (see e.g. speech of Norman Fowler, Secretary of State for Employment, CBI Conference, November 1989).

With shifts in the relative size of the world's population have come changes in age structures. In the industrialised countries the most important feature is the increase in the number of people aged over 60, combined with a decline in the number of school and college leavers entering the labour force. At a global level the proportion of the population over 60 is expected to increase from 6% in 1980 to 14% in 2025. Within this ageing of the population, the number of over 75s and over 85s will increase to 42% and 13%, respectively, of all pensioners by 2000.

In most major industrialised countries (except the USA), therefore, and in Britain in particular, a labour force which is essentially static or declining in size will have to support a growing number of pensioners. Projections of the working age population shown in Figure 2.7 demonstrate Britain's relatively static position compared to other countries. This alone implies the need for a significant increase in productivity to keep total income levels constant. This development will have to take place against a background of a global market in which plentiful cheap labour will be available in developing countries, an increasing proportion of which is likely to be progressively better educated, and where the demand for labour (at least in manufacturing processes) is likely to continue significantly to decline. Demographic trends are likely, therefore, to make a major contribution to the intensity of global competition for markets, employment and wealth-creating opportunities.

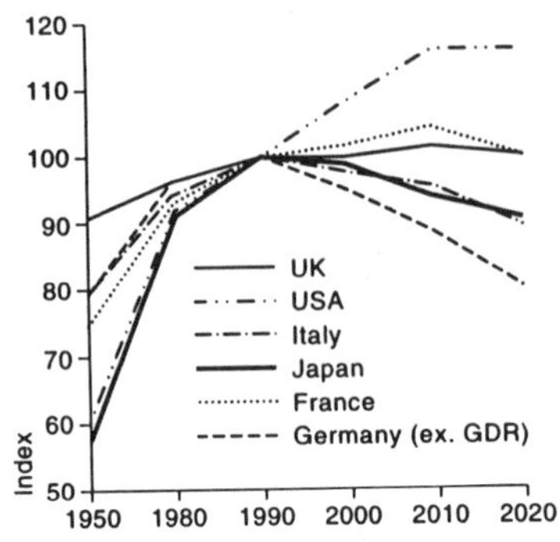

Figure 2.7 Index of working-age (15—64) population
Source: OECD statistics

Resources

Global population growth implies rapidly increasing demands for resources, both renewable and non-renewable. Despite the crisis scenarios in the 1970s, that the world would run out of resources, and the oil stocks of 1973 and 1979, current expectations are that, at a global level, the resource demand can be met. There will, however, be considerable imbalances in satisfaction of demand between countries. The relatively optimistic expectation for total resource supply is surprising in the face of the massive increase in population anticipated. The optimism is possible as a result of the impact of more efficient use of resources through technological development, conservation measures, and innovations in food production. This outcome has been referred to as the "uncoupling" of industrial development from primary products and resources supply.

The declining significance of resources works to the advantage of the industrialised countries as a whole since their supplies are frequently derived from elsewhere. They will still be able to compete in raw material processing and manufacturing, provided that high productivity and further rationalisation can be achieved. That has proved possible in some notable cases, e.g. the UK steel industry, or the German chemical industry. But these competitive pressures will intensify further in the future. In general, however, the declining influence of primary producers and the industrial capacity to process primary products (grain mills, steel, coal, petrochemicals, chemicals, etc.) implies that the comparative advantage of localities and economies in the industrialised economies will have to turn increasingly to their "endogenous" capacity in other respects. Since, as we have already pointed out, there is also an increasing "uncoupling" of production from employment, that endogenous capacity will lie less with local resources and more with the research base, innovative capacity and human skills available in a locality.

Environment

The physical environment has become increasingly important to global development in three respects: first, it has an effect on inter-country competition; second, there is increasing impact on consumer demand for increased environmental awareness in industrialised economies; and third, deriving from increasing environmental awareness, there are significant impacts on global economic development strategies in the face of global environmental interactions.

Inter-country competition up to the 1980s provided, to those countries willing to accept high levels of pollution and contamination, a comparative advantage. For many Third World countries, and for most NICs including Japan, pollution was a price accepted in order to obtain investment and jobs. For Eastern Europe, pollution was an inevitable price to be paid for retaining obsolete productive capacity and using endogenous, rather than the hard currency traded, raw materials (particularly brown coal). East Germany even helped its finances by accepting toxic wastes from West Germany in return for hard currency: it was directly "selling" its environment.

Increased environmental awareness has had a major impact in the industrialised countries in the late 1980s. This is expected to continue in the future. This impact has meant, first, that "exporting" pollution to developing countries or Eastern Europe has become politically unacceptable (when discovered). Second, environmental awareness has influenced the materials, design and marketing of products (e.g. to make them biodegradable, conservative in use of resources, minimal in environmental impact, or recyclable). Third, these influences affect the production process to reduce toxic by-products, pollutants and environmental impacts (including noise, traffic congestion, etc.). Fourth, these developments, in turn, have stimulated markets in recycling equipment and pollution control equipment, etc.

These developments cannot take place easily within one country in isolation. Many environmental impacts have cross-border effects, e.g. water and air pollution, acid rain, the impact of CFCs on the ozone layer, global warming. Hence, heightened environmental concern has increased the motives for global economic cooperation. In addition, most economic responses to environmental awareness cost a considerable amount. Hence, any one country implementing product change would be disadvantaged by the higher costs unless a significant market exists for the higher cost, environmentally friendly product. The 1990s are likely to see increased global cooperation to develop joint economic actions in response to environmental concerns. In addition increased environmental awareness is likely, of itself, to stimulate changes in design, production and marketing since a significant market will exist for more environmentally friendly products. Hence, heightened environmental concern is a further stimulus to global markets, internationalisation and an emphasis on product design and adaptability.

Peace dividend

A rather different influence on national economic growth is the effect of the so-called peace dividend. Rapid changes of military strategy have followed the political and economic reforms of the former communist block and the end of the Cold War. Uncertainties surround the development of these reforms in the USSR, as evidenced by the August 1991 coup. The USSR is crucial because it is the lynch-pin of the economic as well as the military changes. However, in Eastern Europe the process of political change is now regarded as irreversible, even thought its path may be slow and often unsteady. The collapse of COMECON and the withdrawal of Soviet troops from Eastern Europe is complete in Czechoslovakia and Hungary, and looks unlikely to be delayed beyond the deadline for total withdrawal (from Germany) in 1994.

These changes have offered new market opportunities in Eastern Europe. But these are balanced by the cuts in military spending consequent upon reviews of defence needs now that the Cold War is finally over. The medium term consequences, over the next 5–10 years, are:

- Expanding scope for specific industries that can facilitate economic change in former communist countries; especially banking, economic and management consultancy, telecommunications, computers, electronics, training and education;
- Contracts to facilitate environmental clean-up and infrastructure development: pollution control, pollution clean-up, modernisation of the nuclear industry, chemicals, construction;
- Increasing markets for consumer goods, particularly consumer electronics, retailing and distribution;
- Increasing markets for personal services in health care, education and training;
- Declining markets for home and export defence industries and need for defence R&D.

There will be two chief consequences for Britain. First, different industries will experience the benefits or disbenefits of these changes very differently. Consequently, the areas in which key industries are located will also experience very different changes. For example, parts of the South East are highly dependent on the defence industries and defence establishments; Hertfordshire is one of the most highly dependent, for example, and experienced the most rapid rate of unemployment growth of any county in 1991.

A second consequence affects the long term orientation of Britain's R&D. As we shall see in later chapters, a high concentration of both government and private sector finance of R&D has been for defence-related research (see Table 3.4). This concentration has been diversionary from civil research. A long term benefit of the peace process will be the potential to reallocate R&D resources. This will generally serve to intensify competition in civil R&D as the same potential will be available in other countries, particularly the USA. It should, however, provide a more focused response on civil R&D in Britain and other countries formerly dominated by defence R&D, and this should facilitate their long term capacity to compete with countries which have traditionally had low defence R&D commitments, notably Japan.

Meeting the global challenge

This chapter has analysed how the global context of economic relationships offers both threats and opportunities to countries and local communities. Their capacity to respond will depend on their situation within the global economy and how well they equip themselves for change. For a country like Britain we can conclude that the key elements of a strategy to meet the global challenge requires the following challenges to be met:

- Protectionism is not a significant option for national economies or for local communities;
- International competition will further intensify in the future;
- Environmental quality will become increasingly important and the scope for creating and exporting toxic wastes and pollution will radically diminish;
- The peace dividend will allow a greater focus on civil R&D, which will tend to intensify further the competition in new products and technologies;
- Attracting inward investment, particularly from international corporations, will require bargaining and cooperation to put together local packages which are attractive;
- The uncoupling of production and employment means that these packages are not likely to lead to large gains in number of jobs;
- Major scope for safeguarding and increasing the number of local jobs, therefore, requires complex "partnering" arrangements between smaller (local) and larger (national and international) firms;
- Further significant scope for increasing employment can come from stimulating local innovation, technological development and R&D: so-called "endogenous" development;
- The scope for "endogenous" development will, in turn, depend on both the local innovative capacity and the local capabilities of the workforce, institutions and other production factors – particularly their productivity, flexibility and adaptability;
- Any business decision is likely to have beneficial consequences for only a few years: the pace of change of products and services will make any investment outdated quite rapidly. This reinforces the need for rapid adaptability;
- The scope for national government action is much smaller than in the past, the development of local capability is far more important, and economic uncertainties are higher. Companies need to plan for uncertainty through developing an adaptable capacity;
- Global competition means that "doing better than before" is not enough: long-term success will require being as good as the best and as fast as the fastest;
- These developments will require increased emphasis on design, marketing, quality and reliability, greater customisation to specialised markets, and environmental sensitivity;
- The relative shift in the proportion of the world's population to the developing countries will make it difficult for industrialised countries to compete in labour-intensive processes;
- For advanced economies it is, therefore, natural to "rationalise" production and concentrate on high value-added products and services;
- But loss of capacity in basic industries and core technologies may reduce the capacity to influence their design and use; the spotting and development of significant core technologies for the future will be a key determinant of the size of the future manufacturing *and* service industry base;

- High quality labour skills will be required for all anticipated developments;
- Rapid adaptability of people, work practices, organisations and governments will be a sine *qua non* for competitive capacity.

Meeting these requirements will not be easy for any country. For Britain, as we assess in the next chapters, they will be particularly difficult, but not impossible, to achieve.

Footnotes: Chapter 2

1. For example, there is also the development of Optimised Production Technology (OPT) in manufacture, Electronic Point of Sale (EPoS) in retailing, and a variety of financial sector network services.
2. An alternative way of depicting this is Handy's (1989) "Shamrock Organisation" of three leaves for core, temporary and consultant staff.
3. See particularly Toffler (1985), Handy (1985) who also suggest that this will be associated with reduced working hours and changes in the home– work relationship.
4. Source: Blanchflower and Oswald (1991) from BSA. These top four attributes accounted for 76% of the total desired job characteristics.
5. Chalmers Johnson (1992) argues for the crucial role of MITI, the Japanese industry ministry, but more recent and detailed analysis suggests that whilst MITI has had success in some areas, it has failed in others; and many of its successes have been in rationalising declining industries, not in support to new fields of innovation: see e.g. Morita *et al.* (1987) and Wilks and Wright (1987). Recent emulation of Japan is therefore drawn from management techniques and not government's role: see e.g. Oliver and Wilkinson (1988).
6. The case for a large scale impact of labour relations draws particularly from IMS (1986), Daniel (1987), Hakim (1987), ACAS (1988); but this work has been criticised as too wide in its definitions of labour relations: many features are of long standing and almost any initiative is treated as a change in working conditions even though most are of little significance (see e.g. Pollert, 1987).
7. Other supporting evidence is contained in Porter (1987), Pollert (1987), Oliver and Wilkinson (1988), Pinch *et al.* (1989), Gertler (1988), McInnis (1987), Pettigrew and Whipp (1991).

3. *ECONOMIC CAPABILITY:*

Britain's National and Local Position

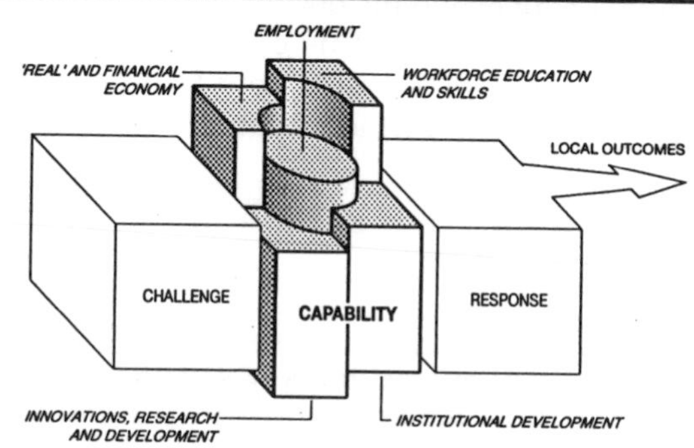

The capabilities required

The assessment of the global challenge in Chapter 2 concluded that the future holds many brutal challenges for the economic progress of advanced economies such as Britain's. These challenges will not be sensitive to national interests and local sensibilities. The success of an economy in the competitive race will depend upon its capacity to meet these challenges. In this chapter we assess the British position. We do this for each of the main dimensions introduced in the previous chapter:

- The economy;
- Employment;
- Population;
- Education and skills;
- Innovation, Research and Development;
- The local conditions.

The discussion in each case is brief, largely descriptive and illustrative of the current position. The detailed development of these themes is contained in the rest of the book.

Our assessment of the British position is bleak. Over the period from the 1950s to the 1970s there were few countries with such a miserable record of economic performance, productivity, profitability, efficient use of human resources, post–16 educational participation, workforce skills, and attitudes to reskilling, training or management development. There is also the strong suspicion that even these phenomena are only the tip of the iceberg in that the quality of some things that are provided may also be suspect from the point of view of economic performance: this is particularly true of schools. Some commentators also suggest that this poor record is part of a long-term decline since the 19th century.

During the 1980s considerable changes took place. These developments have improved Britain's ranking in many respects. Nevertheless, the preconditions were so difficult that a decade is not enough yet to give a verdict. The conclusion to be drawn is also inevitably loaded with political fog, claims and counter-claims in attempting to reach a verdict on the Thatcher administrations 1979–1990 as a "miracle" or "mirage"! We move to assess these verdicts in later chapters.

For the present discussion we see no grounds for complacency. But although the assessment is bleak, there is no inevitability about economic decline, just as there is no inevitability about economic growth. The objective of this chapter is to expose Britain's position in order to allow the later chapters to assess how far that position has recently changed and how far the development of further capability is required in the future.

The economy

Indexes measuring the size and state of the economy are the key starting points for our analysis because:

- Measurement of the size of the economy is the ultimate macroeconomic measure of the national resources available and the contribution of economic development activity to growth;
- The size of the economy determines its capacity to generate endogenous investment on which future growth can be founded;
- The size of the economy is also the long-term determinant of the scope to pursue other objectives (e.g. social policy);
- The state of the economy measures its performance relative to international competitors; key indicators of this are:
    - productivity,
    - profitability;
- The size and state of the economy as a whole, compared to competitors, is a measure of relative success in the economic race.

GDP

Gross domestic product (GDP) is the aggregate measure of the national total wealth and income. It is composed of the personal incomes from wages, profits and rents. Figure 3.1 shows the growth rate of GDP compared to the long-term trends in other major industrial countries. These figures show Britain's steady decline in rate of growth of GDP up to 1980 and the progressive slippage of British performance compared to the rest of the OECD, particularly in the 1960s and early 1970s. The 1980s saw a progressive catching up with the average growth rates of advanced economies, even to slightly exceed them in the late 1980s. This was a remarkable turnaround. But it must be set in the context of comparison with Britain's position in the 19th century, where it had the most rapid economic growth in the world. Thus, although the late 1980s saw a remarkable catching up of the economic performance of Britain with the rest of the world, and a challenge to the best in the world, this must be set against the reduced base for comparison which has seen Britain's growth slip behind other countries since the late 19th century. In addition, renewed worries about Britain's long-term growth capacity have reemerged in the early 1990s with Britain experiencing a much deeper recession, and much lower rates of growth, than other OECD countries in 1990–1.

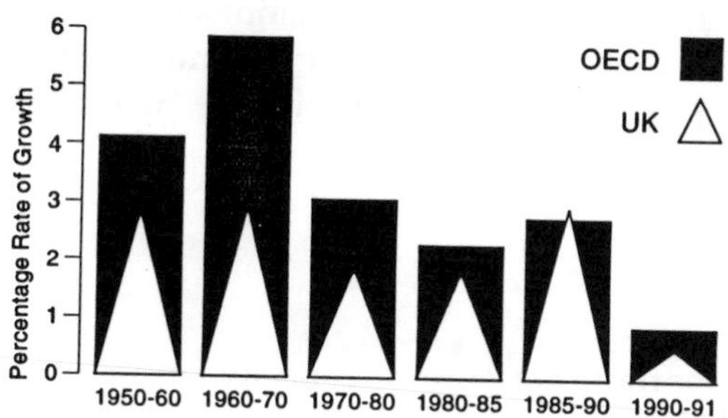

Figure 3.1 Average rates of growth of GDP 1950–1991 of Britain compared to the rest of OECD countries
Sources: OECD and CSO; estimates for 1991 based on part year data

Manufacturing output and productivity

The manufacturing sector in the economy has a special significance because of its historical importance, its political sensitivity, and the argument we examined in Chapter 2 concerning the importance of not only utilising, but also developing, the manufacturing base of core technologies.

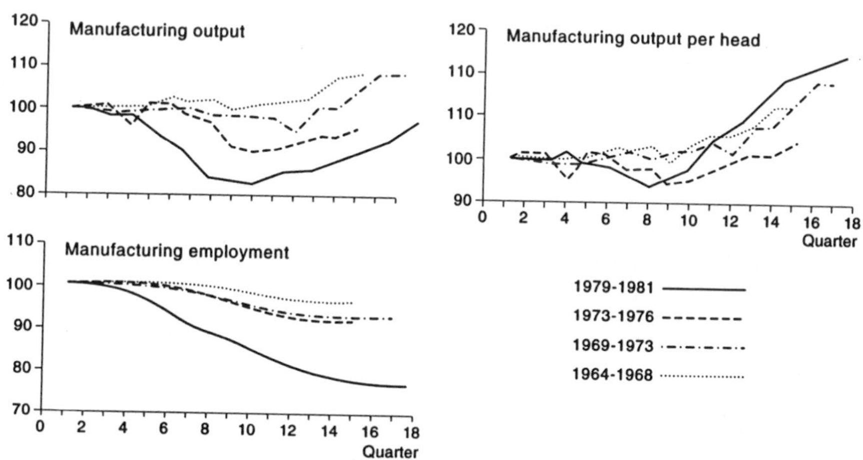

Figure 3.2 Comparisons of UK manufacturing output, employment and productivity over successive cycles, 1964–1984
Source: HM Treasury, *Economic Progress Report*, January 1982, p. 3, with updating

The history of the UK in the 1970s was static or slow decline of manufacturing output, employment and productivity. This trend has tended to accelerate in each recession, and particularly after the middle 1960s when the post-war boom had fully terminated. This pattern is brought out in Figure 3.2. Again, however, a change in the pattern is marked for the most recent period. The recession of 1979–81 resulted, for the first time since 1973, in the output levels of manufacturing before the recession being reattained, and by 1986 exceeded. Manufacturing employment dropped more steeply than in any previous period. But the result of these two trends was a slowing of the long-term decline in productivity.

Profitability

Profitability is an important measure of capacity utilisation and the attraction of a country to external investors. Prior to the 1980s UK profits had systematically underperformed compared both to major competitors and to the OECD average. This is strongly evident from Figure 3.3 which displays profitability of manufacturing measured by net returns to fixed capital. Similar graphs also apply to other sectors. However, again, the steady decline up to 1981 is to be contrasted with the significant growth since that date which has put UK profitability more closely on a par with competitors.

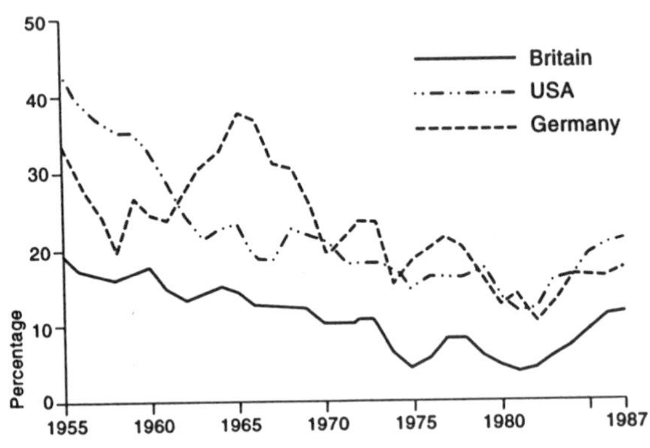

Figure 3.3 Profitability in manufacturing (measured as net rates of return to fixed capital) in Britain, USA and W. Germany, 1955–1987
Source: British Business

The financial economy

The statistics displayed in the Figures 3.1 to 3.4 are each placed in real terms (thus removing the effect of inflation). Inflation was a major factor influencing the economy in the early 1970s, reaching 25% in 1975, and again reaching peaks of 16% in 1980 and 10.5% in 1990. The dangers recognised in such high rates of inflation, and the contrast with much lower rates of inflation in our main competitors, has led to a major influence of Britain's financial economy on economic growth. This issue became particularly important in the period since 1976, when the IMF demanded limits on government spending, through restrictions on the growth of the money supply and the public sector borrowing requirement. However, it was not until the 1981 Budget that a political commitment and organisational mechanism was created, the medium term financial strategy (MTFS) the purpose of which was to establish a control of government spending plans, taxation, other revenues and the growth of the money supply, although even this has proved decreasingly effective. As shown in Figure 3.4, the financial economy in the 1980s came under more control, but there were worrying upturns in inflation and money supply in 1989 and 1990. Despite this worrying reemergence of inflation, Britain's entry into the European Exchange Rate Mechanism (ERM) in 1990, even with a withdrawal in 1992, by restructuring the scope for British autonomous action, should assure a lower and more stable rate of inflation in the future.

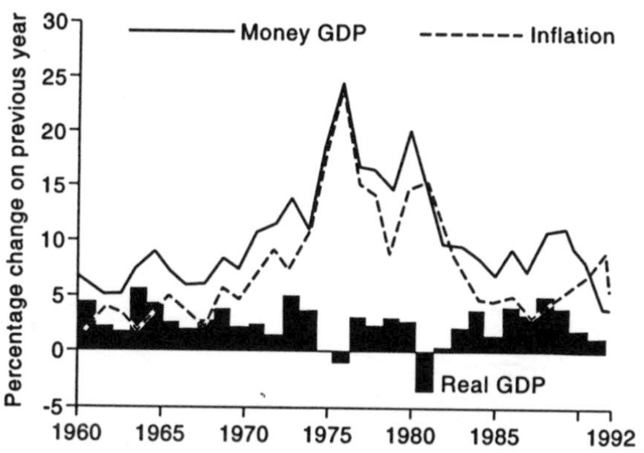

Figure 3.4 Annual percentage change GDP and inflation, 1960–1990
Source: CSO

Concern about the financial economy turns on its interrelationships with the macro- and microeconomic structure of the real economy (which we have briefly outlined above through GDP, productivity and profitability). In simple terms a propensity to allow high inflation is suggestive of weak management, by both government and business, in making more expenditure commitments than are justified by growth in level of receipts. This is the result of self-deception, political deception or over-optimism. We return to this relationship in Chapter 4 where we attempt to account for the difficulties of Britain purging from its systems an inbuilt tendency to allow inflation to occur, instead of imposing tighter financial disciplines.

Employment

Employment represents one of the key outcomes of economic growth, and it is for many commentators its chief "social" objective. Employment has, therefore, a significance beyond its role as a factor input of "labour" or "human resources".

The development of employment in the advanced economies has undergone radical change as a result of global economic developments. Figure 3.5 shows the aggregate change in employment since 1970 in Britain compared to leading competitors. Two features stand out: first, that no European economy can be compared to the growth in jobs in the USA – an increase of over 40% 1970–1987, representing 28m new jobs; second, Britain has a static long-term development of total employment, although it showed rapid growth 1983–90 following earlier steep declines. The job growth over this period in Britain was strong, from 23m to 25.7m, an increase of 2.7m or 12%. But since 1990 many jobs have been lost. Also, compared to other Organisation for Economic Cooperation and Development (OECD) countries, Britain has almost the lowest composition of growth of full time jobs (very slow growth) compared with growth of part-time jobs which show a 36% increase over the longer time of 1973–85.

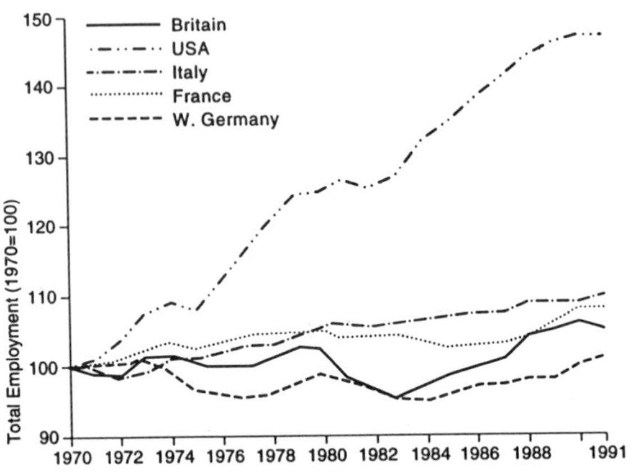

Figure 3.5 Total employment, main OECD countries, 1970–1991
Source: OECD

The relatively static long-term character of British employment is to be compared with rapid increases in manufacturing productivity in the 1980s (see Figure 3.3). Comparing these features demonstrates that increased labour and capital utilisation have played a more important part in Britain than the USA, whilst both countries have shown a rapid increase in service employment compared to manufacturing. In comparing these two countries it must also be borne in mind that the USA has had a rapidly increasing total population since the 1970s through migration and higher fertility, compared to Britain's very slow population increase.

The developments in the global economy anticipated for Britain in the future produce markedly varied demands for different employment sectors. Figure 3.6 shows development of industrial sectors since 1950. Projected changes up to the year 2000 are expected to decrease jobs in manufacturing, whilst service, managerial, professional and technical jobs will have the greatest rate of increase. In terms of human resources this represents a major shift from unskilled and semi-skilled jobs towards skilled manual and, particularly, highly qualified manpower.

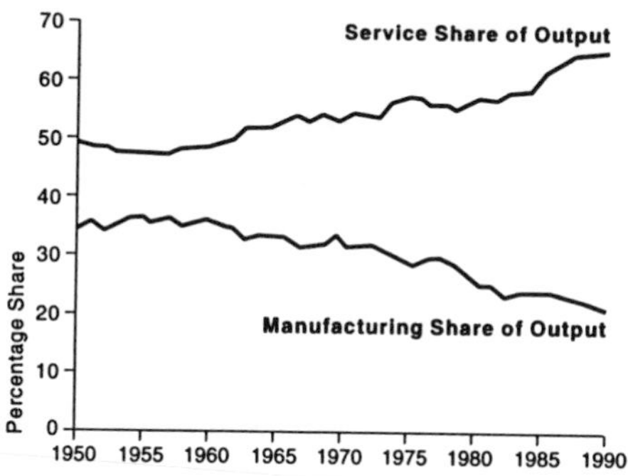

Figure 3.6 Shares of GNP contributed by manufacturing and services 1950–1990
Source: CSO

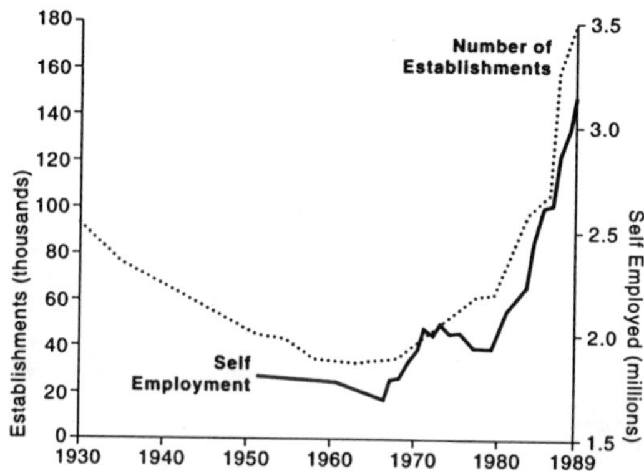

Figure 3.7 Number of self employed and number of establishments with 10 employees or fewer, 1930–1984
Sources: adjusted data from Prais, S.J. (1976) *The Evolution of Giant Firms in Britain*, Cambridge University Press; from 1976, *Business Monitor*, PA 1003, Bannock (1989), DE *Small Firms in Britain* and DE *Gazette*

With changes in the sectors of employment have also come major changes in the character of businesses. Of particular importance has been a shift in relative importance of different sizes of companies. As we note in Chapter 6, there was a steady growth in the dominance of manufacturing output by the largest firms up to the late 1960s, a leveling off in the 1970s, and a decline after 1984 in both output and employment. This recent decline in dominance of large firms is reflected in other data. As shown in Figure 3.7, there has been a steady increase in the number of new companies registered, the number of self-employed and the number of establishments with fewer than 10 employees. The self-employed themselves account for further employees in about one-third of cases (Labour Force Survey) and account for 1.2m new jobs between 1981 and 1989, with a rate of increase of about 200,000 per year. Firms of between 5 and 19 employees accounted for 290,000 new jobs between 1985 and 1987, compared to only 20,000 new jobs in larger firms (DE, 1989). The shift of faster growth rates to smaller firms and self-employment appears to be at least partly a response to the global trends, noted in Chapter 2, towards greater market specialisation and demands for greater flexibility.

The balance between the number of jobs and the available workforce (to be discussed below), in simple terms, determines the level of unemployment. Figure 3.8 shows that unemployment rates rose, in general, in OECD countries up to the mid 1980s. Within this pattern, Britain's position was considerably better than average up to 1970, but during the 1970s and 1980s UK unemployment rates were significantly higher than the OECD average. The cause of this rapid increase in the 1970s was the slowdown in British economic growth (e.g. as measured by GDP in Figure 3.1) and the increase in number of people entering the labour market (see Figure 3.10). But unemployment rates for earlier years in Figure 3.9 show that this was only the last chapter of a story of steadily increasing unemployment in Britain compared to the rest of the OECD since the 1950s.

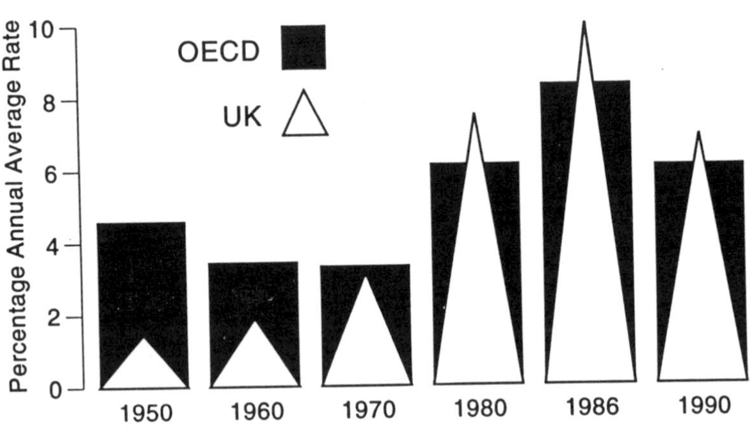

Figure 3.8 Unemployment rates in Britain and OECD countries, 1950–1990
Source: CSO and OECD, 1950 for the six main industrialised countries only

Population[1]

Britain's population represents the source of supply of one of its major factors of production: human resources. The relative importance to businesses of human resources compared to other production factors rapidly increased in the 1980s and, as argued in Chapter 2, is likely to increase yet further in the 21st century. As well as a source of factor supply, people are also a source of innovation, demand and consumption. The balance between supply and demand for labour varies considerably according to people's age and income.

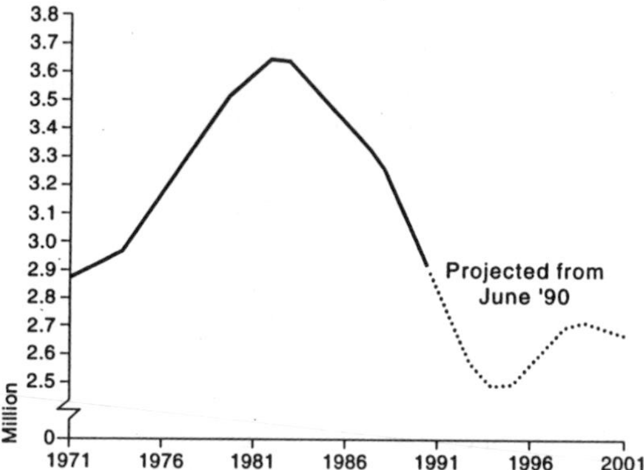

Figure 3.9 Population aged 16–19 in Britain, 1971–2001 (estimated 1990–2001)
Source: OPCS

Because of the effect of the post-war and 1960s baby booms, the development of population and the labour force is not a steady one. In fact it is very unstable. The 1990s are particularly affected by this instability as they will bear the main effect of a reduction in the number of 16–19 year olds (see Figure 3.9). This age group is the main source of entry into the labour force. Between the peak in 1982 and the trough in 1994, the number of 16–19 year olds will reduce from over 3.7m to 2.6m. The interaction of this strong cycle with the rest of the population means that the growth in total working population available slowed down up to 1990, and will remain stable up to the year 2000 (see Figure 2.7). Any growth in the labour force will, therefore, have to come from increased utilisation of the existing working age groups through such approaches as: bringing more women into work (re-entrants); mobilising the unemployed or disabled (who are involuntarily out of work); delaying retirement or bringing the retired back into work. Participation of these groups has been declining (except in the case of women). For example between 1965 and 1990 participation of UK males aged 54–64 fell from 93% to 66%, and for males over 65 from 24% to 18% (source: Labour Force Survey).

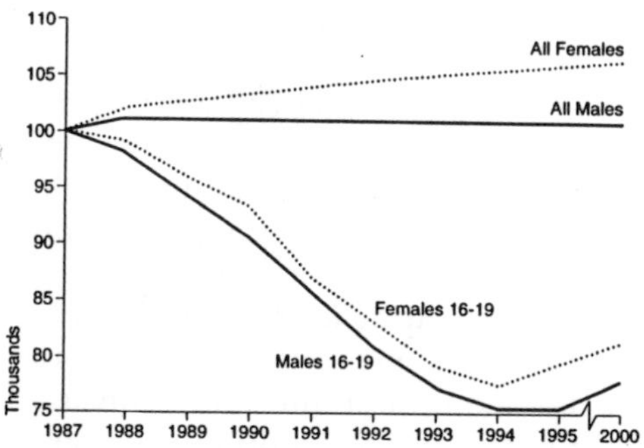

Figure 3.10 Projections of the British labour force 1987–2000
Source: Department of Employment and OPCS projections

Labour force projections are shown in Figure 3.10. These assume continuing growth in the female participation rate. In the 1990s Britain will be more adversely affected by demographic instabilities than most other major OECD countries. In comparison with other countries the shortage of young people will be most severe up to 1995, and then will gradually ease.

Within this pattern, there will also be a further significant shift caused by the relative age concentrations between white and ethnic minority populations. In 1987, 35% of the ethnic population was under 16, compared to 20% in the white population. This means that in the search for young people, employers and trainers will have to rapidly adapt to a shifting balance of needs among the ethnic communities.

A further implication of the demographic impact is that the workforce will become progressively older: the so-called "rise of the gerontocracy"! As shown in Figure 2.7, by 2000 46% will be 35–54 years old compared to 40% in 1988. These changes will be most rapid in the early 1990s. Between 1987 and 1995 the 16–19 age group will fall by 23% and the 20–24 age group will fall by 17%. In contrast, those 25–34 will increase by 16% and those 45–54 by 20%. In the future, this will increase the need for retraining, if the workforce is to remain adaptable and flexible in the face of the global economic challenges outlined earlier.

With the stabilisation of the workforce the dependency ratio of the young and old in relation to the workforce will tend to grow. For example, between 1990 and 2020 the UK dependency ratio will grow from 51.9% to 56.7%. This compares with the average of the 7 major industrialised countries of 47.9% in 1990 and 55.8% in 2020 (source: OECD projections). This means that productivity will have to rise by 9.2% over this period, on average, if average living standards are not to fall.

Education and skills

The discussion of labour force development so far has left out of account the *quality* of the workforce. Absolute numbers of people alone do not constitute a human resource. The extent to which people constitute a resource derives from their level of education, skills, adaptability and entrepreneurship to meet the challenges of the future.

Education

Producing statistics of British educational capacity, and comparing it with other countries, is a hazardous task. Each country's system of education is different and there are many variations within any one system by age, level and mode. However, concern with the quality of the British system has led to preparation of a number of reasonably reliable estimates which are reported here.

A first criterion of education input is the participation rate in education and training in the 16–18 group. This is one of the most important age groups since it is usually considered a crucial one in founding the "transition from school to work". Hence, educational provision to this age group may be taken as a good index of the quality of general skills in the workforce. As shown in Table 3.1, Britain performs very poorly against this measure. Of those countries reported, it is bottom of the league in total participation of 16–18 years olds: 37%, or over one-third of the population, in

1981 received no further education or training after age 16. Of those receiving training, the UK is also almost the poorest in full-time school or other full-time attendance. This means that 69% of the 16–18 population in 1981 received no full time education or training (and this increased between 1981 and 1983). This record compares badly with all the other countries listed, particularly the USA and Japan. The record is even worse when the staying-on rate after 17 is considered. The UK figure for 16–19 full time schooling of 18% is buttressed by a 32% staying on rate at 16, but by 17 this has dropped to 19% and by 18 to only 2% (compared to 20% in most major competitors).

Table 3.1 Participation in education and training of 16–18 year olds

	Full time school	Other full time	Part time	Total full time participation ages 16-18		Total full time participation ages 14-18	
				1976	1989*	1983	1989
Germany	31	14	40	35	47	73	78
Netherlands	50	21	8	64	70	90	92
USA	65	14	–	76	79	–	–
Japan	58	11	3	71	77	–	–
France	33	25	8	54	66	78	86
Italy	16	31	18	44	48	74	77
UK	18	14	30	28	33	68	71

* most non-UK data for earlier years

Source: DES Statistical Bulletins, 10–85 and 1–90; EC DG5 Employment in Europe 1991

This dismal picture is continued at higher education level. Table 3.2 shows that the UK records the lowest number of total enrollments in higher education and the smallest range of subjects usually studied. The Department of Education and Science (DES) (Statistical Bulletin, 4–87) takes comfort in the much better statistics for number of new entrants, since enrollment data are certainly biased by the varying duration of courses and wastage rates. However, even if these data are accepted, the UK still has only a low average participation level. Moreover, that participation is made up, to a greater extent than other countries, of lower level (non-university) education, a high level of part time, and a high drop off after 17.

Table 3.2 New entrants and participation in all higher education (1983–84)

	Total enrollments per 100 of 18–24 population	No. of courses studied in preparation	New entrants per 100	Percentage of new entrants entering university (%)
USA	44	6	60	44
Netherlands	22	6 –7	38	33
Japan	21	8 –10	38	70
Germany	20	5	27	65
France	19	7	34	67
Italy	18	–	28	96
UK	15	3	31	32

Source: DES Statistical Bulletin, 4 – 87

If Britain's education record post–16 measures up as at best a poor average, and on most criteria is the worst of the major OECD economies, concern increases still further with the quality of compulsory 5–16 schooling. A particular concern has become functional *literacy.* Whilst there is no absolute definition of literacy, business leaders have provided their own definition as "the ability to receive and understand simple verbal and written instructions" (see: CBI conference debate, 1989).

The concern with literacy has grown from the experience of business managers, trainers and personnel departments who are the recipients of the products of the education process. National estimates suggest that 13% of adults in the UK have varying degrees of difficulty with reading, writing, spelling, numeracy, etc., whilst 15% of entrants to Employment Training (ET) programmes and 17–26% of entrants to Youth Training (YT) programmes need help in these skills[2]. Even Moser, President of the British Association, claims that *"at least one child in seven is functionally illiterate"*[3]. These claims are borne out by the results of standardised reading tests. For example, a study in Kent (Thomas, 1990) shows that the proportion of pupils with major reading difficulties was 8% in 1987, with no differences between the social and economic character of the school[4]. These results have been put beyond doubt by two recent reports (see: HMI, 1990; NFER, 1990). These show that although there may not be a decline in standards, 20% of schools are judged by Her Majesty's Inspectorate (HMI) (1990) to be "poor" in their teaching of reading and only 30% had standards that were "high". By age 11, pupils were left to read freely with "inadequate guidance" and monitoring: 25% were not as fluent or accurate as they should be, and a significant number are illiterate. These results all suggest a "system" failure rather than a pupil failure.

Interrelated with the problem of functional literacy is that of truancy. For both phenomena, no reliable national data exist; the records at school level do not usually distinguish the reasons for absence[5]. The best general estimate appears to be that there is approximately 8% truancy in primary schools, 10% truancy rate in secondary schools, but rising to 50 or 70% in the final two years (levels 4 and 5). Although the information available suggests that inner city areas have higher truancy levels, the differences are not that great: approximately 15% in Bolton, Gateshead, Manchester and Inner London Education Authority (ILEA), but rural areas such as Cumbria have 10%. This suggests again a system-wide failure. Some have argued that this is indicative of a rational choice which weighs the attractions that exist as alternatives to going to school – economic and otherwise (Baroness Cox, in *Times Educational Supplement*, 23 June 1989).

The discussion of illiteracy and truancy focuses on two specific, but highly significant issues for economic competence. At the same time there is a more general concern by business that the quality and attitudes developed within the educational system are more deeply frustrating to the needs of the economy. This suggests an even wider "system" failure which we address in later chapters.

Skills

There are even more problems in quantifying the relative position of Britain's human resource skills than there are for education. This is because the range of qualifications is large and complex, and the definitions and systems of qualifications differ between countries to an even greater extent than education.

Despite these difficulties, Table 3.3 shows that in comparison with four main competitor nations the skilling of the younger population is lowest in Britain. The proportion of school leavers who do not achieve the recognised standard is also high, although not as high as the USA. These tables also bring out two features: first, that the standards of attainment used are low – one CSE pass is a very low level of minimum qualification; second, there is also a concern that even those attaining the minimum levels are doing this only in the educational field, not with a satisfactory vocational emphasis. The comparison with Germany is the most worrying in this respect. We devote considerable attention to a deeper analysis of this aspect in Chapters 7 and 8.

If the skills of the population give grounds for concern, so also do the attitudes towards those skills. Until recently only a minority of employers or employees recognised the disadvantages of poor skills and qualifications. A Training Agency (TA) (1989a) study estimated that about 7% of total working days of employees in employment were devoted to training and education for post–16 people in 1987. Of this total, 63% is undertaken in colleges, polytechnics and universities, 33% on the job by employers, and 4% by private providers. Management training is one of the largest subjects of private provision. The TA study concluded that participation varies substantially, is overall rather poor, and has least application to the lowest skilled.

Table 3.3 Level of qualifications by country 1980–81

	Workers with recognised qualification as % of population	Definition of minimum qualification	% of labour force qualified to first degree level	Proportion of school leavers going into employment without achieving recognised education standard (3 CSEs or equivalent)
US	78	Higher school diploma	19	29
Germany	66	Vocational qualifications	8	10
Japan	60	Lower secondary school diploma	13	13
UK	50	I CSE pass	7	16

Source: MSC, 1985, Tables 6.5 and 6.6.

The result is a system which in the 1980s ensured that, for those in employment, two-thirds had received no training in the last 3 years. The national Labour Force Survey shows only 14% of employees receiving training at any one time in 1989, although this was up from 9% in 1984. The lack of training experience on the job is worst amongst the lowest skilled, with about 20% of firms giving no training at all, 70% having no training plan, 80% have no formal targets, and 97% make no cost-benefit assessment of the training they do undertake. Training is also the lowest for the over–35s. The lack of training was amongst the poorest in manufacturing processing and manufacturing fabrication, where respectively 27% and 15% of employers provided no training. It was also poorest in small firms: 24% of employers with 10–24 employees and 17% of firms with 25–49 employees gave no training, compared with less than 6% for firms of over 100 employees (see TA, 1989a).

Britain's training record seems, therefore, to cast considerable doubt on the country's capacity to respond to the phenomena we have outlined in Chapter 2, of the need for a high qualified and adaptable workforce to meet the competitive challenges of the future.

The deficiency of provision of training by employers is reflected in the attitudes of employees. Few individuals play any role in funding their development of post–16 skills, and this ensures that the "market" for training is limited compared for example particularly to the US. As a result, only 2% of direct training costs are borne by individuals in 1987 although the figure rises to 25% if account is taken of earnings foregone. A MINTEL (1990) report showed that although more training was the highest rated improvement desired by employees in work (equal with better career prospects and improved working environment), this accounted for only 20% of respondents' rankings; 74% felt they were qualified enough in terms of their job for the 1990s. This shows a strong complacency in the face of the changes in jobs that are likely to occur in the near future. The complacency was highest among factory workers (80% felt sufficiently qualified) and lowest among shop workers (64%), other manual (72%) and managers (72%). These figures are further supported by the response that 32% of respondents have "*got as far as they want to*", only 26% want "*to progress further now*". This lack of ambition is highest among other manual (39%), public sector (34%), shop workers (36%) and factory workers (33%). These results again raise worries about the attitudes to acquiring the skills and responding to change required in the fields of core technologies and products.

The survey evidence suggests that complacency among managers is almost as high as among employees, and their levels of ambition and willingness to retrain are only slightly better than average. Since it is estimated that 7 out of 10 people to be employed in management posts by the year 2000 were already managers in 1987, this again suggests poor prospects for flexible and adaptable management. Controversy surrounds the appropriate training and management qualifications that are required. But on whatever criterion used, Britain's position appears weak. For example, in 1986, 85% of *top* managers have degrees in the USA and Japan, 62% in Germany and 65% in France, compared to only 24% (and 21% of all managers) in Britain; the British output of MBAs is only 12% of that of the USA; 20% of large companies and 75% of smaller companies make no provision for management training, 80% of large companies have no management training at all; only 48% of managers take part in it, and the quality of the management education that is received is routinely criticised as "*too academic*" or "*too discipline-led*" (MSC/NEDC/BIM, 1989). In general, management training is seen as too small in supply and uptake, too fragmented and unrelated to the company's strategy, goals, and staff appraisal, with few companies perceiving management training as an important competitive weapon (AMRC, 1988). Or, in the words of MSC/NEDC/BIM (1987, p.2), Britain just does not "take the preparation and development of her managers as seriously as other countries". Compared to other countries management training is seen as pragmatic rather than professional, with an emphasis on financial skills (especially accountancy) rather than technological knowledge compared to Germany, and with lower entry age (usually 22 in Britain, compared to 27 in Germany).

Innovation, research and development

Britain has often prided itself on its R&D record. Indeed, it has an astonishing record of research in some areas, for example, 26 Nobel prizes in science were obtained by

Britons 1960–89, the second highest total in the world, after 90 in the USA and well in front of the next highest countries of 15 in Germany, 6 in France, 5 in Sweden and 4 in Japan (Rosenberg and Mowery, 1990).

However, there have been increasing concerns about the capacity of Britain's R&D to make the most effective contribution to economic growth. First, the record of Nobel prizes and great discoveries lies mainly in the past. There is a suspicion that current R&D may not be able to contribute as effectively as in the past. This suspicion is based on analysis of statistics such as relative R&D expenditure (Figure 3.11). This shows Britain steadily slipping behind the major industrial economies in proportion of GNP spent on R&D, even though the absolute levels of expenditure have slowly risen.

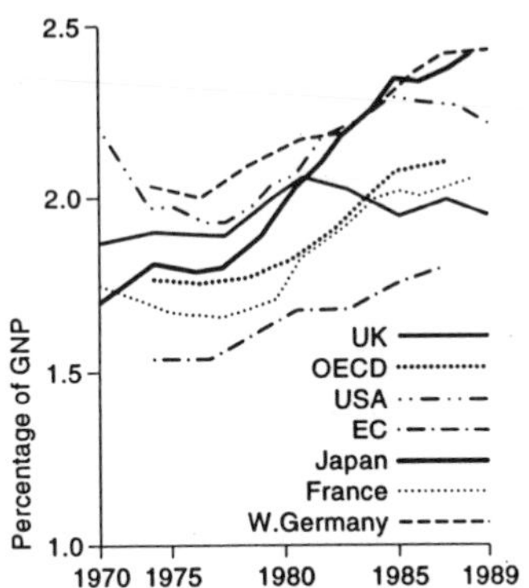

Figure 3.11 R&D expenditure as a proportion of GNP, 1970–1989
Sources: UK CSO Annual Survey; other countries, OECD and Financial Times, 3 December 1990, from STA

A second concern has been that Britain has put too high a proportion of R&D expenditure into defence rather than civil R&D. This has two problems: first, that large scale commercial spinoffs may not be possible from such highly specific investments, and second that the R&D community will have considerable difficulty adapting to the increasing impact of the peace dividend. As shown in Table 3.4, this concentration on defence R&D has particularly affected government funds. As a result it has become an even more focused part of the policy debate (e.g. House of Lords, 1990, 1991). This is the more poignant since it is often argued that long-term and fundamental research usually require a government commitment (see Chapters 4 and 6). There has also been a growing concern that increasing overseas funds may be using UK contracted research organisations for R&D, but product development goes elsewhere (see SEPSU, 1991).

Table 3.4 Sources of R&D funds applied to civil and defence R&D in 1989.

Source of funds	Civil (%)	Defence (%)	Total (£m)
Own funds	82	26	5,328
Government funds	5	57	1,249
Overseas funds	12	17	1,023
Total (%)	100	100	–
Total (£m)	5,947	1,653	7,600

Source: CSO Annual Survey

The gap in government commitment is also evident for changes over time. Figure 3.12 shows that almost all expansion of Britain's R&D spending, since the late 1960s, has come from companies' own funds and from overseas. Hence, Britain's record of relatively constant R&D spend with rising GNP shown in Figure 3.11, comes almost exclusively from non-government sources. As with R&D spend, so also with R&D manpower. Figure 3.13 shows the relatively stable position of the UK compared to the rapid growth of R&D employees in the other major industrialised countries.

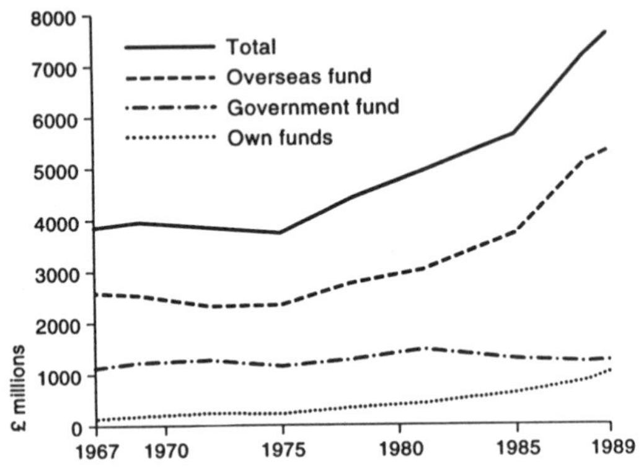

Figure 3.12 Sources of funds for business R&D, 1967–1989 (at 1989 prices)
Note: includes all civil and defence R&D; after 1986 including the UKAEA
Source: CSO annual estimates

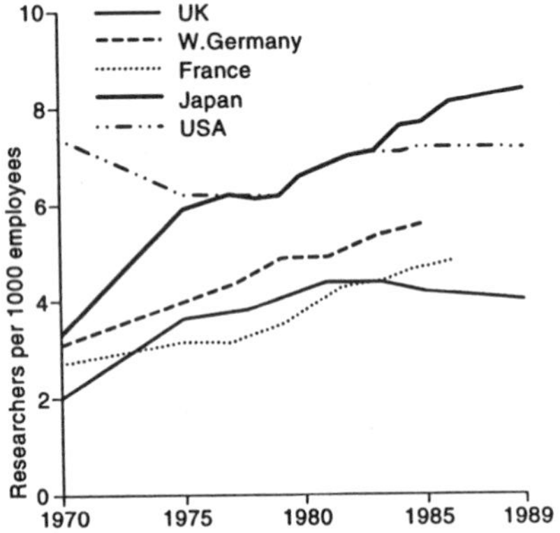

Figure 3.13 Numbers of R&D researchers per 1,000 national workforce, 1970–1989
Sources: UK CSO Annual Survey; other countries from Financial Times, 3 December 1990; The Economist, 16 February 1991, NSF and MITI)

The economic impact of a static R&D commitment relative to rapid expansion of R&D in Britain's main competitors is very evident from a number of indicators. Figure 3.14, for example, shows the decline in British patents granted in the USA compared to the rapid rise of impact in the USA of German and Japanese R&D. A recent R&D scoreboard showed Britain most frequently in the bottom rank position across 18 industrial sectors compared to the USA, Germany and Japan (*The Independent*, "British efforts fail to close the spending gap", 10 June 1991).

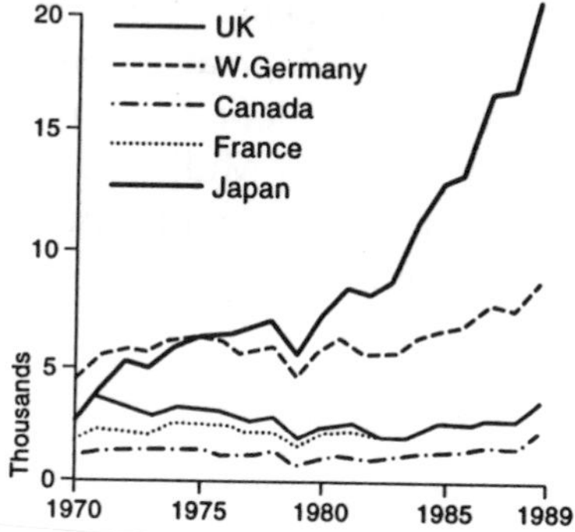

Figure 3.14 Patents granted in the USA to non-USA companies, 1970–1989
Source: Financial Times, 3 December 1990

The form of Britain's R&D problem is discussed further in Chapter 4 and later chapters. What is already clear, however, is that a static or declining R&D commitment is likely to cause severe long-term difficulties for the British economy in facing the economic challenges identified in Chapter 2. The emphasis on development of core technologies, quality, customisation and speed of delivery all require extensive R&D commitments. The evidence presented here suggests that Britain has lagged in this commitment since at least the early 1970s.

Local conditions

The development of the economy, both in its long-term decline and in its recent economic growth, has not been uniform. The contrasts between areas have been considerable, and differences have even tended to increase. Since an economy is a combination of its parts, examination of local conditions is as important as understanding the national picture. It is also an important part of our argument that, since so many economic decisions are made in a local as well as a global context, it is the local capacity that is essential to responding to the challenge facing the economy as a whole. The detailed examination of local capacity is the subject of later chapters. Here we give a brief outline of local variations in employment, business growth, unemployment and education.

Employment and business growth

Very marked differences in regional growth of employment and business occurred in the 1980s. The largest absolute growth 1984 – 89 was in the South East, which accounts for 27% of all new jobs measured in the Employment Census (Table 3.5). However, it was some of the smaller, and traditionally more peripheral regions, which experienced the most rapid rates of growth; for example East Anglia, the South West and Wales. There was thus some evidence of catching up between regions in level of economic growth during the second half of the 1980s.

The picture is a little different when looking at the number of new businesses in Table 3.5. The South East now has a much greater dominance in absolute numbers and growth rate. But as well as the traditionally more peripheral regions of East Anglia and South West, the West and East Midlands have also experienced rapid business growth. The more detailed map of country business growth rates 1979–89, shown in Figure 3.15 exhibits the north–south difference more clearly. The Employment Census data in Table 3.5 largely exclude the self-employed and micro-businesses (under 5 employees), whereas the new business data in Figure 3.15 includes all businesses registered for VAT, including the self-employed. Hence the difference in relative growth rates between the two sources of statistics in Table 3.5 is almost entirely accounted for by the higher rates of growth of self-employment and micro-business in the South East and Midlands. We turn in detail to these differences in enterprise patterns in Chapters 6 and 11–14.

Table 3.5 Employment 1984–89 growth and net business growth 1979–89 by region

Region	Growth in employment 1984/89		Net new business 1979/89	
	(000s)	(% growth)	(000s)	(% growth)
South East	379	5.3	170	40
East Anglia	84	11.7	16	31
South West	201	12.9	37	30
West Midlands	120	6.1	21	26
East Midlands	117	8.0	25	29
Yorkshire & Humberside	130	7.2	22	21
North West	136	5.9	21	16
North	56	5.3	10	19
Wales	101	11.4	15	21
Scotland	64	3.4	20	21
Northern Ireland	28	5.6	9	21
UK total	1,416	6.6	373	29

Sources: Employment Census and British Business VAT registration data

Unemployment

Unemployment differences between regions have shown a tendency to widen in recessions and narrow in periods of rapid growth. This is particularly marked in the period of emergence from the 1981–82 recession, where regional unemployment differences only began to narrow after 1984 (see Figure 3.16).

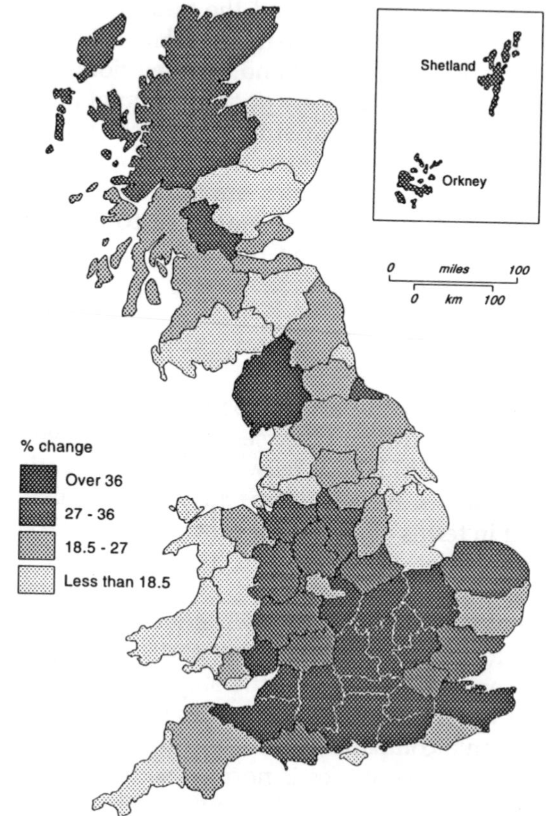

Figure 3.15 Percentage increase in the stock of VAT registered businesses 1979–1989
Source: Employment Gazette, November 1990, from CSO

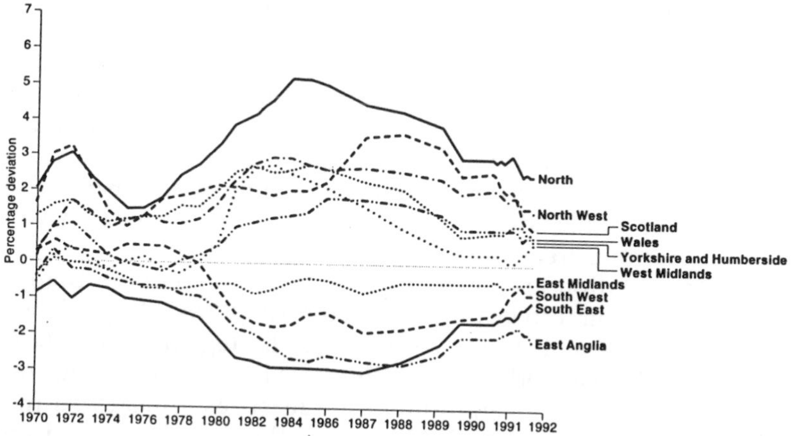

Figure 3.16 Percentage deviation of regional rates from the national unemployment rate 1970–1991
Source: Department of Employment data

Across these changes there has been considerable stability, the North West, North, Scotland and Wales being above average, and the South East, South West and East Anglia being below the average unemployment rates. However, Figure 3.16 shows the considerably improved performance of Scotland, the deteriorating performance of the West Midlands, and the continued extremely poor position of the North West.

Within these regional trends are considerable local variations. Particularly significant are the differences between inner city and outer more suburban areas. Generally differences of unemployment rates are 6 to 10% higher in inner cities. In some inner city pockets, unemployment may rise to 60–80% of the potential workforce. We discuss this in more detail in Chapter 11.

Education and skills

Like international comparisons, comparisons between areas in Britain in education and skill levels are fraught with difficulty. Assessment of local variations is also made of less relevance by the mobility of labour between places depending upon the supply and demand for different skills. Nevertheless, the focus of our discussion is on the local institutional context in terms of how far it contributes to the economic capacity of its area. Hence it is appropriate to assess the contribution of local education and training to the local skills base.

A variety of criteria could be employed to assess educational contributions. However, because it has been the focus of the adverse international comparisons surveyed in Tables 3.1 and 3.2, we concentrate here on the staying-on rate post–16. Figure 3.17 displays the variation for Local Education Authorities (LEAs) in 1987–88. Unfortunately the data are not collected on a comparable basis for England, Scotland and Wales. As a result the LEAs in each of these countries is normed so that Figure 3.17 represents the quartile distribution of LEAs relative to the distribution separately in England, Scotland and Wales, i.e. LEAs can be compared only within these areas, not between.

In general, staying on rates are highest in outer London, the South East, Scottish Islands, South Glamorgan and Dyfed, and lowest in the North, Yorkshire and Humberside, the small industrial towns in Scotland, West Glamorgan and Powys. There is also an urban – rural differentiation, so that more metropolitan areas have the lower staying-on rates. But this is not a generalisation holding for all places. For example, Bury, Haringey, St Helens and Wigan all have staying on rates in the top quartile, whilst Dorset, Durham and Essex have staying-on rates in the bottom quartile.

The differences in staying-on rates at the extremes are very significant. The lowest six LEAs all have under 50% staying on rate at 16 (Sunderland, Barking, Gateshead, Wakefield, Doncaster and Sandwell) whilst the highest six LEAs all have staying on rates above 74% (Harrow, Brent, Bury, Surrey, Barnet and Sutton).

Skills in the population are even more difficult to compare than education. However, some indications can be drawn from the TA (1989a) study of training. Table 3.6 shows the levels of training on and off-the-job by region. It is highest in Wales, East Midlands, East Anglia, Yorkshire and Humberside, and the North, and lowest by far in London. These data compound three features: variations in employer commitment to training; the training needs of the workforce; and the training demands of the industry in each region. The training rates can be compared with the staying-on rates in education, also shown in Table 3.6. The relationship is far from clear, which is to be expected given the number of factors involved and the high degree of variation likely to be present within each region. However, it is the case that of the five regions with the highest training inputs three have the lowest education staying-on rates (depending on how the Scotland and Wales data are compared with England). Conversely, of the five regions with the lowest training inputs, two have the highest post–16 staying on rates and two have average staying-on rates. The relationships require considerable further analysis, but there is some evidence to suggest that employers in regions with the lowest staying-on rates in education are having to invest more in training. We look in detail at the contribution that education and training can make to local economic networks in later chapters.

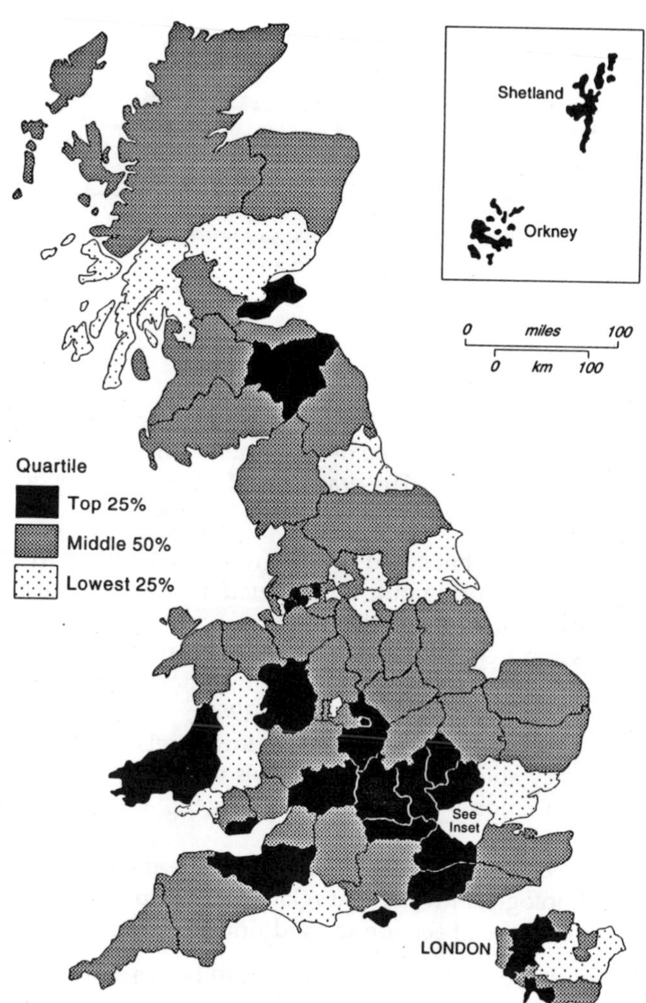

Figure 3.17 Staying-on rate post–16 in education
Sources: England–DES Statistical Bulletin 3–89; Wales–Welsh Office; Scotland–Scottish Office

Table 3.6 Training days per employee in 1989, and staying-on-rate in school post-16, by region, 1987–88

	Training days per employee			
	On-the-job	Off-the-job	Total	% post-16 staying-on in school
London	3.0	2.2	5.2	62
Outer South East	2.8	3.1	5.9	66
South West	3.1	2.7	5.8	65
West Midlands	3.1	3.3	6.4	62
East Midlands & East Anglia	2.9	3.9	6.8	62
North	3.0	3.0	6.0	58
North West	3.2	2.6	5.8	62
Yorkshire and Humberside	3.2	3.2	6.4	57
Wales	3.5	3.3	6.8	32*
Scotland	3.0	2.9	5.9	52*

Sources: Training Agency (1989a); staying-on-rates, as Figure 3.18, * with similar comments on the direct comparability between England, Scotland and Wales

Implications

This chapter has sought to assess Britain's relative capability across the key dimensions that determine its economic development. The conclusion to be drawn on the performance up to the late 1970s was one of bleak prospects in almost every dimension. The chief points can be summarised as follows:

- Steady slippage in GDP per head and rate of growth in GDP up to 1981;
- Steady decline in manufacturing output, productivity and employment up to 1981;
- Steady decline in profitability up to 1981;
- High inflation rates and instability in the financial economy;
- Steady growth in unemployment levels from well below the OECD average up to the 1960s, to well above in the 1970s and early 1980s;
- Low participation rates in post–16 education, low levels of educational attainment, high levels of illiteracy and truancy; Low levels of skills and training, complacency and lack of ambition among workers and managers, and low levels management training;
- Low levels of resources and priority to civil research and development, innovation and long-term technological investment relative to competitors;
- Considerable variations in all economic conditions in different parts of the country.

The 1980s gave some hope that the problems were both recognised and were being addressed:

- The growth rate of GDP by 1989 was equal to the best 10% in the world economy;
- A rapid increase in manufacturing output and productivity 1981–89;
- Stabilisation of the long-term trend in the level of manufacturing employment since 1986, with some evidence of continued modest growth;

- Marked increases in profitability 1981–89;
- Stabilisation of the extremes of the financial economy (despite doubts about money supply and inflation in 1989 and 1990, re-entry into the ERM should provide a long-term stability previously unattained);
- Reduction of unemployment to the OECD average since 1988;
- Rapid growth in the number of jobs, number of self-employed and number of business start-ups;
- A slow increase of participation in post–16 education and training and some evidence of increases in attainment since about 1983;
- Improved attitudes of workers and managers to training and development since about 1987;
- Recognition of priority needed for civil R&D, innovation and technological investment, although little in the way of new government resources;
- Some evidence of a narrowing in differences between places in rates of business growth and levels of unemployment.

These achievements represent a very significant turnaround of the long-term trends.

However, a more considered verdict must be based on assessing how far these recent changes have tackled the underlying causes of the historical weaknesses. In 1990–92 the depth of the recession significantly reduced many of the 1980s gains in employment, business growth, profits and outputs. The form of recovery from this recession will allow answers to the key questions of how far the major gains of the 1980s can be sustained, how far they represent a long-term shift in Britain's economic performance, or are merely a catching up after the deep recession of 1980–82.

The discussion here has suggested that Britain's steady slippage in relative global economic performance did not arise solely from inefficiencies and inadequate application of resources. Rather there are strong indications that underlying the indicators of poor performance is a wider structural problem, of system failure, that even if more resources were applied they would not necessarily solve the economic problem, because they would be applied to the wrong thing. It is to assess this possibility that we turn in the next chapter. From that discussion we provide the basis for the detailed analysis in the subsequent chapters which seek to answer the question of how far the 1980s have gone far enough in developing sufficient system-wide changes to assure economic prosperity in the future.

Footnotes: Chapter 3

1. All statistics in this section are based on OPCS or Department of Employment analysis and projections.
2. ALBSU estimates reported in *Employment Gazette*, June 1991, pp.347–350, "Basic Skills at Work".
3. Sir Claus Moser, Presidential address to the British Association for the Advancement of Science, *Financial Times*, 21 August 1990.
4. See also Times Educational Supplement, 6 July, 13 July 1990.
5. In 1991–92 the DES is obliging schools and LEAS for the first time to record reasons for absence and these data will be made public.

4. BRITAIN'S INSTITUTIONAL CAPABILITY

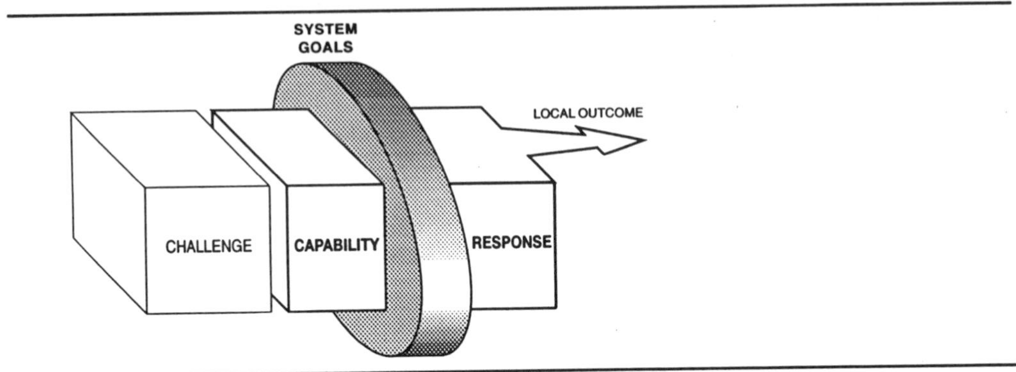

Britain's systemic problem

Recognising the long-term slippage of Britain's economic position up to the early 1980s, and the beginnings of a possible reversal since then, is only the start in seeking to answer the fundamental question which is the purpose of this book: how to provide a capability to respond to the economic challenges of the future?

In this chapter we move to seek an explanation of the key factors that have shaped Britain's long-term position. In so doing we move to controversial ground. We also accept that, in the space we can devote to this question here, we cannot do full justice to the complexity of the historical and economic analysis required. However, there are now available a number of extremely thorough studies which are sufficiently similar in their conclusions that it is possible here to draw out the main implications for our argument.

This chapter argues that Britain's long term economic slippage is indeed one that is system-wide. It arises from deep within the structure of the country's institutions and attitudes. It is a strong characteristic of system problems, though not always fully recognised, that it can be normally expected, that when new resources are applied to overcoming a problem they will not improve the situation. They may even make the situation worse. There is a so-called "perverse policy syndrome".

System failure, we argue, arises from the goals and performance of the policy communities, institutions and the networks developed between different institutions. We argue that there are six key dimensions to this problem:

- Business strategy;
- Employment and the labour market;
- Education and training;
- Economic policy and the welfare compromise;
- Government: central-local relations;
- The impact of Europe.

These have tended to mutually support each other and to lead Britain into economic slippage. Our presentation of these dimensions here lays the foundation upon which the analysis of the rest of the book is based where we argue that economic decline is not inevitable; but it requires major development of institutions if it is to be reversed. Some of our remarks will appear highly critical, but it is our argument that it is not from individuals, as such, that difficulties arise, but from the institutional system within which they work and respond. We start by introducing a framework for the economic appraisal of institutions and define the meaning of the "perverse policy syndrome".

The economic appraisal of British institutions

The central question with which this book is concerned is how Britain's historically poor and degenerating economic performance can be reversed. Our approach to answering this question is explicitly economic. In the discussion here we start with presenting the approach we shall adopt in economic assessment of institutions.

The system-wide character of a country certainly depends on its individual people and their response to incentives and the needs for learning, adaptability and flexibility. This is basic for the concept of *human resources* which is a key part of our argument. However, individuals alone do not shape an economy. No modern economy is a pure market of atomistic individual decision making. Instead an economy is chiefly shaped by organisations and institutions – such as companies, interest groups, government, unions, societies and other organisations. It is these institutions that link individuals together, support networks of exchange of information and incentives, represent individuals' views and, through government and bureaucracies, provide information, products, services, employment and take economic decisions. A country's economic system is therefore a subtle combination of individuals and these collective organisations.

Once we recognise that organisations as well as individuals shape a country's economy we are drawn to assess not only the relationships of macroeconomic and microeconomic indicators, which relate "people" to the "economy". We also have to assess the performance of a country's institutions in relation to its economic goals. The importance of institutional performance has been long recognised. But the traditional view, associated pre-eminently with Adam Smith's *Wealth of Nations*, was that markets assure the best economic allocation decisions and hence the highest level of prosperity: what they need is as little government as possible. It is only recently that it has been recognised that the converse may, in fact, be true: that strong government may be needed to assure as close as possible an approximation to market allocation decisions, because only strong government can keep the power of other institutions in check in order to allow economies to work better. Of course, in this assessment, strong government means a government that works strongly to stimulate economic forces, not to conflict with them.

But in recognising the importance of government lies a further dilemma. No-one better than Mancur Olson (1982) has made the argument that institutions, including government, are subject to a perverse policy syndrome. This is an observation about the long-term behaviour of institutions in a stable society. It is an economic explanation for the phenomena that other, more popular writers, have observed: that "every change is likely to achieve the opposite of what was intended" (the so-called Howard's law) and that "resistance to new ideas increases as the square of their importance" (the so-called Russell's law) (see e.g. Sampson, 1982, p. xiii). In other words, strong government is required to keep markets operating efficiently, but government itself is also subject to the development of cartels and networks that, if not kept in check, will pervert economic objectives.

How does the perverse policy syndrome arise? Olson's argument is essentially an economic one, but it also touches on the "anthropology" and "sociology" of organisations and their bargaining relations. Olson's argument is that no economy will be able to attain a position in which all groups and organisations have equal power. It will not therefore be possible, in general, for economically efficient outcomes to be achieved through comprehensive bargaining because more powerful groups will always assert their interests over weaker groups: a typical organisation *"will have little or no incentive to make any significant sacrifices in the interests of society; it can best serve its members' interests by striving to seize a larger share of society's production for them"* (Olson, 1982, p. 44). This tends to reduce overall economic efficiency over time because monopolies, oligopolies and cartels are developed by organisations in order to prevent change, or loss of influence, or to extort higher prices than are justified by productivity.

The argument continues with the observation that stable societies tend to accumulate more organisations attuned to specialist purposes over time: hence the longer that time progresses, and the more stable a society is, the greater will be its accumulation of special interest groups and organisations. With this accumulation comes a greater control by cartels, and the greater is the distortion of decision making away from economic objectives. The development of the perverse policy syndrome is the result of this accumulation of interests. Over long periods of time a stable society tends to become "top heavy" in that a small number of people, representing the top of each organisation's management pyramid, have a disproportionate strength. This top management group, which normally approximates and includes the county's elite, tends to use that strength not only to defend the interests of their organisations, itself a major economic distortion, but the elite itself may increasingly respond to their own personal interests and beliefs. A smaller and smaller range of views thus enters economic management decisions. A form of bargained consensus emerges. The concentration of power, therefore, tends to limit the breadth of response by society, its adaptability and flexibility, and thus its capacity for economic growth. Politically, too, there will be organisational sclerosis since the effect of voting in elections is unlikely to change anything significantly. *"Institutional systems mean serfdom"* argues Dahrendorf (1990) in that individuals become subjected to institutional or elite objectives at odds with their own long-term interests.

At the same time the increasing importance of organisations, as opposed to individuals, tends to shift a greater proportion of decision making into a context of bargaining between interests, rather than of individuals responding to market potential. The concept of policy networks and policy communities has been used by Rhodes (1981) and others to describe the way in which organisations and governments then deal with each other. "Distributional coalitions" have to be developed in order to obtain a consensus on a given policy. The bargaining required to make decisions between and within organisations tends to be slow, usually very slow, and in many cases may be incapable of reaching any decision. Hence economies with a large institutional density tend to be sluggish, less adaptable and relatively inefficient.

The accumulation of long-term interests may also have a cyclic structure related to Kondratieff long waves (see Chapter 2). Middlemas (1990) argues that a political cycle covered the period from 1918 to the 1970s in which each major interest group – industry, labour, government and the financial sector – grew in maturity and learnt to work with each other: so-called corporatism. This cycle of accumulation was linked to a particular cycle of industrial practice: large scale industries with very narrow management elites which strongly reinforced the already narrow base from which Britain's elite was recruited. The cyclic notion suggests that the emerging fifth Kondratieff wave is providing both the stimulus and a process for recruiting new members to the elite and for changing the institutional power base.

The negative effects of slow and inefficient decision making will be the greater, the more rapid is the rate of change in their environment. We have argued in Chapter 2 that the 1990s will be subject to an unpredicated rate of economic change. Not only is there likely to be the influence of a general world squeeze on profitability and rate of economic growth, but also there will be major technological changes. Hence, at no time should our concern with institutional sluggishness be greater than in the next 10 or 20 years.

The effect of sluggishness in one sector also tends to spill over into other sectors. As observed by Malinvaud (1977) if the price set in one market for factors or products is allocatively inefficient, this will contribute to either underemployment or excess capacity in another market. When prices are completely out of line with market conditions, excess factor utilisation in one product area will lead to deficient product outputs in other areas, or vice versa, until the point at which the whole economy seizes up. This is a special interpretation of the more general process of "crowding out" usually associated with excess public sector activity reducing the extent of private action. Kornai (1980), in his study of the economics of shortages, has been particularly eloquent in showing how economic sluggishness in individual Hungarian economic sectors contributed to a macroeconomic underproduction for the economy as a whole under the extreme cases of state socialism in Eastern Europe.

Because of the breadth of implications of the perverse policy syndrome, and its hypotheses about the role and evolution of organisations, it is virtually impossible fully to assess empirically. There are, however, some notable analyses that attempt to do so. In the rest of this chapter we draw on a number of previous studies to demonstrate how Britain has been particularly subject to the effect of organisational rigidity and the perverse policy syndrome.

Business strategy

The economic success of a country no longer derives very significantly from anything special about a country as such. Instead, national economic development derives essentially from the success of a country's businesses. The same applies to each region and locality. Local employment, incomes and future developments depend on the success of local business.

Many studies have attempted to analyse the performance of Britain's businesses. At a generalised level, Porter (1990) gives an analysis of wide scope and compares Britain with seven other countries. He argues that the competitive success of nations and localities derives from four mutually reinforcing attributes, all of which underpin business strategy:

- *Factor conditions*: the availability and quality of skilled labour, infrastructure, capital necessary for business, including motivation;
- *Demand conditions*: the availability of a home demand that allows the accumulation of information, assets, skills and commitment, stimulates quality and development, and provides conditions that are transferable to other places;
- *Related and supporting industries*: the presence of suppliers and customers that are world leaders;
- *Business strategy, structure and competition*: the conditions governing how firms are created, organised, managed and compete or cooperate with each other, including the role of government.

He argues that Britain suffered post-war decline because of significant weaknesses in each of these areas, but particularly in human resources, motivation, lack of competition and eroded demand conditions. Negative reinforcement of the problems of one industry hurt other industries. His comparative analysis strongly supports our economic appraisal of institutions. He argues that:

> *The British case illustrates why it is so hard to turn around an economy once it starts to erode. There was no shock or jolt to reverse the cycle; indeed a victory in the war bolstered confidence, and lingering market positions and customer loyalties may have allayed a sense of urgency about the need to change* (Porter, 1990, p. 506).

Porter finds some recent encouraging trends:

> *The distress of many British companies in the 1970s and early 1980s finally made it clear that the choice was to compete or go under. A flurry of takeovers has shaken up staid companies and led to more aggressive managements. Privatisation has created more competition in some industries such as telecommunications and electric power generation. Deregulation is increasing competition in others such as financial services where Britain's competitive advantage will benefit. Competing aggressively is becoming more socially acceptable, and rivalry shows signs of being on the rise.*
>
> *Entrepreneurship is increasing, and the Thatcher government has sought to celebrate the entrepreneur. A venture capital industry has developed that ranks well ahead of the rest of Europe. Finally, foreign investment in assembly facilities, much of it in distressed areas, is creating welcome new jobs. The recent experience of Britain illustrates the change in climate that accompanies a series of vigorous policy shifts which triggers responses and counterresponses throughout an economy (op. cit. p. 507).*

But he doubts that the changes have yet been fundamental enough to reverse Britain's decline:

> *However, the renewal of British industries appears fragile and spotty. A large pool of unemployed persists. Renewal is also confined, in many industries, to one-shot restructuring and cost cutting, made possible in some cases by a new balance of power between unions and management. Mergers are prevalent, but the benefits to real competitive advantage are less clear. Especially in manufacturing, British firms have undone some past sins, but most have yet to create the basis for future advantage. This requires new products and new processes; it requires innovation (op. cit. p. 720).*

More detailed appraisals have been made of the history of many British industries in comparison with competitors. Each of these demonstrate in one way or another that Britain's corporate problem has been poor business strategy, poor management, sluggish response to change and slow innovation[1].

Some interesting studies have recently highlighted the differences between successful and unsuccessful growth among firms. Particularly informative have been the matched pairs of manufacturing firms examined by O'Farrell and Hitchens (1989). They demonstrate that successful firms had developed quality and product assurance control, a proper link between managerial and workforce training, and marketing strategy. The less successful firms in terms of productivity, profitability, competitiveness, and hence further growth potential, have major gaps of: quality control, product design, marketing, the correct mix and use of production machinery, managerial training (particularly in production scheduling, inventory management, planning of production methods and financial management) and the relation between management, supervisory and shop floor training. At the core of these features is the relation of management to strategic thinking and R&D.

Comparing with other countries, two recent studies argue that Britain has a myopic approach to business innovation (Freeman *et al.*, 1991; Roussel *et al.*, 1991). This means that technological activities are treated just like other activities in response to market demand and price stimuli, with similar discounting for risk and time. This leads to the result that Britain has a tendency to produce yesterday's products better. Dynamically innovating businesses, in contrast, treat technological products as occasions to change organisational and commercial approaches, looking for new product opportunities, with different appraisals of risk.

Britain certainly spends less on R&D than its major competitors, and more of this is directed to defence which has equivocal commercial benefits. However, Britain's R&D problem goes much deeper. It reflects the more general gap in business strategy that so many studies have observed. Figure 4.1 exhibits some of the key difficulties through comparison of R&D in Britain and Germany. This shows not only the larger volume of German R&D, but also its very different makeup. There is a strong division in Britain between government and private research, a strong centralisation in government funds, a much smaller volume of research goes to the further development and testing phases. In contrast Germany has a large number of jointly funded public-private research institutions, strong localisation and intercompany links, and a much deeper mix of fundamental and applied research[2]. The contrasting British focus is on research councils and the Ministry of Defence (MoD) who concentrate on long-term research, higher education following the same route, and a strong polarisation from private sector applications of R&D. Of course there are no guarantees of success in R&D, and more expenditure does not guarantee success. But if the relations between industry and research are distant, it is likely that resources will be customarily misapplied: a system failure will exist.

In the circumstances shown in Figure 4.1 there is no ready environment or system which brings business managers into contact with long term research, and vice versa. Commenting on this phenomenon a Centre for the Exploitation of Science and Technology (CEST) (1991) study concluded, *"like a chef cooking a meal, a German company has at hand most of the ingredients it needs to innovate. In contrast, British companies have to reach a long way for what they need, whether it is technology, staff or finance. Their cooking has to be constantly interrupted by visits to shops to get ingredients* (*Financial Times* "No chance of an even match", 18 June 1991; see also NEDC, 1991; and Wilkie, 1991). The problem is of long-standing, as noted by Sir Alan Cottrell (quoted in Sampson, 1982):

We have the extraordinary result that, after thirty years of government science policy in which the primary aim has undoubtedly been to apply the results of scientific research more purposefully to our national production effort ... the practical effect of government policies has been to make pure science strong and industrial science weak.

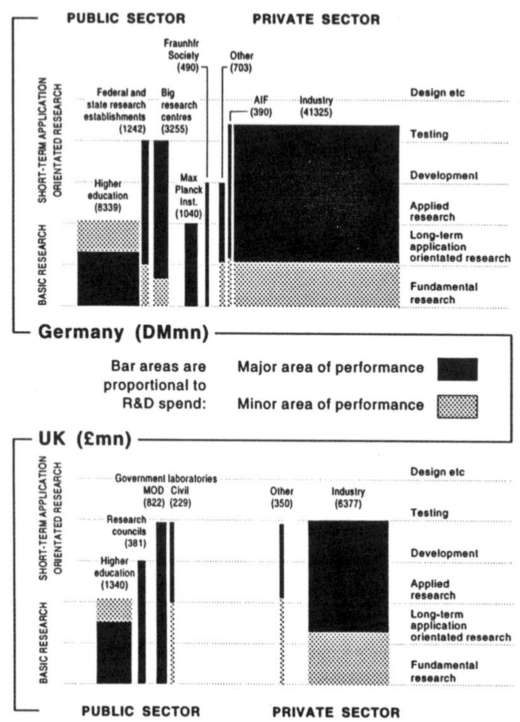

Figure 4.1 R&D expenditure in Britain and Germany by institution and emphasis
Sources: Financial Times, 18 June 1991, p.20, "No chance of an even match", from Meyer-Krakmer, BMFT; SEPC and CSO annual review

Not only does this phenomenon mean a slowly responding business sector, in a period of accelerating technological changes, it is likely to leave whole industries floundering with out-of-date core technologies and products. Hence the gap between innovation capacity and business strategy is one of the most crucial for Britain's long-term economic development. It is a critical ingredient of systems failure. Simply putting more resources into R&D will not alone solve the problem because the institutional gaps will often prevent resources being properly applied.

Employment and the labour market

Also at the core of the economic performance of nations is the way in which human resources are applied to produce economic output. This determines a nation's productivity and hence its scope to provide incomes. Human resources are also the key elements in the economic appraisal of institutions since it is people who make organisations respond, and provide the overall economic capability of a country. Most of all, human resources are affected by the framework of incentives at individual, institutional, local and national level to which everyone responds, from the humblest employee to the company director or cabinet minister.

The straightforward economic diagnosis of Britain's labour market problems, using the economic assessment of institutions introduced above, is that institutional resistance by both employers and workers has prevented the changes in work practices, skills and management that would allow the economy to perform better and be better able to adjust to change. Trade unions certainly played a part in institutional resistance and have affected industrial performance (e.g. Layard and Nickell, 1985; Minford, 1983; Blanchflower *et al.*, 1988), but a number of analyses now show that the level of unionisation of industry per se does not explain its poor economic performance (see e.g. Metcalf, 1988; Nickell *et al.*, 1991). Deeper analysis can be approached through three aspects: unemployment, management, and industrial relations. All three interact.

It has long been observed that Britain has an *"unnaturally high natural rate of unemployment"* (Meade, 1982). Such unnaturally high rates imply a higher rate of *involuntary* unemployment than comparable countries. Olson (1982) explains this by arguing that if involuntary unemployment exists this must be because someone has an interest in preventing mutually advantageous bargains being worked out between unemployed workers and employers. The main groups that can have such an interest are: (i) other workers with similar skills, since their own wages would be lowered, and (ii) a monopolistic employer's cartel that is seeking to benefit from an uncompetitively high price (in order to protect super-normal profits or to prevent changes in production to a cheaper more competitive level). High unemployment can thus result from worker demands that set wages above the market level – the wages will be at too high a level to make it economic for employers to hire more workers; or from employers attempting to control competitive pressures that limit long-term market expansion.

Olson goes on to argue that the forces that seek to maintain this uncompetitive position encourage two further responses: (i) protection of markets, and (ii) the closer cooperation of individuals in order to maintain their interests (of employers, or of groups of workers). Both, he argues, are pre-eminently exemplified by Britain's experiences.

There is considerable evidence from historical analyses to support Olson's position. Correlli Barnett (1986), for example, argues that the combination of the two forces of protection of markets and complacency among employers and workers presented a formidable barrier to change in post-war Britain. Most British employers and most employees, he argues, have been blind to the economic importance of developing the long-term capability of the workforce. The home market seemed assured, guaranteed by various protective measures. Even in 1982 Sampson (1982, p. 455) was able to write that *"only if the British people are confronted with their real predicament, without the concealments of politicians and the obstacles of defensive institutions, can they be expected to respond to the global economic challenge"*. The origin of this situation is argued by almost all commentators to have arisen from Britain's 19th century advantage of having an industrial base that had experienced the first industrial revolution and controlling an empire which essentially set and controlled prices, policies and the evaluation criteria for assessment of a large number of subordinate economies elsewhere. This insulated British industry from competitive pressures. This tended to inculcate a strong sense of business complacency.

If complacency protected investment and trading decisions, it also encouraged the separation of the interests of workers and employers. Both groups were prevented from realising the improved economic benefits of cooperation by the forces of institutional resistance that sought to keep their interests apart. Indeed it developed a concept of "class" rather than "people". These forces, *"operating simultaneously in thousands of professions, crafts, clubs and communities, would, by themselves, explain a degree of class consciousness. This in turn helps to generate cultural caution about the incursion of the entrepreneur and ... helps to preserve ... prejudice against commerce and industry"* (Olson, 1982, p. 85).

Correlli Barnett goes so far as to claim that, by 1850, Britain had attained *"a workforce too largely composed of coolies, with the psychology and primitive culture to be expected of coolies"* (Barnett, 1986, p. 187). This view is reinforced by others, such as E.P. Thompson (1974, p. 486) who has observed that there was a deeply imbedded separation between workers and managers and hence between workers and the purposes of business effort: in Britain *"industrialisation ... was unrelieved by any sense of national participation in communal effort ... its ideology was that of the masters alone"*. This stimulated a strong separation of "the working class" and a strong sense of their own identity: in Hoggart's (1971, p. 20) words a *"sense of being a group of their own ... that they are "working class" in the things they admire and dislike, in "belonging" "*. But whilst there have been eulogies, as well as sentimental and nostalgic studies of the character of the working class and its neighbourhoods (see e.g. Seabrook, 1985; Blackwell and Seabrook, 1985; Young and Wilmott, 1957), Barnett sees the 19th century creation of the working class as one of the most destructive forces and a formidable barrier to Britain's economic development. For *"the worker ... the productive process, let alone success in the market, was no responsibility of his"*; this *"degree of motivation explains the performance; the performance demonstrates the degree of motivation; and the nature of the historical experience of the working class accounts for both ... it determined their human quality - their all-round capability and effective intelligence, their aptitude for more and sophisticated tasks"* (op.cit., pp. 191–2).

This situation had been relieved, but not substantially changed by the 1950s (Hoggart, 1971). That it is still a problem for the British economy as a whole, and has an extreme concentration in inner city areas often accorded the status of an "underclass", shows the immense capacity for attitudes to be reproduced and to be passed between generations.

Among managers and elites the situation has often been no better, from an economic point of view. Wiener (1981) notes that already by the mid-19th century there were strong desires among the elite to keep trade at arm's length and return to country roots and nostalgia for the rural past in search of more "lasting" or "respectable" values. A sense of aversion to trade developed: that it was a scarcely respectable activity and this tended to cultivate a national perception that "the pursuit of wealth was vulgar". This position had only slightly changed up to the early 1970s: that there was a lower status to be accorded to business careers compared to the civil service, military, clerical or purer academic activities (considerable historical evidence for the domination of this tradition and its imperial values is available from AST, 1956; Thomas, 1959; Stanworth and Giddens, 1974; More, 1980; Wiener, 1981; Hampden-Turner, 1984 and Rubinstein, 1986).

The outcome, therefore, was a long-term degeneration of industrial relations due to a separation of the interests of workers and employers, a strong demotivation of the workforce which gave little stimulus to the acquisition of skills or adaptation of working practices, an elite increasingly pursuing objectives irrelevant or perverse to the needs of the economy, and a passiveness and complacency about such issues as adaptation or delivery of products to rigorous performance criteria of delivery time or quality. Moreover, until recently, the situation was not even generally recognised by most employers as inhibitive to business growth.

Recognition of this situation has strong implications for policy. The labour market is a major example of the perverse policy syndrome: simply applying more resources will normally make matters worse rather than better. This forces a shift of thought from Keynesian concern with macroeconomic management to emphasis on microeconomics. Jobs must be recognised as not just the outcome of the aggregate demand in the economy, but derive from the profitability, to a firm, of employing people. *"With extreme rigidities in the process of adjusting the price of labour, simply pumping money into the economy (along Keynesian lines) resulted not in the creation of more jobs, but more inflation"* (Ball, 1989, p. 45). In such a situation there is no way that Keynesian demand management can work; thus, emphasis must shift to effective stimulus of factor supply. This means unravelling the set of regulatory and institutional forces that affect supply – of workforce and skills, land, premises, and capital. Recognition of the need for a supply-side focus, achieved through institutional learning, is a key element of our analysis to follow.

Considerable changes have occurred among Britain's business elite since the 1970s, and these changes have accelerated during the 1980s. There is every reason to expect that they will continue. A new attitude to management effectiveness and productivity has developed which is separating the high-performing and less well performing companies. A major contribution to this change appears to derive from the different attitudes and backgrounds of the emerging business elites. Mrs Thatcher, in particular, stimulated a new conception of what she felt was required, especially vaunting the success of those major business leaders who emerged from outside the traditional elite (see Young, 1990; Paxman, 1990; Fay, 1988). Hannah (1990) has analysed the backgrounds of the chairmen of Britain's top 50 companies and shown that between 1979 and 1989 the public school percentage reduced from 58% to 24%, with a corresponding increase from Grammar and other maintained schools from 36% to 70%. Other analyses give wider evidence. For example, the proportion of male graduates with first class degrees going into industry and commerce in 1950 was under 40%, this increased to 67% by 1968 and to over 80% by 1988 with a particularly rapid growth after 1982. Together with the massive rise in total graduate numbers over this period, this represents an increase from under 200 to 1,400 first class graduates per year going into industry, compared to approximately constant numbers going into other careers (Hannah, 1990, p. 26a; Sanderson, 1972; Goldsmith and Ritchie, 1987, *Business*, May, 1989, pp. 52–59). However, Hannah (1990, p. 2) notes that *"this contrasts strikingly with the experience of academically weaker graduate students: business has not recruited an increased proportion of graduates with third class honours or pass degrees who have also been produced in increasing numbers (who have gone) to the public sector and particularly the local authorities."*

Education and training

Education and training is a crucial ingredient to the systems failure we have outlined. A need for radical change in British education's relationship to industry has been only properly recognised in the aftermath of the then Prime Minister Callaghan's speech at Ruskin College Oxford in 1976. The "Great Debate" on education that Callaghan initiated, led, through a series of reforms under the Thatcher administration, to the 1988 Education Reform Act. Interestingly, these reforms have largely been led by the Department of Employment (DE)[3] with Department of Education and Science (DES) resistance at almost all stages, until recently. The reforms of the 1980s sought to reverse the problems that the 1950s and 1960s had created: "the golden age of teacher autonomy" over the curriculum and the "ideology of teacher professionalism" that excluded all other interests. The analogy of the "secret garden" as a description of how educationalists handled any discussions of the curriculum has become a source of infamy that has led ultimately to the central prescription of a national curriculum (see Lawton, 1982, 1989; Broadfoot, 1980). Whether an effect or cause, Callaghan and others have seen businesses *also* to blame for the separation that emerged of education from the needs of the economy. As Barnett notes (*ESRC Newsletter*, June 1991, p. 2), there has been no habituation of links as occurs in other countries, particularly Germany and Japan. As we show in Chapters 7 and 8, Britain's employers have traditionally given low priority to training and have been largely unable or unwilling to play a more active role in vocational education. Many employers, indeed, are not clear what they need in skills from their workforce and have failed to use the potential channels of communication open to them to develop a coordinated, coherent approach to education.

The origin for the separation of education from the needs of the economy lies in the education values of the 19th century. These developed a strong separation between the approach, and especially the status, given to different disciplines. In general it tended to develop a false antithesis between, on the one hand, "cultural" subjects for "enriching the mind" and "inspiring a moral sense", and on the other hand, "other" subjects which are more mundane, vocational, concerned with "nuts and bolts" or less theoretical issues. It was therefore an antithesis of "pure" and "applied", "cultural" and "vocational". Barnett traces the origin of this division to religious revivalism and the romantic movement. However, Britain's empire reinforced the system because it was suited to its educational products: in civil service and military pursuits alike, the cultural emphasis supported the British imperial role as one of *"civilisation and enlightment ... profoundly pre-industrial, conservative nostalgic"* rather than concerned with economic growth and exploitation (Barnett, 1986, p. 221). In the words of Sir James Goldsmith (quoted in Sampson, 1982, p. 128): *"schools were meant to create a rather pleasant non-specialist gentleman who would hand on the British civilisation throughout the world. They weren't trained for doing business"*.

Barnett's careful historical analysis is the basis for his contention that, once established, this scholastic tradition was able to frustrate the reform of state education because *"the development of state education in Britain at critical junctures fell directly to members of that governing elite"* (Barnett, 1986, p. 223). Barnett traces this process through the demise of the 19th century recommendations for reform such as the failure of the attempt to produce a set of *Realschulen* for vocational education in Britain, following the 1869 recommendations of the House of Commons Select Committee on Scientific Instruction, through to the absence of implementation of the technical schools that had been legislated in the 1889 Technical Instruction Act and in the 1902 Education Act, and to the 1944 Education Act.

The 1944 *Act* forms the foundation for much of the period of our detailed analysis in later chapters. Barnett (1986, p. 291) comments that:

the vaunted 1944 Education Act offered not so much an executive operational framework as an opened gate to an empty construction site on which local authorities might or might not (depending on their zeal and the effectiveness of the ministry's nagging) build the technical and further education system that Britain so desperately needed. Yet even the most zealous local education authority would have to work within government limits on expenditure. What therefore followed in the next forty years was yet another halting, spasmodic, spotty advance like those following the Technical Instruction Act of 1889 and the Education Act of 1902.

The 1988 Education Reform Act is the latest milestone in this evolution and, as we shall argue, it still remains to be seen whether it has successfully overcome the key criticisms voiced in Callaghan's 1976 speech by rebalancing the emphasis of state education. *Rebalancing* is the correct concept to use since we argue that the antithesis that has developed in education is a false one: both elements are required. Much "cultural" material can be gained through "practical" teaching, and "practical" education has as much capacity to "cultivate the mind" as "cultural" subjects, it is no narrower in style, subject matter or approach.

The absence of sufficient links between practical and cultural educational skills in the past is confirmed in the miserable education and training statistics of Britain compared to other countries outlined earlier (Chapter 3). But the gap in education skills also contributes strongly to the other dimensions discussed in this chapter: the British institutional resistance to change, the shape of the welfare compromise, and the character of employer-employee attitudes in industry and commerce. It is this set of relationships which has led many to conclude that no other single area has played a greater role in Britain's economic decline than its educational and training system. This is not a criticism of Britain's teachers as individuals, but of the system within which they work which structures their objectives and incentives.

Economic policy and the welfare compromise

Economic development, education and training inevitably involves a crucial role to be played by government. This role concerns both priorities for public expenditure on economic-related activities, and how other government services contribute to economic prosperity. But how government balances its economic role with its other concerns is an issue not only of public expenditure and service quality. It also concerns how government affects the climate, or environment, within which economic decisions are made. It is in this sense that Britain's welfare compromise assumes a central relevance.

The form of the post-war development of public services has stimulated a lot of recent discussion. It has often been referred to as a period of "post-war consensus" by those seeking to defend existing practices (the more thoughtful examples are Middlemass, 1990; Deakin and Wright, 1990). However, even Deakin (1987, 1988) recognises that consensus was short-lived and might have characterised only the period of office of two chancellors, R.A. Butler and Hugh Gaitskell: hence the term that is sometimes used of "Butskellism". Others have seen it as fundamentally a "Keynes-Beveridge" structure: the coming together of the ideas of macroeconomic management and social policy (e.g. Glennerster, 1985). The concept of compromise is, however, we believe the most useful phrasing since it emphasises, first, the tensions implicit in the government's role, and second, the feature that compromise is the result of bargaining between institutional and interest groups, thus reminding us of the perverse policy syndrome. Indeed Middlemas (1990) refers to the period as one of "pluralistic stagnation".

Three extremely penetrating historical analyses are available to help in the understanding of this debate: Greenleaf (1983a, b; 1987), Himmelfarb (1984) and Barnett (1986). (Other key sources are Thompson, 1990; Barnett, 1972; Middlemas, 1990). Each, in their different ways, sees the post-war legislation that created the welfare state in Britain as a specific settlement made in the circumstances of that time. The implication, of course, is that as circumstances change, the form of settlement required will need to change. The settlement was one of balancing social with the economic interests: a compromise, not an integration. Barnett describes the battle in terms of the success of Beveridge's social policy founded on a "romantic idealism" of "dreams and illusions" over Kingsley Wood's (the then Chancellor) economic "realism" concerning how everything could be paid for. Barnett argues that it was inevitable from the brutal exploitation by early nineteenth century capitalism, that a sentimental view of the worker as "noble savage" should develop and that this should be combined with "pity, guilt, remorse and moral indignation". For Himmelfarb as well as Barnett, the precursors of the welfare state represented a success of the concept of social responsibility over that of individual responsibility. The "poor" were separate, identifiable and a class created by society to whom a social responsibility was owed. For Himmelfarb this represents the ascendancy of moral puritanism over individualism. Greenleaf extensively chronicles how this ideology of collectivism then became institutionalised as the government's social responsibility.

Although rethinking of these ideas of the welfare state has become a general debate to all OECD countries, the British welfare compromise is strongly specific since it interrelates with the other dimensions we have highlighted here – the role of post-empire adjustment, employer-employee relations, British institutional structure, and the education tradition. The form of the British welfare compromise provides the basis for the claim by one of the system's most extreme critics that it provided the "incentives to fail" (Murray, 1984, p. 154; 1989); and from incentives for individuals to fail comes the failure of the economy. Thus, increasingly, the welfare compromise has been seen as another example of the perverse policy syndrome.

The tensions for the economic growth of the country created by the Keynes-Beveridge compromise have been highlighted before by Bennett (1990a). Employment policy after the 1944 White Paper represented a compromise between the notions, on the one hand, of competitive markets, economic growth and efficiency, and on the other hand, of social policy. It institutionalised a government responsibility to ensure high and stable employment. Keynesian management became the mechanism for employment to acquire the status of a claim of "rights" against society that had to be addressed by the state. Hence employment almost acquired the character of a public "service". The welfare compromise, therefore, resulted in economic policy becoming largely subordinate to social policy. Conveniently forgotten was the problem that employment has to be justified by the product of labour, and that productivity provided the economic prosperity and resources that were available for social distribution. This was the argument that was the source of the vigorous clash between Beveridge and Kingsley Wood.

The main planks of government industrial policy in the period up to the late 1970s variously followed strategies of:

- Spotting and supporting strategic industries;
- Spotting and supporting national champions;
- Often linking strategic and national champion industries with nationalisation;
- Selectively channelling investment and support through subsidies, tax privileges and protection;
- Regional selection to prevent growth or divert industries from the congested South East through IDC/ODP controls, subsidies and tax allowances;
- Focusing on compensatory and "worst first" policies rather than investing in success – between sectors and between regions;
- Increasing use of inflation solutions rather than limiting investment to the resources available, this stimulated a culture of paying more than the labour product.

In general, the government responsibility for the economy stimulated a system based more on patronage than performance.

Some flavour of the climate that these policies stimulated can be gained from Sampson's (1982) comments on the 1970s: *"private industry ... was increasingly dependent on government favours"* (op.cit., p. 182). Sampson even compares the situation to Elliot's (1970) account of 17th century imperial Spain: where the number of workers, not their effectiveness, gave Castilian aristocrats their status. Employment itself had become the government's conception of the purpose of industry; the indication of success was the number of employees, not their contribution to the nation's prosperity.

The sea-change which has now begun to occur was becoming evident even by the mid 1970s: *"stately old corporations, and even nationalised industries, were beginning to realise that they could no longer be run as if they were part of the public service, with committees, managers and boards of directors retired from Whitehall. The whole concept of the semi-permanent corporation was coming into question ..."* (op.cit., p. 335). The changes wrought by the 1980s, by government policy and by the effect of the 1982 recession, produced *"a fundamental change in social and political climate. In the seventies most executives, even under worsening conditions, were not prepared to be ruthless; they often felt themselves circumscribed not only by the fear of the unions but by their own social conscience ..."* (op.cit., p. 342).

The Thatcher government's view of this change is exemplified by the recent Department of Trade and Industry (DTI) statement: *"government intervention directly affected the fortunes of companies and industries ... the result was an inefficient economy. The symptoms were readily apparent: reduced and inefficient use of investment, low productivity combined with high wage growth, poor industrial relations combined with weak management and a continuing lack of technological innovation"*. Now the government's responsibility is seen entirely differently: *"the main responsibility for efficiency and the achievement of prosperity lies with industry ... industry is responsible for its own destiny ...* (the role of the government) *will be to produce a climate which promotes enterprise and prosperity"* (DTI, 1988, pp.1, 38–41, emphases added; see also DTI, 1991). This has led to the preeminent emphasis turning to government as *enabler*, facilitator or catalyst to the economy.

Key planks of the reforms that have taken place since the late 1970s have been: acceptance of financial rigours to control inflation, culminating in joining the Exchange Rate Mechanism (ERM) in 1990; focusing government policy on providing the regulatory environment for strong internal national competition, following Porter's conclusions[4]; privatisation of major industries to remove political patronage;

focusing of regional policy on startups and support for foreign direct investment; shifting the national climate to investing in business successes.

The change in the view of government's role away from intervener, patron and guarantor to enabler was bound to have an effect on other parts of the system – particularly on education, and on government itself. Again to use Sampson's (1982, p. 342) insight: in taking tough decisions in employment redundancies in the 1980s, company chief executives *"became more conscious of the gulf between the insecurity of their industries and the more protected world of the city, academia or the professions ... a gulf which was part of Britain's predicament; for all those other comfortable and secure superstructures ultimately depended on Britain's industrial exports"* (Sampson, 1982, p. 342). This interaction of business climate with other parts of British institutions is the main subject of the rest of this book.

Government: central-local relations

The failure of national systems of incentives is bound to affect each local community. But the local level also has a more central importance in our analysis. With a greater emphasis on the importance of supply-side factors and a diminishing capacity of national governments to protect and act as patrons, the *local* environment becomes a key ingredient in business success. Releasing Britain's economic potential has an even stronger focus when it is noted how locally concentrated are some of the system problems we have outlined:

- Large scale older industrial sectors are concentrated in certain regions, mainly outside the South East;
- Public sector and nationalised industries are also concentrated, mostly in inner city and older industrial areas;
- Traditional government assistance of sectoral, defence industry and regional policy support has propped up these areas using a strategic and compensation principle;
- This has been associated with low rates of business formation in these areas and a lack of ability to adapt;
- High public sector control, usually associated also with high union power, has encouraged uniform social grouping – so-called "working class areas";
- This in turn has stimulated local political control that has sought to maintain high public sector involvement, local public intervention, high levels of public housing, and planning restrictions emphasising social needs ahead of those of business.

National systems, therefore, have produced strong variations in local conditions that support or inhibit business. And this has had its own local government flavour.

Traditionally the policy differences between political control of local government tended not to be strong in terms of economic policy. Indeed, most local authorities followed Hicks' (1947, pp. 342–5) assessment that the local public sector was a key aspect of national economic policy. But from the mid-1970s, accelerating in the early 1980s, many Labour-controlled areas took up highly interventionist economic policies and the "creation" of jobs through local authority employment (see e.g. Mawson and Miller, 1986; Chandler and Lawless, 1985). This was associated with a "new left" ideology which brought local government into direct conflict with the reforming Thatcher government. The Audit Commission (1986, 1987) has argued that this led to "management by elected council members" with a proliferation of committees and subcommittees. As a result it became difficult to recruit both officers and members. These problems were further compounded by "interest" group politics. For example, elected members who were also council employees or municipal trade unionists in Inner London boroughs comprised between 33% and 50% of the council members, with 61% in the former Greater London Council (GLC) (Walker, 1983a,b). As a result they have found it difficult to distinguish their roles as politicians, employees and trade unionists.

These developments have interacted with the natural processes of social filtering in the inner city areas. Poor housing, low educational attainment, high youth unemployment and public service costs and inefficiency have each contributed to further social filtering. This process has been set amidst changes in the economic structure of the inner city economies as a whole which have made the dependent groups more dependent and less and less able to participate because of inappropriate training or labour skills.

Analysis of the financial consequences of these developments demonstrate that between approximately 1979 and 1985 "new left" Inner London boroughs had changed from rough parity in local tax rates to a situation of tax rates 36% higher than comparable areas, of which 26% (or three-quarters of the increase) was accounted for by "new" expenditures (Bennett and Krebs, 1988). As a result the burden of rates on business in the city of Sheffield, as a percentage of trading profits, for example, was up to three and a half times higher than in comparable areas (Bennett and Fearnehough, 1987).

Major changes in thinking by most "new left" local authorities have taken place since 1987. But the results of the decade of politicisation from approximately 1977 to 1987 have strongly evidenced the difficulty of local government adaptation in periods of rapid economic change. This forced central government into taking greater power to coerce local authorities into the changes they deemed necessary (cf. Davies, 1990).

Central government sought to draw local government into its economic reforms since 1979 by a variety of targeted initiatives. The shift from *planning and compensation* policy to *enterprise* policy led to multiple initiatives from central government directly into local areas (Enterprise Zones (EZ) and Urban Development Corporations (UDC), City Action Teams (CAT) and Task Forces (TF)); joint central-local activity (mainly through Urban Programme Areas); and a strong emphasis across all these initiatives on collaboration of local public initiatives with the private sector. This led to a strong refocusing of central government support away from regional policy grants to very localised urban policy, as shown in Figure 4.2.

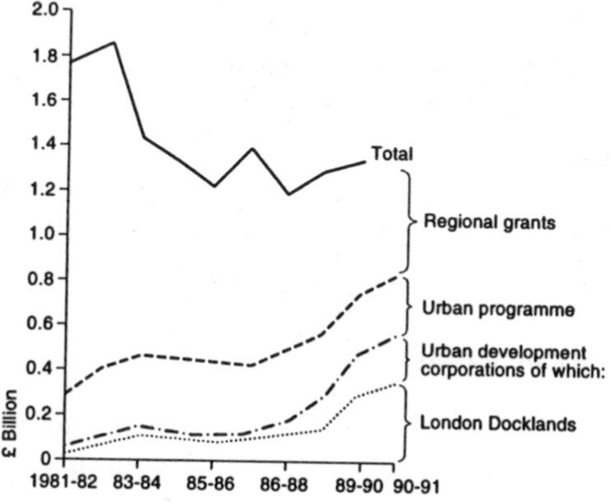

Figure 4.2 Changes in emphasis of regional and urban policy expenditure, 1981–1990

Business opportunities are also being affected by future attempts to increase the rate of contracting out of local government services and increases in local management effectiveness that seek to achieve improved responsiveness of services to consumers (see e.g. OECD, 1987; Davies and Powell, 1992). The "citizens charter" is a particularly focused attempt to achieve this. These policies have not been without their difficulties. Indeed they have contributed to the substantial confusion of agencies that act on behalf of the public sector in many areas (see Chapter 5). They have been an important attempt to change the system structure at local level. As a result economic objectives have been achieved that would have been impossible by use of the existing system of central-local relations. Central government intervention in local areas represents, therefore, an attempt to overcome system failure. From it, later chapters argue, many lessons can be learnt which allow major steps towards further improvements in economic systems in the future.

One of the major negative consequences of recent reforms has been the establishment, since 1990, of a national rate poundage on the previously local non-domestic rates. This so-called Unified Business Rate (UBR) has had a dramatic effect in undermining many of the incentives for local government to consult effectively with business, and vice versa. This, combined with the increasing influence of central government on local authorities, has left a very awkward vacuum in local government-business relations which must be filled in the future. The lack of an effective mechanism of local links is a problem that must be addressed urgently. We feel that one means of introducing an effective mechanism is to reform non-domestic rates in the direction of giving some control to local business bodies. We discuss this further in Chapter 15.

The challenge of Europe

We have not so far isolated for attention the impact of developments in the EC, particularly the single European market due for completion by 1993. We have argued that the economic challenges that lie ahead do not have a specifically European dimension, rather they are global trends. We view European integration, therefore, as just one specific dimension of market integration and growing global economic interdependence. There are opposed optimistic views (Cecchini, 1988) of employment and market growth consequent upon European economic integration, and pessimistic views (e.g. Rajan, 1990) that there is a zero-sum game in which half of Europe's companies will disappear. However, this argument is not a specifically European but a global one. We argue that the outcome for any one area depends less on the total impact of integration on business growth, but mostly on the capacity of an area to attract, adapt and retain investment. There are also opposed views of whether the single market will continue economic liberalism, or seek to maintain subsidy-based economies with external barriers to trade entry – so called "fortress Europe". The balance will ultimately be a politically driven one.

What European integration will certainly do, however, is to radically change the role of local government and its relations both with Whitehall and with other key local agents such as businesses, Chambers of Commerce and Training and Enterprise Councils (TECs). The local authority is the key level through which many EC programmes are directed. Excluded formally from programmes affecting nations by the principle of subsidiarity, the Commission has developed a wide series of programmes which support activity at the regional and local level. With the single market, these programmes will increase in importance.

Examples of this now stretch beyond the more traditional concerns of the Social Fund or Structural Funds (the European Regional Development Fund (ERDF), European Social Fund (ESF), etc.) to economic development. Examples of these developments are (see e.g. Bongers, 1990; CE, 1991):

- ELISE (European Information Network on Local Development and Local Employment Initiatives) which exchanges information between local authorities;
- LEDA (Local Employment Development Action) programme to exchange knowledge on policy best practice;
- SPEC (Special Employment Creation Projects);
- BC-Net (Business Cooperation Network) a computer network to help Small and Medium-Sized Enterprises (SMEs) look for suppliers and customers;
- EIC (European Information Centres) for small firms documentation access;
- R&D programmes through COST (Committee on European Cooperation in the field of Scientific and Technical Research), e.g.
  - BRITE (Basic Research in Industrial Technologies in Europe),
  - DRIVE (Dedicated Research Infrastructure for Vehicle Safety in Europe),
  - ESPRIT (European Strategic Programme for Research and Development in Information Technology),
  - FAST (Forecasting and Assessment in Science and Technology),
  - RACE (Research and Development in Advanced Communications Technology in Europe);
- EUREKA to aid industry-led European collaborative projects;
- SPRINT (Strategic Programme for Innovation and Technology Transfer).

Almost all of these are primarily focused on agents at regional and/or local authority levels, through joint bids with central government.

To access EC economic development funds often requires a local business involvement or the development of a local innovations or R&D strategy. To be effective this needs an effective local agent to channel local business projects to the attention of government and to act as a broker on behalf of business with local authorities and the EC. This requires an enhanced *local capacity* to be able to respond to such initiatives (see e.g. Vazquez-Barquero, 1987; Stohr, 1990; Martinos, 1989; Bennett, 1989a). Britain's system of local business support is ill-equipped to answer this challenge, as we shall see in Chapter 5, although the development of TECs / Local Enterprise Companies (LECs) and the Chamber of Commerce national network are steps moving in the right direction.

The character of EC initiatives falls awkwardly across the spectrum from intervention and subsidy to true market support. It is understandable, therefore, that the EC has had equivocal support from a reforming Conservative government since 1979. Indeed, overcoming Britain's systems failure will be put back if the EC supports outmoded practices that substitute and divert from the needs for change. This dilemma is the more acute since many analyses show a large part of the EC lagging behind the USA, Japan and the NICs, and suffering on a wider scale a variety of different forms of system failure (see e.g. Porter, 1990; Dicken, 1990). Transforming the political arena to a European stage, therefore, may just increase the number of interest groups to be balanced with the result that it becomes even more difficult to achieve meaningful economic reforms.

Reversing the "perverse policy syndrome"

This chapter has sought explanation of Britain's poor and degenerating economic performance in the period up to the 1980s. It has argued that the explanation is to be found chiefly in the institutional structure of the country. Because of Britain's long period of political stability, the number of its institutions inexorably increased, their power came to dominate economic decision making, and objectives considerably at odds with economic performance came to direct more and more activity away from beneficial economic outcomes. The result has been the development of an institutional structure that will normally subtly pervert the objectives of economic policy.

It has long been recognised, by Disraeli amongst others, that Britain is one of the most difficult countries in which to achieve change and innovation. Many commentators have tried to explain why this should be so. Sampson (1982, p. xiii), for example, argues that *"the unique dangers of a nation in the aftermath of empire"* was to be trapped in *"self deceptions and resistance to change, the loyalties to tribal groups and the reassertion of old patterns of behaviour."* In a statement which we will draw upon a number of times in this book he makes the key observation that *"governments ... liked to assume that civil servants, scientists or teachers would cooperate in reforms from within; they shied away from statutory changes or imposing their own direction ... the institutions remained largely immune in their autonomy while they had become increasingly separated from the centre and from each other"* (Sampson, 1982, p. 420). The effect of these phenomena has been that much well-intended government action has been frustrated by defensive institutional interests. The problem has been diagnosed, but when handed to the "professionals", the old solutions have usually endured, if under a new name.

This is a vivid expression of the perverse policy syndrome and is reinforced by Correlli Barnett's (1986) evidence, from detailed historical analysis, of how institutions founded in the 19th century have managed to endure through the influence of the relatively closed recruitment to and perceptions by the British administrative elite. Their influence, through access to power, has been so strong because of the strong imitation by other schools and higher education institutions and by the inability of legislators to change delivery structures in business, in the public services, or elsewhere. From a different perspective Noel Annan (1990) shows how little the leaders of the post-war era adapted earlier values.

The effects of this "perverse policy syndrome" lead us to the conclusion that more resources alone will change nothing; indeed *more resources may make matters worse* by strengthening the power of the institutions allocating those resources. The only way to break out of the perverse policy syndrome is to *break away from the institutional priorities and economic values of the past and to develop new institutional goals and systems of economic support*. This has not, on the whole, been the fault of individuals, but the outcome of a *system failure* within which people work.

We have seen, in Chapter 3, that a considerable change in Britain's economic performance occurred in the period covering approximately 1981–89. But the verdict is still to be given on whether these changes are permanent or not. In the rest of this book we turn to examining progress in institutional development at national and local level in the 1980s and early 1990s.

Footnotes: Chapter 4

1. Examples are Chandler's (1989) comparison of 200 of the largest firms in Britain, the USA and Germany; various NIESR studies and Prais (1987); Jones' (1990), Carr's (1990), and Whipp and Clark's (1986) analyses of the motor industry; Lorenz (1991) on the shipbuilding industry; Singleton (1991) on the cotton industry; Campbell et al. (1989) and Northcott et al. (1985) studies of micro-electronics; Hendry (1990) and Oakley and Owen (1990) studies of computing; computer manufacture (SI, 1990) and consumer kitchen manufacture (Steedman and Wagner, 1987); elements of the defence industry (Mackenzie, 1991) and more general studies of management (Thurley and Wirdenius, 1989; Lane, 1989).

2. A similar set of outcomes from a different set of institutions is also present in Japan (NEDC, 1991).

3. Through the former Manpower Services Commission (MSC), subsequently (1989–90) renamed the Training Agency (TA), and since 1990 termed the Training Enterprise and Employment Department (TEED).

4. Porter's (1990) comparisons of national industrial success are quoted extensively by DTI (1991), particularly his emphasis on the positive benefits of internal competition.

5 REACTIONS TO ECONOMIC CHALLENGES:

The Current Response

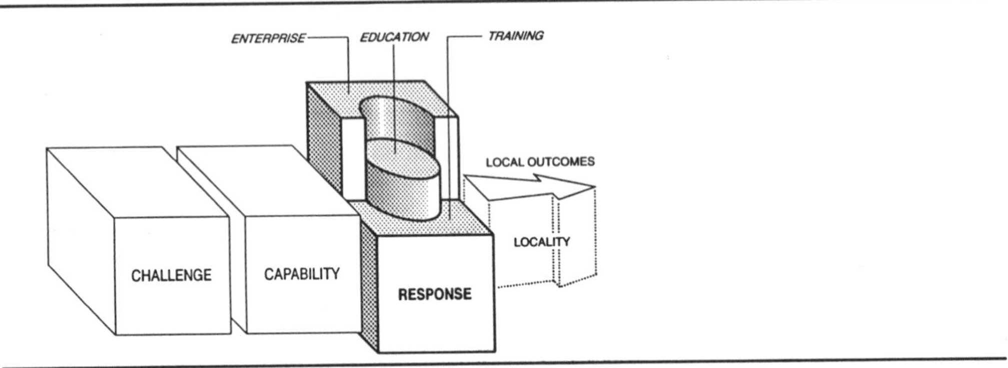

The current response

The earlier chapters have documented the first two parts of the sequence:

CHALLENGE – CAPABILITY – RESPONSE

This chapter lays the foundations for addressing the third element, *Response*. The detailed assessment of Britain's response capability is the subject of the rest of the book. This chapter argues that the basis of that capability must be derived from the extent to which "vertical" programmes of activity such as enterprise, education and training are integrated by the "horizontal" structures that provide a management capacity to respond. Generally, the vertical programmes are national in origin, the horizontal capability is local.

Integration is the antidote to the "systems failure" that we have argued above is Britain's endemic problem. Reversing the slippage of Britain's economic capacity is not, as we have seen, just a question of changing macroeconomic policy or applying new resources. Because of the effect of the "perverse policy syndrome", merely putting more resources into programmes or manipulating national aggregate demand and money supply is as likely to make matters worse as better. But similarly, tackling capacity building as a purely microeconomic issue will also leave gaps in effectiveness. Individual programme performance can, should and is being significantly improved by various reforms that address each programme field individually. However, improving each programme in an isolated manner rapidly leads either to its demands outstripping the capacity of agents to provide them, or to the improved programme outputs being wasted because they cannot be properly applied by the programme consumers. The resulting inefficiencies can be extreme.

This can be readily understood in the case of training. On the one hand, devoting increased macro resources to training, by government or business, will be largely wasted if the training programmes available do not lead to the demonstrably improved or applicable skills that are needed by business. On the other hand, devoting resources to micro improvements in the quality and applicability of training programmes that lead to improved skills will also be wasted if businesses either have not developed a capacity to employ those skills, or have not developed the innovations in products and marketing that can sell the outputs produced from their training investments.

The same difficulties beset attempts to improve each of our chief focuses of attention: enterprise, education, and training,

The characteristics of systems failure mean that effective action, in the long term, can only be achieved by *tackling simultaneously* the macro and microeconomic issues across a wide range of fields of activity. This draws us in this chapter to suggest a framework for policy development that links national and local levels of action, across fields of activity, through programmes, institutions and process. This is assessed below in three parts:

- The targets for system quality;
- Extent of economic network integration; and
- The local pattern.

The concept against which we assess the British system of support can be summed up in the single message of integration: the capacity to attain a client focus directed to the local needs of business and the local economy within the context of national programmes and global economic processes.

This capacity builds on earlier ideas of "integrated economic management" and "partnerships" for economic development. But it goes much further in seeking a system-wide set of mechanisms that have the true capability *to deliver* links between the macro and micro, national and local, into improved system development overall. This vision is used to assess vertical programmes in Part 2 of the book (Chapters 6–8) and locally contrasted experiences (Chapters 9–14), before advancing in Chapter 15 our assessment of the improvements required.

Targets for system quality

One of the chief aspects of improving the quality of response has to be overcoming the aspects we have identified of Britain's systems failure. We argue that a major aspect of this has been the absence of integration between different delivery institutions and their separate programmes of activity. In the introductory diagram to this chapter improved integration is presented as the better linkage of separate vertical programmes and fields of activity, both with each other as a horizontal structure, and with the delivery structures that translate requirements, through institutions, to a delivery process.

A network of links, interactions, "partnerships", contractual arrangements or other mechanisms can be used to achieve these linkages. But, whatever mechanism is used, it is important to recognise that there must be *effective* links that add proper *value* to assure the quality of outcomes that are required.

All individuals and businesses operate within networks of relationships. As we have observed in Chapter 4, an atomistic market rarely exists, however much it may be desirable. Instead, Britain's economic system is a subtle combination of individuals, businesses and collective institutions. Improving economic performance, therefore, requires not only individuals and businesses, but also institutions to be developed. This development, in turn, requires improvement in the performance of each separate institutional and programme field, but also the integration of performance development in one field into that of other fields.

The institutions that we are concerned with are: individual businesses, including their relations with each other and the community; Chambers of Commerce; enterprise agencies, enterprise boards, venture capital funds, research and innovation centres; education bodies deriving from central or local government; training bodies; local authorities, through their wider role in providing public goods and services; central government national programmes, as well as agencies for national and local delivery and support, particularly SE (SDA), HIE (HIDB), WDA, RDC, UDCs, CATs, TFs, etc. and the recently constituted TECs and LECs[1].

The development of improved networks between these agents requires, in simple terms, the implementation of a system for *managing externalities*. Effective networks mean that key producer agents work closely together, and that clients receive support from different producers of services for different requirements, but each producer works within an integrated concept, or *system*, of service delivery. For example, different agents may help firms during growth from small to large; different agents may support finance, product development, marketing, workforce training; but in aggregate all gaps are filled and each agent is working towards a common goal.

One approach to achieving properly integrated business support networks is to apply the concept of quality management. The achievement of quality in the economy is based on the quality of the management systems of the institutions supplying the factor inputs that contribute to the production of goods and services. Since output can be achieved only by incurring costs, development of improved systems must relate output to their value added. From value added derives relative profit, incomes and return on investments to the economy as a whole. Hence, the major emphasis of the system development we seek is a capability that is focused on:

- Outputs and their quality;
- Value added in the production of output.

Central elements in achieving the improved capability required are:

- Each agent must orientate to the needs and requirements of the economic customer, instead of producer or agency objectives;
- Agents must be organised for frequent changes in demand to achieve a flexibility to respond to changing requirements;
- Agents must ensure that the concept of why a product or programme is needed is well understood; this then becomes the focus for systems that manage services to meet that need;
- Each agent must disseminate the requirements of its programme or product to all staff, and to all related agencies, subcontractors and suppliers to which it is networked, so that each understands and responds to the same economic requirements relevant to its role;

- Quality control should be developed over linked agents and suppliers, and similar controls must be accepted in return, rather than relying on progress chasing and bureaucratic oversight;
- Relationships with other agents and subcontractors should be infused with the concept of win/win so that long-term relationships develop that can assure quality, rather than just drawing down the unit price;
- Each agent must think long-term about innovation so that it can lead change, rather than merely managing response in terms of products and services;
- The long-term goals of each agent should be related to short-term satisfaction targets;
- Agents that do not need to be involved should be kept out of networks, otherwise their involvement may introduce barriers and may induce them to fail in their own purposes; i.e. make sure each agent in the network addresses the most appropriate targets.

These concepts of developing network and agent capability have become familiar in companies through the development of Total Quality Management (TQM), but their application, as phrased above, is equally appropriate to the wider network of relations between firms, agencies, organisations and government that underpin the economy as a whole. In simple terms, this approach seeks to focus action on developing "fitness for purpose".

Recognition of the broad applicability of a quality standards approach has become one of the emergent global thrusts of the 1990s identified in Chapter 2. It is a key part of our assessment of how to improve Britain's economic capability in this book.

Extent of economic network integration

Although there have been major steps to improve integration, in general it can be said that in many fields of activity Britain's networks of local economic relationships are deficient. Many networks exhibit: fragmentation; significant areas of competition and overlap between agencies; significant gaps; relationships which are needlessly complex and confusing to the business client; and organisations focusing more on their own needs as producers rather than on their business clients.

Britain's present delivery structure, therefore, does not measure up well on the criteria of quality outlined earlier. Although each agent may be good in itself (although not all are), the system as a whole cannot attain the integration required. Our analysis which follows differentiates the four elements of (i) enterprise support, (ii) education, (iii) training, and (iv) physical development.

In Figure 5.1, the proportional expenditure devoted to each major field of activity is analysed among the nine key agents of:

- Businesses;
- Banks;
- Enterprise Agencies;
- Chambers of Commerce;
- Training and Enterprise Councils;
- Local Enterprise Companies;
- Local Authorities and Education Authorities;
- Scottish and Welsh Development Agencies;
- Urban Development Corporations.

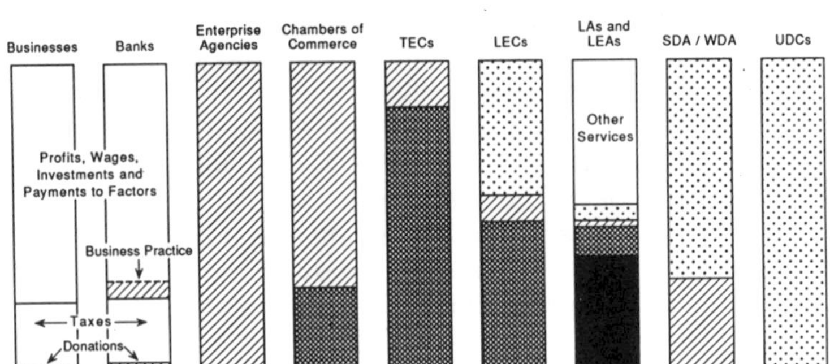

Figure 5.1 Relative proportion of expenditure devoted by main local agents to each field of economic development activity (in 1990–91)
Notes: Statistics for training, in businesses and banks derived from *Training in Britain*; enterprise support by business refers to donations and in-kind support; enterprise support by banks as for businesses, plus estimated role in consulting and advice; local authorities derived from LSE surveys and National Expenditure Accounts; statistics of distribution of functions in all other organisations based on LSE surveys; all these estimates are approximate and subject to major local variations. The LSE surveys are explained at length in Chapters 6–8.

Whilst some agents focus on specific areas, no major field of activity has less than five agents involved. And of course each agent itself is not monolithic but subject to its own departmentalisation and local variation. Quality assurance is very difficult in this situation. The example of enterprise support is particularly illustrative. This is part of main business practice and is the subject of subcontracting through business-to-business links; it is also a substantial part of banking practice through advice and finance; counselling and finance is also the main focus of Enterprise Agencies; it is also a major focus of Chambers of Commerce, particularly on exports, representation and "peer" support; it has become an important part of TEC and LEC activity; local authorities, as well as WDA and UDCs also have support systems. Enterprise support is thus spread across nine major agencies. It also derives funding from at least four central government departments.

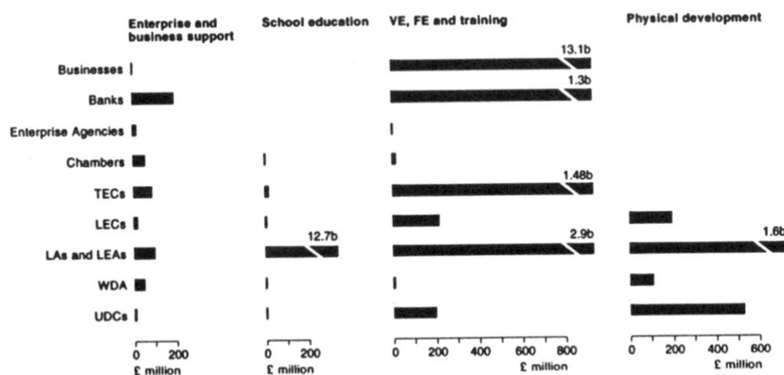

Figure 5.2 Relative scale of expenditure by each main agent in the different fields of economic development activity 1990
Source: based on National Expenditure Accounts and LSE surveys, as in Figure 5.1

Turning to the absolute level of expenditure (Figure 5.2) by different agents we find considerably more focusing. For example, 36% of enterprise support is funded by just one agent (banks), and 85% of support comes from four agents (banks, Chambers, TECs/LECs and Local Authorities). However, this seemingly greater coherence masks the extensive fragmentation and overlaps of the services often provided, and the gaps that often remain unserviced.

The nature of overlaps becomes clear when we look at the specific fields of activity that different agents undertake. As shown in Figure 5.3, some activities have major *overlaps* and the potential for competition, e.g. business counselling and training. Other activities are very *focused* on a few agents, e.g. export advice and export centres. Yet other activities are spread across many agencies with an *uneven* provision by those agents giving a potential for significant *gaps* to occur, e.g. education links, youth enterprise, marketing and workspace premises.

Activity (Direct Provision)	7 Businesses	7 Banks	1 Enterprise Agencies	Chambers of Commerce 2	3 TECs	3 LECs	5 LEAs	8 Local Authorities	4 UDCs
Direct education support (e.g. compacts)	0%	0%	10-49%	10-49%	50-79%	50-79%	80%+	0%	<10%
Training provision (to NVQ or equivalent)	10-49%	80%+	10-49%	10-49%	80%+	80%+	80%+	80%+	10-49%
Vocational education (WRFE) support	0%	0%	0%	10-49%	80%+	80%+	80%+	80%+	0%
Youth enterprise	<10%	<10%	80%+	10-49%	10-49%	10-49%	10-49%	0%	0%
Enterprise support (full counselling service)	0%	80%+	80%+	50-79%	80%+	80%+	0%	10-49%	0%
Small firms management courses / seminars	0%	0%	80%+	50-79%	80%+	80%+	0%	10-49%	0%
Small & large firms management courses / seminars	0%	0%	<10%	50-79%	80%+	80%+	0%	0%	0%
Export advice	0%	0%	<10%	80%+	0%	0%	0%	0%	0%
Export centre	0%	0%	10-49%	10-49%	10-49%	10-49%	0%	10-49%	0%
Trade missions	<10%	0%	0%	50-79%	0%	0%	0%	0%	0%
Marketing centre / support	0%	0%	10-49%	10-49%	0%	0%	0%	10-49%	0%
Direct provision of loans & grants to SMEs	0%	80%+	10-49%	<10%	0%	50-79%	0%	10-49%	0%
Owns workspaces / premises	<10%	0%	10-49%	<10%	0%	50-79%	0%	50-79%	80%+
Land provision	0%	0%	0%	0%	0%	0%	0%	50-79%	80%+
Infrastructure	0%	0%	0%	0%	0%	50-79%	0%	80%+	80%+
Environmental improvement	0%	0%	0%	0%	0%	50-79%	0%	80%+	80%+

Key: 80%+ | 50-79% | 10-49% | <10% | 0%

Figure 5.3 Proportion of agents undertaking specific activities concerned with economic development (estimated number of agents as a percentage of the national total in each group)
Sources: 1. Enterprise Agencies from BITC Directory and LSE survey of 18 agencies; 2. Chambers from LSE survey of all Chambers 1989; 3. TECs and LECs from LSE surveys in 1990 and 1991; 4. UDCs from NAO and HoC reports; 5. LEAs from national data and LSE local surveys in 1989–90; 6. Local authorities from LSE surveys in 1989; 7. Businesses and banks based on a wide variety of sources (as Figure 5.1) plus LSE interviews.

The fragmentation and gaps in coverage by economic agents would not be so important if it was clear that a system was in place that provided effective integration.

Although there are emergent local examples of such systems (discussed in later chapters), there is no evidence of a general approach that satisfies the quality requirements we have outlined, that is in place across the whole economy.

Unfortunately a major responsibility for these gaps lies with government itself. Figure 5.4 presents the pattern of spending and control by the major government departments that affect the national and local economic process. Each department is again analysed by its proportional contribution to each of the main fields of activity of enterprise, education, training, and physical development. It is accepted that any approach to classifying government programmes in this way will be rough-and-ready. However, Figure 5.4 emphasises that, however the classification is drawn in detail, there is a major fragmentation and overlapping of programmes between government departments.

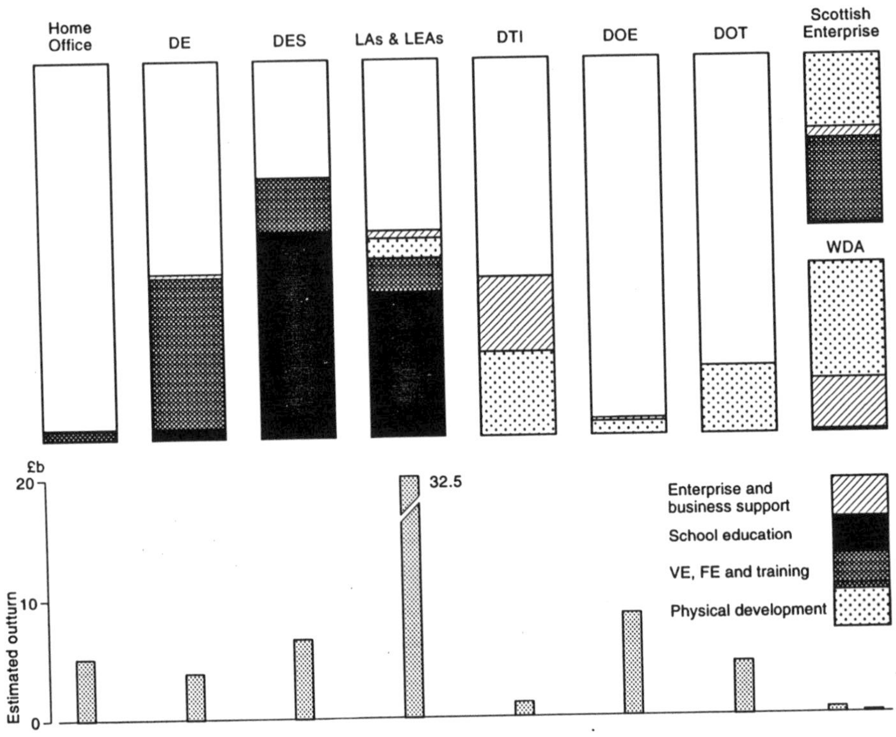

Figure 5.4 Proportion of expenditure devoted to different fields of specific economic development activity, estimated outturns in 1990/91
Source: based on National Expenditure Accounts and Chancellor's Autumn Statement 1990

This fragmentation and the resulting need for coordination have been recognised by government which has argued that disparate initiatives are interdependent and form part of an integrated strategy that can be varied to fit local circumstances. Attempts have been made over the years to improve coordination; the most recent are the "Action for Cities" programme and "Investors in People" initiatives. But these have stimulated yet further agencies that seek to coordinate. For example, CATs and TFs, Training Access Points (TAPs), Local Employer Networks (LENs), TECs and LECs can all be seen as specific government-stimulated coordination bodies. Many of these bodies also seek to stimulate coordination of government services with outside bodies, particularly the private sector.

Despite these manifold attempts at coordination, government is generally not good at bringing its departmental programmes together. There are many forces that limit government's attempts at better coordination[2]:

- Financial accountability for the use of public funds imposes a necessity for (a) strong vertical structures upwards to central departments and to the Treasury, and (b) strong limits on the degree of virement or flexibility in use of funds in any specific field;
- Political accountability reinforces the financial pressures to a strong vertical structure of civil service accountability and management upwards to the top of the civil service, to ministers and to parliament;
- Departmental, ministerial and political rivalries tend to stimulate strong pressures for "ownership" of programmes. This encourages a departmental unwillingness to pool resources, and a central government reluctance to pool credit for programmes with other actors – often particularly local government;
- Public accountability, access to information and the form and speed of the public administrative processes tend to impose a long timetable and caution on use of public funds. This tends to limit the speed of response and extent of risk-taking possible. In addition wide consultations are usually required. This slows the speed of decision making, but also undermines the possibilities for commercial confidentiality. The private sector, in contrast, needs rapid and efficient decisions, commercial confidentiality, and a capacity to seek opportunities in exchange for acceptance of often high degrees of risk. The result is a tension. Simply stated, it is difficult for government or its agents to be entrepreneurial, and it is often difficult for the public and private sectors to work at the same pace or with the same commercial effectiveness;
- The personnel, administrative policies, career structures and training programmes within the civil service naturally reinforce a lack of entrepreneurism and instead focus on financial and political accountability, departmental needs and administrative practice. For example:
  - there is little responsibility delegated downwards in the administration hierarchy,
  - many tiers of administration are necessary to implement programmes making decision takers remote from technical knowledge,
  - increasingly strong public sector unionisation has generally reinforced the forces that stimulate civil servants to look inwards rather than outwards from their fields of concern,
  - rapid rotation of staff between areas of responsibility tends to assure a lack of technical expertise at the expense of a high quality of administrative expertise.

The result is a personnel that is often relatively poorly equipped to link outwards beyond government, often does not have the equivalent technical skills as the external agents with which they have to deal, and tends to slow down or bureaucratise decisions that the private sector and other agents expect to be executed quickly through delegated discretion to the individuals with whom they have been dealing.

It should also be noted that most of the attributes listed above conflict with the aims of client-orientation, flexibility and the seeking out of opportunities necessary to achieve a coherent and effective economic support system. The outcome has often, therefore, been a tension of cultures between government and the private sector, and between government, local authorities and other actors.

The patchwork quilt

The national system of economic support outlined in Figures 5.1 to 5.4 shows a general pattern of fragmentation and overlaps which is confusing, complex and offers no assurance that quality networks can be constructed. These problems are particularly evident at the local level. Britain's economic agents are not spread evenly across the country. They have a varied geography with a varied organisational capability, and operate over very different scales of geographical coverage. Figure 5.5 compares the main agents by the size of area they cover and the size of their budget. Included in this are Chambers of Commerce both at their existing scale and within their new national network (see Chapter 6). Many of the other data derive from original surveys described in later chapters.

Figure 5.5 shows a wide range of diversity in size. Generally in *geographical area*, local government is both large and medium in size (local authority counties/regions or boroughs and districts). Central government local agents are generally either very small and focused (EZs, UDCs, CATs, TFs) or very large (TECs and LECs). Private sector bodies are intermediate or large (Chambers and Enterprise Agencies). However in *expenditure*, government funded bodies are very large (except non-metropolitan districts) whilst private sector bodies are small, and central government local agents are intermediate.

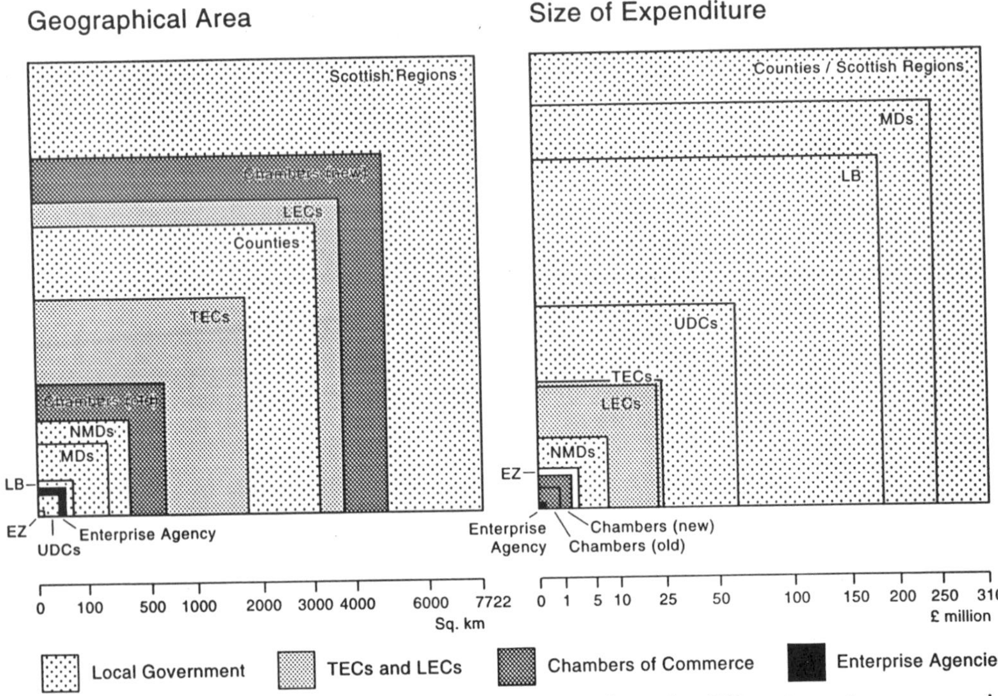

Figure 5.5 Average geographical area and average expenditure by different agents on economic development activities (in 1990/91)

Generally the greatest mismatches of resources and geographical area are for the private-led bodies which have larger areas than their resources can adequately cover – this leads us to important policy issues discussed in later chapters.

Apart from a confusing range of scales of agents, their geographical focus is also very variable – some agents exist in some areas and not in others, and some areas are only partially covered. Local government and TECs/LECs are present everywhere. But, although local government certainly exists everywhere, there is often confusion because of the division and lack of cooperation between tiers in non-metropolitan areas. Central government has also imposed on local government a wide variety of criteria that restrict local government expenditure and limits to specific areas the use of local economic development grants, loans and guarantees, as shown in Figure 5.6.

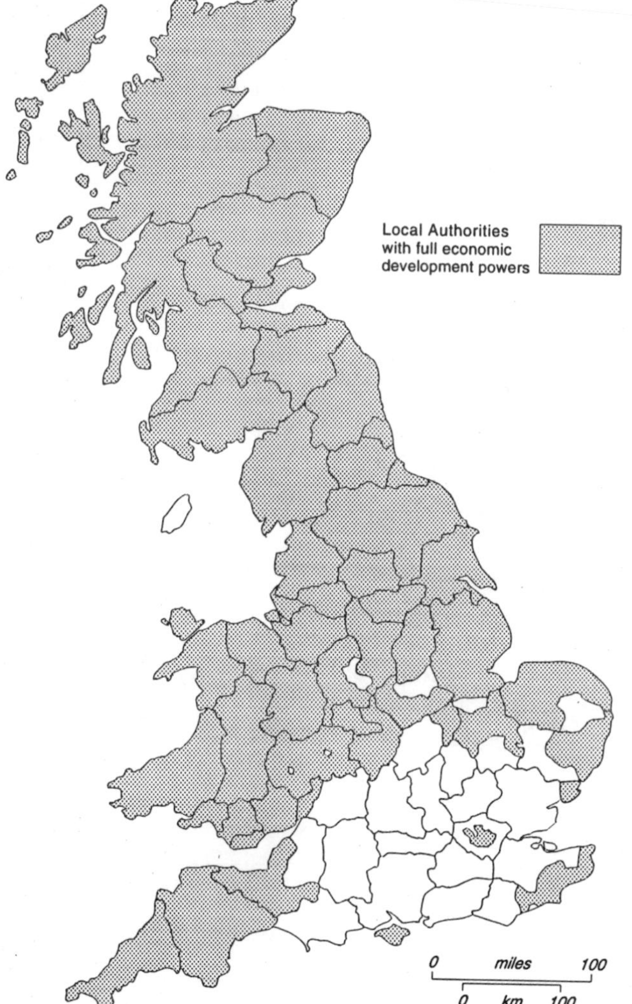

Figure 5.6 Proposed areas where principal local authorities were to be given the power to provide grants, loans and guarantees of borrowing to undertakings conducted with a view to profit
Source: DoE, 1989

There is also a range of central government local agents. These are very focused on specific places (see Figure 5.7) and, when their programmes are undertaken through local authorities, support is not uniformly available everywhere. Important differences of support and resources apply in Urban Programme Areas (UPAs), TF, CAT and UDC areas. EC Structural Funds criteria add further dimensions of selectivity to local authority areas eligible for external support. The main Structural Funds categories applicable to Britain are shown in Figure 5.8.

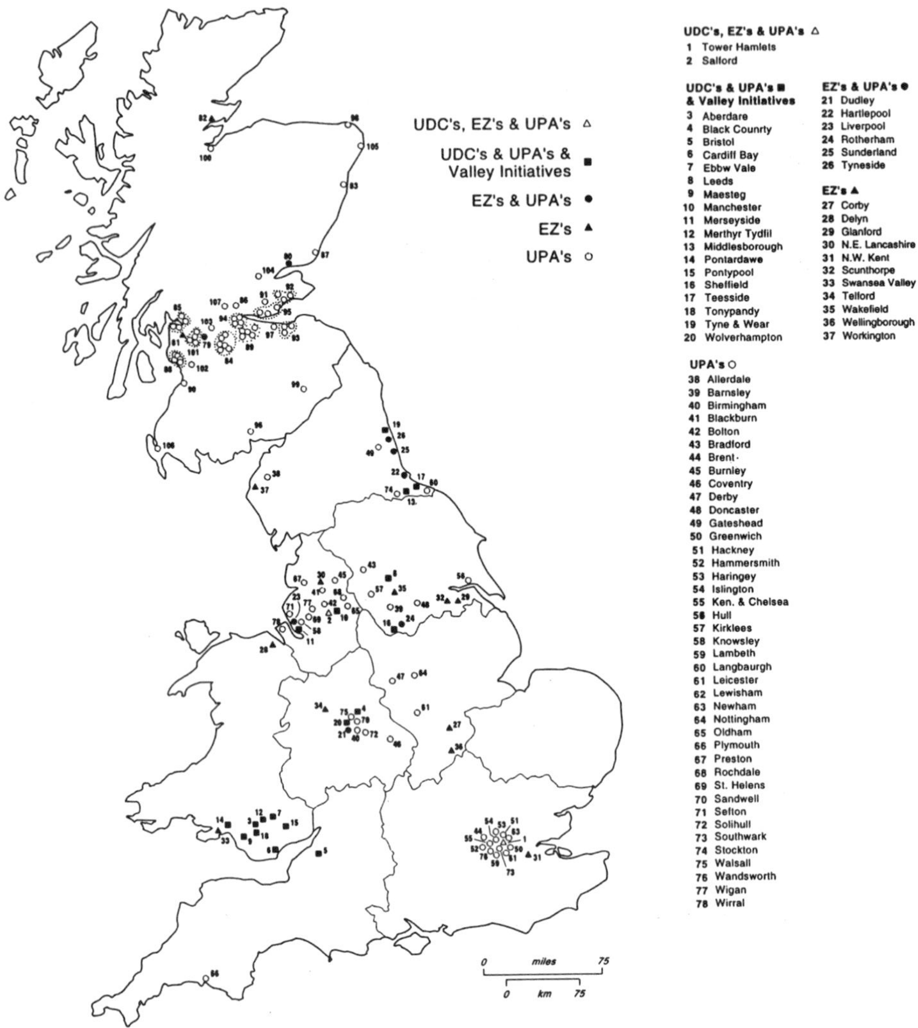

Figure 5.7 Central government local activities, 1990 (UDCs: Urban Development Corporations, UPAs: Urban Priority Areas, EZs: Enterprise Zones. 'Valley Initiatives' apply only to South Wales)

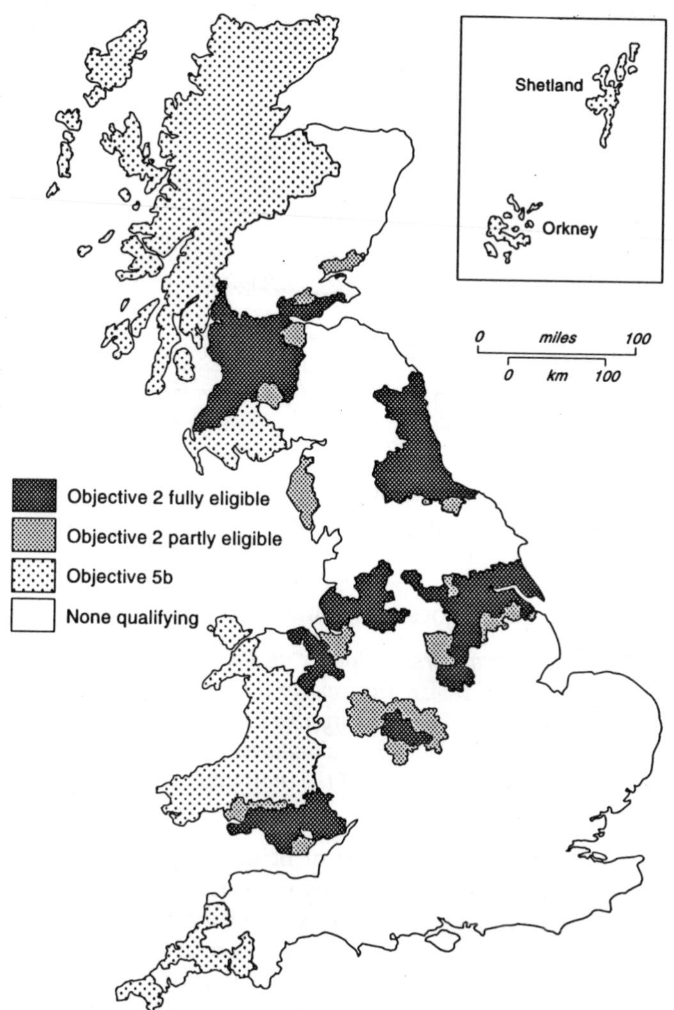

Figure 5.8 Areas eligible for EC Structural Funds support in 1991
Source: LSE Cartographic Unit from EC sources

These agents are all governmental. The Audit Commission (1989, p. 1) has been very critical of this governmental systems failure. It refers to the resulting outcome at local level as *"**a patchwork quilt** of complexity and idiosyncracy. (Government programmes) ... baffle local authorities and businesses alike. The rules of the game seem over-complex and sometimes capricious. They encourage compartmentalised policy approaches rather than a coherent strategy; ... Key organisational structures have fallen into disrepair. Some* *partnership schemes do not in practice operate."* The resulting programmatic fragmentation is shown in Figure 5.9.

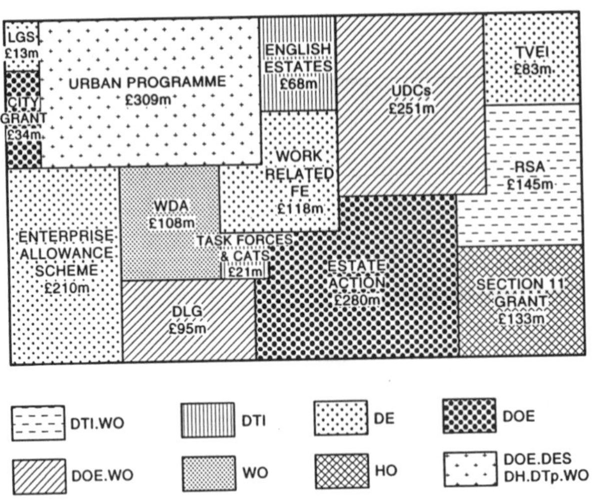

Figure 5.9 The "patchwork quilt" of governmental programmes that seek to assist urban economic development. Size of square is proportional to magnitude of expenditure in 1988–89
Source: Audit Commission, 1989, exhibit 2

The Audit Commission (1989, p. 16) goes on to note that

> *Nothing is likely to have a greater adverse influence on the private sector's perception of an area than evidence of disunity between the two branches of the public sector. Many business people ... simply fail to comprehend why there is so much concern about precisely which agency disbursing other people's money should take the credit for doing so. ... it is hard to escape the conclusion that at the level of the individual city there can be programme overkill with a strategic vacuum (ibid, p. 32)*

Thus the Audit Commission sees a major part of Britain's system failure in economic support at local level being the result of failure by government.

The fragmentation of government's response is often matched by an equal level of fragmentation among other agents and institutions. Part of this phenomenon derives from the impact of governmentally fragmented initiatives. Some government departments favour one institution, other departments favour others. The establishment of departmental "ownership" and vertical lines of accountability is a strong influence on the agencies that deliver government programmes or collaborate with government.

But other agencies are equally subject to the same forces that influence government departments: financial accountability, vertical line management, pressures to retain "ownership" of programmes, and personnel policies that induce fragmentation of capacity. Hence, the potential for fragmentation and a lack of a client-focused response is also a major problem for non-governmental agents.

Figure 5.10 shows the geographical coverage by enterprise agencies. Enterprise agencies are numerous, over 300 in number, but most are very small, and a number of significant business centres are not covered. They overlap significantly in coverage in most metropolitan areas, and leave major gaps in rural areas. Their services are also extremely variable, most having only a limited range of service support, but approximately 15% of agencies have a large and wide service coverage (see Chapter 6).

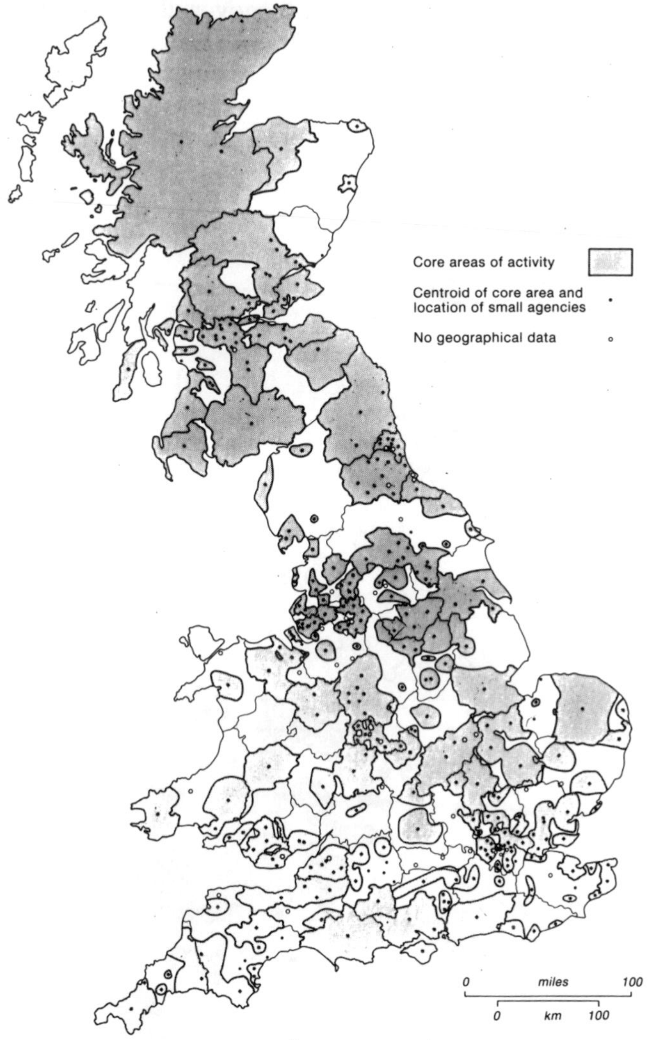

Figure 5.10 Geographical coverage of enterprise agency core areas of activity, 1989
Source: LSE survey

Turning to Chambers of Commerce, these also, at present, have an uneven incidence across the country. Their *core* catchment areas of activity (Figure 5.11) cover only 26% of Britain's surface area, although these areas do cover 73% of all business units (Bennett, 1991a). The present coverage is thus concentrated in the main economic centres, but like enterprise agencies their presence is often small or absent in rural areas. There are also many Chambers that are too small in membership, staff or resources to provide a quality service. Chapter 6 discusses the present variability of services provided. This had led to the adoption of a development strategy for Chambers (Bennett, 1991a), the mapped outcome of which is shown in Figure 5.12. Each of these Chamber areas is seeking to satisfy minimum requirements of critical mass of at least 1,000 members, 30 staff, £1m turnover, the capacity to grow, and a service management structure capable of accreditation to BS5750.

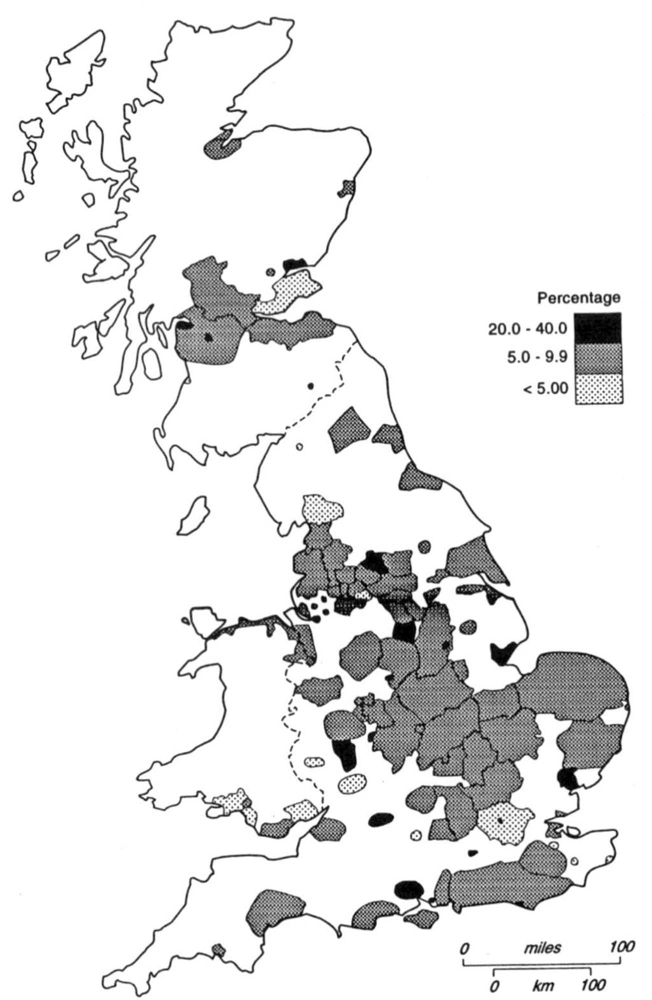

Figure 5.11 Geographical coverage of Chamber of Commerce core areas of activity, 1989 and their density of coverage of local businesses
Source: LSE survey; density is defined as the ratio of Chamber members to local businesses as assessed in the Census of Employment, which largely excludes the self-employed: see Bennett, (1991a)

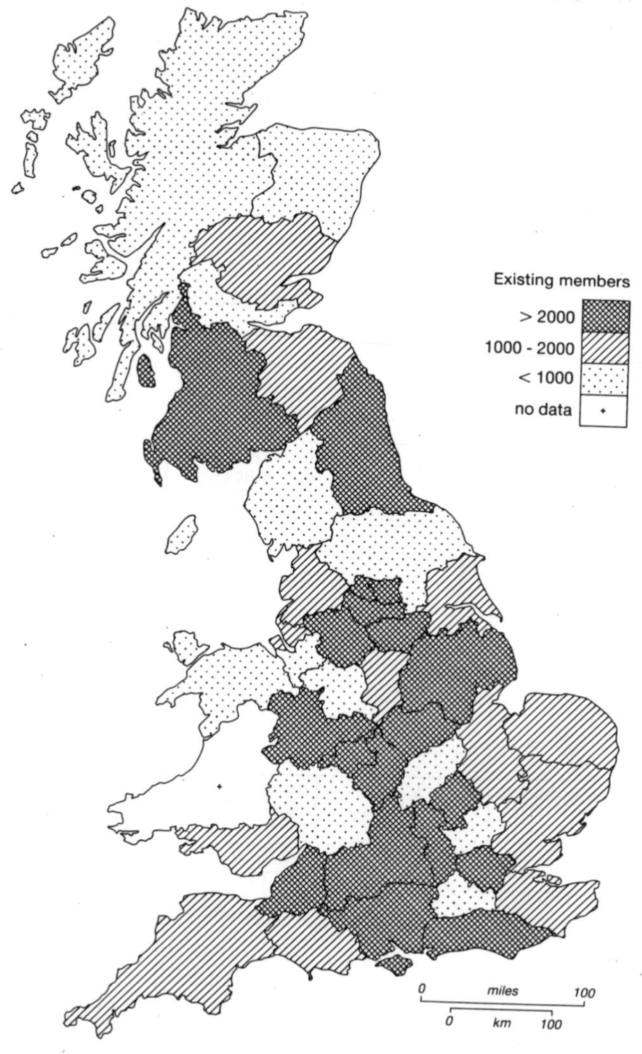

Figure 5.12 National network of core Chambers with size of 1990 membership. Proposal by Bennett (1991a)

The pattern of local agents is not static. The map is changing all the time and major developments are taking place. Important changes are: the development of TECs and LECs; the integration of enterprise agencies into TECs and LECs; the national development strategy for Chambers of Commerce; and the continuing assimilation by local authorities of the new economic development power which has been available to them since April 1990 and is implemented in local economic development plans that had to be drawn up by April 1991.

The result of fragmentation of programmes by both government and other agents can be illustrated by a "typical area" shown in Figure 5.13. Later chapters present the empirical material from which this generalised illustration is derived. What is clear from this illustration is that the characteristics we have noted in general between institutions are blatantly evident at local level, namely:

- There is major fragmentation;
- There are significant overlaps between many fields of activity and places;
- There are often significant gaps with no coverage at all;
- There is considerable complexity, making it difficult for the client to know where to go for what service;
- The overall structure is focused on the needs of producers rather than clients.

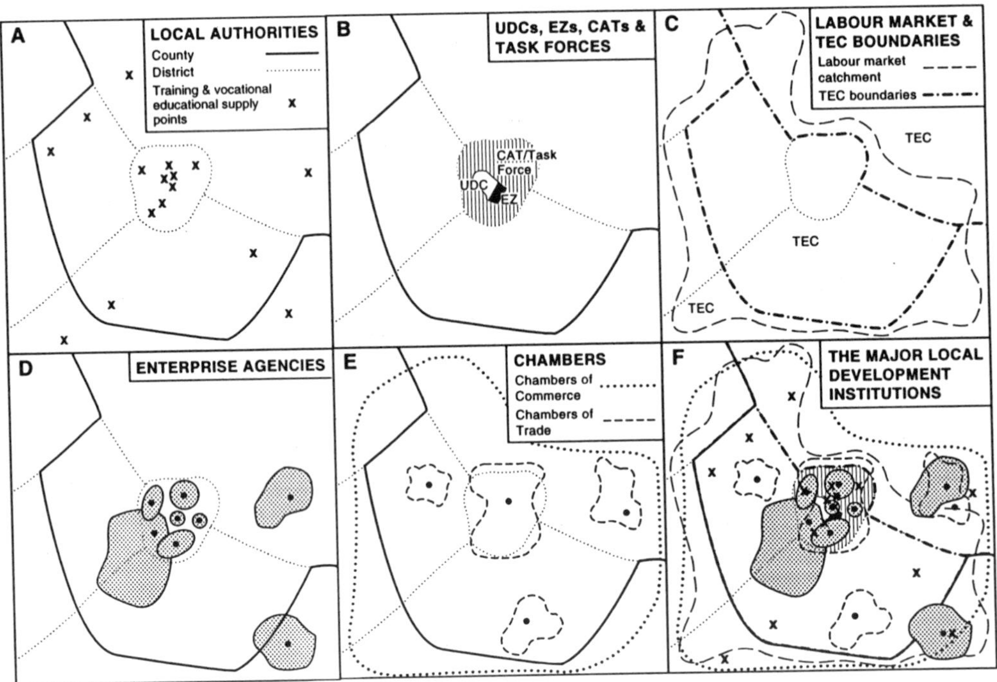

Figure 5.13 Schematic illustration of geographical coverage by the major agencies concerned with local economic development

The geographical map can be complemented by the organisational map. Figure 5.14 illustrates a specific example of organisations concerned with business delivery in Oxfordshire in 1990. This is typical of the organisation map of many areas, and is indeed less complex than many of the larger metropolitan areas such as London shown in figure 5.15. How this fragmentation arises and can be overcome is the focus for the rest of this book.

Figure 5.14 The network of economic development activities in Oxfordshire in 1990
Source: D. Stanley, N. Oxford LEN manager

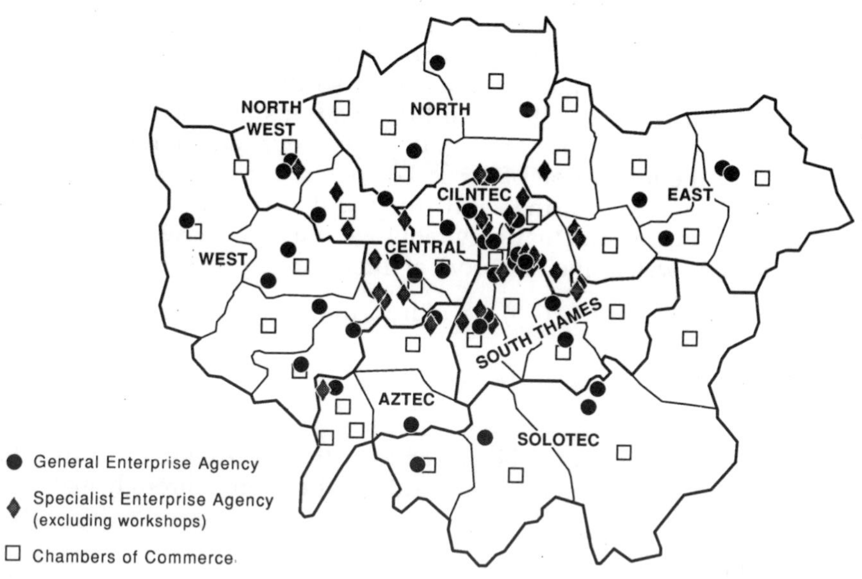

Figure 5.15 Business organisations in London in 1992
Source: LSE and TEC surveys

System development

This chapter has established the framework which is to be used in the following chapters *to assess* Britain's economic and institutional developments of the 1980s and early 1990s and to provide a basis for outlining *ways forward on policy*. The chapter has argued that *systems failure* can be overcome only by *systems development*. Local capacity building is a key part of system development. This requires both the development of networks linking agents, and the development of each agent's own programmes and services. We have referred to this as developing a quality response that offers a capacity focused on the needs of the economic client.

Our analysis here has shown that the present complex multi-agency structure of programme delivery at the local level makes it very likely that gaps and overlaps will occur. As a result, resources can be wasted and major deficiencies of client support can arise by dispersion of programmes. A client-focused approach necessitates a stronger coherence to be built across the programmatic fields. Demonstrating how these gaps and inefficiencies can be overcome and how a quality management structure can be built at local level is the purpose of the following chapters.

Local capacity building cannot be achieved in a fragmented environment. But capacity can be enhanced by encouraging agents to work effectively together linking their programmes. The DTI proposed one-stop shops attempt to encourage this, but our assessment goes wider in terms of the number of agents that need to be integrated.

Our focus of attention is on national programmes and local response. As introduced in Chapter 1, this concerns the interaction of three main fields of vertical programme activity (enterprise, education, and training), with the organisational and management structures that are responsible for making the economic development decisions in local situations. Such a structure is required in order to deliver a true local capacity, which we refer to as horizontal syntheses, since it attempts to bring a coherence between programmes. Because it is so difficult to gain a horizontal synthesis at national level, and because the situations in which many economic development decisions take place are so often local, our main emphasis will be on local capacity. But the interaction of vertical, programmatic fields of activity, which are often dominated by national statutory and informal norms, with local management structures means that inevitably we must appraise both national and local organisations, as well as their network of interactions.

In Part 2 of the book (Chapters 6–8) we address the vertical fields of:

- Enterprise;
- Education;
- Training.

In Part 3 of the book (Chapters 9–14) we address the horizontal structures that can integrate vertical programmes in different local situations, first through analysis of:

- Local networks;
- Dimensions of local capability;

and second, in the context of different types of areas:

- Large cities and metropolitan cores;
- Metropolitan fringe areas;

- Dispersed industrial areas;
- Central places and rural areas.

Footnotes: Chapter 5

1. SDA is the Scottish Development agency; HIDB is the Highlands and Islands Development Board; WDA is the Welsh Development Agency; RDC is the Rural Development Commission in England; UDCs are Urban Development Corporations; CATs are City Action Teams; TECs are Training and Enterprise Councils in England and Wales; LECs are Local Enterprise Companies in Scotland (in April 1991 the SDA and HIBD were merged with the Scottish part of the Training Agency to form Scottish Enterprise (SE) and Highlands and Islands Enterprise (HIE), respectively).
2. For detailed demonstration of these limitations see e.g. Widdicombe (1986), Audit Commission (1989), SQW (1988), HoC (1988), Committee on Public Accounts (1989).

PART II

Fields of Activity: Vertical Programmes

6. *ENTERPRISE*

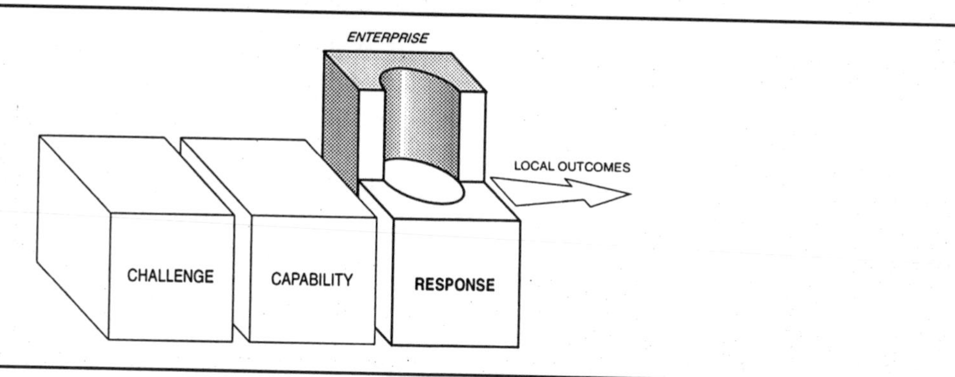

The development of enterprise

Enterprise development concerns business start-up, business growth and development of main business practice. Enterprise evidences many of Britain's difficulties of system failure. But it is also an area in which many developments have been taking place.

This chapter analyses these changes. It argues that *responsive* economies derive from both encouraging small firms and "down-sized" larger companies. The case is argued for business support services which enable firms to gain market access and help them cross significant growth thresholds. Since responsiveness necessarily places chief emphasis on the capacity to change, to innovate, and to grow, the chief focuses for this chapter are naturally enterprise in (i) start-up, (ii) growth, and (iii) adaptation and development of existing main business practice.

The chapter devotes most space to analysis of the chief existing agents that help business start-up and growth: businesses themselves, banks, enterprise agencies, Chambers of Commerce, trade associations, local authorities and TECs and LECs. The chapter reviews the very considerable progress that has been made by each of these agents in the last 5 to 10 years. But it also concludes that there remains in Britain a systems failure in which enterprise support is still too fragmented, both nationally and locally, between agents who fail collectively to address the broader structural barriers that inhibit Britain's economic progress. This leads directly to the policy conclusion developed in Chapter 15.

The contribution of enterprise

Enterprise concerns the pursuit of business for the creation of profit and wealth. Definitionally, it is concerned with capital formation derived from increased total productivity and/or increased total output. We set our analysis within the context of the global challenges to business development outlined in Chapter 2. Enterprise is being profoundly affected by the internationalisation of markets and the development of possible transition to the fifth Kondratieff wave of communications-based technology. The key aspects we have identified are shifts to high quality, high value-added products; increased needs for flexibility and responsiveness to the speed of change related to enhanced customisation; and increased emphasis on design, organisation and marketing.

The developments of the global economy affect different businesses in different ways. In the subsequent discussion, it is particularly important to differentiate different sizes of business. Although definitions vary, we use as guidelines the following categories:

- Micro-businesses of less than 5 employees (including self-employment);
- Meso-businesses, often to be distinguished into two sub-groups: 5–20 employees, and 20–200 employees;
- Large businesses of greater than 200 employees.

The first two groups of micro- and meso-businesses are sometimes collectively referred to as SMEs (small and medium-sized enterprises).

Associated with changes in the global economy, the 1970s and 1980s saw a shift of emphasis both to smaller firms and to the "down-sizing" of larger firms. The rate of growth of larger firms decreased and the rate of growth of small firms increased rapidly in the 1970s and 1980s. First brought to attention in the UK by Prais (1976), the trend is shown in Figure 3.7. This pattern is repeated in the USA and other OECD countries (see e.g. Storey and Johnson, 1987a).

Birch (1979) showed that in the USA over 60% of new jobs created over the period 1969–1976 came from firms employing less than 20 employees. This finding has had a major impact on government perceptions of the importance of the small firms sector. Studies replicating Birch's findings in the UK by Gallagher and Stewart (1986) and Doyle and Gallagher (1986) showed that between 1971 and 1981 firms with under 20 employees, although having only 12% of the UK workforce, created 36% of new jobs: a "fertility ratio" of 3.1. For the 1982–84 period they showed that 46% of new jobs derived from firms with under 20 employees accounting for 23% of the workforce, a fertility ratio of 2.0. These statistics contrast with the decline in employment in large firms which had fertility ratios of approximately 0.5. Although subject to controversy as to the detail of these estimates, there is no dispute as to the general importance of SMEs to employment growth in both the US and UK in the 1970s and 1980s. Confirmation is to be found in a variety of studies using different data sources. In the UK particularly important is Macey (1982) and a whole range of regional studies reviewed in Storey and Johnson (1987a, Chapter 4).

Despite the importance of growth of SMEs in the 1970s and 1980s, the late 1980s have seen a slowdown in the importance of small firm growth, in both employment and in their contribution to GNP. It is uncertain at this stage whether this represents the start of a new phase of concentration of economic activity into larger firms as a result of mergers and acquisitions, or whether it is just a short-term differential impact of economic slowdown in some of the sectors in which SMEs are prominent and which have been particularly affected by the cuts in consumer spending of the 1990–92 recession (especially services).

One possible explanation of the slowdown in the contribution of SMEs activity may derive from lessons learnt by larger firms from small firms. The attractions of SMEs for many of the most talented workers and managers have been the greater variety of work, greater responsibility, availability of equity stakes and profit sharing, flexibility of employment conditions and lack of big firm bureaucracy (Blanchflower and Oswald, 1991). These advantages are being increasingly offered by big firms seeking to act like small ones. Firms like IBM, Eastman-Kodak, 3M, Hewlett-Packard and Hanson are splitting themselves into smaller and smaller core operating groups, and giving greater flexibility and responsibility in work practices to people in divisions or sub-units; what Rothwell and Zegveld (1985) term "internal entrepreneurship". This allows large firms to copy the benefits of small firms, but they can usually offer better pay and other benefits to their core staff than normally available in small businesses. This may give them a competitive edge which will lead to a new phase of corporate concentration, but with decentralised internal structures. In this sense, enterprise development has diffused to affect the business community as a whole. Indeed, we choose to treat enterprise here as a concern of the management and employment structures equally of large and small firms.

Recognition of the contributions that can be made to economic growth by both large firm decentralisation and small firms has had an important effect on the debate about management of both national and local economies. It has shifted discussion from Keynesian macro-economic demand management and regional policy concerned with stimulating inward investment and relocation of industry, to the search for means to stimulate enterprise and enhance local capacities by indigenous growth. This involves working to a greater extent with the supply side factors in the local economy. As the experience of the early 1990s unfolds, it is evident that the development of local growth capacity is not an issue associated specifically with small firms, but arises across the size spectrum of firms. Thus it is the *responsiveness* of a firm to the challenges of change, rather than its size, that is the key determinant of growth potential (the recognition that responsiveness and flexibility can be achieved in both large as well as small organisations also allows us to understand better the process of entrepreneurship, examined later). Among the factors stimulating the growth of smaller business decision units in both SMEs and decentralised large firms are:

- Increasing emphasis on service industries, including marketing and producer services (see e.g. OECD, 1985);
- The reduced benefits now available from economies of scale as a result of technological change;
- The need to restructure traditional industry through job rationalisation, improved industrial relations, job spinoffs, cost cutting, redundancy schemes, management buyouts, subcontracting, etc. (see e.g. Bluestone and Harrison, 1982; Keeble and Wever, 1986);
- The desire to stimulate a greater capacity to innovate (see e.g. Rothwell and Zegveld, 1985);
- The search for greater managerial flexibility (see Handy, 1985, 1989; Pettigrew and Whipp, 1991);
- The search for greater employee job satisfaction, especially among managers (see Handy, 1985, 1989; Pettigrew and Whipp, 1991);
- The restructuring of the public sector through privatisation and contracting out of public services (see e.g. Bennett, 1990a);
- The opportunities offered by reduced sizes of decision units to relocate to places which afford a better quality of life for workers and managers (see Chapters 9 and 10).

The variety of these factors confirms the conclusions of most analysts that emphasis on responsiveness to diversity is the chief aspect of current change in business structures.

Thus the programmes that seek to stimulate enterprise must also be diverse and should reflect the variety of each business situation, and the different local possibilities for success (see e.g. Meyer-Krahmer, 1985; Keeble and Wever, 1986; Keeble and Kelly, 1988; Storey and Johnson, 1987b; Nijkamp et al., 1988; Bannock, 1989). The rest of this chapter is devoted to assessing how existing enterprise institutions operate.

The case for an enterprise policy

The need for a specific policy to enhance business performance is not self-evident. Businesses are usually the most competent to make decisions on their investments, factor inputs, marketing and strategy. Indeed, much theoretical economics suggests that, if we assume profit maximisation, perfect information, free mobility of resources, freedom of entry and neutrality of government policies, then the market will achieve all that is required. Businesses will make optimal decisions and no enterprise policy is needed. Maximum economic output of the economy will be achieved at the lowest costs with the optimum mix of sectors, firm sizes, and factors of production.[1]

The limitation of the economic argument is, of course, in its assumptions. The market does not work perfectly such that all parts of all businesses work to maximise profits. Information and mobility are not perfect, and there is not equal entry into the market for all types and sizes of firms. This has stimulated the evolution of enterprise policies

Table 6.1 Market imperfections, their causes and areas of action required

Market gap	Cause of market gap	Action needed
Supply of entrepreneurs	Social and economic bias in favour of employment rather than self-employment	Social security system Education Tax system
Supply of innovations	Inadequate R&D	Education and research policy Misallocated R&D expenditure Tax system
Lack of capital	Distortions in capital markets	Tax system Subsidised lending Monopoly policy Credit guarantees
Labour shortages	Imperfections in labour markets	Social security system Social environment Housing policy Training and education Monopoly policy Labour relations policy
Lack of premises	Imperfections in property market	Urban redevelopment Planning regulations Infrastructure investment Tax system
Bureaucracy and compliance costs	Growth of government	Simplification, exemption, changes in local taxation Reorganisation of central and local government
Purchasing	Imperfections in supplier markets	Monopoly policy, tax system, government "crowding out"
Marketing	Imperfections in seller markets	

(developed from Bannock, 1981, 1989)

that seek to fill the gap where markets do not work. These gaps arise in situations in which businesses alone cannot overcome barriers to entry or access to opportunities. This argument was the basis for the recommendations of the Bolton Committee (1971) on small firms. The Bolton Committee also went further by identifying the limits on government policy if it departed from giving equal treatment to all businesses: intervention by government could create a displacement effect where the aided business would occupy the market previously filled by a non-aided business. The Bolton Report has underpinned the subsequent evolution of UK enterprise policy.

The case for support to enterprise rests on developing government's role as enabler or filling the gaps where markets fail to ensure equal treatment to all firms. The gaps in the market process can be analysed in three ways – national, sectoral and local. At a *national level*, enterprise development needs the supply of each factor of production to be available on an equal basis to all businesses, and equally between the public and private sectors. The difficulties arising from the chief gaps in the market which commonly occur are listed in Table 6.1, together with their causes and fields in which action is required to overcome them. This analysis, developed from the influential work of Graham Bannock, directs attention to a long list of governmental policy areas that can remove obstacles and improve the general environment for business developments in Britain (see Bannock, 1989, 1990). Bannock forcefully argues, in particular, that most of the national barriers and distortions to enterprise arise from government or EC policy. Thus they can be removed by changes in government policy.

At a *sector level*, there are two chief issues – first, that relating to firm size, and second, that relating to industrial sector bias. All of the imperfections in the market listed in Table 6.1 apply not only to the general environment of business development, but tend to apply with disproportionately adverse effect on *small firms*. Writers on small firm policy agree on the common adverse affects of (see e.g. Bolton Committee, 1971; Bannock, 1981, 1989; Storey, 1982; Storey and Johnson, 1987a; Curran, 1986; CEC, 1987; DE, 1989, 1990):

- *Taxation*: which distorts incentives and the capital market and places proportionately higher burdens of compliance costs on small firms;
- *Regulation and bureaucracy*: is highly regressive with firm size (proportionately much higher on small firms);
- *Purchasing*: large firms and public sector purchasing is heavily biased towards other large firms and public sector suppliers;
- *Competition policy*: is a largely discretionary aspect of government activity and generally has to reach high levels of abuse before government acts; it thus tends to strongly weaken the possibilities of entry by small firms;
- *Education and research*: has little focus on business and enterprise, particularly in the small firms sector: it is biased towards either management or employee status rather than entrepreneurship, and pure research rather than technological innovation and development;
- *Social legislation*: the effects on incentives to individuals, costs to businesses (especially labour costs) (see, particularly, Layard and Nickell, 1985 and OECD, 1986b) and forms of employment (part-time, full-time) all have regressive effects on SMEs.

All of these areas have been tackled by reforms of government policy, but much still requires to be done.

At a *local level*, national and sectoral issues come together and are reinforced by the specific local conditions that support or inhibit enterprise. These determine how fertile the local environment is, both to new firm formation and to the development of firms once they have been founded. Some areas have a more positive supporting environment to market development than others. A good deal of analysis has gone into assessing these factors (see e.g. Oxenfeld, 1943; Mansfield, 1962; Gudgin, 1978; Johnson and Cathcart, 1979; Cross, 1981; Keeble and Wever, 1986; Lloyd and Mason, 1984; Storey, 1982; Storey and Johnson, 1987a; Sweeney, 1987; Beesley and Hamilton, 1986; Hamilton, 1989). The main factors identified are listed in Table 6.2 together with the indicators that are frequently used to measure and assess local conditions. In general, it has been found that the extent of existing entrepreneurism and growth of small firms in an area is a strong stimulus to enterprise, along with occupational structures related to commerce, services, management and the professions. High rates of job loss can be

Table 6.2 Chief factors that promote the local enterprise "environment"

General factor	Variable normally measured in empirical studies
1. Size of "incubator" firm	High % of total employment in plants employing <10 persons Low % of total employment in plants employing >500 persons
2. Occupational experience	High % of population in managerial and professional groupings Low % of population in manual groupings High % of population self-employed
3. Education and training	High % of population with higher degrees High school attainment level High level of skills attainment
4. Access to capital	High savings per head of population High house-owning population Low local-authority renting population
5. Entry into industry	High % of population in industries with low entry barriers Low % of population in heavy industry Low % of population in mining and quarrying industries
6. Non-production entrepreneurship	High % of total employment in services High % of total employment in commerce, retailing and wholesaling
7. Market demand	High regional income distribution Increase in production employment Increase in total employment
8. Institutional environment	Supportive local agents in regional or local government Presence of other key actors
9. Business climate	Good labour relations Attractive environment
10. Communications and accessibility	Links to national communications networks Closeness to communications nodes
11. Turbulence	High rate of employment loss in manufacturing plant closures
12. Industrial specialisation	High level of diversity of economy
13. Premises	Availability and low cost of premises
14. Unemployment	Low % level of long-term unemployment High % increase in the rate of unemployment in short time
15. Rurality	Low % of population living in towns of over 5,000 population
16. Degree of local autonomy	High % of total manufacturing employment in indigenous plants Low % of firms in branch plants
17. Age of investment	High % of total manufacturing employment in "young" plants

(developed and amended from Moyes and Westhead, 1990, and other sources, chiefly: Cross, 1981; Keeble and Wever, 1986; Lloyd and Mason, 1984; Storey, 1982; Beesley and Hamilton, 1986; Storey and Johnson, 1987a; Aydalot and Keeble, 1988; Westhead, 1989; Hamilton, 1989; Martinos, 1989; Bennett, 1989a; Hepworth, 1989)

strong "push" factors, whilst long-term unemployment and high levels of employment in branch plants are usually impediments. More general factors such as high levels of educational attainment, availability of skills, premises, local capital and general business climate are also important in allowing enterprise to develop. However, one of the strongest forces that can promote or impede enterprise is the general institutional structure of an area (see e.g. Stohr, 1990; Martinos, 1989; Bennett, 1989a; Bennett and Krebs, 1991 and contributions to Bennett *et al.*, 1990). This has led to the general conclusion, phrased particularly strongly by Sweeney (1987), that enterprise development is as much a social as a technological or financial phenomenon.

As well as barriers and market imperfections, it has been increasingly recognised that *growing firms* experience particular difficulties. Most economic theory has ignored this problem, instead focusing on growth as if it were merely an issue of increasing volumes. However, business growth is more complex. It usually requires significant thresholds to be crossed for information, innovation, finance, labour force and managerial skills, marketing, management and accounting systems. Within small firms, crossing each of these thresholds requires disproportionately higher levels of knowledge and self-confidence, and high investments of staff time and finance, as entirely new systems are built from scratch. In larger firms, growth can often be more easily tackled since it can draw on existing managerial, financial and other resources. In large firms, however, growth frequently requires the development of new working and managerial practices which may have difficulties similar to those of start-up or small firms. Indeed, the adaptation of existing practices in larger firms often meets resistance from bureaucratic inertia which can be very difficult to overcome. These problems may be more difficult if contraction of existing employment or changes to productivity deals are involved. Thus growth requires significant thresholds to be surmounted by firms of all sizes. In the next section we examine how recent developments have sought to tackle this problem.

Support for enterprise

A large number of providers have sought to support enterprise. This section analyses these services and their mode of provision. The key elements of services provided usually consist of (see the guidance given particularly in SQW, 1988; also BiTC, 1989, 1990a):

1. *Signposting*: Provision of information on the business services available, potential business partners, suppliers and markets, sources of finance and technical expertise. This function is best developed in part through general media to raise awareness, but is most effective through referral systems between each organisation providing business services. The importance of effective referral is greater the more frequent and regular is the contact with the firms needing assistance. Of greatest importance for referral usually are local banks, accountancy and solicitors' firms.
2. *Business skilling*: The transfer of know-how to businesses so that they can undertake tasks themselves. This can consist of a variety of techniques:
   - Open learning media such as videos to change the general perception and base of business skills;
   - Informal exchanges and seminars;
   - Management training and education;

- Counselling (this is the most expensive as it can cover only one firm at a time).

3. *Business advice*: Advising a firm on what to do for commercial or technical developments. This can be undertaken through either counselling or consultancy. The areas where advice is most commonly required are:
   - Exporting-importing procedures and contacts;
   - Personnel and labour market information;
   - Contacts to R&D institutions;
   - Patents procedures;
   - Taxation and financial management;
   - Sources of venture capital.

4. *Business assistance*: Undertaking tasks for a firm either as an advisory/consultancy partner, or through a subcontract or management agreement, e.g. marketing, payrolling, product development, etc.

5. *Business support*: Various approaches to helping factor inputs in the fields of:
   - Finance;
   - R&D and technology;
   - Premises;
   - Staffing / secondment;
   - Facilities (as in a managed workspace).

   This is the most expensive area of service and throws into question the issue of equity, since support at this level to some firms can displace others. It may also lead to a long-term dependency of the firm on the network of support. This is in conflict with the enterprise goal of encouraging a self-sustaining structure.

As we have noted earlier, one of Britain's system problems is the fragmentation of business services between different support organisations. This has produced competition, overlap, major gaps in provision and a patchy geographical coverage. We assess below each of the key agents in enterprise development:

- Individual businesses;
- Banks and venture capital funds;
- Enterprise agencies;
- Chambers of Commerce;
- Trade Associations;
- Local authorities;
- TECs and LECs.

This is a long list of agents and each has its own substantial complexities. We highlight here the chief aspects, assessing their strengths, weaknesses and national pattern of contribution. We then examine how they fit together and the extent of the systems problem that has to be addressed.

Individual businesses

Enterprise development centres on investment, entrepreneurship, innovation and business growth. The chief contribution individual businesses can make to enterprise development is to remain competitive, retain and expand markets, and to continue growing. In this way a business makes a major contribution to the creation of wealth in the local and national economy through wages, direct and indirect employment, local and central taxes as well as the production and sale of its goods and services. The prime task of business is thus to:

- Invest in R&D (develop new products, expand markets, or invest to exploit new technologies);
- Plan successful new projects (produce business plans, develop new inputs (labour, capital), develop new structures, find new customers, design new products);
- Plan long-term financial structure (diversify funding sources, control costs, plan and implement growth strategy);
- Communicate (identify audiences, develop strategy and produce best image, prepare and secure publicity, market strategy);
- Evaluate and respond to progress (measure outputs, secure feedbacks from customers, respond to evaluation);
- Motivate and train staff (development of personnel through training, career structure, development of internal communications, handling quality problems with staff, clients and local actors).

One of the most important areas for business development of enterprise is in the field of R&D and new product development. Here, a wide range of different approaches have been recognised by which firms are trying to make themselves more innovative and entrepreneurial (see e.g. Rothwell and Zegveld, 1982, pp. 82–4; Pettigrew and Whipp, 1991):

- *Stimulate entrepreneurial personnel* within existing organisational structures, e.g. by encouraging entrepreneurism, diversification and product teams (scope for only limited success in large, bureaucratic companies unless strong decentralisation also occurs);
- *Venture capital operations* derived from the company's own resources of personnel and finance that may lead to a new product group or division (this can be a very successful means of diversification, e.g. ICI industries);
- *"Venture nurturing"* where the parent firm provides not only cash and ideas, but also gives production, distribution and further R&D support (can be inhibitive because of dominance by demands of existing company);
- *"Venture packaging" and spinoff* where a separate firm is set up by entrepreneurial personnel of the parent company with small equity capital from it, but then left on its own. This leads to a formal joint partnership.

Various management writers (see e.g. Kanter, 1988; Rothwell and Zegveld, 1982; Handy, 1985; Deming, 1986; Peters, 1987; Harvey-Jones, 1988; Pettigrew and Whipp, 1991), argue that these processes require the businesses themselves to be able to adjust radically and to lead change, rather than merely to respond to it. They suggest that the most radical changes are required when at least two elements of – product, technology or markets – together require development. Such changes require a new leader, team and structure of corporate support. If all three elements change together, then a new business company is required.

These are the things that business does on its own, as part of its business strategy. In this way it contributes income, skills and products to itself and the local community. Many businesses, especially large ones, need no support to facilitate their development in this way, beyond the provision of a generally supportive environment and good "business climate". However, each business also looks wider than itself. In the discussion below we look at progressively wider interlinkages: first, at business-to-business links; second, at links of firms with the community through donations; and then at the wide range of links of businesses with support agencies.

Business-to-business links

Businesses are not isolated entities, but prosper and develop through links with other businesses as product suppliers and markets for goods produced. These normal trading relationships can be supplemented by longer term links. These may be at an *informal* level (purchasing and marketing initiatives), or may develop to the point where there is a *formal* contract and long-term partnership in business development (alliances, joint ventures or strategic partnerships). Each link can cover:

- Purchasing and subcontracting;
- Marketing, sales and distribution;
- Research and development, technology transfer;
- Corporate venturing through equity and other stakes.

Usually links are between large and small firms, but not exclusively so.

Informal links derive from the stimulus of the restructuring of an enterprise. They have been stimulated by decentralisation and down-sizing of companies, changing labour practices, and advances in communications technology. These developments allow a much wider range of links to occur and to be effectively managed. Links tend to emerge (Chandler, 1989; PW, 1991; Linzey, 1990; BiTC, 1990a):

- Because they offer greater flexibility of supplies and/or markets;
- Because products of different companies match as compliments of one another;
- Because small distributors are close to markets and because manufacturers, who need closer customer relationships, are more distant;
- Because small manufacturing concerns need a national marketing partner;
- Because technology exchanges can occur, because joint technological investments save costs, and because joint R&D can save costs;
- Because local links can improve quality of supplies (especially for just-in-time (JIT)) as well as contributing to local community support and credibility.

To support these links, a number of initiatives have been developed. The chief focus for enterprise policy has been on improving the awareness, capacity and training of managers of SMEs so that they are better able to take advantage of the opportunities offered by:

- Other private sector businesses: particularly the larger companies or major suppliers to them;
- Central government's 36 government departments, requiring £7 billion of goods and services per year (excluding MOD and NHS) (see HM Treasury, 1991);
- Local government's purchases of goods and services.

Although the demands of each purchaser are very different, in general large purchasers should open up their procedures to become more accessible to other organisations, particularly small firms, and new contractors should be aware of the quality requirements and other demands that will be placed upon them.

A variety of initiatives can facilitate business-to-business links, for example (BiTC, 1990a; PW, 1991):

- *Meet the buyer events* (helpful but generally rather diffuse and one-off);
- *Directory / contact service* provides a list of potential suppliers or purchasers (useful to look for possible partners, but passive and offers no readily available intelligence on companies);
- *Sourcing services* based on a coordinating agency linking larger and smaller companies (useful but tends to diffuse lines of accountability);
- *Group marketing* by a number of small firms jointly (very useful where clearly defined common needs link SMEs);
- *Local purchasing clubs* supported by data bases and contact networks, sometimes supplemented by a guidance service (often very useful and longer term).

Each method is useful but, in general, the more targeted the organisation, and the more direct the introduction of customer and supplier, the more effective are these approaches. Successful examples are those of the Northern Development Company (SQW, 1988) and London Business in the Community / London Enterprise Training Agency (BiTC/LEnTA), whilst Coventry and Bassetlaw have local authority-stimulated local purchasing schemes (see *Financial Times*, 14 August 1990).

Formal links extend purchasing and marketing initiatives to the point where business-to-business developments became part of a partnership with a formal contractual arrangement extending beyond one particular set of transactions. This leads to alliances, joint ventures and "strategic partnerships". These require long-term legal relationships so that each party can plan the scale of the different inputs required of them, and there exists a legal statement of how any R&D or other products will be owned and subsequently developed.

Such partnership networks are little developed in Britain compared to Germany or Japan. Recent surveys show that there is considerable potential for major payoffs to individual businesses from wider links (see e.g. DE/Newchurch, 1990). At present most partnerships and alliances aim at technology transfer and product development (SQW, 1988).

Many technological-based links arise spontaneously, but considerable attention has been directed to how they can be stimulated. The focus for most programmes of stimulation has been to make the links easier to achieve, or to shorten the time taken in the process of moving a new product from its inception to its marketing (through its R&D, prototypes, testing, scale-up, manufacturing, marketing and distribution stages). Much of the activity to stimulate these processes can be handled between firms directly. But a number of initiatives have focused on trying to create innovative milieux, technology transfer centres, technological incubators or science parks (see e.g. AGF, 1988; Premus, 1988; Malecki and Nijkamp, 1988; Stohr, 1990). These are often seen as best situated in collaboration with universities or large research institutions so that they can exploit the local R&D spinoffs. In Germany and Japan these have been built into major technological centres (see e.g. Bennett and Krebs, 1991). In general, the analysis of creative milieux has tended to suggest that an agglomeration of technical workers, urban facilities and an institutional environment generating new research products are critical in such initiatives (see Chapter 9; see also Mansfield, 1982; Oakey, 1984; Rothwell and Zegveld, 1985; Keeble and Wever, 1986; Amin and Goddard, 1986; Hall, 1986; AGF, 1988; Hepworth, 1989). However, it is not easy to encourage development: government policy cannot create entrepreneurs, though it can impede them; and government policy cannot easily create critical mass if a strong base does not already exist. This has led to the concentration of the most successful technology centres and science parks in areas with a strong existing research base.

In Britain the number of operating science parks has grown from 2 in 1982 (Cambridge and Heriot-Watt, Edinburgh) to 21 in 1985 and 38 in 1988, with a slow-down since (*Financial Times*, 10 October 1989). In some cases Enterprise Zone (EZ) tax incentives have been used in addition to more traditional stimuli as an incentive to investment (e.g. in London Docklands and Dundee Technology Park). A major focus has been high tech links to electronics, chemicals/pharmaceuticals and to IT. It is estimated that 807 companies are now accommodated on UK science parks. As in Germany, their performance is patchy and is likely to remain unpredictable. The critical ingredients for success are good R&D links to existing university/research institution programmes with strong management education links (see Chapter 8), and a wider vision to bring in new businesses which can feed stimuli for new developments to university researchers since exploitation of existing R&D usually has relatively short life. Also, if they are not sufficiently integrated into the local innovation strategy of other firms, or lack the support of the key local enterprise organisations, then the number of innovative firms will be far too small to fill a centre. As a result of such gaps there are a number of science parks that have become no more than managed work-spaces, and have not been true technological centres (SQW, 1985; Segal, 1985; Marshall, 1985; Heuer, 1985; Bennett and Krebs, 1991).

Business-community links

Some firms go beyond their direct business needs to develop external links to the local or national community. Such links are sustained by a variety of mechanisms:

- *Donations of cash and gifts in kind* (often transport vehicles and facilities). Sometimes this support may be set as a per cent of profits (as in Per Cent Clubs);
- *Secondment of staff* to other local businesses (particularly start-ups and small firms), community projects, training schemes, specialist investment agencies, etc., to provide specialist skills;
- *Secondment* and work experience placements into the business;
- *Location and investment*: investment projects are supported in disadvantaged areas (such as inner cities or declining regions) rather than on green field sites, in order to provide employment and other benefits;
- *Employment and training*: recruitment policy and training can be targeted to disadvantaged groups or localities; this may extend to making available surplus training capacity, premises or facilities for local community use;
- *Involvement in public affairs* by staff and management, e.g. membership of school governing bodies and support to education-business partnerships, area health boards or voluntary organisations.

Much activity has focused on corporate "social responsibility" as a means of generating private solutions to public problems (see e.g. Sawyer, 1979). This has been stimulated in Britain primarily by BiTC. But is has also occurred autonomously, as well as being stimulated by government and the EC to facilitate industrial restructuring, e.g. early retirement schemes, lump-sum payments, intra-company transfers, use of job placement consultants, career counselling and business advice for those thinking of self-employment options. Indeed the largest community support schemes by businesses have had substantial public sector aid.

Business support can follow one of three routes, shown in Figure 6.1. No reliable statistics are available on the relative importance of each route, but it is likely that many donations follow the route of going to agencies (charities, voluntary bodies and enterprise agencies), of which enterprise agencies are one of the smallest recipients compared to charities and voluntary bodies (inferred from CAF, 1988). The largest cash and in-kind volume of support, however, is linked to government schemes, including regional assistance, EC aid, as well as work experience and training on the job in Youth Training (YT) and Employment Training (ET) (see CAF, 1988; TA, 1989a). Only a relatively small volume goes directly to recipients.

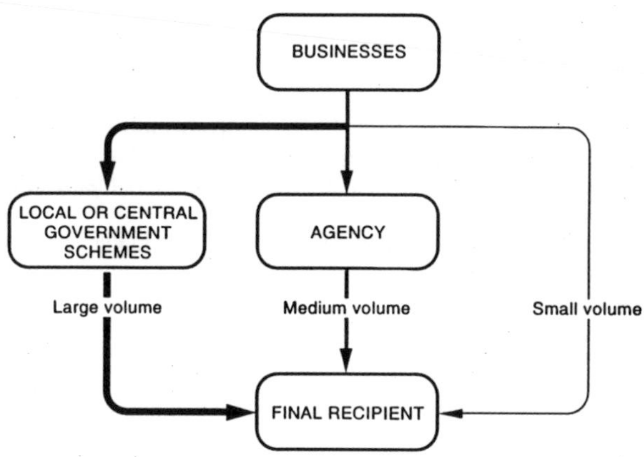

Figure 6.1 Types and volumes of community support by business (after Metcalf *et al.*, 1989)

The schemes with the largest volume of activity involve businesses working with government (the left hand stream in Figure 6.1). This can be on the basis of single contracts for trainees or work placement participants. This area is now being developed rapidly by TECs. The largest single company schemes, however, are Economic Development Partnerships which arise when business retains direct control over an initiative but acts with a number of other sponsors, e.g. central government, EC, local authorities, consultants or special purpose agencies. Economic development partnerships usually have specific targets and direct returns to the partners, e.g. as returns to equity investment. Many science parks have aspects related to such partnerships, but some of the most extensive in Britain have arisen from the attempts of companies to cope with redundancies and industrial restructuring, usually with the help of central government, local government and EC money.

The chief aspects of three of the largest and most successful of these schemes are reviewed in Table 6.3. They differ in emphasis, but each has a package of business start-up capital and counselling assistance, job search and career counselling, and training measures. British Steel (Industry) (BS(I)) has the largest start-up capital activities, whilst British Shipbuilders Enterprise Ltd (BSEL) has the greatest emphasis on training, career support and relocation. Each represents a very considerable partnership of central government, local government and local agencies, using large EC grants, to cope with the problems of restructuring within very large businesses.

Corporate sponsorship of community bodies

We concentrate here on how businesses use their donations and what their scale of activity is. The experience of business sponsors working with enterprise agencies is reviewed later in this chapter.

Analyses of company donations normally show a preference for the fields of children, youth, medical and welfare programmes over enterprise. For example, Norton (1989, p. 20) quotes a sample survey of 100 companies in which these fields all received preferences from 36–58% of companies. Education was a preference in 35% of cases,

Table 6.3 Main programmes of three business-led Economic Development Partnerships

A. British Steel (Industry) Ltd (BS(I))

Subsidiary of British Steel plc;
Set up in 1975 in areas where steel jobs were being lost; 19 **BS(I) Opportunity Areas**: Lanarkshire, Cambuslang, Garnock Valley, West Cumbria, Derwentside, Hartlepool, Teesside, South Humber, Rotherham, Sheffield, Corby, Dudley, Deeside, Llanelli, West Glamorgan, Methyr, Blaenau Gwent, South Glamorgan, and South Gwent;
All areas qualify as Assisted Areas and can receive ECSC low interest loans;
Package of assistance includes:

- unsecured loans up to £25,000,
- secured loans up to £200,000,
- training in business and management skills,
- share capital options,
- regional advice centres in Glasgow, Middlesbrough, Sheffield and Newport,
- managed workspaces;

Through other agents (enterprise agencies, Chambers, local authorities), further counselling and advice services.

B. British Coal Enterprise Ltd (BCE)

Subsidiary of National Coal Board;
Set up in 1984 to support restructuring and job losses in coal industry;
Mainly uses ex-NCB premises through seven regional managers;
Most areas qualify for Assisted Areas and ECSC supports;
Package of assistance includes:

- preferential loans over 5 years,
- managed workspaces,
- advice and counselling services and career guidance,
- training allowances;

Support to enterprise agencies to run advice services.

C. British Shipbuilders Enterprise Ltd (BSEL)

Government established company with £5m start-up as subsidiary to British shipbuilders;
Set up in 1986 to cope with expected redundancies;
Initial concentration in 6 areas: Govan, Troon, Tyne, Wear, Tees and Appledore;
Package of assistance includes:

- local "job shop" with counselling and training,
- selection of training programmes and job opportunities,
- skill-shortage training,
- business start-up assistance,
- free financial counselling,
- marketing grants to relocate;

Special TA grants;
Close links to local authority and enterprise agency support services.

Sources: interviews plus company reports

enterprise and training in only 26% of cases. Hence, the concerns that are central to this book come low down the list of most companies priorities, and are only above the fields of support to the arts, elderly, heritage, environment and overseas aid (see also CCS, 1986; CAF, 1988; Knox and Ashworth, 1985; Reid, 1986; Metcalf *et al.*, 1989). This is comparable with the USA.

Detailed analysis of company support is, however, extremely difficult. Only a few large companies have declared statistics of their contributions, some may not even know the full extent of their support as it is spread between a head office, separate plants, branches and subsidiaries. Total contributions to the community vary downwards from BT (£11m), and others of the top 15 companies which all give over £2m per year (of total support including in-kind donations). Many small contributions are made by thousands of small local firms.

Norton's (1989) estimate of total annual donations of £250m covers only large companies; hence it certainly underestimates the total. Whatever the figure, it is a comparatively small one compared to total charitable support from trusts, government gifts to charities, and benefits of tax and rate relief (excluding business donations) of £3,910 million (Norton, 1989; see also CAF, 1988). Whatever the real level of business donations, therefore, it is clearly dwarfed by the charitable gifts derived from elsewhere.

The total size of donations has been growing. From Norton's (1989) survey of 200 companies, support grew from £40m in 1979 to £63m in 1987. However, donations stayed fairly stable as a percentage of profits. Thus growth of donations appears to be strongly linked to economic growth as a whole. Statistics from Exstat and our analysis of an annual survey of over 1,000 firms in 1989 confirm these trends. As shown in Table 6.4, donations appear to fall in recession (as in 1982) and increase in periods of rapid growth. The effect of recession on donations is again marked in 1990–92 (based on interviews). Table 6.4 also shows that donations are generally higher from service sectors than manufacturing, which in turn are higher than donations from construction, mining, etc.

Table 6.4 Levels of donations 1979–86 and 1989 by business sector.

Donations	Year			
	1979	1982	1986	1989
Mean as % of profit:				
• services	0.14	0.13	0.33	1.42
• manufacturing	0.26	0.02	0.13	0.48
• construction, agriculture, utilities, mining	0.10	−0.08	0.03	1.02
Mean as % per £1,000 turnover:				
• services	11.1	14.2	14.0	53.9
• manufacturing	11.7	10.1	10.4	17.0
• construction, agriculture, utilities, mining	11.5	8.1	6.3	14.7

(Note a negative number appears when profits are low)
Note: sources of data differ for 1989 and earlier columns and are therefore not comparable
Sources: original calculations from: 1979–86 *Exstat* data base – Extel Financial Publishing; 1989 from *Guide to Company Giving* (DSC, 1989)

There has been considerable effort to stimulate donations by the charities, government and by BiTC. One concept that has been used is that of a Per Cent Club. This seeks to encourage businesses to devote a percentage of pre-tax profits. In the late 1980s the average financial contribution was about 0.2% of profits (Norton, 1989), although analysis of large company donations, shown in Table 6.5, demonstrates that the total "community contribution" (including in-kind support, secondments, etc.) is closer to 1%. This table also shows that there is a very wide range of company donations: from small sums up to £2.9m. This accounts for the very large standard deviation in Table 6.5. Separate analysis of BiTC members shows that whilst their mean donations may be lower at 0.4% of profit, the variation between firms is comparatively small. The same applies to an even greater extent to firms that are both BiTC and Per Cent Club members. The target for the Per Cent Club launched in 1986 was one-half-of-one-percent : Table 6.5 demonstrates that the 123 firms analysed do nearly achieve this, on average. By 1988 the members of the club had reached 175 so development of this concept has, as yet, been slow and confined to a few large companies.

Table 6.5 Level of donations and relation of donations to profit and turnover for BiTC, Per Cent Club and non-BiTC / Per Cent Club firms in 1989

Donations	Mean	Standard deviation	Size of sample of firms
Mean donation (£000s)	65	207	1,194
Mean as % of profit:			
• all firms	0.88	8.12	1,166
• BiTC members	0.38	0.86	160
• BiTC % club members	0.38	0.65	123
• not BiTC or % club	0.94	8.58	1,043
Mean as % per £1,000 of turnover:			
• all firms	28.3	205	1,120
• BiTC members	32.6	64	124
• BiTC % club members	39.0	73	98
• not BiTC or % club	27.2	213	1,022

Source: original calculations from sample of firms in *Guide to Company Giving*, 1989

Among small companies there are fewer statistics available. The CAF surveys, of 500 small firms of under 100 employees for 1987 and 1988, show that their median cash contribution was just over £200, 89% of which was in the form of single cash gifts. Of small firms 95% gave cash, but there was also substantial support through gifting products (54% of firms), supporting their staff's activities in fund raising (35%), sponsorship (28%), job training (25%), use of premises (21%), and enterprise agency support (14%) whilst 8% used secondments. The focus on enterprise is likely to be a small proportion of most of these activities.

The total scale of business donations and social responsibility activities in Britain is significant and growing, although it is still small compared to that in the USA. Within the growth that has occurred, large companies are increasingly focusing their activity in terms of the location and fields of action to which they give priority, and the assessing of its contribution. Particularly important has been the effect of decentralisation within large companies to give local plants and branches more autonomy. This has meant that many companies that have a major presence in a locality have become key leaders and supporters of enterprise, e.g. ICI, BP, Shell UK, Hanson Trust, Wellcome (based on interviews in 1989–91). Other companies with a broader presence (like the banks, BT, Marks and Spencer) have usually chosen a few local initiatives on which to concentrate their support (Norton, 1989; see also CAF, 1988). Within this trend, increasing attention is also being given to assessing effectiveness. This follows earlier trends in the USA (see e.g. Barnes, 1974; Dennis, 1976).

A particular concern has been to ensure that company support is "genuinely" gap-filling or pump-priming. Firms have generally moved away from areas in which they feel a government role is required, or which require their continued long-term support because no self-sustaining base is available. The limits to the effectiveness of business contributions are noted particularly by Milton Friedman (1970). He terms the social responsibility movement *"hogwash"* and a *"fundamentally subversive doctrine"*. Business social responsibility, he argues, is *"spending someone else's money for a general social interest"*. If the consequence is a price rise, then the consumer pays, if wages fall, then the employee pays; if profits fall, then the shareholder pays. In effect, social responsibility activity, he argues, is a *"tax"*. As a tax, such activity should be managed by a political process of democratically and properly elected representatives in government, not by self-appointed business people. Moreover, social responsibility activities can deflect businesses from their main objectives.

The increasing concurrence of businesses with this conclusion is confirmed by the evidence we have reviewed above. Business support in general is small, and the largest and most effective schemes are generally those which have combined business support with government and EC funds, e.g. British Steel Corporation (BSC), National Shipbuilders. These have usually aimed at retraining redundant workers, setting up small firms, reusing redundant land or property assets, facilitating new technology, and responding to local political and union pressures to soften the impact of plant closure or workforce reductions.

Banks and venture capital

Banks act as business advisers, financiers and, in some cases, may be leading forces in local partnership development. Their roles as advisers and financiers are normally strongly related to each other. Banks are frequently the first point of contact by a business with external advisers. This is the result primarily of the needs for business finance; but it is also a result of the traditional role of banks as advisers and their ubiquitous presence. In recent years banks have also significantly increased their support to small businesses through changes in the level of local discretion they allow their managers and through vigorous marketing. As a result, banks play a very important role in enterprise support in Britain. Although we point to inadequacies in their support below, it remains true that banks are by far the largest of all financial agents and that they are almost uniquely the best qualified in the management support which they can offer to small businesses.

Banks and venture capital funds are also businesses. They seek to make a return to their owners and to keep costs to a minimum. These objectives may often be different from the needs of the businesses they serve. This has resulted in areas of business needs that may not be fully met – a so-called *"funding gap"*. This explains the irony that whilst there is normally no shortage of capital funds available, and no shortage of proposals, businesses nevertheless experience a funding problem (see e.g. NEDO, 1986a, 1986;

OECD, 1986a; Wilson Committee, 1980; Bayliss and Butt-Philip, 1980; Kozmetsky *et al.*, 1985). This irony has been of long standing (see e.g. the Macmillan Report (HM Government, 1931); the Radcliff Report (HM Government, 1959); as well as the more recent Bolton, 1971 and Wilson, 1980 Reports).

The funding problem arises chiefly because of the difference in risk level of many enterprise investments and the level that will be accepted by venture capital funds. The main clearing banks have spent many years in developing their business practice so that they can achieve low ratios of bad debt of 1–3%. Naturally, even this level is one that they seek to reduce. In contrast, business investments in SMEs typically have a 20–30% level of risk of failure and bad debt (*Investors chronicle*, 13 November 1981). The result is that the clearing banks and most venture capital funds will accept only a small proportion of the proposals submitted to them; typically no more than 10% – "*banks are thus not venture capital*"! (Stevenson, 1990). The problem for enterprise development is, therefore, how to provide for that proportion of the remaining 90% of proposals which are viable.

The difficulties of using banks and venture capital funds for enterprise development are considerable:

- High risk levels lead British banks to support businesses as debt rather than equity participation. This is in contrast to Germany and Japan;
- The rates charged often discriminate strongly between SMEs and larger companies (by commonly 3–6% higher interest rates), although banks argue this is still not high enough to cover their risks (see e.g. *Business Briefing*, 6 June 1991; *Financial Times*, 18 July 1991);
- Banks prefer to be sole providers of finance (so as to be the first call on debt to reduce risk) and this can inhibit wider joint financing schemes; this is in contrast to Germany and Japan;
- Risk leads banks to seek a high proportion of security on their debt (usually on the business owner's house or other assets) which is most inhibiting to enterprise;
- The size of most proposals from SMEs is very small, at £50,000 – 100,000. These proposals take as much, or more time, to assess as a proposal for many millions of pounds, and this time often cannot be repaid by the fees paid by the business or the benefits of greater returns to the business;
- Many proposals by SMEs require not only finance but also considerable help in management development and business planning, as well as post-investment help and aftercare (see e.g. Kozmetsky *et al.*, 1985; OECD, 1986a). This is all extremely expensive in terms of time and demands for high level expertise which cannot be justified by the returns to the business or the bank; "*We are looking for quality among management teams as well as the quality of the businesses they are running*".[2]

These impediments have been the focus for a wide range of initiatives. Primarily the focus of such initiatives has been to give advice, business planning support, or "aftercare" service. In some cases, there has also been the development of equity participation. These developments have come from a variety of sources:

i) *The clearing banks* themselves, in part chastened by criticism, and in part seeing a business opportunity, have set up venture capital offshoots. For example, by 1989 the Barclays venture capital fund had been allocated £20m for start-up and business expansion in loans of £100,000 to £500,000 (*Financial Times*, 19 July 1989). It initially used another venture capital company to handle preliminary enquiries, to assess them and to monitor progress. National Westminster Bank has developed a

Growth Options Scheme of subordinated loans with the option to convert into equity. This has run at approximately £10m per year since 1989. National Westminster and other banks have also piloted direct equity participation schemes;

ii) *Large companies* have set up venture capital subsidiaries to stimulate developments in related areas with a view to retrenching their main business, developing markets and developing innovation in component supply. Such examples are few in number in Britain compared to the USA. British Steel and British Coal have been involved in retrenchment schemes, British Gas was one of the first British companies to set up its own £15m venture capital scheme to share the burdens of R&D with smaller partners, and to gain the advantage of higher levels of innovativeness in smaller firms (*Financial Times*, 20 February 1990);

iii) *Private sector joint ventures* by the banks have been used to set up assessment and advisory groups to reduce and share risks. The chief example has been 3i and the major clearing banks. But, in the late 1980s, many banks set up regional venture capital bases, often in conjunction with other financial institutions, most commonly the pension funds and building societies. These have partly reduced risk by greater help to business planning. But most developments have benefited from changes in business structure itself. Up to late 1989 there was an emphasis on down-sizing through management buyouts. More recently the concern has shifted to larger scale start-ups. These funds have been much more willing to take equity participation, with the result that debt-equity ratios have been considerably reduced: to around 2.5:1 from the 5:1 more common in the early 1980s (see LEL, 1986; McKean and Coulson, 1987; Gunnell, 1990; *Financial Times*, 4 December 1987, 30 November 1989, 22 November 1990). In an increasing number of cases in the late 1980s this has led to the potential subsequently to float the business on the main stock market or Unlisted Securities Market;

iv) *Public and public-private enterprise boards*. It is a natural extension of the private sector joint venture for the public sector to provide a widened base. Sometimes public sector funds may be the sole resource. The ratio of private to public sources for Boards is about 1:6. There are a number of regional venture capital funds and enterprise boards. The largest are Lancashire Enterprise, West Midlands Enterprise Board, Yorkshire Enterprise and the former Greater London Enterprise Board (BiTC, 1990a; PW, 1991), but there are also many small boards based on single district council areas, e.g. Dundee, Derby. These enterprise boards can normally deal with far smaller investment requirements. Some have also linked funds to urban regeneration initiatives, in part supported by city grant or other public sector subsidy (e.g. Inner City Enterprises set up in 1983 by the Church Commissioners, and a consortium of banks and insurance companies: it had an investment worth about £8m in 1989) (*Financial Times*, 19 August 1989). Public sector support has allowed the higher counselling costs of many small start-ups to be covered where the counselling:investment ratio is high. They face the danger, however, that they can underweight risk and costs (see e.g. Stevenson, 1990). Estimates in 1985/86 suggest that Boards had invested about £42m at a cost of £2,000 – 6,000 per job. This is more than, or comparable to, other forms of assistance. They have been most successful when supporting new firm growth rather than propping up ailing companies[3]. With the abolition of the metropolitan counties in 1986, most Boards diminished in status, and resources as a result of being run by a sometimes difficult coalition of districts. Some have been abolished. Their hopes of having the potential to be comparable to the Welsh Development Agency (WDA) or Scottish Development Agency (SDA) (McKean and Coulson, 1987; Mawson and Miller, 1986; Lawless, 1988; Gunnell, 1990) were never realistic without greatly enhanced resources and a different management ethic;

v) *Small loans and grants.* Even with the enterprise boards a gap has remained for the administration of very small loans and grants, in the range of £500–10,000. This field of activity has been associated with the DTI Enterprise Initiative, as well as a number of other private and government programmes. These have frequently been run by enterprise agencies, Chambers of Commerce and more recently TECs (q.v.). Because of their size, they have often been linked with initiatives to stimulate self-employment and micro- businesses, rather than firms capable of major growth, but the distinctions are blurred. Detailed discussion is given in the relevant sections below. There is clearly considerable scope for expansion through informal investors, following their success in the USA (see e.g. Wetzel, 1986) (i.e. wealthy individuals and speculators) (see Mason and Harrison, 1991, 1992; ACOST, 1990). Business Expansion Scheme (BES) is one mechanism to stimulate this, but further match-making and other services are also required. There are, however, strong limitations to this expansion in Britain arising from a relatively low proportion of wealthy individuals, tax disincentives, and the need for match-making agencies to charge fees or subscriptions for services.

These developments have seen a rapid growth of venture capital funds available for enterprise, with a growing interlinkage of these funds to advisory and support services either internal to the financial organisation, or in an external network. The growth of available funds is shown in Figure 6.2. Each sector has shown significant growth, but the most rapid expansion has come from the venture capital funds set up as subsidies of banks and as independent funds with several funders. These together now outstrip 3i and account for over £1 billion per year. Although smaller, government schemes, the BES and investment trusts (publicly quoted companies that raise money from the stock market) are also increasingly significant players in the market.

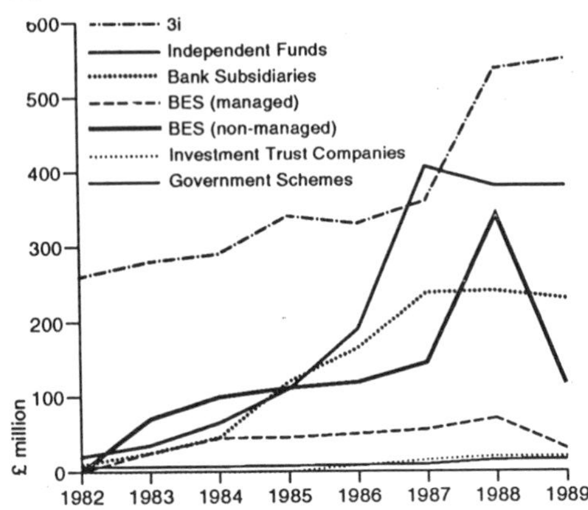

Figure 6.2 Annual investment by venture capital funds in Britain 1982–88
Sources: Venture Economics and *3is Annual Reports*, Mason and Harrison (1992); BES excludes the extension to private rental housing since 1988

The growth record is remarkable. But its support to enterprise growth is somewhat exaggerated. The sources of capital have shifted significantly to a dominance by pension funds and insurance companies, which increased from 34% to over 60% of the sources between 1982 and 1988. Whilst private individuals (mainly through BES and investment trusts) increased from 11% in 1982 to over 15% in 1988, the banks, foreign investors and industrial corporations declined as sources. The problem with this bias has been the strong support of the institutional investors for buyouts and acquisitions. For example, in 1989 61% of investments were for buyouts and acquisitions, less than 9% for early stage and 6% for start-up investments, and 23% for expansion schemes (Mason and Harrison, 1992). Apart from lower risk, buyouts offer a quick return on investments, usually being floated within 2 years with major capital gain potential, whereas start-ups require 5–10 years before they return on investment or can be floated (or refloated) on the stock market. The result is that non-government venture capital funds loans average £3.4m, with the smallest being £54,000 (Cary, 1989).

There remain, therefore, major dilemmas in the support for business available from the banking and venture capital industry. First, a major gap still exists for start-up and expansion in the small enterprise sector, mainly in the sub-£100,000 level, but extending up to the £0.5m to £1m level where the advice cost:investment ratio is high. This appears to need a stronger advisory support system than presently available that can reduce costs to venture capitalists. Moreover, this advice covers a broader range of areas than finance alone. This is a field where enterprise agencies, Chambers of Commerce, local authorities and TECs are becoming increasingly involved, as discussed in later parts of this chapter.

A second gap arises from the regional bias of equity funds, particularly towards London and the South East, and secondly towards the main urban centres. Estimates vary, but approximately 60% of venture capital is invested in London and the South East, although it has only 34% of new VAT-registered businesses (see e.g. Mason, 1987; Martin, 1989). It is often more difficult to attract finance in more peripheral, rural or small town environments. However, regional venture capital funds have grown rapidly and they have normally a stronger bias towards small firm start-up and expansion (see e.g. Wright *et al.*, 1984; *Financial Times*, 30 November 1989, 22 November 1990). This indicates that, although they receive a smaller proportion of the total available venture capital, the regions may receive a stronger proportion of that which is oriented towards enterprise needs rather than buyouts and acquisitions. However, the regional bias of venture capital funds is still a most disturbing element, and appears also to be reflected to a lesser extent in some of the major government schemes, such as the BES (see Mason and Harrison, 1989; Mason *et al.*, 1988; Harrison and Mason, 1986).

A third gap stems from the still low level of willingness of venture capital holders, especially the banks, to get involved in wider development schemes on a longer term basis. Whilst complex syndications grew rapidly from the mid-1980s, these were normally oriented towards property development rather than enterprise and business growth. The British experience contrasts strongly with France and Germany. For ex- growth. The British experience contrasts strongly with France and Germany. For ex- ample, in Germany, the banks, Länder governments and Chambers of Commerce have been frequent participants in developing joint enterprise and economic development projects, e.g. in Köln and other parts of Nordrhein-Westfalen, Hamburg or Siegen (see Bennett *et al.*, 1990; Bennett and Krebs, 1991; Martens-Jeebe, 1990). Britain has by far the largest number and volume of venture capital funds in Europe (43 funds with over £1.5b in 1988) compared to Germany (3 funds with £200m) and France (19 funds with £460m). But this very size dominates the market (60% of all venture capital compared to 8% in Germany and 18% in France) and tends to squeeze out joint support to enterprise (all statistics quoted are from *Financial Times*, 30 November 1989). This effect is further exaggerated by the dominance of public listed companies in Britain compared to Germany or France which has further tended to emphasise the bias of British venture capital towards short-term interests (see Wrobel, 1979; Bennett *et al.*, 1990; Bayliss and Butt-Philip, 1980 and OECD, 1986). Deutscher Bank, for example, readily acknowledges that it is not concerned with short-term projects but with looking 5 to 10 years ahead.[4]

These gaps involve start-ups, particular regions, and longer term partnership networks. This is indicative of the problem of systems failure in the enterprise field that we have outlined in earlier chapters. We turn to solutions to the system problem after addressing, below, the role that has been developed by other agents.

Enterprise agencies

Enterprise agencies (sometimes termed enterprise trusts) play an important role in advice to small businesses and self-employment, as well as in a wide range of other activities.[5] Their main services to enterprise are in counselling, follow-up and after-care of SMEs, promotional exhibitions, business training, and youth enterprise. As shown in Table 6.6, exhibitions, training and youth enterprise have been the most recent generally developed services. A small proportion of agencies is involved in finance or loans to business, premises, marketing or exports. Thus, although enterprise agency services are broad, the base level of service available across the system is counselling, advice and business training. This is generally focused on the micro-business (less than 5 employees) and has been chiefly a service to the unemployed seeking self-employment and their "after care".

Table 6.6 Enterprise agency activities in 1986 and 1990

Services provided	1990 (%)	1986 (%)	%Difference 1986–1990
Business counselling	100	100	–
Follow-up and aftercare	94	N/A	N/A
Access to loan/grant funds	52	32	20
Member of LINC	18	N/A	N/A
Managed workspace	48	22	26
Business competitions	31	16	15
Marketing centre	17	14	3
Tourism projects	19	N/A	N/A
Export centre	15	N/A	N/A
Regular newsletter	56	35	21
Promotional exhibitions	73	35	38
Business training courses	80	41	39
Small business club	54	29	25
Links with educational estab.	41	37	4
Youth enterprise centre	83	19	64
Total number of agencies	323	245	–

Source: original analysis of BiTC *Directory*

The network of agencies receives considerable stimulus from Business in the Community (BiTC; ScotBiC in Scotland) which, since 1981, has championed enterprise agencies, diffused information, attempted to standardise their development through the creation of a model legal structure allowing them to satisfy the requirements of legal status under the 1982 Finance Act (CEI / BiTC, 1985), and has organised training/ development programmes for their directors. Since 1991, BiTC has offered an accreditation charter (BiTC, 1990b) which has been developed into a quality assurance manual aimed at helping agencies to be accredited under BS5750 (BiTC, 1991).

Table 6.7 Proportion of enterprise agencies with different numbers of activities and staff size in 1989/90

Number of activities or staff	Proportion of agencies by number of activities* (%)	Proportion of agencies with staff size†	
		Executive (%)	Clerical (%)
1–3	3	64	78
4–8	43	30	17
9–12	47 }	6	5
13–16	7 }		
Total (%)	100	100	100

* from original analysis of BiTC *Directory* (323 agencies) in 1990
† from LSE survey of 244 enterprise agencies in 1989

Table 6.8 Sources and extent of income of a sample of 18 enterprise agencies in 1988

	Proportion of agencies receiving support (%)	Mean level of support of those receiving from source (£000s)	Range: Min	Range: Max	Mean contribution to total budget (%)
Cash income					
• Private sector	89	29	7	67	30
• Local authority	72	19	0.4	52	18
• Central government:					
• LEAGS	55	16	7	24	11
• LEAPS	17	10	5	20	2
• EAS	33	8	3	16	4
• Urban Programme	22	30	20	48	8
• TA (TEED)	39	17	1	40	8
• DTI Task Forces	11	11	5	16	1
• WDA	100	9	8	10	11
• Other income	56	11	0.2	45	7
Total cash income	–	82	3	110	100
In kind income (imputed income)					
• Private sector industry	39	28	1	67	35
• Local authority	28	6	0.4	10	6
• Private professional advice	39	47	3	132	59
Total in kind	–	38	0	140	100

* percentage of Welsh sample (of 3) *Source*: original LSE/BiTC survey

These efforts have been aimed increasingly not only at diffusing the enterprise agency concept to more places, but at assuring an even level of quality across the system. Table 6.7 demonstrates that there is considerable variation in the size of agencies, their staff, and their number of activities. Most agencies are relatively small with less than 4 operational staff, but have a wide range of activities. This is indicative of variation in the depth of support that can be offered to each activity and an attempt to fill too many gaps. Total annual cash income in 1988 in a sample of 18 enterprise agencies was an average of £82,000, with a range of £3,000 to £110,000 (see Table 6.8) (the figures are in line with earlier surveys: CEC, 1985; BiTC, 1988, 1989).

Enterprise agencies were stimulated by the experience of US Community Development Corporations. Early examples in the UK, set up from 1975 by the charity, Alternative Society, were voluntary sector initiatives, e.g. in Oxford. Other early examples were developed either from the lead of local businesses (St Helens by Pilkington Glass; Runcorn by ICI Mond; Bristol by Wills; Clyde workshops in Glasgow by BSC) or from local authorities (Hackney Business Promotion Centre). This mix of local business and local authority leadership has continued as the movement has grown (see CBV, 1981; DHS, 1984; CEI, 1986; DoE, 1988).

In 1981, BiTC was formed in part to shape and develop the enterprise agency movement. Its founding twelve organisations were Marks and Spencer, IBM, Shell, BP, GEC, ICFC, Pilkington, Prudential, NCB and the government departments of Industry, Environment and Manpower Services Commission (MSC) (later the Training Agency / Training, Education and Enterprise Directorate (TA/TEED)). Rapid growth in the number of enterprise agencies followed. From 23 agencies in early 1981, there were 61 in 1982, 103 in 1983, 245 in 1985. By 1991 421 agencies were in operation, of which 408 had been approved by the Department of the Environment under the statutory provisions for tax relief on donations to them (source: Eric Forth, *P.Q.*, 3 July 1991), of which 320 were in the BiTC network. Their number has since reduced with the end of Local Enterprise Agency Grants (LEAGs) and the emergence of TECs.

The rapid growth in the early 1980s was in part the result of a central stimulus from BiTC, but particularly reflects the stimulus of government grants following the 1982 Finance Act. The main grants were the Local Enterprise Agency Grant Scheme (LEAGS) and LEA Project Scheme (LEAPS),[6] with Rural Project Grants (RPGs) launched in 1987 in rural areas.[7] These grants each require matching from private sector sponsors, at an increasing rate over time. By 1988 most enterprise agencies were dependent for 63% of their cash income from government, both local government (18%) and central government agencies (45%).[8] The breakdown of detailed income sources is shown in Table 6.8 for a sample of agencies. This also shows the wide variety of government departments supporting enterprise agencies, each, of course, with different programme objectives.

The financial dominance of government is offset both by the importance of the private sector in matching government funds in many cases, and by the substantial in-kind support of industrial and professional services. As shown in Table 6.8, 94% of in-kind support derives from the private sector (the remainder being local authority). A large proportion of in-kind support comes from *pro-bono* work within the supporting companies. But a growing trend has also been the use of secondments, most starting in 1987 or 1988. In 1987 there were 300 secondees in enterprise agencies making up 40% of their staff (CEI, 1986, p. 81). Table 6.9 demonstrates that the private sector is the major provider, 56% in our sample of 21 enterprise agencies. Moreover, in-kind support through secondments tends to be targeted at both senior and operational levels. As shown in Table 6.9, at least 33% of secondments are at director, chief executive or manager level,[9] and 33% are counsellors. Secondments also tend to be relatively long-term contributions, 71% are 2 years or longer in our sample of 27 secondees in 21 agencies.

There is a source of tension in the imbalance between the dominance of governmental financial support and private sector in-kind support. Private sector support was initially given primarily through major local businesses and professionals offering support services to other, mainly small, local businesses needing help. Typically, this support derived from one or two major local employers (as with Pilkingtons in St Helens, BSC in Glasgow, and other examples listed earlier) as well as local solicitors, accountants and, more occasionally, banks. Only later, in 1987 or 1988, have secondments become the more significant element of private sector support. Often, this was the form of matching that the private sector could provide to meet the criteria for government support.

It is clear that many businesses, particularly those that are large nationally, initially went into enterprise agency support as an element of their community support programmes. This could be done without major financial implications. DHS (1984) suggested that their role was (i) a source of business information, (ii) a sounding board, (iii) a business consultant, (iv) a business trainer, and (v) a stimulant to other bodies. Later, as government grants came to dominate the scene seeking to spread the concept to many more areas, the private sector was increasingly levered into giving direct sponsorship, donations or secondments. Companies justified their support as short-term pump-priming. But they have often been unwilling to sustain support at this level for more than a few years, seeing such sustained financial effort as being a governmental role.[10] This was likely to lead to a crisis in 1990 or 1991, therefore, as the 2 to 4 years of pump priming which began in most areas in 1986–88 ran out. It has been at this point that TECs and LECs have come on the scene.

The tension of governmental and private sector priorities can also be seen in the form of support enterprise agencies offer. The original objectives were normally:[11]

- To encourage existing local businesses;
- To encourage businesses to relocate into the area;
- To encourage start-ups; and
- To foster the local business climate.

Table 6.9 Secondees in a sample of 21 enterprise agencies in 1988 by seconding organisation and job description

Seconding organisation	No.	%	Job description in enterprise agency	No.	%
Manufacturing	8	30	Director / Chief Executive	4	15
Banks	6	22	Asst. Director / Manager	3	11
Other prof. services	1	4	Business Devpt. Officer	2	7
Local government	8	30	Counsellor / Advisor	9	33
Central government	1	4	Research	2	7
Other public sector	1	4	Consultant	1	4
Higher education	1	4	Secretary	2	7
Church	1	4	N/A	4	15
Total	27	100		27	100

Note that all but one secondment is full-time. The Research jobs are filled by the central government and higher education secondees. The secretaries come from local government.
Source: LSE/BiTC survey

But government grants and local authority involvement have tended to shift the emphasis from enterprise towards unemployment counselling, much of which has led to the foundation of micro-service businesses with little potential to grow (such as window cleaning, garden maintenance services, etc.). BiTC (1989) found that 53% of clients counselled were unemployed. From our sample of 23 enterprise agencies in our case study areas in 1988, 55% of those counselled were unemployed, with a range up to 90% in some agencies. A larger LSE survey of 244 enterprise agencies in 1989 showed that 8% of agencies had no counselling for established businesses, and only approximately 16% of all counselling sessions in the 244 samples were for established businesses, whilst 24% were for early start-ups and 60% for the unemployed.

Generally, the agencies appear to fall into three broad categories. First, those which are mainly private sector-led with either a large number of counsellors and private sector secondees or a strong access to local pro-bono inputs from firms focusing on existing small business growth, e.g. St Helens, LEnTA, Teesside. Second, those with a large number of managers and an emphasis on counselling the unemployed. These tend to be local authority-led or set up by local authorities, e.g. Manchester, Tyne and Wear, Walsall and Cardiff.[12] The third group may have either of the previous emphases, but has taken on a major training function as a contractor to TEED and this dominates its activities, e.g. Cardiff.

There appears clear evidence, therefore, that central government grants and local authority support has drawn enterprise agencies more closely towards unemployment counselling and the foundation of micro-businesses, rather than the wider enterprise objectives we are chiefly concerned with in this chapter. Such an emphasis is of considerable importance in itself, since it diffuses enterprise concepts to a wider population and has also been an important stimulus to the growth of self-employment. But it appears that few of the 323 enterprise agencies in existence in 1990 have been able to make a significant contribution to the growth of businesses with 5–20 or 20–200 employees ("meso-businesses"), still less to the down-sizing and strategic partnership concepts. Those enterprise agencies that do make a significant contribution in this field tend to be predominantly private sector led and to be in locations in which major *locally-based* companies are available to provide the necessary support (mainly in-kind). These are locations such as central London, Teesside and Glasgow. We pursue the impact of these major locally-based companies in Part 3 of this book.

The emphasis of enterprise agencies on counselling the unemployed into self-employment is being further increased by the development of government funding associated with TECs and LECs. The LEAGs and LEAPs grants have been terminated and the main programme money available to enterprise agencies is the Enterprise Allowance Scheme (EAS) which seeks to help the unemployed into self-employment. There are also parts of Business Growth Training (BGT) and Business Enterprise Training (BET) and the Small Firms Service which focus on either self-employment or micro-businesses. Many enterprise agencies have received one year contracts from TECs/LECs to run EAS or part of BGT. Approximately 80% of TECs/LECs gave such contracts to agencies in the year 1991/92.[13] However, more general TEC/LEC support for enterprise agencies "core costs" applies to only 35% of cases. Those TECs in 1991/92 prepared to give core support see it as "bridging" period support only.[13] At the same time, the effect of the recession in 1990–2 and the end of the "pump priming" phase of private sector sponsorship begun in 1986–8 has reduced the scope for corporate financial and in-kind support. At the time of writing, therefore, uncertainty hangs over the future of many enterprise agencies. This is likely to be resolved by the further closer integration of their role into TECs/LECs. However, the gap of support to established meso-businesses, that was part of the initial stimulus to enterprise agencies, will remain unless TECs/LECs or other agents develop their services.

The future role desired by BiTC (1988) for enterprise agencies includes:

- Provision of sophisticated information on local firms, linking business data bases into the European Business Information Networks;
- Marriage broking between investors and investees including technology transfer and licensing;
- Assisting in preparations for European integration; and
- Providing services modelled on Japanese trading houses.

The potential role of enterprise agencies in each of these areas overlaps with Chambers, TECs/LECs and other agents. Hence, it will be shaped by the development of the enterprise support system that emerges in Britain as a whole. We develop these areas of debate further below.

Chambers of Commerce

Chambers collectively constitute a large representative organisation with 90,000 member businesses in 104 Chambers affiliated to the Association of British Chambers of Commerce (ABCC). There are, in addition, over 300 other, usually smaller, Chambers of Trade, and a few other non-affiliated Chambers of Commerce. The affiliated Chambers have a national coverage of 8% of all UK businesses. Although their core areas cover only 26% of Britain's surface area, these cores cover 73% of all business units, 80% of firms over 200 employees, 77% of all employees and 71% of the UK population. Their area of coverage is highest in Northern Ireland (100%) and England (41%) than in Scotland (12%) or Wales (8%).[14] The considerable contribution that Chambers make, therefore, is in offering a large representative membership base with a presence that can speak on behalf of business to local and central government in most of the important parts of the British economy.

Chamber services have shown rapid development during the 1980s, and have transformed further in the early 1990s as part of the Chambers' development strategy. Figure 6.3 shows the pattern of development of Chambers services in 1991. Comparison with an earlier survey in 1989 (Bennett, 1991b) demonstrates that Chambers are both widening and deepening their services. In some categories evolution has been rapid – particularly for local promotion, economic surveys, local directories and trade missions/exhibitions, which are provided in 4 out of 5 Chambers. More than one-half of Chambers have export agencies or centres, and arrange senior management seminars. Other significant services provided in at least one-fifth of Chambers are national and international promotion, local purchasing initiatives, 1992 coordination, advice to start-up and small firms, provision of youth business support, full counselling service, small business clubs and direct participation in trade fairs and exhibitions. The least developed areas of Chamber services are financial and premises support.

Chambers are also increasingly collaborating with other agents in service delivery. This reflects both increasing activity by Chambers, but also the greater activity by other actors. Chambers are, at the same time, developing a significant focus to their provision. One of the major changes observed between 1989 and 1991 is the very significant growth in the direct provision by Chambers of local promotion, economic surveys and directories which were previously mainly collaborative activities. This is doubtless linked to the search for sources of revenue and is likely to be seen in other service fields in the future.

Despite their significance, it has become increasingly recognised that British Chambers suffer from a number of disadvantages. Their low levels of resources, small numbers of personnel and only partial geographical coverage is no worse, indeed better, than most other business support deliverers in Britain; but it is very different from the depth and general coverage offered by European Chambers, particularly in France and Germany. Because they offer an obvious European comparison, Chambers evidence the particular aspects of the more general problem of Britain's inability to compete with the large and professional business support bodies in Europe. This has led some to call for merger with the other large representative business body, the CBI, or to attract the public law support that French and German Chambers have (e.g. Forster, 1983). A more recent target has been the possible contracting by Chambers of a number of DTI export services (ABCC, 1991c). In the late 1980s and early 1990s, however, the Association of British Chambers of Commerce (ABCC) has been moving Chambers forward first in the direction of developing their own resources and capacity, with the objective that this might provide a stronger basis for government or other support in the future.

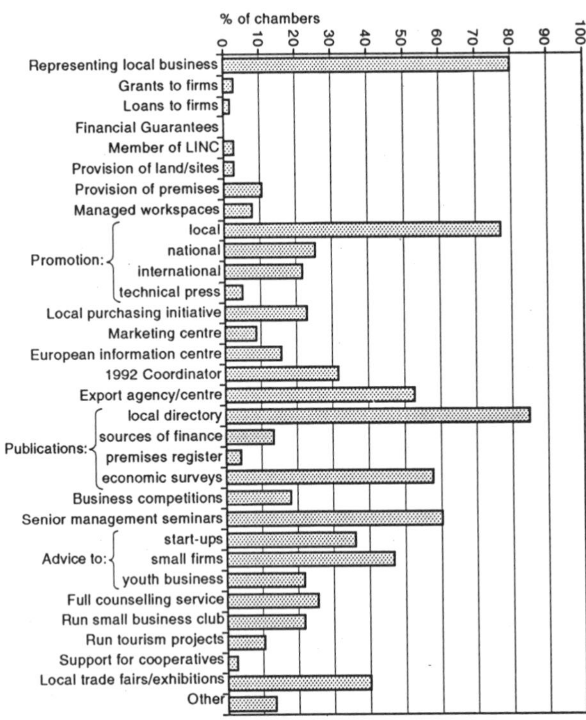

Figure 6.3 Direct provision of services by ABCC Chambers in 1991: Percentage of Chambers offering particular services
Source: Sample of 84 Chambers (79% response rate) from an original survey; Bennett, 1991b

With this objective in mind, the ABCC launched a strategy document in October 1990 (ABCC, 1990), which was followed up by a commissioned study – the Bennett Report (Bennett, 1991a). This has been complemented by a report from an internal ABCC Working Party on minimum standards that will allow Chambers to move towards accreditation for BS5750 (ABCC, 1991b). Together, these have formed the framework for the ABCC's development policy up to 1994 (ABCC, 1991a). This policy seeks to develop a new network of core Chambers each of which will seek to attain minimum levels of staffing and service quality. Indicative criteria for the required critical mass have followed the Bennett Report:

- At least 1,000 members with a capacity to grow initially to 2,000–3,000 members and to at least 5,000 eventually;
- Income to satisfy on expenditure requirement of at least £1m (with variation possible for location and joint financing of some services);
- Personnel of approximately 30 with at least 10 at executive level;
- A premises requirement of approximately 8,000 sq. ft.;
- A membership density of at least 14% of local businesses as Chamber members, growing further over time.

The network suggested by Bennett (1991a) is shown in Figure 5.11. This is based on the strengths of existing Chambers, the catchment of potential business members, the geography of each area, and local authority or TEC/LEC boundaries. This is the basis for development, but some detail has been modified in some areas. The map is likely to be finalised in 1992. It will have about 50–55 core Chambers, with two of special status for the Channel Islands and Isle of Man. Within the core Chambers will be a variety of arrangements for service delivery which will vary to take account of the layout of settlements, business communities and labour markets. Some models of branch/outreach and central site cooperation are shown in Figure 6.4. In general, the system will evolve through either (i) more intensive cooperation between existing Chambers, or (ii) through the expansion of Chambers to cover areas not previously covered in depth (particularly in rural areas of Wales and Scotland).

Inter-Chamber cooperation is following a variety of resource models:

(1) Links or federation, involving joint meetings and exchange of information, e.g. Kent, London;
(2) Affiliation and confederation, where usually a large Chamber offers to small Chambers affiliation status and access to services including dissemination of information, e.g. of Hampshire Chambers to Southampton, in Sussex, and in Northern Ireland;
(3) Self-nominating joint membership whereby members join two Chambers on a reduced joint subscription, e.g. between St Helens, Warrington, Halton, Chester and Merseyside;
(4) Management agreements and subcontracting for specific administrative services such as payrolling, e.g. Dudley to Birmingham; or member services such as exports and missions, e.g. Calderdale to Bradford;
(5) Branches and sections: outreach offices or support to local areas, e.g. Thames Chiltern, London, Chester and North Wales, Manchester, Birmingham;
(6) Consortium and merger with full pooling of resources, staff, services and strategy: being developed between Blackburn and Burnley to form an East Lancashire Chamber, and between Hull, Goole, Grimsby and Scunthorpe to form a Humberside Chamber.

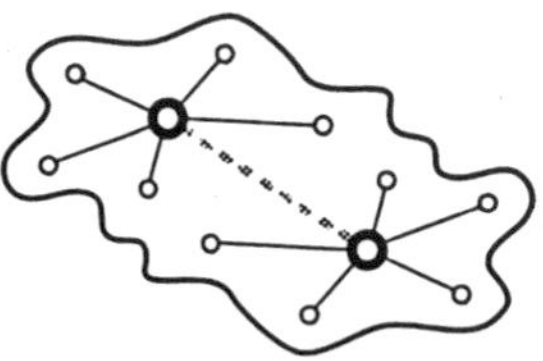

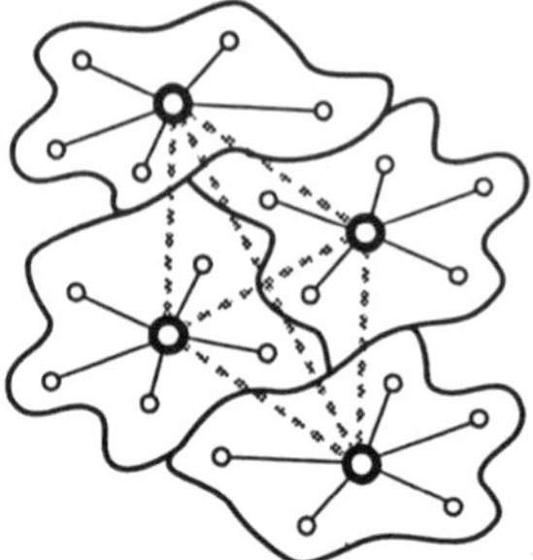

Figure 6.4 Possible modes of collaboration between Chambers of different sizes. The same models can be applied to other local agencies (see Chapter 15)
Resource models are defined in the text.

Different models are being developed in different places. In some cases models (1), (2), (3) or (4) may offer stages of learning to a structure such as (5) or (6). Such mergers and developments are part of the history of the Chamber movement, most local Chambers now in existence having been formed from mergers of numerous smaller Chambers in the past.

Within the new core Chamber structure, smaller existing Chambers, branches or outreach developments will be part of a hierarchical system of service delivery. Above the core Chambers, core-clusters will offer higher order services particularly in the

CORE-CLUSTERS OF CHAMBERS

- National and Regional Prominence
- Economic Research
- R and D and Innovation Stimulus
- Export Advice, Missions and Exhibitions
- International Promotion
- Major Information Sources and Data Bases

CORE CHAMBERS

- Local Prominence
- Management Information
- Technical Information, Advice and Enquiries
- Strategic Policy over all Business Programmes for area
- Export Certificates
- Training Policy within Firms
- Enterprise Support
- Links to Education, Policy and Local Authority Policies
- Contributes to and uses Data Base

LOCAL CHAMBER BRANCHES AND OUTREACH SERVICES

- Local Representation
- Meeting Point and Social Functions
- Contact Point for Information on where to go for Advice
- First Call for Enquiries and Liason
- Training Agent / Job Centre
- Fax / Telex etc. Facilities
- Data Base Terminal

Figure 6.5 Organisation of Chamber services at different levels; each higher level includes all lower level services

fields of export missions, research and data bases. The core clusters may have a lead Chamber – as in the case of Manchester for the North West, or Birmingham for the West Midlands. Or there may be a pooling of effort by a group of larger Chambers to gain economies of scale and specialisation in some services – as is emerging in South Yorkshire and appears to be emerging in West Yorkshire. The possible hierarchical structure of Chamber services is shown in Figure 6.5.

Chambers have already moved a long way towards attaining these targets. Table 6.10 demonstrates the general increase in size of Chambers since the 1970s, and Table 6.11 shows their increase in staff. However, it is clear from these tables that only perhaps 30 Chambers meet or have the capacity to meet the minimum criteria listed above. When the income level of Chambers is studied (Table 6.12) there appear to be perhaps no more than 26 Chambers at present close to the income criterion of £1m, although this number has increased rapidly since the early 1980s. Of this income, only a very small number raise a significant proportion from their own subscriptions (Table 6.13). Moreover, after a significant increase in subscription income among Chambers in the 1979–82 period, there has since been relatively little increase in the real level of subscriptions. What appears to have been happening, as shown by Table 6.14, is that the smaller Chambers have been coming up closer to the medium-sized ones in subscription rates (few Chambers now have subscriptions of less than £50 per year), whilst the larger Chambers have kept their rates, and hence their total subscription income, relatively stable since the early 1980s. Bennett (1991a) suggested a target for subscriptions of 35–45% of income in order to provide a stable core resource. For Chambers of 1,000–2,000 members with an income requirement of £1m, this requires subscriptions of approximately £200–300 (at 1989 prices).

Table 6.10 Proportion of Chambers of Commerce 1976–1990 with different sizes of membership

Size of Chamber membership	1976 (%)	1979 (%)	1982 (%)	1990 (%)	Annual growth rate 1976–90
>1,000	16.5	18.5	20.2	24	3.2
500 – 1,000	13.2	15.2	22.5	33	10.7
100 – 499	52.7	52.2	46.1	39	–1.9
<100	17.6	14.1	11.2	4	–5.5
Total number in sample	91	92	89	100	–

Source: LSE analysis of ABCC annual surveys

Table 6.11 Proportion of Chambers with different staff numbers (total FT and PT numbers) 1979–1989

Number of Chamber staff	1979 (%)	1982 (%)	1989 (%)
>40	6	4	23
20 – 39	6	8	19
10 – 19	13	17	15
2 – 9	37	43	35
<2	39	28	9
Average number of staff	11	10	26

Chambers have made up their income in the 1980s largely from non-subscription sources. Of these, the most important source has been training income, either as a managing agent or training provider for government YT and ET schemes. Additionally,

Table 6.12 Proportion of Chambers with total income (turnover) at different levels 1976–1989 (at 1989 prices)

Income level (£) (%)	1976 (%)	1979 (%)	1982 (%)	1989 (%)
>2.5m	1	1	1	10
1.0 – 2.5m	–	–	–	11
750,000 – 1.0m	4	3	2	5
250,00 – 149,999	7	9	12	22
100,000 – 249,999	12	16	18	14
10,000 – 99,999	47	46	43	30
<10,000	28	24	23	8
Average income level (£)	148,000	152,000	144,000	750,000

income has been derived from magazines, mailing, information bases, directories, publications, export services and seminars. Some Chambers have been more innovative through development of child care and employer services (e.g. Kirklees). A number of small government schemes have also provided some support where many Chambers have acted as host bodies, e.g. Local Employer Networks (LENs), Compacts. However, most government schemes have yielded increasingly modest returns, and in many cases, such as LENs and Compacts, have required subsidies by the Chambers to keep them alive. The relatively modest yields, or the need for subsidies, have also applied to many government training programmes since April 1991. This has led to the argument that Chambers need a more sustained and reliable base which could be provided by compulsory registration of companies or a form of public law status (see ABCC, 1991a).

Table 6.13 Proportion of Chambers with subscription income at various levels 1976–1989 (at 1989 prices)

Membership subscription income (£)	1976 (%)	1979 (%)	1982 (%)	1989 (%)
> 200,000*	2	2	2	4
100,000 – 200,000	6	11	12	14
50,000 – 99,999	15	14	21	21
20,000 – 49,999	22	20	18	21
10,000 – 19,999	13	18	9	17
<10,000	42	35	38	21
Average subscription income (£)	33,500	39,400	41,800	64,400

*London and Birmingham are the members of this group in 1976–82, plus Manchester and Westminster in 1989

Table 6.14 Proportion of Chambers with average annual subscription rates at a given level 1979–1989 (at 1989 prices)

Average subscription (£)	1979	1982	1989
>120	2	2	2
80 – 120	20	20	27
60 – 79	27	23	34
40 – 59	21	31	14
<39	30	24	24
Overall average per year (£)	60	62	82

The present Chambers, when analysed in terms of the new core network (Figure 5.11), have 32 at or above 1,000 members, 16 at or above a membership density of 10%, 25 at or above an income of £750,000, and 16 with subscription income exceeding £100,000 (with 9 having subscriptions exceeding 15% of income, and only 4 with subscriptions exceeding 30% of income). The Chambers have thus developed very significantly since the early 1980s, and promise considerable deepening of quality and widening of services in the future. However, like most other enterprise agents, they suffer considerable lack of resources and are adversely affected by not being part of a *system* that links them, with other agents, into a coherent approach. We develop this theme further below.

Trade associations

Trade associations, like Chambers of Commerce, are representative bodies. They have a higher proportion of income derived from subscriptions, and levy subscriptions at much higher rates, typically £350 – £1,000 per member. Like Chambers they have also been seeking to develop their activities beyond representation to provide services to members. Their main activities, however, remain lobbying and representing members' interests to government, and increasingly to the EC, both the Commission and the European Parliament. The services that they have recently developed relate to marketing, agency work, business directories and data bases, export advice and overseas missions.

Like Chambers, they have also felt themselves increasingly disadvantaged by the large, well resourced and highly professional bodies present in France and Germany. These benefit from compulsory membership at the Chamber level. In Germany, although national trade and craft bodies are private law organisations, they are recognised or licensed by government. This offers the potential for a representational monopoly and considerable economies of scale. In the field of German crafts there is a particularly strong hierarchical relationship between national associations and local and regional guilds. German industry and commerce, however, is divided between Chambers and trade associations, as in Britain, but with the benefit of (effectively) compulsory membership (see Fröhler, 1965; Wernet, 1965; Streeck, 1989).

In response to the European challenge, many British trade associations have sought to work more closely with each other. Some of the most successful examples are the Chemical Industries Association (CIA) and the Mechanical and Metal Trades Confederation (METCOM) which was formed in 1988 as the final outcome of a 1979 DTI initiative to bring the engineering trade associations together. Smaller associations have tended increasingly to join these groups, e.g. the British Federation of Printing Machines and Supplies (BFPMS) can access 40,000 members through these links, thus greatly extending beyond its own specialist membership base of 150. The trade associations tend to see their strength in specialisation allowing a simpler approach to lobbying, that does not try to represent a range of conflicting interests.

The movement towards large sectoral groupings has been stimulated by the DTI which does not want to talk to 200–300 separate associations. It is seen as offering considerable potential in Brussels. However, in 1991 there were a number of tensions emerging. First, the CBI has fought shy of sectoral structures that could allow the associations to draw together from sectoral groupings into one "mega-body". The CBI tends to prefer a regional structure and to draw on a few large companies to represent sectoral interests. This is seen by the associations as a weak approach, which they have rejected.[15]

A second dilemma has been the development of the Chambers of Commerce movement. Most trade associations desire no local presence and so have normally been complementary to, rather than competitive with, Chambers. However, the development of stronger Chamber services in the fields of databases, exports and foreign missions has brought the two organisations into potential competition – both for the support of their member companies, and for any possible contracting out of DTI services. Third, like all enterprise support bodies, the trade associations have also been struggling with lack of resources and sufficient critical mass. Thus the development of British trade associations, like each other element we have discussed, suffers from a lack of a national systemic approach to enterprise support.

Local government

Local government provides a wide range of services, some of which directly benefit all businesses, some of which are targeted on specific economic development activities, and some of which have indirect benefits to business. Their specific role in support to enterprise has been increasingly recognised and they received a new permissive economic development power as a result of the Local Government and Housing Act (1989).

Direct benefits to all businesses include roads, traffic regulation and lighting, refuse, police, fire, promotional services, and education and training of the workforce. Indirect services include social, community and welfare support that may help unemployed or disadvantaged groups into the workforce, environmental improvements, housing policy, leisure services and a wide range of other local services. These can all be seen as important supply side supports to business. There are also some specific services by local authorities which are targeted to specific firms. These are relatively small in extent in most places, but are often locally significant. They include small business and start-up advice services (often targeted at special needs or community groups), managed workspaces and small grants/loans.

Local authorities (like central government) can also be inhibitive of business. Most commonly this arises in the case of planning restrictions, or weak education and training policy. But it may also affect their wide range of services and thus the "business climate" of an area. Clearly local government's approach is affected by its own political and ideological stance (for an analysis of political differences in emphasis that arise see e.g. Martinos, 1989; Chandler and Lawless, 1985; Gyford, 1985; Mawson and Miller, 1986).

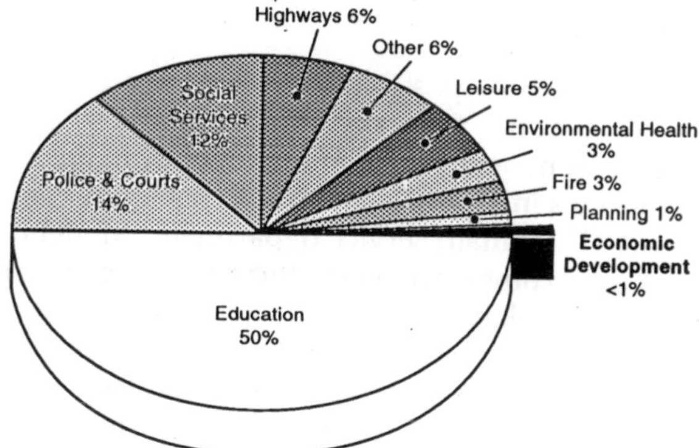

Figure 6.6 Local authority current service expenditure (1989–90) (excluding housing revenue account and debt charges)
Source: Audit Commission, 1989, from CIPFA estimates

In general, local authorities have far more budget for their "mainstream" services than specific economic development support, which frequently is less than 1% of total local spending (see Figure 6.6). This has led many commentators to conclude that the most significant contribution local authorities can make to enterprise is to get their mainstream activities efficiently and effectively organised so as to create a supportive environment that leads to a good business climate (Audit Commission, 1989, 1990; JURUE, 1981; Chandler and Lawless, 1985; Lawless, 1988; Morison, 1987; McKeown,

1987; Bennett and Krebs, 1991). Whilst specific economic development services to business may aid a few small firms, the care, maintenance and encouragement of existing enterprise is a far more important field of activity than local authorities, through their mainstream services, can contribute much to stimulate, or inhibit: "*Almost every mainstream local service – social services, policy, libraries – can play a part in creating an area that is attractive to people and industry*" (Audit Commission, 1989, p. 33).

This conclusion has led to the view that local authorities must concentrate efforts on their mainstream services, whilst in targeted economic development they must work increasingly in partnership with business and other agents to get the best local business climate. For local government this means developing a broad and pervasive approach to *all* its services. Local economic development is too large and too important a problem to be handled by a small local economic development department or LED officer alone. To give greatest support to enterprise requires the whole of the Council's approach to be planned to achieve a proper local economic support system and to balance this with wider service demands. This in turn stimulates the need for a corporate and integrated management vision by the local authority: it is also a business and needs a strategy. This strategy is the key element in building the capacity of local government to participate in economic development.

A key aspect of best practice local authority support for enterprise has, therefore, to be management arrangements. The Audit Commission (1990, pp. 123–6) recommends that three elements should be in place: (i) main service contributions to enterprise should be identified and managed, (ii) specific economic development services should be effectively coordinated, and (iii) corporate direction should ensure that all policies are coordinated to produce a cross-service economic development strategy, ensure its implementation, coordinate it with other agents, and act as a local ambassador with non-local agents.

The Commission identifies three possible locations for an Economic Development Unit (EDU), as shown in Figure 6.7. Typically, local authorities have had separate units (Model A) but these suffer from being small and remote from the mainstream services. This covers 11% of authorities in 1989. To overcome this limitation, most local authorities have located their EDU in a main service department (Model B), usually Planning or Estates (46% in 1989). This can be beneficial, but suffers from being submerged in a larger department which may have a culture "*at odds with the more entrepreneurial approach needed by an EDU*" (Audit Commission, 1990, p. 126). Model C locates the EDU within the chief executive's office. In general, the Audit Commission favours this approach, "*especially if the unit is small, since it should ensure that it receives top level support*",[5] and can be more effectively coordinated with the other major programmes of local authority services. It can also be the means of most effectively *delivering* the authority's economic development support in negotiation with other actors. This overcomes the gap in empowerment of chief executives, or councillors, to deliver the effective action of their authorities which is recognised as often a major problem in the partnership process outlined below. Despite its advantages, only 28.5% of authorities in 1989 follow Model C, although their number is growing (statistics from Coulson *et al.*, 1991).

Within each field of activity, the Audit Commission (1990) has developed an audit guide to best practice.[16] A key aspect of the recommended approach is "working with others" – or *partnership*. Since local government is not itself a direct producer of wealth and economic growth, it can be only a participant in most economic development

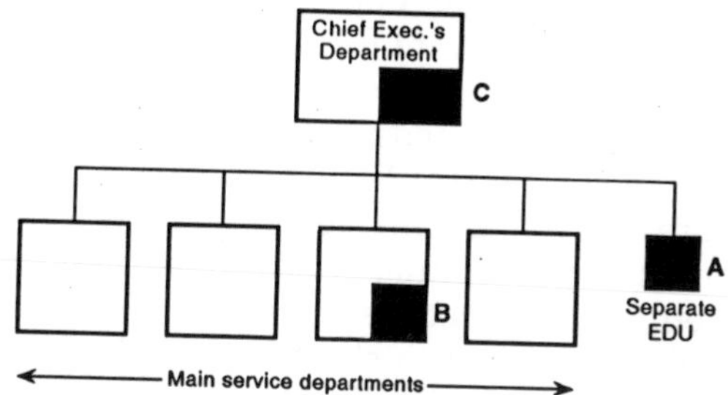

Figure 6.7 Alternative locations for the economic development function within local authority administrative structures
(after, Audit Commission, 1990, p.128)

actions. However, they are very important participants. Local authorities can block development (through planning powers), they can mediate the form of development (by having a wider social and community representation), they provide important supply side services to business, and they can facilitate and catalyse change. But to fulfill these roles effectively they usually need to work in collaboration or partnership with other agents (see Bennett and Krebs, 1991, Chapter 12).

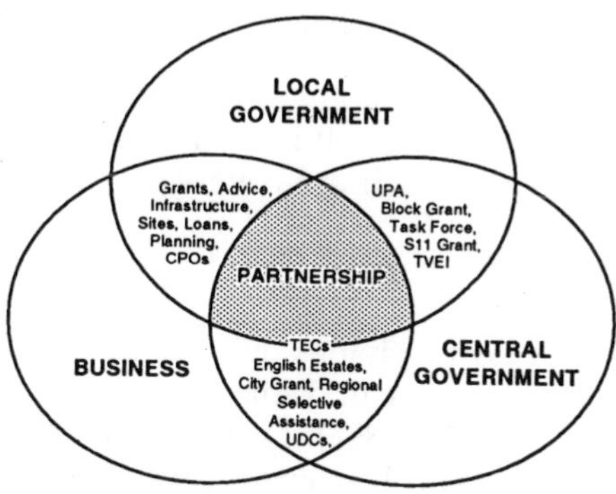

Figure 6.8 Partners in economic development
(after Audit Commission, 1989, p.7)

The partnership concept involves each organisation drawing on its different skills, knowledge, powers and resources but making their activities "*consistent with each other ... guided by a similar view of how the local economy will develop and not duplicate or conflict with each other*" (Audit Commission, 1990, p. 33). The importance of partnership approaches has increasingly permeated the discussions of local authority economic development. The Audit Commission depicted this, as shown in Figure 6.8, as a process of working independently and jointly with both central government and the private sector, in different combinations for different purposes.

Partnership also involves local authorities working more *closely with each other*. This is necessary because the local economic geography is not bounded by local government boundaries, but has its own structure of local labour markets, business trading links, business organisation areas (such as Chambers) and TEC/LEC areas. Cooperation between local authorities is a major lacuna in British behaviour. Historically, there has been an arena of competition, both between local authorities, and between local and central government. Each has wished to claim "ownership" of particular initiatives. These problems characterise both metropolitan and non-metropolitan areas. There are many "doughnuts" where old county boroughs and their overlying upper tier counties do not work well with each other. In the metropolitan areas conflicts and apathy about the relations between districts are common, yet integration of economies and labour markets makes most local government boundaries irrelevant for economic processes. Central government has also been an intrusive actor in urban areas, through UPAs, UDCs, EZs, CATs and TFs (see Chapter 5). Local authorities need to recognise the constraints under which they operate. They are both a major contributor to local fragmentation and a major potential support to its solution. To increase local coherence they must work more effectively together with each other, with local business organisations and with central government if they are to have any chance of offering a supportive local environment to business.

The bulk of activities relate to mainstream programme areas of local authority services. However there are also important specific economic services. Various surveys have been undertaken that demonstrate the rapid growth of these specific services. Some general patterns of expenditure and staff in EDUs are shown in Table 6.15. Expenditures doubled, and in many areas staff doubled, between 1978 and 1986, although they experienced slower growth 1986–89. Generally, metropolitan areas have much higher staffing than non-metropolitan, whilst non-metropolitan counties have a staffing much larger than their districts. It is clear that, except in a few areas, EDUs are small. In the majority of areas, which are covered by non-metropolitan districts, the staffing consists of only 1, 2 or 3 people. This reinforces the Audit Commission's preference, reported earlier, for small EDUs to be located in the chief executive's department.

The specific enterprise support activities undertaken by local authorities across their EDU and other functions is shown in Table 6.16 (see also Mills and Young, 1986; Armstrong and Fildes, 1988; DHS, 1989a). This demonstrates that the main activities of local authorities are preparing and brokering sites and nursery units, and providing advice and information. There was a rapid growth in financial assistance over the period shown. The advisory function has been stimulated among other things by central government and EC programmes: a local officer is needed who can stimulate and pilot applications to central government or EC programmes such as ERDF and ESF, as well as being a full time catalyst or link with local outside bodies such as TECs, UDCs, CATs, TFs, etc.

The rapid growth of local authority economic development activity in the 1980s was initially stimulated by the 1981/82 recession and high unemployment levels (see e.g. Bennington, 1985; Hawkins, 1985). Subsequently, however, the process has spread and taken on a far wider set of characteristics (Mills and Young, 1986; Young, 1986; Sellgren, 1987, 1988):

- Rippling out: spreading of interest in economic development from older and declining areas to prosperous and more rural locations;
- Filtering down: a growing concern with economic development in lower tier authorities (districts) as well as counties;
- Diversification: widening of the range of activities, particularly in the fields of education, training and SMEs advice;
- Collaboration: increasing joint action of local government in collaboration with other agents.

The consequence of these developments is that almost all areas, even smaller local authorities, now have an economic development office.

As a result of expanding interest, a wide range of different enterprise programmes have received local support. Many of these programmes evidence relatively low costs per job created or sustained. For example, Davies *et al.* (1986) find a range of £330–770. This estimate is low compared to that of central government's Regional Selective Assistance of £3,500 or Regional Development Grant of £9,100; but these contain substantial capital investment effects. Whilst costs per job have been low, however, there has been considerable concern about the *displacement* effects of local authority assistance. This is the concern that subsidised firms reduce the potential or lead to the closure of non-subsidised firms. Such assistance is frequently in the form of a grant or employment subsidy. Since most assisted firms are small, have a purely local market and are low tech, their multiplier effects have been small. Their benefit appears to be mainly in reducing unemployment rather than contributing to the wider enterprise goals outlined in this chapter.

Table 6.15 Expenditure and staffing levels in local authority economic development activities in England and Wales 1978–85

Expenditure or staff	1978–9	1980–1	1985–6	1989	% of total local expenditure (1986) or staff (1989)
Mean capital expenditure per head (£)	2.6	5.0	5.1	–	0.4
Mean current expenditure per head (£)	–	1.9	2.2	–	0.2
Mean number of staff	2	2.5	4.0	7.1	1.2
Non-met. counties	4.9	5.7	9.8	12.0	0.08
London boroughs	8.9	8.4	8.9	10.6	0.1
Met. districts*	9.3	9.3	14.3	29.3	0.4
Non-met. districts	1.6	1.8	2.5	3.3	0.01

* excluding the GLC and metropolitan counties which were abolished in 1986. They had EDU staff of 299 and 27.3 respectively in 1986.

Source: 1978–80 CIPFA data, recalculated from Sellgren (1989) (reported in Bennett and Krebs (1991) Table 6.2); 1989 from Coulson *et al.*, 1991

Local authorities have been given an important stimulus to the expansion of their activities by the permissive powers of the Local Government and Housing Act (1989). Traditionally, local government has had to use permissive power under Section 137 of the Local Government Act (1972) in England and Wales, and its equivalent Section 83 of the Local Government (Scotland) Act (1973). Under sections 137/83, local authorities were able to incur expenditure for local economic development, as well as for other purposes in the interest of their area, up to a maximum of a 2p product of the rates. Although not large, a 2p rate product can be significant in a large authority, e.g. in Birmingham it provided a maximum of £3.2m. Most authorities used at least 1.5p of this power, increasing their collective spending from £17m to £90m, from 1981 to 1984 (Ramsdale and Capon, 1986). The new powers have sought to regularise local approaches under Section 137/83 powers. The legislation was strongly influenced by the Widdicombe Committee which concluded that the existing powers used under Section 137/83 should be clarified by "defining more precisely the degree of benefits (to the local area) which must be achieved" (Widdicombe, 1986, para 8.85). The Committee recommended limits on local powers and for local government to work with other actors.

The new legislation confers many benefits (see Bennett and Krebs, 1991, pp. 47–9):

- It is focusing the minds of all councils on economic development issues, in conjunction with their wider roles in other service sectors;
- It requires economic development to play a key role in corporate planning in local government;
- It introduces more clearly a balance of businesses' needs into the wider social and political questions which tend to dominate council discussions;
- It simplifies the legislative provisions and thus allows better appraisal and clearer policy formulation;
- This in turn allows simplified audit (as developed by the Audit Commission, 1990),

Table 6.16 Proportion of local authorities engaged in different local economic development activities in Britain in 1983 and 1986

Activity	1983 (%)	1986 (%)	% change 1983–86
Preparing serviced land	65	64	−1.5
Preparing sites <2 acres	86	94	9.3
Preparing sites 2–10 acres	87	93	6.9
Preparing sites >10 acres	64	75	14.1
Factory development	32	38	18.7
Nursery units / managed workshops	63	76	20.6
Provision of premises:			
• <2,500 sq.ft.	91	99	8.8
• 2,500 – 10,000 sq. ft.	93	96	3.2
• >10,000 sq. ft.	74	83	12.2
Financial assistance:			
• loans / grants	51	59	15.7
• rent concessions	42	46	9.5
Key worker housing	71	73	2.8
Business advice	38	76	100.0
Business information services	85	98	17.0

Source: Sellgren (1987) from *Industrial Development Guide* (reported in Bennett and Krebs, 1991, Table 6.3)

and the development of best practice through proper performance assessment and monitoring (a 1989 ADC survey showed that only 15 per cent of respondents had any arrangements for the monitoring of performance in the field of economic development).

However, there are some important restrictions on the use of the new power. The most important are (DoE, 1989a):

1. *Restrictions on the range of activities*: exclusion from banking, investment business, insurance, estate agency, manufacturing, media, and other professional services, trading businesses, etc. (except those ancillary to training, management of land and buildings and information provision).
2. *Restrictions on wage subsidies.*
3. *Restrictions on loans and grants*: to a rate representing the true cost, with subsidised assistance to borrowing identified as a grant.
4. *Geographical restrictions*: grants, loans, and guarantees of borrowing are restricted to £10,000 in any one year to any one business (unless the support is for training, for specified unemployed or support for individuals on government or EC schemes) unless the area is an urban programme area, development area, intermediate area, derelict land clearance area, rural development area, travel-to-work area where unemployment is above the England or Wales average; in Wales, a WDA and Development Board for Rural Wales (DBRW) area; and the whole of Scotland.
5. *Restrictions on local authority companies (DoE, 1989b)*: controls on the range of activities; capital finance; accounts and auditing; personnel involvement; access to information, political activities, contracts procedures, land transactions, etc.

These restrictions have sought to prevent local authorities acting in fields in which the government believes the private sector is the preferable provider. *"This approach will ensure that local authorities can continue ... without trespassing on areas in which the private sector is fully able to provide private cover"* (DoE, 1989a, p. 6).

Whilst the expansion of local authority activity has been rapid, its focus on the development of its mainstream services have been slower than that of those specific to business development. Given the number of other actors in the fields of advice and SMEs support (e.g. TECs, LECs, Chambers, enterprise agencies, central government grant schemes) the local authority role is not usually crucial, whilst its mainstream services are. This is reinforced by the deep suspicions that exist about both the displacement effects and the sustainability of many local authority-financed enterprises. This suggests that a key role they can play in the development of enterprise is in the enhancement of their own corporate management to deliver mainstream activities. This can ensure that local authorities offer to other actors a reliable input that ensures their effective collaboration in partnerships. We address these specific roles further below.

TECs and LECs

The Training and Enterprise Councils (TECs), and their equivalent Scottish bodies, Local Enterprise Companies (LECs), are a new development among local agents. The first TECs became operational in April 1990 and all were operational by October 1991. There are 82 TECs in England and Wales, and 22 LECs in Scotland. The TECs vary in size considerably in terms of the number of businesses and employees covered. Their boundaries are usually coterminous with those of local authorities.

TECs/LECs are a major initiative designed to decentralise the administration of the main central government programmes for training, as well as some enterprise and education programmes, to local private sector-led organisations. For each area the TEC is supposed to act as a strategic body developing a strategy and awarding contracts to public and private sector providers to supply training and enterprise programmes, and work-related further education. Their budgets vary considerably, being based on the size of their population, numbers of unemployed and similar factors. The national budget allows for approximately £20m per TEC. Within their budget each TEC has the following major programme responsibilities derived (largely) from the former Training Agency:

- Youth Training (YT);
- Employment Training (ET);
- Business Growth Training (BGT);
- Enterprise Allowances;
- Small Firms Service;
- Trainer Training;
- Training Access Points;
- Work-Related Further Education (WRFE);
- Education-business partnerships (EBP).

In addition Scottish LECs have major programmes covering:

- Enterprise advice;
- Environmental improvement;
- Community Development Action (CDA) (in Highlands and Islands Enterprise (HIE) areas only).

Scottish LECs are divided into two groups. The first group, mainly outside the Highlands, is under Scottish Enterprise (SE) and has a high level of decentralised power. The second group of LECs is in the former Highlands and Islands Development Board (HIDB) area, and is under HIE. It has considerably less decentralised powers, particularly for environmental and enterprise functions. HIE LECs do, however, have the additional CDA grant.

In addition to these areas of programmatic finance, TECs and LECs can bid in 1991/92 for Development Grants for approved local projects (typically £10,000 – £20,000, but up to approximately £100,000). There are also special grants for those TECs acting as pilots for national schemes, e.g. for training credits. In the future, TECs/LECs may gain further programme moneys through reforms of the Careers Service and FE college funding. There is also a Local Initiatives Fund of up to £100,000 – £500,000 in Year 1 (with about 10% of this sum annually available thereafter). Further funding is "won" from TEED on a project-by-project basis or depends on generating a surplus by efficiency savings.

TECs are companies limited by guarantee which contract with government to provide programmes. The TEC is managed by a Board of up to 15 members, each acting as individuals (not as representatives), of whom two-thirds must come from private sector businesses. Local authority, union and other public sector bodies including public employers, therefore, have a maximum of five places. The staff of the TEC are mainly seconded civil servants from the former Training Agency Area Offices, except for the Chief Executive who in an increasing number of cases is appointed from other sources.

The main budget for TECs, and the main elements of their contract with the Government, concerns training. They also have a significance for Work Related Further Education (WRFE) because they control approximately 15% of LEA's further education (FE) budget. They have only a small budget to allocate to enterprise, and depend almost exclusively on bidding for extra funds when it comes to education and other initiatives. They are thus dominated by training and secondly by WRFE. In all other fields, to have any major impact, they will have to work closely with other agencies to gain the advantages of economies of scale or a significant critical mass of resources. Indeed, even in training their government budget is only a small part (approximately 20%) of all training expenditure (TA, 1989b), so that even here they have to develop strong cooperation.

The LECs, however, have very significant additional resources in the fields of enterprise and environmental improvement. This has meant that, although seeking to work with other local agents, LECs are emerging as larger forces in Scottish local economies. They have been able to act more independently or to effect greater leverage on other actors – in both the public and private sectors. LECs have also gained considerable advantage from the experience of the former SDA and HIDB which had considerable local presence in many parts of Scotland, generally had strong local support and had a base of experienced staff to draw on (many of whom have moved from SDA/HIDB into the LECs). Early surveys support the view that they have been able to develop more rapidly their goals and operational procedures than TECs at the same stage of development (Bennett *et al.*, 1991a, 1991b, 1993).

TECs and LECs are the recent major entrants on the enterprise scene. Although England and Wales TECs have only small enterprise resources they are in a position to start to bring local programmes together. Scottish LECs, with their greater resources and environmental powers, are even better placed to do so. However, both TECs and LECs suffer some important constraints arising from: first, their dominance by civil service staff and programmes driven by TEED – this limits severely their freedom of action; second, they have a limited capacity to draw from local agents and business because of their external and appointed origin of Boards – this limits their acceptance by other agents and restricts their capacity to transmit change, particularly to smaller firms.

Filling the gaps

This chapter has assessed the development of enterprise in Britain. Enterprise is the most crucial of all the building blocks of vertical programme discussed in this book because it is the core of business development, income and wealth creation. We have observed that a major force behind developing enterprise is the need to increase the responsiveness of businesses. This frequently requires small business development, or downsizing and restructuring of larger businesses. This in turn is fed by the global requirements of closer market-producer links; reduced benefits that can be derived from technical economies of scale; pressures to reduce costs and the need to stimulate innovation.

We have argued that enterprise development is primarily a spontaneous process which businesses themselves undertake. But there is a range of gaps that arise from reliance on a purely spontaneous approach. These arise at national, local, and sectoral level. They particularly affect *growing firms*. We have analysed the network of agents that seek to support enterprise development and we have found a number of crucial gaps. *First*, on a geographical basis the network of agents is uneven across the country and uneven in depth or quality. Most agents have had only imperfect procedures for assessing and achieving quality outputs, although major improvements have been made in the early 1990s as many Chambers, TECs and enterprise agencies move to adopt quality accreditation.

Second, there is considerable overlap resulting in implicit or explicit competition between agents to deliver services, whilst leaving some areas of strategic gaps. Whilst competition itself may be healthy, it tends to lead to wasted resources, may be furthering conflicting objectives, and offers a baffling confusion to the entrepreneur needing support.

Third, the scope for voluntary support from business donations and sponsorship has provided only limited potential for diffusing broad enterprise objectives. Whilst there have been important and undoubted successes, the greatest benefits have usually derived from strategic alliances and partnering arrangements. These latter seem to have benefitted from the *formality* of such relationships: formal and contractual relationships normally yield the most reliable outcomes.

Fourth, it also appears that the emphasis of much sponsorship activity, and a major range of other support services (particularly in local government and TECs/LECs) is strongly towards getting the unemployed into self-employment. Whilst this provides strong support to micro-businesses, we would argue that it leaves a strategic gap for meso-businesses. These businesses usually have the greatest potential to grow. Meso-businesses also tend to focus on higher level technology, and higher value added, than micro-businesses. There is thus a strategic gap in support for those enterprises that could offer most to Britain's required longer term need for high quality, high value added products.

Fifth, there appears still to exist a significant funding gap for meso-businesses, although micro-businesses and large company downsizing or restructuring appears well-served by the rapid growth of venture capital funds in the last 10 years. The discussion of venture capital also draws out a strategic gap in the whole enterprise process. This centres on the need to integrate financial with each other element in the economic process: from innovation, research and development, through product design and production, to marketing and distribution. Where a system failure exists for enterprise, its core problem is the lack of a structure of support, care and aftercare through the entire, long development process of new goods and services. It is clear that this is a system-wide, and hence a national, problem. But it is also a local problem because of the variable incidence of support agencies across the country.

Sixth, a wider aspect of the system-wide difficulties of business relates to the lack of proper skills at each level, from management and supervisor to operative. This leads us to our examination in the next chapters of the education and training base. It is upon these elements of human resource development that enterprise ultimately relies.

Footnotes: Chapter 6

1. Useful summaries of these arguments applied to enterprise policy are given by Bain (1956), Baumol et al. (1982), Curran (1986) and Bannock (1989).
2. Michael Joseph, Head of Lloyds Bank Development Capital (Birmingham and Leeds), *Financial Times*, 22 November 1990.

3. Estimates of cost per job also range above £6,000 with additionality of only 40% (Monk, 1991).

4. Interview with Bernard Direen, Industrial Editor, *Yorkshire Post*.

5. There are also a range of other agencies which may be locally significant, e.g. local cooperative development agencies, worker cooperatives, town development trusts, etc. These are generally rather small in number and limited in geographical coverage (see CBVU, 1981; Gibbs, 1983).

6. LEA here means Local Enterprise Agency: elsewhere we use this to refer to Local Education Authorities.

7. BiTC (1986, 1987, 1988). LEAGs amount to £2.5m in 1986/87 and 1987/88, reducing to £1m by 1990/91 and zero in 1991/92.

8. The statistics quoted in Tables 6.8 and 6.9 are derived from a sample of 24 enterprise agencies surveyed at the end of 1988. The sample size varies in each table depending on the responses. The sample was drawn from the case study areas discussed at length in Part 3 of this book and is broadly representative of different sizes and locations of enterprise agencies, except that rural-based agencies are excluded. The sample includes: Birmingham Venture, Sheffield Enterprise Agency, Glasgow Opportunities, Dundee Enterprise Agency, The Barras Enterprise Trust, Manchester Business Venture, Cardiff and Vale Enterprise, Cleveland Business Development Agency, Oldham Enterprise, Merthyr-Aberdare Development Enterprise, Leicestershire Business Venture Limited, Leith Enterprise Trust, Ogwr Partnership Trust, North East Thames Business Advisory Centre, Edinburgh Old Town Trust, Salford Hundred Venture, Sandwell Enterprise Limited, Walsall Small Firms Advice Unit Limited, Nottingham Business Venture, East London Small Business Centre, Trafford Business Venture, Greater Easterhouse Partnership, Agency for Economic Development (Moss Side).

9. This confirms earlier surveys, e.g. CEC (1985), Metcalf *et al.* (1989).

10. Based on interviews with corporate social responsibility managers in Marks and Spencer, BP, IBM and Wellcome Foundation.

11. e.g. Hackney Business Promotion Centre and St Helens Trust articles of association of the 1970s and interview comments in 1989.

12. This is confirmed by the analysis of nine agencies by Metcalf *et al.* (1989).

13. Derived from an LSE survey sample of 40 TECs and 12 LECs in 1991 (Bennett *et al.*, 1993).

14. All statistics from Bennett (1991a); see also Figure 5.11.

15. Interviews with trade associations, May–July 1991. The CBI has now created a National Manufacturing Roundtable comprising large companies and trade association representatives.

16. These expand on the more specific evaluation methodologies previously developed, e.g. Coulson (1990).

7. EDUCATION

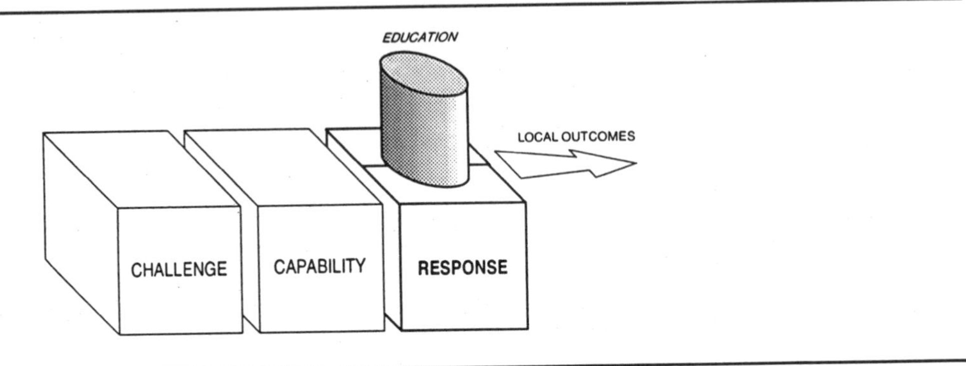

The education response

Education makes a crucial contribution to a country's potential for economic progress. Although education policy has been one of the most hotly debated areas, as we have seen in Chapter 4, it has been unquestionably one of the fields where Britain[1] has been least adequate in providing a system that measures up to competitors in its support of the economy.

The inadequacy of education's response to economic challenges has been recognised for many years and goes back in many ways to the debates of the 1870s. However, the recent focus of attention dates from the now famous Ruskin College speech of October 1976 by the then Prime Minister, James Callaghan (1976). This sparked a so-called "Great Debate" in education. At the same time a series of major developments in thinking about policy in vocational education and training, discussed in Chapter 8, led to a progressive "rebalancing" between the economic and wider cultural objectives of education. The result has been a rapid development of many institutions and initiatives in the 1980s; and in the 1990s some consolidation has occurred. This chapter seeks to address how far the developments that have occurred have produced a structure that can now be relied upon to provide the quality of education the economy requires. We emphasise, in particular, the inseparability of changes in management from changes in the curriculum.

Our discussion is not an assessment of education across all its dimensions, but focuses on the key aspect of how far it serves the needs of the economy. The discussion therefore focuses on the relationship between education and businesses' needs. We outline, in turn, the development of initiatives that focus on this problem:

- Recognising malaise;
- Early learning;
- New solutions based on integration;

- Towards partnerships;
- Assessment of Compacts;
- Development of education-business partnerships (EBPs);
- TECs and EBPs;
- The impact of the Education Reform Act.

Recognising malaise

The "Great Debate" that followed James Callaghan's 1976 Ruskin College speech focused on the inability of British education to support the level of economic performance that was sought. As we have already suggested, there are two issues of concern:

- General educational standards;
- The balance towards vocational needs.

James Callaghan gave prominence to both issues. He noted the *"complaints from industry that new recruits from the schools sometimes do not have the basic tools to do the job that is required"* and the *"need for a more technological bias in science teaching that will lead towards practical applications in industry rather than towards academic studies"* (quoted in Maclure, 1988, pp. 154–157). It was a question of striking the right balance between equipping children for *"a lively, constructive place in society"* and fitting them *"to do a job of work"*. Better cooperation between business and education was required, but this did not necessarily entail more vocational *skills*. It was more a question of vocational and practical *experience*. Callaghan's arguments have been reiterated and reworked countless times and were developed by the Conservative governments of the 1980s.

The malaise falls into four components. *First*, Britain compares poorly with her major international competitors in terms of educational attainment. A key factor in accounting for this is the dominance of the school curriculum by an examination system dictated largely by university entrance requirements. By this route, universities, which have catered for a small elite, have come to have an enormous influence over both *what is taught* and the *mode of assessment* for *all* pupils. This occurs despite the fact that "O" levels and CSEs were designed for only the top 60% of children by ability. Until the advent of GCSE, the system left 40% of children following courses which were either not designed for them or which had become low-status "residual" courses with no final target for pupils to aim at. The system was thus designed to fail a large proportion of its clients. In the words of Sir Peter Swinnerton-Dyer, former chief executive of the Universities Funding Council, *"it is designed almost exclusively for those going on to the next stage"* (quoted in *THES*, 5 April 1991, p. 2); or, in the words of Correlli Barnett (ESRC Newsletter, 10 June 1991, p. 2), education has played a major role in developing a culture of "habituated" failure. Handy (1985, p. 133) calls the system *"disabling"*.

Apart from the stigmatising and demotivating effects of the British system on pupils, the examination system has had a *second* consequence for businesses. Reliance on the traditional modes of assessment and certification have meant that businesses have used "O" levels and CSE results as an initial method of "screening" applicants, even when they often know that these examinations do not properly test the skills they require. Screening is a controversial issue, but has been identified by a variety of analysts as a barrier to entry to jobs, to specific jobs, or to progress in career stages (see e.g. Taubman and Wales, 1973; Arrow, 1973; Stiglitz, 1975; there is also evidence that YT has been used as a screening device, see Gleeson, 1989; Finegold, *et al.*, 1990). Macro-economic and econometric tests show equivocal evidence of the effect of screening. But many surveys show that businesses use examination attainment as a crude index of basic skills (numeracy and literacy) as well as of other attributes that are desired (such as attendance and work discipline in terms of being able to accomplish tasks). However, the result of using examination results for screening often leads to inappropriate decisions because the system of examination assessment is so poorly tuned to employers needs. Hence the use of examination results will lead to the rejection of candidates who are, in fact, perfectly well qualified. There has been no means of crediting other capabilities. Whilst GCSE has improved the situation over "O" levels, it is only by Records of Achievement linked to the national curriculum and more diversified vocational qualifications based on National Vocational Qualifications (NVQ) and General National Vocational Qualifications (GNVQ) that these major systemic problems can begin to be overcome. However, as we show below, doubt still remains as to the adequacy of current developments.

A *third* consequence of the examination system has been a poor staying on rate. Geared to the traditional examination system, education after the age of 16 has been seen as the preserve of those destined for higher education. Age 16 has been seen as an inflexible end-point for most pupils, with little opportunity for slow-learners to stay on and thus reach a certain level of attainment. The Scottish system is notably more flexible in this respect. As a result, in England and Wales particularly, those not destined for qualifications have either gone straight into work or have had to enter FE or tertiary colleges. But the route into FE is far from automatic or obvious and the multiplicity of courses is bewildering. Moreover, there is considerable variation in the type, quality and appropriateness of FE courses available in different areas because of the discretionary nature of past local authority responsibilities and spending in this area.

But the final and *central* problem has been the gap between professionalised education and the needs of business. A "system failure" has occurred because each has stayed aloof from the other[2]. As Callaghan pointed out, the failure of the educational professional was at least equally matched by the unwillingness of employers to take any major responsibility for vocational training. However, the culture and organisation of Local Education Authorities (LEAs) has been a formidable barrier to overcome. Even educationalists recognise a culture of departmentalism, top-down direction, and multi-tiered LEA officer functions.[3] These features have made education inaccessible to business and other "outsiders" and has isolated it from its wider objectives in both economy and society. Overcoming these gaps has to be the central objective for achieving increased quality in education.

The gap between education and business is all the more startling when the educational areas in which business most commonly states its priorities are analysed. One of the most recent studies found the chief areas of concern to be:[4]

- Lack of a standard leaving certificate;
- Poor basic educational skills (basic arithmetic and functional literacy);
- Personal and communication skills;
- Specific skills in word processing, typing and foreign languages.

This study reflects similar priorities found in earlier studies (e.g. IPM, 1981, 1984a; Cleverdon, 1988; Warwick, 1989) which also tend to include emphasis on:

- Acceptance of quality standards;
- Punctuality;
- Teamwork;

- Persistence;
- Ability to plan and solve problems;
- Maturity;
- Readiness to learn.

In the words of Chris Marsden, Manager of BP's Educational Relations Unit (in Blandford and Jamieson, 1989, pp. 55–6; see also Marsden, 1991): "*The emerging partnership between education and business is about Total Quality. It is about increasing the quality of performance of both education and business and the contribution each can make to the other. ... A business is driven hard by its bottom line ... education, on the other hand, has apparently never had the importance of its bottom line similarly questioned by the public.*"

None of these concerns of business differ from what anyone expects of education. Almost all of what business is seeking from education is in line with mainstream educational objectives. The surprise is that these concerns should have to be asserted and pressed by those outside the main educational process. This leads us to two main conclusions:

First, raising general educational standards is an issue which has been highlighted by economic imperatives but is *not* an issue which *centres* only on business needs. Much can and should be done without business. Indeed, as we show below, the national curriculum has in any case made this inevitable. Raising standards is a social as well as an economic necessity. However, business can nonetheless make an important contribution in all areas.

Second, reorienting the curriculum so that it is more attuned to business is necessary, but does not just entail the teaching of specific vocational skills. It is also part of a "system" shift which focuses on moving the curriculum away from more abstract knowledge towards issues in the "real world". It is in this area that business arguably has the greatest role to play and it is this area on which we focus most heavily in the rest of this chapter.

These findings also have consequences for the nature of business involvement at different levels of the education "system". Quite clearly, the general raising of educational attainment ought to be a *national* concern, and there are leading businesses (such as BP) and business organisations (e.g. CBI, BiTC, ABCC) which have been active in influencing the national agenda. But, especially in the development of vocational dimensions to the curriculum, businesses have a crucial role to play at a *local* level. It is here that they can help affect change by being incorporated into *the local management of education* and help to facilitate local solutions to education-business liaison to suit differing local circumstances.

Given the importance of business involvement, the key question which remains to be answered is: *what are the best means of ensuring the effective participation of education with business?* This chapter is devoted to answering this question. In the following sections we describe the various attempts mounted by the educational "policy community" to involve business, detailing their successes and deficiencies, before moving on to discuss the emergence of new approaches emanating from other sources. This analysis sets the scene for analysis of the most recent developments, chiefly Compacts and EBPs.

Early learning: SCIP and TVEI

Arguably, recognition of a problem often means that we are well on the way to its solution. This has not been true of education. Recognition of the inadequacy of the educational system to meet the needs of the economy dates from at least the 1870s. But, as discussed in Chapter 4, almost every attempt at improving quality since the 19th century has been thwarted by institutional barriers to change. As a result, achieving the central objective of integrating into education the needs of business has been a slow and difficult process.

At the time of Callaghan's speech and well into the 1980s, education's attempt to cater for business needs can best be described as *ad hoc*. As a result, it is very difficult to obtain an accurate picture of the nature of education's response in this period. LEAs' response was certainly weak or absent: schools were left very much to their own devices, which usually left any response to business needs to the initiative of a head-teacher or deputies. This pattern fitted the tradition of an education system characterised by a "dispersal" of power between central government (DES), LEAs and schools. As a result *links* between businesses and schools were the main means of schools knowing about the needs of business. But links tended to depend on personal relationships: there were rarely any formal structures through which co-operation could be shaped. Very few schools, and even fewer businesses, had individuals with designated responsibility for responding to business needs, although many School-Industry Liaison Officers (SILOs) had been appointed. Teachers and managers took on business links as an added task and, when their main duties became too burdensome, these "peripheral" activities were often left aside. As a result, there was considerable variation between schools, and even between classes in the same school. Also, when the individuals left, the links usually just disappeared with the person. This outcome explains the very considerable variation in both the number and quality of links between schools, and between LEAs. This generally *ad hoc* pattern continued to exist in the majority of schools and LEAs at least up to 1990, as we demonstrate in an analysis below.

Slowly through the 1980s changes began to take place. At national level, the most important initiative was probably the development of the Schools Council Industry Project (SCIP), launched in 1978. With the abolition of the Schools Council during the 1980s, SCIP changed its name whilst retaining its acronym, to the School Curriculum Industry Partnership. Its nature has, however, remained largely unchanged. SCIP is concerned with the development of new schools-industry practice in the curriculum, seeking to improve pupils' understanding of industrial society. Through a network of coordinators based in LEAs[5] and, above them, a series of Regional Coordinators, SCIP develops specific innovative projects, and gathers and disseminates best practice.

Bottom-up initiatives are a key element of SCIP's work. "*The essence of SCIP's approach is on drawing upon the uniqueness of each school's local economic community and giving teachers 'ownership' of the activities developed by them and the local trade unionists and industrialists with whom they collaborate*" (SCIP, undated). SCIP encourages schools to make use of what it terms "*adults-other-than-teachers*" from the "*local economic community*" often in active and experiential learning situations which support existing innovation in education.

SCIP originated from within the educational community and this has coloured its approach. SCIP coordinators are educationalists, and there has been a tendency to emphasise the benefits to education rather than the mutual benefits of partnership. Nonetheless, SCIP continues to be a major actor in the field of education-business links. That said, the importance of SCIP coordinators and the nature of their role varies between LEAs, depending not least on the commitment of LEAs to a clear education-industry policy. At the beginning of the 1980s, such policies were usually vague and ineffectual, where they existed at all, so that coordinators were rarely able to perform a clearly defined function as part of a coherent local system. Their resources also varied considerably between LEAs. Hence SCIP coordinators, whilst possessing the potential to act as a focus for the integration of local link activities, have not often fulfilled this role. Instead, they have tended to be facilitative and encouraging, with the result that progress has been slow and patchy.

The growth of links has also depended upon economic circumstance. In the late 1970s and early 1980s, economic recession and high unemployment dampened the development of links. Contraction reduced the incentive of employers to be involved since there was no economic rationale for encouraging pupils' interest in particular industries when there were no job opportunities in those industries when the pupils left school. As a result the development of links was more difficult and vocational developments relied instead on post-16 training schemes such as Youth Training (YT) and its predecessors.

Cognisant of the need for more radical change in schools' approaches to businesses' needs, the government launched, in 1983, the Technical and Vocational Education Initiative (TVEI), which has arguably been the most important single curriculum initiative since the 1944 Education Act. TVEI was aimed at the development of vocational education across the whole curriculum, for all pupils in the 14–18 age range, by increasing the relevance of what was learnt and enhancing the practical application of skills, knowledge and understanding. It affected the whole range of activities at the education-business interface and had significant consequences for management as well as for the curriculum. It provided much important experience on which many later developments have built (see e.g. DES, 1991). Because of its significance, we discuss it in some detail.

TVEI was launched by the then Manpower Services Commission and not by the Department of Education and Science (DES). The Conservative administration was unimpressed by the apparent inability and/or unwillingness of the DES to impose national policies on LEAs and schools because of the dispersed nature of power in the educational system. The government, with the support of the Treasury, felt more effective results could be achieved through a direct agent – the Manpower Services Commission (MSC). The MSC would also be free of the types of attitudes to education which the government felt was contributing to the resistance to more vocational curricula (see Chapter 4 and Dale *et al.*, 1990). TVEI was also in many respects a natural follow-on to national youth training programmes by encouraging developments in schools.

TVEI began in 14 pilot LEAs in 1983/4. LEAs bid for the considerable TVEI funds available (around £2m per LEA over 4 years) and were accepted or rejected according to government-set criteria. In the context of the reduced funds available to education in the early years of the Thatcher governments, there was a considerable incentive for LEAs to bid for these new funds. Central government was, in effect, re-routing educational finance through a new channel in order to stimulate a significant shift in the nature of the curriculum, and a high level of monitoring and evaluation was built into the system to see that real change occurred. In July 1986 the government announced a further £1,000 million over 10 years to extend TVEI to cover all schools in Britain.

One of the chief characteristics of TVEI, especially during its pilot phase, has been its variability between LEAs and between schools. This variability makes it difficult to draw general conclusions about its impact. Nevertheless TVEI's main characteristics and outcomes can be summarised as follows:

The curriculum

- TVEI's impact here is ambiguous. On the whole, there is little evidence of schools having used TVEI to bring about radical change across the curriculum (Barnes *et al.*, 1987). However, given the unpredictable nature of MSC funding, a cautious approach on the part of schools is perhaps not surprising;
- There has been great variation in the extent of change in what was taught from the introduction in some schools of whole new tranches of "TVEI subjects", which previously did not exist, to the use of TVEI resources to teach existing and unmodified syllabuses more effectively (Dale *et al.*, 1990, p. 63);
- TVEI did little to bring about increased curriculum "relevance". Its main contribution has been, firstly, to develop and demonstrate the effectiveness of new ways of bringing about curriculum change and, secondly, to challenge the traditional curriculum. This has meant challenging established subject boundaries *"not just (as) a matter of integration but more centrally ... (as) doing rather than knowing"* (Barnes *et al.*, 1987, p. 120). TVEI *"made some progress towards dislodging the academic from its perch of taken-for-granted pre-eminence. It was bidding to establish a parallel, if not yet equal, set of justifications, contents and practices"* (Dale *et al.*, 1990, p. 118). It made important headway in boosting the status of existing technical and vocational subjects such as Craft, Design and Technology;
- TVEI pioneered a number of important innovations. In general, TVEI represents a fusion of the MSC's version of "experiential pedagogy" based on "real world" experiences and practical activities with existing currents in progressive education (Dale *et al.*, 1990, p. 27). The result has been (TVEI, 1988, 1989; Sadler, 1989; Storey *et al.*, 1986; Bridgwood *et al.*, 1988a,b):
  - highly successful *modular* systems which have been seen to raise choice and motivation (Barnes *et al.*, 1987; Black *et al.*, 1988),
  - further development of new forms of *assessment*, notably profiling and records of achievement (ROAs) which have opened up the possibility of a nationally agreed qualification. This has always been difficult both because of the embedded academic emphasis of education and the patchiness of education-business activities which made accreditation problematic (TVEI, 1988, 1989; Sadler, 1989; Storey *et al.*, 1986; Bridgwood *et al.*, 1988a,b),
  - the development of cross-curricular approaches.

Management and the involvement of business

- TVEI represented a new means of managing education. The MSC had conceived a new model for TVEI, i.e. a local steering group consisting of education, business and perhaps voluntary groups, along with the project director/coordinator, who were responsible for "delivering the contract". However, in the event, the MSC was compelled to work within the existing organisational structures of LEAs. This occurred because of educationalists' success in controlling the system, and because education far more enthusiastically embraced TVEI than did business. Businesses' reluctance can be explained by the lack of any form of institutional mechanism through which to draw on a wide business base (a key gap we discuss at length later). The existing structures of LEAs were highly decentralised, and the LEAs were reluctant to give power to a new structure partly because of problems of political accountability and also because of a fear of being left saddled with a costly management tier due to the uncertainty of long-term MSC funding. This has meant:

(a) considerable school-level autonomy with few LEA-level strategies,
(b) monitoring is not part of a management process, but based on dipstick tests by HMI,
(c) "bolt-on" TVEI teams, not integrated into mainstream LEA procedures, too few TVEI advisors recruited from outside education (almost all were ex-headteachers). Hence there was little outside vision or experience, and they also suffered from rotation between posts,[6]
(e) ineffectual steering groups, which, devoid of a clear role, have been unable to attract and retain the interests of business (Dale, *et al.*, 1990);

- TVEI's location within the education community reinforced the poor record of developing inputs from business. Barnes *et al.* (1987) found that *"little had been achieved in a concrete sense in encouraging employers to take an active role in the overall construction and planning of TVEI curricula"* (p. 135). Businesses' main input had been at classroom rather than school or LEA level, and then employers had been happy to be treated as a resource. Thus, *"developments (have) tended to look inwards, to the educational service for both their broad aims and the intended strategies for delivering these"* (Dale *et al.*, 1990, p. 163). This is strongly supported by a number of our case studies and in detail by the Richmond case study (Bennett *et al.*, 1990b);
- Subsequent study has also demonstrated that the results of TVEI could not be easily separated from other funding. A NAO Report (1991) found that the Department of Employment had inadequate monitoring of the programme and could not differentiate reality from LEA claims. Many of the benefits of TVEI therefore cannot be independently confirmed;
- Despite these drawbacks, TVEI did act as a "seminal force" in drawing to schools' attention the need to develop links with business (Sims, 1988). It was the first national school-based scheme to make work experience mandatory, and stimulated many new activities. However, links developed *"pragmatically rather than in compliance with a master plan"* and only in some areas had *"strategic decision-making ... begun to supersede previously uncoordinated and fragmented approaches"* (*ibid*). Moreover, whilst TVEI was generally successful in persuading teachers of the value of business links, it was less successful in persuading business of the fact (Sadler, 1989). Thus the impact on links has been mixed, being much more effective generally in stimulating work experience than curriculum involvement or other innovations;[7]

TVEI has now been transformed into an extension phase, Technical and Vocational Education Extension (TVEE). It is hoped that this will being about important changes. Evans (undated) suggests that TVEE is a fundamentally different animal, concerning the development of the whole curriculum for 14–18 year olds. Dale *et al.* (1990, p. 173) speak of a switch from a "resource-led" to a "management-led" initiative. However, these comments must now be treated sceptically given the termination of funds for TVEI/TVEE and the effects of the wider changes entailed in the Education Reform Act and the impact of Compacts and EBPs.

The first phases of TVEI point to four key lessons for the interaction between business and education. These are:

(1) TVEI has remained too separate from mainstream education, both in its curriculum and management;

(2) TVEI has not been able properly to involve business, both strategically (LEA level) and in the curriculum (school level);
(3) TVEI was not designed to bring coherence to the increasingly confusing field of link activities; it sought to lever change, but has instead tended to add to the list of uncoordinated developments;
(4) The development of records of achievement in TVEI demonstrated the centrality of assessment and certification in bringing about sustainable shifts in the curriculum. This has been one of its major long term results.

Despite its shortcomings, TVEI prepared the ground for later developments, and, in particular, the search for ways of stimulating the increased participation of business. However, the extent to which the lessons from TVEI actually fed into later developments, either at national or local level, is a point of debate to which we return below.

New solutions: towards integration

During the early 1980s recession it had been the public sector which had mainly financed education-business links. TVEI, in particular, entailed considerable costs. Such an approach was clearly at odds with general government policy on public spending. Since the private sector manifestly stood to gain from the development of effective links with schools and colleges, the Government sought to look for increased use of private resources. Direct business involvement was also more likely to improve the quality of links and the development of ways of addressing the needs of business in the curriculum. Around the middle of the 1980s, a further stimulus to business involvement was given by skill shortages which began to become a problem in certain areas, exacerbated by the declining number of school leavers.

As a result, the second half of the 1980s saw a number of attempts to deepen business involvement in education. 1986 was declared Industry Year. The Royal Society for the encouragement of Arts, Manufactures and Commerce (RSA) became the main promoters of the initiative which was designed to change attitudes between education and business. Industry Year subsequently spawned Industry Matters (IM), under the auspices of the RSA. IM was essentially a campaigning body which *"helped to transform the ways in which industrialists and educationalists perceive each other"* (BiTC, undated a). It ceased to exist at the end of 1989, having fulfilled this overall aim and aware of the danger of competition and duplication of bodies involved in links. Apart from its cultural objective, IM was involved in a number of practical activities. It set up more than 200 local partnerships between education, industry and the local community using its network of Regional and Local Coordinators, many of whom were business secondees. It also played an active role nationally in the promotion of the DTI's Enterprise and Education Initiative with a number of its local groups playing host to the advisers appointed under the scheme. It thus filled some important gaps in the national pattern of business organisation (see below).

It is difficult to measure the overall impact of Industry Year and IM. Its overall aim of changing attitudes cannot be quantified. However, it clearly played an important role nationally and its Education/Industry forum was retained for the first half of 1990 in an advisory capacity to the Foundation for EBPs, so clearly it fuelled future developments. Locally, its record was more varied. In some areas, activities proceeded without much influence from the local IM coordinators, whereas elsewhere they performed an important role. The scenario for any one area depended on both existing levels of organised business activity in education and the talents of individual coordinators. In our case studies IM probably had more of an impact on business than education. In Sheffield, Industry Year was one of a number of strong catalysts of change in attitudes in 1986–7. But most of our case study interviews comment on the failure of Industry Year to establish sustainable activities.

If Industry Year was an attempt to bring about a change in attitudes, the development of City Technology Colleges (CTCs) was the first national attempt to stimulate business to commit substantial resources to education. CTCs were conceived along the lines of US "magnet" schools. Either built *de novo* or through the refurbishment of old schools, CTCs are designed to be centres of excellence for vocational education, selecting pupils on the basis of both academic and technical ability. They are intended to generate competition amongst local schools and, through this market mechanism, raise standards. The intention was that they would be a means of regenerating inner city education and would be funded primarily through business sponsorship.

The first CTC opened in September 1988 and by the end of 1990 15 were either planned or in operation (*TES*, 23 November 1990, pp. 1,4). But, contrary to the Government's hopes, businesses have not been eager to sponsor this initiative and as a result the government has had to inject large sums of public money into the CTCs rather than face the demise of the concept. By November 1990 the government had agreed to spend £140m on the capital costs of CTCs, in contrast to business' £43m (*ibid*). It is also clear that CTCs have not been an exclusively inner city phenomenon, with colleges also appearing in suburban Solihull and Dartford.

The reasons behind the uneasy development of the CTC initiative offer important contrasts to the notions of partnership now offered as the key solution to the education-industry problem. CTCs have proved unpopular with business and education alike. Our interviews indicate that business has been, on the whole, unwilling to sponsor CTCs simply because the level and the nature of the commitment required is not what business is prepared to offer. CTCs represent high initial capital investment and a long term commitment with little in the way of guaranteed return or advantage to the "investor". Business manifestly prefers to offer in-kind support to public-private initiatives rather than direct financial contributions. Those CTCs which have found sponsors have tended to rely on large national or multinational companies such as Dixons or Queensway which have their own reasons for wanting to be identified as sole backers of what tend to be high profile projects. Many businesses, along with education, object to CTCs on the grounds that, rather than generating competition, they generate an elite group of pupils attending extremely well resourced schools. This clashes with many businesses' community policies and compromises their existing link activities. Local supporters have also attempted to introduce CTCs outside mainstream education-industry links. In Cleveland, for example, the first the local Chief Education Officer heard of a proposed CTC was when it appeared in the local press, despite the existence of good links with the local business community. The existence of CTCs outside of the mainstream is, of course, indicative of their failure to secure more widespread support. CTCs were designed to generate competition rather than coordination and have thus tended to become just another initiative contributing to the "patchwork quilt" we have noted earlier.

Proliferation and variation in links

The 1980s saw a burgeoning of national link organisations and initiatives (see Figure 7.1). The major national initiatives achieved considerable expansion of their programmes and secured a presence in most LEAs. By 1988/89 Understanding Industry was providing more than five times as many courses as it had in 1982/83 and was serving over 80 LEAs. It had also expanded into Scotland through its involvement with Young Enterprise. Project Trident increased its number of work experience placements from over 35,000 in 1984 to over 57,000 in 1988, its number of secondees from 35 to 48 and its number of project directors from 37 to 62, giving it 43 "project bases" throughout Great Britain (Project Trident, undated). *SATRO* (the Science and Technology Regional Organisation) expanded its range of activities and by 1988 had established a network of 39 regional centres covering all but 13 LEAs and parts of two more in England and Wales and covering two authorities in Scotland (SCSST/SATRO, 1988). Although established back in the 1960s, Young Enterprise saw its most rapid expansion in the 1980s, nearly quintupling the numbers of participants and companies during the decade (Young Enterprise, undated).

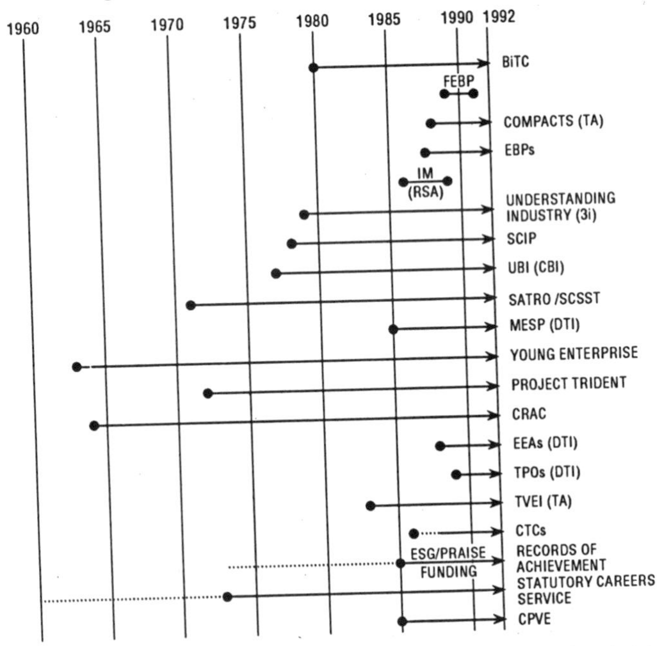

Figure 7.1 The proliferation of education-business link organisations and activities into the 1990s

Despite this burgeoning of the national initiatives, coverage is still patchy both between LEAs and amongst schools within LEAs. The CBI Schools Survey (Cadbury Report: CBI, 1988) for the 1986/87 year, revealed the varied perceived effectiveness and form of links and link organisations. It demonstrated that a wide range of effective links existed between schools and businesses, with most links working well. Only 7–10% of links received a "low" rating for effectiveness. But existing links were nowhere near as extensive as was desirable: over half the respondents to the business survey had no regular links at all with local secondary schools in 1987; less than one-third of schools had sufficient local links to meet the work experience targets required by Government; 37% of schools had no regular links with business at all; and over half of businesses and 70% of schools believed that more links were required.

The Cadbury Task Force identified four barriers which had to be overcome if local links between business and education were to be increased:

i) Better understanding and knowledge of each other;
ii) Better appreciation by business of the costs of failure due to impending youth labour shortage and higher skill requirements;
iii) Gaps in knowledge of effective best practice; and
iv) Gaps in the organisational structure in both companies and schools.

The Task Force report concluded with a number of specific recommendations to CBI members to develop their link activities. These were mainly aimed at encouraging clear company policies on links. The report suggested a local site manager, acting with whichever local organisation was best placed to promote links, and joint national action by business to provide leadership and spread best practice.

Our reanalysis of the data derived from the CBI Schools Questionnaire shows that most links in most authorities came into operation after 1981 (Bennett *et al.*, 1989c). In 12 of the 91 LEAs and Scottish Regions for which data were available less than 20% of links predate 1982. By contrast, in only 9 of the authorities were more links in operation from before 1982 than after 1981. The effectiveness of links, as judged by the schools, was also highly varied. More recent DES surveys confirm, in less detail, these findings (DES Statistical Bulletin 10/90; see also Kirby, 1989a,b).

It is difficult to find more objective measures of school involvement with business. Readily-available national statistics do not, on the whole, concern themselves with the specifics of school practice. In general, there is considerable variation between LEAs in educational expenditure, and this gives a very rough indication of the magnitude of variation in resources potentially available for link activities, but the translation is, of course, in no sense automatic. The only other readily available indicator is the number of careers officers employed by LEAs, which gives a general idea of commitment to the world of work. The range in number of careers officers per 1,000 secondary school pupils is from under one to over 5, with most LEAs having under 2. Even these differences do not reflect the extent of variation in the quality of the careers service nor the role it plays; our detailed case study work shows that in some LEAs it clearly has a pivotal proactive role in link development, whilst in many others it is moribund.

All evidence, however, points to major expansion of links during the 1980s. Though laudable, this was largely uncoordinated. Some LEAs attempted to weave the different initiatives together but to varying degrees of success. Some, such as Salford, had established education-industry units to try to bring the diverse projects together. On the whole, there was a lack of high-level strategic lead from senior officers, not least because of the immense increase in the demands on their time from other directions, most importantly the 1988 Education Reform Act. Links initiation and maintenance was still left to individuals, usually in schools. Many, if not most, LEAs had no accurate idea of the nature of links by their schools nor who to contact in them in order to gain an overview. It was not surprising, therefore, that there was no systematic, structured involvement by employers (see also Warwick, 1989; Blandford and Jamieson, 1989).

Towards partnership: the Compacts initiative

Whilst much had been done to foster links, there was a clear need to fill the system gap by finding a means of binding business and education into closer collaboration. A concept from the USA provided the opportunity: the Boston Compact. Originating in 1982, the Compact was a series of agreements between the Boston Public School Board, local employers, trade unions, universities and community groups designed to raise educational attainment and bring about a closer matching of pupils' qualifications to the needs of industry. The key mechanism to bring this about was the agreement on the part of employers to *"endeavour to provide job opportunities to Boston public high school graduates"* provided the schools improved *"the quality of secondary education"* (Employers' Letter of Intent, 1982). The Boston School Board undertook to produce measurable improvements in attendance and drop-out rates and in attainment in reading and maths, for which employers pledged to give *priority* to Compact graduates. Allowing employers to decide on students' suitability for jobs was seen as crucial to the scheme (Rossano, 1985; Hargroves, 1987).

The Boston Compact provided a clear incentive for employers to play a leading role in developing links. Its potential to forge strong and lasting education-business collaboration in Britain was first realised by the London Enterprise Agency and officers of the Inner London Education Authority (ILEA) who launched the first British Compact in September 1987 in East London. With signs of successful partnership emerging in London and Boston, the Department of Employment through the then MSC launched a national initiative in 1988 to fund initially 15 Compacts in Urban Programme Areas (UPAs) in Britain. However, so overwhelming was the response to the invitation for bids that the number was increased to 30, and eventually all 57 UPAs developed Compacts.

The British Training Agency-funded Compacts have, in many ways, gone further than the original Boston scheme. The most important feature, in this respect, is the employer's undertaking: in Boston this was simply a pledge of priority; in Britain it was a *guarantee*: if students attain specified targets, they are guaranteed a job, or training leading to a job, with a Compact employer. As we shall show, this has become an important difference between USA and British Compacts.

Key features of Compacts

Compact clearly differs from past initiatives in a number of key respects. First, whilst significant *resources* have been committed to Compact, these are pump-priming grants which last only for approximately 2 years. It is a central feature of the concept that LEAs will draw on existing resources both in the school and, most significantly, outside in the wider community, principally amongst business. Second, Compact is unique amongst educational initiatives in the centrality of *target setting* and *monitoring*. Whilst TVEI has done much to move in this direction, Compact takes the concepts one step further and provides incentives for the pupils themselves and targets for the schools, rather than simply making further funding dependent upon the achievement of certain goals. This is something new for the culture of the education service and its impact could be profound.

Third, Compacts are based on a *signed agreement* requiring not only the LEA and schools, but also employers, to commit themselves. This was a crucial innovation. Fourth, Compact involved *individual schools* rather than LEAs. This was a crucial lesson from the Boston experience which showed the gaps that could emerge between managers and schools if schools themselves did not sign up to the commitment.[8] Fifth, Compact provided the opportunity to bring *coherence* to activities at the interface of business and education. As the *Compacts Development Handbook* states (TC, 1988) *"Compacts should provide a framework for structuring and focusing business-education activities ... YTS, TVEI and the Careers Service represent invaluable expertise and resources for the*

Compact. Partnerships will need to examine how best to integrate these and other programmes under the Compact umbrella" (p. 13). As one Compact bid states, Compact is *"an umbrella delivery mechanism"* which, apart from guaranteeing jobs, *"can also be used to coordinate and promulgate other schemes and initiatives"* (Kirklees submission for development funding, p. 1). For Wester Hailes, Compact is seen as *"a logical extension of initiatives already underway"* (bid for development funding, p. 1); for Doncaster, *"a facilitator whose role is to enhance the existing links and to initiate new ones"* (Application for Full Funding, 1989, p. 1).

Sixth, and most importantly of all, Compact has acted as a vital catalyst for *partnership*. This is likely to prove the most significant and enduring outcome of the initiative. In Boston, Compact had been preceded by many years of close cooperation between business and education, culminating in 1981 in the formation of the Boston Private Industry Council and the Jobs Collaboration through which companies hired students for periods of work experience (Rossano, 1985). Few areas in Britain could boast such a high degree of collaboration by the late 1980s, as indeed could few in the USA (see Stratton, 1989). Though it can be argued that such collaboration should precede a Compact agreement, there is no doubting Compact's role as a stimulus and lever of change. Because of its importance to our discussion, we examine it in some detail.

Developing partnerships through Compact

Partnership was important to Compact from the outset. In granting funds, the then MSC laid down *"strength of partnership"* as one of its criteria (MSC, 1988). However, at first, little thought was given to the nature of partnership or how it should come about, other than stating that *"... Compacts must have strong leadership ... commitment and involvement ..."* (ibid, para 1). It was not until the publication of the *Compacts Development Handbook* (TC, 1988) that further elaboration was made. The *Handbook* states that a "strong" EBP is *"the essential foundation for a successful Compact"* (p. 3). The elements of a successful EBP are given as:

- Common ownership and sharing of benefits;
- Backing of top leaders;
- Measurable objectives within a long-term strategy;
- The establishing of monitoring procedures;
- Development of ways to adapt to changing circumstances.

But *"... partnerships are (not) synonymous with Compacts"* (ibid): *"by establishing clear measurable goals, Compacts take business-education partnerships a stage further"* (ibid). But whether these goals need include a job guarantee as the TA stressed or, indeed, whether a partnership can deliver a guarantee which works, is debatable.

As to the nature of that partnership, the TA's position has undergone further change. In its guidelines for the second round of development grants (TA, 1989c), the TA states:*"The first and most important condition to be met is that there must be a partnership between employers and education authorities* ***at a senior level****"* (para 9, our emphasis) based on a *"solid record of local partnerships"* (ibid, para 25).

Despite these requirements, it is clear from our analysis of the bids for funding[9] and our case studies that the various "partners" who bid for the first tranche of development grants were in different states of readiness for the scheme. The final allocation of grants was clearly designed both to encourage the relatively advanced partnerships and to stimulate them in places where the chances of one "spontaneously" arising were slim. Among LEAs receiving first round Compacts, Sheffield, Humberside and Leicestershire had formal education-business partnerships already in place or about to be ratified, whilst in Liverpool and Newham such ideas seemed remote, even if there were established networks of school-industry links. In Wolverhampton the type of partnership envisaged in Compact had "*no history of its own but the constituent elements and their respective track records (in education, training and employment) will stand close scrutiny ...*" (bid for development funding, p. 7). This was the type of situation prevailing in the vast majority of areas.

The extent to which areas were "ready" for Compact obviously depended upon both the degree to which local business was organised and the extent of previous links. Table 7.1 shows the way in which the employers were represented in the first wave of Compacts. (Although there are 30 schemes, the four London projects are all based upon the single LEBP, and for this reason there are only 27 partnerships.) The table shows the importance of having an existing business organisation that can be used for organising the employer commitment. This is a Chamber of Commerce in 56% of cases. Our case studies show that, where there is a history of business organisation and, moreover, a history of public-private liaison, as in Birmingham for example, Compact has been added to the broad canvas of initiatives. Other areas, however, have clearly had to work very hard to find a voice for local business interests (see Bennett *et al*, 1989c). This is often related to the underlying industrial structure (see Chapter 10). Where local businesses are predominantly small, as in parts of the West Midlands, this is a particular problem because of the lack of what the TA called "lead companies". In Newham, it was necessary for a limited company to be formed, around which a nucleus of businesses could be linked, in order to secure operational funding beyond the development phase. Lead companies simply do not exist in many localities, and, even where they do, as with ICI in Cleveland, or Whitbread in London, the representation of small businesses, which collectively may account for a significant proportion of local employment, remains a problem.

Table 7.1 Employer representation in Compact partnerships (first round)

Organisation	No. of Compacts	%
Chamber of Commerce	15	55.6
Chamber of Commerce with other bodies	3	11.1
Formal forum, partnership, committee, etc.	5	18.5
Training Association	1	3.7
LEN	1	3.7
CBI (Regional Office)	1	3.7
Other (Clydebank Economic Development Company)	1	3.7
Total	27	100

Source: LSE analysis of 1988 first round bids for development funding

As far as the state of readiness of education is concerned, Bennett *et al.* (1989a) have indicated the nature of the variation in local authority experience in Vocational Education and Training (VET) and the substantial differences between areas. More direct evidence has come from an internal DES paper (King, 1989; see also Bennett, 1992) which has identified a variety of levels of school-industry links. In most cases in 1987 a poor LEA base was available from which to develop Compact and other link activities (q.v. below). A very varied and generally weak preparedness existed when Compacts were introduced in 1987 and 1988.

Despite their lack of guidance on the nature of partnership, the TA rejected a number of bids for development funding in the first round primarily because of gaps in business links. In all, 14 LEAs failed in the first instance, though all finally secured support. Interviews in key areas, and with TA officials, have shown that concern for lack of support at high levels led to the failure of certain bids, e.g. Sandwell. Other bids only subsequently succeeded because they were recast. Thus, in Tyneside, the bid from five LEAs for one Compact encompassing the whole of Tyne and Wear was deemed by the TA to be unworkable and smaller areas were subsequently considered.

In a number of cases, the TA has tried to make local partnerships run before they can walk. This is not unique to Compact, however. Indeed it is typical of the TA's approach, which eschews rigorous piloting in favour of "learning by doing". Such an approach has the advantage that an initiative can be spread rapidly, and it is true that initial phases of Compact can take place without "major new structures or administrative procedures" (Wester Hailes bid) at the start. However, whether Compact is sustainable without the development of major local partnership structures in the long run is debatable. Many partnerships rely upon *individual* relationships, particulary in their early stages; but suffer from gaps in commitment or the lack of vision of how to establish appropriate structures to sustain them.

Two Compacts have had major difficulties because of these problems. In Dundee, our case study interviews show that the Compact's initial failure to win second year funding rested on the wish of the local authority rather than the Chamber of Commerce to be the main signatory. In Derby, the lack of high-level support for Compact together with problems associated with interlocking county (then Labour-controlled) and city (then Conservative-controlled) boundaries has led to difficulties. Both exhibit the problems of a central city within a rural area, discussed at length in Chapter 14.

Assessment of Compacts

Compacts have achieved a great deal. By 1991/92 they had covered about 92,000 children in nearly 500 inner city schools with nearly 9,000 employers and training providers involved.[10] But Compacts have not been without their problems. Indeed, during 1989 the Boston Compact which provided the examplar for Britain, seemed to be on the verge of falling apart. Although there had been success on a number of fronts (Rossano, 1985), the main target of the scheme, the drop-out rate, had not been substantially reduced (Hargroves, 1987). The central problem had been the failure to transmit targets and incorporate fully those most central to the scheme – the schools, teachers and pupils (Stratton, 1989). The Boston Compact has since been reformulated. Its central difficulty, of existing at too high a level of management, was foreseen in Britain by firmly locating the commitment at school as well as LEA level. We assess below the key lessons of Britain's Compacts.

The Training Agency conception and the job guarantee

Compacts have been a central government initiative and have therefore been coloured by Training Agency conceptions of their purpose. Unfortunately, the Training Agency seems to have adopted, especially in the early stages of the scheme, a narrow conception of Compact, which contrasts with the interpretations often sought by business leaders. There appear to be a number of reasons for this. First, it was important for the TA to be able to justify to other government departments and to the Treasury a new scheme, given the existing and planned substantial investment in TVEI. Compact could be justified by arguing that, whilst TVEI focused very much on the curriculum (i.e. what took place *in school*), Compact was essentially about what happened *after school*. Much more than TVEI, Compact was about linking education and employment and was therefore more likely to be acceptable to both DES who feared that Compact would encroach on TVEI and the Treasury who held the purse strings. Second, Compact was focused on inner city areas and was part of the DE's commitment to the Action for Cities programme. The third reason for the narrow vision stemmed from the TA's need to enforce the terms of the contract under which Compact was operationalised. TVEI had been subject to the criticism that it had been "captured" by the education policy community (e.g. North, 1987) and that it was difficult to assess quantitatively. Compact was to be given clearly measurable objectives in the shape of the job guarantee and other targets.

The outcome was an over-preoccupation with the jobs guarantee and an unwillingness to allow the Compact concept to be broadened beyond the terms of its contract. For local actors this was unhelpful. Our interviews revealed that the TA had to spend considerable time and effort persuading not just educationalists but also employers that the guarantee was both necessary and achievable. Many remained unconvinced, and some non-TA funded partnerships (e.g. Waltham Forest) eschewed the notion. The first results of the East London Compact showed that only 10 of the 200 guaranteed jobs were taken up (ILEA, 1987a,b,c), thus demonstrating the contradiction inherent in having a guarantee based on pupil achievement when raising achievement is likely to bring about a welcomed rise in the staying-on-rate! Our interviews also show that the guarantee can generate false hopes and expectations amongst pupils and employers which can lead to misunderstandings and recriminations. The centrality of the guarantee for the TA also flies in the face of US results which stress that it *"should not be overemphasised – it is an important instrument but should be seen as part of a wider strategy"* (Kirby, 1989a, p. 5).

In the long-run, the value of the guarantee will probably be shown to have been in stimulating business involvement by catching the imagination of some employers. Compact has acted as a means of engaging business so that they might become involved in deeper and more meaningful curriculum development. Once the value of links *per se* are demonstrated, the need for a guarantee arguably disappears. Our interviews indicate the receding importance of the guarantee, over time, amongst local partners, its maintenance in order to satisfy the TA contract being seen as an increasingly irrelevant nuisance, rather than something of value.

Despite the TA's agenda, Compact has in practice become concerned with what goes on in schools, as much as about what comes after. With the development of EBPs, the TA concept of Compact has remained narrow, so much so that Compacts and EBPs are differentiated and seen as existing alongside one another. "On the ground" in local areas, such fine distinctions are meaningless, and the conception of the two as somehow distinct, whilst necessary for contractual purposes, generates confusion and appears more as an attempt by the TA to "hold on" in the face of the growing effectiveness of the DES who have been able to claim a greater role in EBPs because of their curriculum links. As a result local actors have broadened the vision in a patchy way, and often by stealth, against TA resistance.

Outcomes

It is not our purpose to make a major assessment of the outcomes of Compacts in terms of pupil achievement. This has been done, with fairly positive conclusions, and is being carried out in great detail elsewhere (see e.g. Nuttall et al., 1991; Lawler and McKay (in Warwick, ed., 1989)). However, here we highlight the main findings on pupil outcomes and indicate other findings supported by our own interviews.

A key outcome is that there is every indication that Compacts are stimulating pupils to stay-on at school. The first results from the East London Compact were somewhat mixed, but later results (see e.g. Nuttall *et al.*, 1991; see also *Financial Times*, 13 March 1991; *TES*, 15 March 1991) indicate an important rise in the number of students staying on at school beyond the age of 16.

In terms of stimulating business interests, Compacts have undeniably had a major impact. In East London, the vast majority of Compact businesses wanted to increase their involvement after 1 year and, irrespective of the extent of their previous links, all companies had shown greater involvement as a result of Compact (ILEA, 1989c). Our case study interviews show that there has also been a significant increase in employer involvement. One director, from education, was "amazed" at employers' commitment and their willingness to undertake work for Compact at short notice. Business has seconded staff to act as directors, and in-kind support in the form of office equipment, stationery and office space has proved invaluable to many Compacts. Compacts have also increased the mutual understanding between employers and educationalists. The process of setting goals for education has been a new experience for business. It has entailed major learning in many cases. A number of interviewees reported to us the unrealistic assumptions many employers had about the constraints that operate on what children can be reasonably expected to achieve. In Salford and other areas, for example, employers were surprised to learn that there is a local practice whereby older children have to assume responsibility in the home for young siblings (in single parent, Asian and two-working parent households) which makes a 100% punctuality record impossible for many pupils.

Linking the initiatives

One of the hopes surrounding Compact was that it would improve *integration* of the various education-business activities and the actors involved in them. However, there must be reservations about the extent to which Compacts have acted as "umbrellas". A distinction needs to be drawn, too, between the different degrees of integration which have been achieved by different Compacts. Compacts can simply be umbrellas for loose agglomerations of activities, or they can become the means through which genuine integration can take place, involving common decision-making and working towards agreed objectives, rather than simply contributing to a general trend of events. Our researches suggest there are far more areas in which Compacts act as either a "loose agglomeration" or "just another initiative", than there are Compacts which have "fully integrated" education-business links.

Perhaps greatest cause for concern is given by the failure to bring about an integration of Compacts with EBPs and TVEI. This has been a problem as much for the TA as for local actors and, indeed, much derives from governmental and TA fragmentation of activity. We have already demonstrated the significance of TVEI and the lessons it provides for EBPs. However, there is reason to believe that, at the centre, there was little feeding through of conclusions from TVEI into Compacts. There was certainly physical isolation of the two, the TA's TVEI Unit moving from London only in 1990 to be housed under the same roof as Compacts at Moorfoot in Sheffield. Moreover, Compacts and TVEI were conceived and *set up* as separate entities with *different* local management structures. Hence, at local level there has been a tendency for TVEI, Compact, and LEA-based EBPs to remain compartmentalised, sometimes with the replication of the physical separation found in central government. TVEI units in local authorities now have established traditions and staff with vested interests (see Dale *et al.*, 1990, p. 173) who are unlikely to acquiesce to being subsumed by Compact, which has been a goal sought by the TA. Moreover, in some areas TVEI consortia have provided the basis for EBPs, especially in non-Compact areas (Foster, 1990). Whilst many LEAs have established committees or forums on which sit representatives of Compact, TVEI, etc., the extent to which this has led to shared objectives beyond the banal is highly questionable.

The national picture is clearly highly varied. But it has been a significant achievement of Compacts to "ratchet up" employer involvement in their communities and it is this which may further stimulate integration by creating a force for change from outside education which was missing from TVEI.[11] However, there remains great scope for bringing together the management achievements and potential of Compacts, and the curriculum and curriculum management achievements of TVEI.

Beyond Compacts: the development of Education-Business Partnerships

In the long run, the Compact initiative's main achievement will probably have been to have demonstrated the importance of formal structures and targets, and to have acted as a major stimulus for the formation of EBPs. By offering the potential to coordinate local links, Compacts have stimulated debate and the development of concepts regarding the *effective management of links* and the most appropriate organisational form to achieve this. There has, however, been an emerging tension between Compacts and EBPs.

EBPs have developed more autonomously than Compacts. They have been stimulated by LEAs' own awareness of a coordination gap in their efforts to link with business and by general publicity about the need for improved structures associated with Compact, the CBI (1988) Task Force, and the activities of BiTC. As a result of a variety of trends, therefore, a national pattern of EBPs has been developing. Figure 7.2 shows the emerging pattern at the end of the 1990–1 year, based on LSE research for the CBI. This map is based on a conception of 5 levels of EBP development developed by the authors for FEBP and the CBI.[12] It can be summarised as follows:

- *Level 1*: Links exist only for single schools with no LEA commitment, no designated liaison teachers, work experience isolated from classrooms, no recognisable business liaison structure with LEA, no specification of link objectives and low frequency of link activity.
- *Level 2*: A number of schools engage in *ad hoc* activity with some LEA support from below level 3, some schools have designated liaison staff and there is debriefing in the classroom or use of essays about work experience, there are recognisably stable commitments from businesses with some designated liaison staff, an occasional

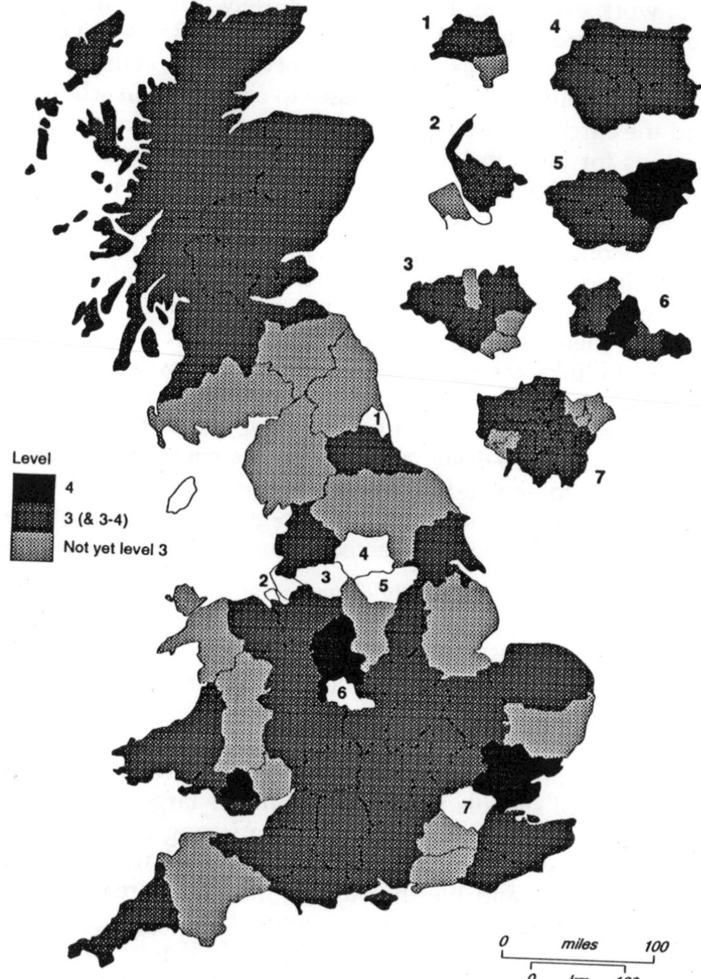

Figure 7.2 Map of status of LEAs by level of EBP in 1991 (City of London, which has one primary school, is omitted)
Source: Bennett, 1992

"forum" or "taking shop" between the LEA and business, a statement about the values of links and a high frequency of links.

- *Level 3*: There is an organised structure for business-education links over at least a proportion of schools, with a formal LEA commitment. Most schools and colleges have designated liaison staff and work experience contributes to GCSE project assessment, a stable and recognisable business organisation is in place which meets regularly and formally with the LEA at least 4 times per year with some designated business liaison staff committing a significant amount of time to links. Links are monitored to a specific set of objectives. All pupils have significant link experiences at year 4 and above. Compact, to a basic Training Agency contract, is at this level.
- *Level 4*: Almost all primary and secondary schools and colleges are involved with links and have designated liaison staff, there is substantial LEA commitment at

above level 3, work experience is integrated closely into GCSE *and* A level in some subjects, the LEA coordinates links across most of the fields of TVEI, Careers, SCIP, and across most heads of primary and secondary schools, colleges and special needs, there are significant initiatives for businesses to contribute in schools, including staff appraisal and the curriculum. All children are involved in links, and there is a strong curriculum focus for links in the classroom. There are frequent meetings between business and school/LEA partners with a formal structure, action agenda and some delegated powers to set, achieve and monitor a wider set of targets. This is satisfied by an expanded Compact.

- *Level 5*: A committed, signed partnership is in place with staffing and an action plan involving *all* schools and colleges such that *every* young person 5–19 will have a significant part of their learning experience through link activities. LEA staff commit substantial time to links across all main departments, with *all* schools and colleges having designated liaison staff with a proportion of time release. Work experience is a strong part of the classroom curriculum of GCSE and A level in *all* subjects. A large number of businesses have designated staff, some contribute secondments or other significant resources to demanding targets, e.g. mentoring, curriculum projects. The Partnership has strategic meetings, action sub-groups and strong delegated powers to agree and monitor annual targets across *all* main departments. A full EBP.

This set of criteria is plainly not entirely clear cut, and it is quite possible for an LEA to have some developments at one level, whilst other developments are at other levels. Thus classifying a given school or LEA into any level is hazardous because it over-simplifies. There are also a number of other constraints on interpretation, which we discuss elsewhere (see Bennett, 1992).

Figure 7.2 shows that whilst a large area of Britain has now reached level 3 or better, a considerable number of LEAs remain below level 3. Level 3 is a minimum target for an EBP (a limited set of schools involved, or limited targets), so the map shows the areas where most progress is required. There is a strong concentration of the level 3 areas in metropolitan and urban centres. The greatest relative progress is required in outer London and English and Welsh counties, in order to reach level 3. But all areas have the similar problem of needing to get beyond level 3.

The assessment of EBPs is analysed in more detail in Figure 7.3 for a matched sample of 76 LEAs for which sufficient data exist to evaluate their change over time. The figure shows the very considerable progress from 1986/87 to 1988/89. Almost all LEAs were at level 2 in 1986/87, but by 1988/89 most (59% of the sample) had progressed to become either close to level 3 (28%, denoted level 2–3) or had attained level 3 (31% of the sample). Thus from a position where 96% of the sample was at level 2 or below, 59% had attained a level of 2–3 or above. This was a major achievement over a 2-year period and shows that a process of catching up occurred.

The catching up process was most marked in the metropolitan areas. A higher proportion of the metropolitan districts (67%) progressed to level 2–3 or 3 than for the non-metropolitan counties (57%). This was particularly true of the movements to level 3, where 47% of metropolitan districts attained level 3, but only 19% of non-metropolitan counties. The explanation for this lies mainly with the impact of Compact. Compacts supported by the Training Agency were only available in Urban Programme Areas (UPAs), almost all of which are in the metropolitan districts and London. Our classification of levels makes a Compact (or its equivalent) one of the criteria for level 3. As well as being responsible for the metropolitan bias of the progress to levels 2–3 and 3, Compact is thus also responsible for the catching up process.

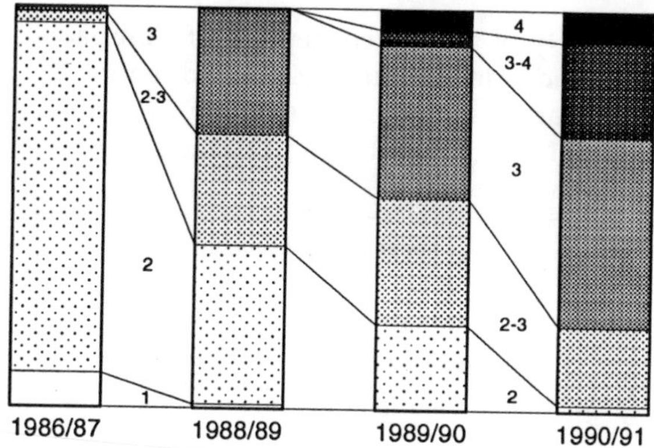

Figure 7.3 Progress of LEAs between 1986/87 and 1990/91 from a matched sample of 76 LEAs
Source: Bennett, 1992

Over the period 1988/89 to 1990/91 considerable further progress was achieved. No LEAs are below level 2: level 2 is reduced to 1%, and 78% are at level 3 or above. Of these, 28% are at level 3–4 or above. Figure 7.3, therefore, records steady progress towards a deepening of EBPs in the matched sample. As in the earlier analysis, TA Compacts are responsible for a large proportion of the changes occurring. Of 66 LEAs attaining level 3 or higher in 1990, 52 (79%) had a TA Compact at least in its development phase.

However, by 1990/91 there is some indication that the process of EBP development is slowing down. Only 6% of LEAs have reached level 4 and above; most are making marginal developments from level 3 to reach a level 3–4. Of these, almost all are developing from Compacts.

The reasons for this slowing down derive from a number of factors. One has been the uncertainty of how TECs would relate to EBPs and the level of their funding. Another was the delay in the announcement of funding for the government's EBP programme, discussed in the next section. But probably the greatest problems have been (i) getting partnerships going in some of the most difficult areas, and (ii) raising a vision of what is required. A certain complacency may have set in that level 3, a Compact, is good enough. There is some evidence of this in the surprisingly indecisive phrasing in the Department of Employment's Partnership Primer and Partnership Handbook (EDG, 1990a, 1990b) in which the impression is given that very broad variations in targets sought are acceptable. Although it is certainly important to encourage flexibility to local needs, flexibility appears more often to be urged as a result of indecision between the rival pressures of DES on the classroom curriculum and the DE on the relevance of education to the world of work.

These difficulties have to be set in the context of the strong variations in local conditions and institutions which we discuss in Chapters 9–14. Our detailed studies demonstrate that the prime-movers in EBPs differ depending upon the strength of local institutions. As shown in Figure 7.4, where business organisations are weak, the LEA may be the only leadership available that is capable of organising coherent local links. Where businesses are strong, the leadership of that link may differ considerably: in some cases it may be large local firms (as with ICI on Teesside or Whitbread in the former ILEA); in other cases it may be a Chamber of Commerce (as in Sheffield, Birmingham or Manchester); in other cases it is an enterprise agency, as in Mid

Glamorgan. The inflexibility of the TA conception of Compacts created problems in all the areas on the left hand side of Figure 7.4. The advent of TECs may make this no easier since, as we shall argue below, the leverage of central government-funded EBPs is too small to affect LEAs unless they are already progressing in this direction.

LOCAL EDUCATION AUTHORITY	LOCAL BUSINESS ORGANISATION: Weak	LOCAL BUSINESS ORGANISATION: Strong
Weak	Waltham Forest Richmond-upon-Thames	
(centre)	Dundee/Tayside Teeside Mid-Glamorgan	
Strong	Sandwell Newham	Birmingham Manchester / Salford Sheffield former ILEA

Figure 7.4 Leading local agents in EBPs, 1989–91, depending on local institutional strengths

As a result of interactions between the local education and business environment and government funding criteria, EBPs can be viewed as placed along four possible dimensions of organisation and management (shown in Figures 7.5 and 7.6). In Figure 7.5 is contrasted (i) whether EBPs are single initiatives within school; multiple activities; or form a coherent general school policy, with (ii) whether EBPs are based on *ad hoc*, informal agreements; or constitute formal contracts between the parties. In Figure 7.6 is contrasted (iii) whether EBPs involve individual students, cohorts, or single schools and colleges; groups of institutions; or cover the whole of a local education authority or even groups of local education authorities, with (iv) whether EBPs are based on a number of individual businesses; business organisations; or use a general business agreement covering (as far as possible) all individual businesses and business organisations in a given area.

The interrelations between these dimensions shown in the Figures allow us to contrast the *London Compact*, as originally developed by LEntA / ILEA, which appears in the centre of Figure 7.5 (informal agreement to specified targets initiatives), and in the left centre of Figure 7.6 (individual businesses making an agreement with a selected group of schools), with *TA Compacts*, which are located in the right centre of Figure 7.5 (formal contract for a group of initiatives with specific targets), and in the left centre of Figure 7.6 (cover a selection of schools or colleges through agreement with a particular business group offering job guarantees). *TECs* have ambitions to be located in the lower right of Figure 7.5 (agreements, formal and informal, as part of a coherent general policy), and in the lower right of Figure 7.6 (a general business agreement for a whole local education authority or a group of local education authorities). Some TECs are beginning to put such an ambitious plan in place. But most appear to be located in a similar place to Compacts, but covering whole LEAs.

Our various case study areas are shown located in different parts of the figures to exhibit the local contrasts in the 1990 year. These contrasts are used to exhibit key

	Individual and adhoc initiatives	Informal and sustained agreements	Formal contract and performance assessment
Separate initiatives in individual schools	Waltham Forest Richmond-upon-Thames Sandwell		
Groups of initiatives		London Compact	TA/TEC Compacts Manchester Salford Newham Dundee Birmingham
Coherent general policy			Sheffield Teesside Mid-Glamorgan Coventry

Figure 7.5 Possible forms of education-business relationship and the spread of policy pursued in 1989–91

	Individual businesses	Business Organisations	General business agreement
Individual students, classes, schools or colleges	Waltham Forest Richmond-upon-Thames Sandwell		
Groups of schools and colleges	London Compact former ILEA	TA Compacts Mid-Glamorgan Dundee Manchester Birmingham	
Whole LEA or group of LEAs	Newham	Salford TECs	Sheffield Teesside Coventry

Figure 7.6 Possible forms of business groups involved in education links and the extent of education involvement in 1989–91

institutional issues of local networking in Chapter 9–14. Clearly there are simplifications involved in these figures; but they do show the *dominant* mode of articulation of business interests in the various cases.

TECs, Compacts and EBPs

Compacts have provided an important stimulus to the establishment of EBPs in Britain. But both Compacts and EBPs are being affected by the advent of TECs. For Compacts the link is a direct one, with TECs being given responsibility for their finance. For EBPs, the impact of TECs is likely to vary from place to place. EBPs will receive some finance from the Partnerships Initiative, under which local EBPs can bid for grants to support development through their respective TECs. Our research reveals that even without the

Partnerships Initiative and the shift in formal responsibility for Compacts, close links would in any case have been forged between Compacts/EBPs and TECs. This had already happened in lead areas such as Mid Glamorgan and Coventry.

A key factor compelling such links has been the need to have a sustained and stable business commitment and to develop a local vision amongst senior leaders of education and business. Stability and vision are absolutely crucial if EBPs are to succeed in bringing about a genuine integration of activities at the interface of education and business. It may well be the TECs rather than EBPs which offer the greatest potential to develop that vision. This is a result of the different ways TECs and Compacts/EBPs have been set up.

TECs are intended to be run by senior local business leaders and to have a much higher profile than Compacts; the stakes are noticeably higher for TECs. Compacts, by contrast, have received much less attention as far as organisation is concerned, employer *bodies* have tended to be the main business signatories and there has been a high profile *national*, as opposed to local, company commitment to the initiative. For example, in September/October 1989 some 19 of the 27 Compacts then in existence had managers on secondment from national companies – often at Director level. Notwithstanding their major contribution, which has sometimes been pivotal (as in Ogwr in Mid Glamorgan – see Chapter 13), it is doubtful that these line managers are capable of providing the same calibre of leadership that it is hoped TECs will offer. Similarly, Compact entails the involvement of *organisations* to *represent* business whilst TECs involve individual chief executives, in theory, representing no-one other than themselves. This arguably places Compacts in a disadvantageous position. The need for strong local leadership has been given a much higher priority for the TECs project than for Compacts. Consequently, there is the danger of an imbalance emerging which will lead to Compacts being subsumed by TECs. At the same time, however, it is likely that those people who choose to become involved in TECs will also be those who choose to be part of an EBP, so the distinction in practice may be of little consequence in many places. This is especially likely where the geographical boundaries of a Compact and a TEC are coterminous, as in Sheffield. It is least likely where Compact forms a small part of a large LEA, as in London TECs and the UPA core cities of many non-metropolitan counties, where tensions appear to have been greatest. This gap in vision between EBPs and Compacts was recognised as early as Kirby's (1989a) study of the USA, but has not fully informed TA practice.

In leading partnership areas, a synergy is being developed between EBPs and TECs with ideas from one feeding into the other. In Newham, employers active in the development of the Compact formed a core nucleus for the formation of the London East TEC. In Teesside, EBPs were recognised early on as a crucial part of TEC activity and a coherent plan developed – mainly through the Cleveland LEN and Cleveland LEA (CEN/CEA, 1990; and interviews with TEC Board, chief executive, and LEA). In Sheffield, it was discussions over education which provided key concepts for the growth of a wider partnership leading to the launch of the TEC. But in other areas the links between TECs, Compacts and EBPs are not coherent. TECs may cover more than one LEA or, more rarely, only part of an LEA. They may encompass both Compacts *and* EBPs. In these areas, the sorting out of arrangements is an important priority.

How TECs, Compacts and EBPs interface in practice is only beginning to emerge. With central government backing away from the prescription of national models, considerable flexibility is possible, but targets are becoming confused. This also appears to be the line followed with respect to TVEI, where TECs have also been given no responsibilities. TVEI still has its own management structure involving local TVEI groups. Logic would suggest some connection between TECs and TVEI groups. But no mandatory link has so far been introduced so local areas are being left to sort out these connections. This is likely to lead to great variation in the effectiveness of TEC-TVEI-EBP interactions; the LENs initiative suggests that such voluntarism in education planning does not auger well (see Bennett *et al.*, 1990a).

In this regard we would argue that, with the Partnership Initiative, a major opportunity was lost. Funding of this initiative is orientated via the Department of Employment, but only at a relatively low level (£10,000 development phase; £50,000 in year 1 and £25,000 in year 2, per LEA). This is not enough to lever mainstream education nor does it offer to business a long-term commitment. The announcement in October 1991 of Training, Education and Enterprise Directorate's (TEED) intention to extend the Compact approach to all LEAs represents an attempt to regain the initiative. Compacts are now to become the general vehicle for education-business links rather than EBPs, so that the Partnership Initiative may be shortlived. This strengthens the hands of the DE, has allowed it to win money from the Treasury, and provides larger scale resources for up to £100,000 per year for 4 years. But it confuses the purpose of Compacts. It usefully extends the concept to general goal setting by pupils and meaningful involvement of local employers in a committed "deal". It also provides enough money to lever some change. However, it still leaves education-business links struggling for identity.

Left outside mainstream DES practice and curriculum developments, it is clear that the government has so far stepped aside from properly integrating business links into the *system* of education. As a consequence, it is still too easy for an EBP or Compact to be a "bolt-on", effectively running a structure for certain kinds of links and work experience, but remaining outside of the mainstream of classroom practice (see Cleverdon (1989) in Bennett *et al.*, 1989b). This is why we believe there has been a slowdown, shown in Figure 7.3, in the rate of progress of EBPs beyond level 3 to levels 4 and 5. The deeper explanation of these trends thus leads us to examine more closely developments in mainstream education following the Education Reform Act.

The impact of the Education Reform Act, 1988

The developments we have discussed in this chapter are being crucially affected by the enormous changes introduced to education by the Education Reform Act (the ERA) in 1988, particularly the national curriculum and Local Management of Schools (LMS). TVEI, Compacts and EBPs have emerged from a different part of central government to the ERA and, as a result of this, tensions have been introduced. TVEI, Compacts and EBPs have involved the introduction of new management structures at LEA level and new and effective forms of cooperation between schools and colleges. These management initiatives are somewhat discordant with the thrust of the management changes of the ERA, which emphasise the school, choice and competition (see e.g. Ball, 1990; especially pp. 59–69). The ERA involves a redefinition of the role of the LEA and a major increase in the autonomy of schools through LMS. Yet the structure of EBPs and TECs has emphasised partnership structures at the LEA level. These tensions can be resolved only by a school-based and curriculum-based approach by EBPs and other link initiatives.

The ERA has introduced the national curriculum. This establishes 10 "foundation" subjects which, it was originally intended, all students would take up to the age of 16. The attainment targets, programmes of study and assessment procedures which are an essential component of the national curriculum are still under development (for further discussion, see Maclure, 1988). The national curriculum is designed to bring about a general uplifting of standards which is generally identified as an imperative for Britain. However, considerable debate has surrounded the intermeshing of the national curriculum with existing and developing modes of assessment. Indeed a reconsideration has now taken place of the view that all pupils should take all ten foundation subjects to the age of 16, because there is insufficient space on the timetable to allow both the taking of options and the pursuit of all subjects to GCSE. As a result, fears have emerged that a two-tier system will come into existence in which the brightest pupils take GCSE, with the less able pursuing vocational courses or simply sitting assessments for the national curriculum's attainment targets. At the time of writing, only the three core subjects, English, Mathematics and Science, are now to be taken to GCSE level by all pupils.

These trends point to a failure on the part of the government to decide upon whether the aim should be a general education common to all, or streaming, with specific vocational subjects for the less able. The argument we have pursued here is of the need for a general vocational education for all and for businesses' involvement to be built into the whole curriculum and mainstream educational practice. A system which streams in the 14-16 phase according to academic and vocational subjects is likely to downgrade the status of the latter leading to the same old problems of demotivation of less able students and an academic bias for the brightest. Exhortations for "parity of esteem" (e.g. Tim Eggar, M.P., *Today*, BBC Radio 4, 11 February 1991) will not remove the structural, social and economic supports of status differentiation in education.

Whether a proper rebalancing in favour of greater vocational education for all is now possible under the national curriculum is in doubt. In particular, the fate of the alternative curricula developed under TVEI, of cross-curricula subjects and of Records of Achievement is unclear. For example, "*TVEI faces an uncertain future ... despite the shift in the culture of schooling created by TVEI, the implementation of the national curriculum will eventually result in a considerable realignment of teacher priorities and school practices. Perhaps, in the longer term, TVEI will be more influential in its impact on the way changes are orchestrated and maintained than on the educational processes it has attempted to enhance*" (Saunders and Halpin, 1990). In particular, TVEI's integrated approach and modular courses are felt to be in jeopardy.

The final form of cross-curricular subjects in the national curriculum is still to be decided. It is here that vocational aspects may receive attention, through Economic and Industrial Awareness and other elements of the curriculum. However, there remains a major concern that the reform of the national curriculum will once again pass to one side a proper integration with wider functional and industrial needs. The historical pattern has seen the marginalisation of links and business involvement from schools, and the difficulty, for both sides, of making links more than a bolt-on activity which is dropped when other pressures are stronger. The national curriculum is such another very strong pressure. Since this curriculum reform has not, so far, fully grasped the need to bridge the vocational-traditional divide we can only conclude that there must be considerable doubt about the future of effective links with business and what BP's Head of Educational Affairs, Chris Marsden (1991, p. 9), calls "*the appropriate, balanced role for vocational preparation in the education process*".

Filling the gaps

We have argued in this chapter that to introduce the "systems" changes needed to fit British education to the needs of the economy requires a new means of developing and maintaining *productive* links between education, business and the wider community. This argument is not uncontroversial. Howarth (1991), for example, argues that setting up a *"vocational"* curriculum in opposition to a *"traditional, academic"* curriculum is unhelpful; the Japanese system, he argues, shows that *"the best vocational preparation is good and prolonged general education, not vocational education"* (p. 14). Indeed, he goes on to suggest that business involvement with education at local level may be *"damaging"* (p. 137). In the Japanese context, Howarth's comments are undoubtedly true. But lessons cannot be simply transferred in this way. We suggest that the British context is fundamentally different from the Japanese and this necessarily affects the action that can be recommended for education. Concentrating solely upon the raising of general educational attainment in Britain at this time is insufficient because it leaves the systemic problem of education's isolation from businesses' needs unreformed. The Japanese education system seems to work because it intermeshes with an economic and institutional system which is attuned to the importance of human resources. To put it crudely, Japanese education produces a better prepared product and Japanese business knows what to do with a highly educated population: British education does not prepare a very good product, staying on rates are low, and functional literacy questionable; whilst British business has no proper approach yet to its subsequent training strategy and no sustained *local* organisational structure to make local links readily available.

More fundamentally, the argument we have advanced is that the British education system itself is part of a system failure that contributes to economic malaise by perpetuating an academic liberal tradition inimical to the needs of the late 20th century. Thus Howarth's plea for a "general education" fails to recognise the needs of economic regeneration if it leaves these traditions untouched. We do indeed require higher levels of general education but within the context of a reorientated system. But we stress again that this shift must be for *all*. Current changes to the national curriculum are in grave danger of leading to a two or a three tier system, with "vocational" subjects seen as an option for the less able. If there is one lesson we can take from the Japanese, it is the need for a *common system*. Recognition of this common framework of linkage is indeed now running through the debates in most industralised countries (see OECD, 1991).

This chapter has led us, therefore, to recognise a number of deficiencies in current practice that must be overcome.

First, the general educational product, of pupil quality, must be enhanced, particularly in *functional* skills. Many of the developments required relate to schooling methods, syllabus, school objectives, management and finance; they do not require a direct business involvement. The Education Reform Act should allow many of these basic needs to be addressed.

Second, however, effective links between business and schools still require radically to be enhanced. Although significant progress has been made, most business link activities are still relatively loose and too easily treated as "bolt-ons" to school practice. The major gap that has existed has been the absence of a proper presence of business needs in the curriculum across all disciplines, and at all levels. This gap appears to be being left unfilled by the new national curriculum. Although significant steps have been made, there remains a significant gap between the national curriculum, driven by the DES, the links to workplace needs driven by the DE, and the wider needs of business, some of which have yet to be fully articulated; i.e. there is still a strong *system gap*.

Third, this gap has tended to be exacerbated by the rather rigid conceptualisation of the form of links deriving from TA Compacts. Born chiefly to help problem schools in inner city areas with high peer unemployment pressures, the Compact model and its methods have proved much less appropriate to other areas; indeed Compact is often regarded as a purely "inner city" mechanism and hence held in ill repute by many other areas. Although evolving, since 1991, to offer greater flexibility in the criteria applied to the Partnership Initiative and Compact Extension, this flexibility appears more as an attempt to retain a DE presence in response to DES pressures which de facto leave EBPs and Compacts as peripheral to the curriculum. Thus government backing for wider EBPs, beyond Compact, still lacks a clear focus, commitment, finance or conception. Most importantly, as Partnerships and Compact Extension are peripheralised from the national curriculum, they are likely to remain as bolt-ons for teachers and schools, with TECs caught in the middle of this awkward debacle trying to develop a stronger employer commitment. In effect the short-term political pressure has shifted to FE, discussed in the next chapter, and left school level links for the future.

Fourth, there are still too many separate education initiatives with different link objectives and organisations. This is government's contribution to the "patchwork quilt" of initiatives in the field of education. SCIP, TVEI, Compacts, EBPs, and TEC-based partnership initiatives are all still too separate from each other. They are also too separate from mainstream education, from the Careers Service, and from other initiatives in the fields of enterprise and training. We expand on the developments needed between school and the training / work transition in Chapters 8 and 15.

Fifth, the experience of SCIP, TVEI, Compact and EBPs has amounted to an important period of learning from which a number of key lessons have been learnt:

- Clear targets are important for each party (individual, school, and business);
- A formal organisation for links is required to guarantee proper commitment and a stable involvement;
- A stable employer organisation is essential to make the employer side of links work effectively and to diffuse links across a number of companies and down the size spectrum of firms;
- Major commitments are required of staff time and finance to make everything work;
- Business is reluctant to provide much finance, seeing this as the proper role of government, although in-kind support and secondment of staff is often viewed very enthusiastically;
- Seconded business staff, if carefully chosen, have proved critical catalysts to successful EBPs in many areas: they have the credibility of business involvement, can more easily bring businesses into commitments, and have the right vision to lever the changes needed in education;
- There is still major confusion resulting from a plethora of link bodies with often different objectives which government activity has done little to simplify;
- Links work best when they are part of mainstream school practice, i.e. classroom-based curriculum activities.

Our conclusion is, therefore, that the creation of new and successful partnerships will depend on *change on both sides*. For *education* the critical imperative is to *embed links in the curriculum*. For its part, *business* needs (i) a management body to facilitate links, and (ii) to embed links more deeply into its central management. TECs and LECs provide a beginning in the direction of providing a general employer body to sustain links, but usually suffer from insufficient breadth and depth of employer coverage (see Chapter 8). The development of deeper company commitment requires explicit policies to make link activity a part of managers' career development, especially in large national companies. Only by integrating the notion of partnership in day-to-day activity in these ways will both sides be clear on their objectives, and be able to realise the potential of partnership in full. To improve this situation requires a stable commitment by government to a common system.

Footnotes: Chapter 7

1. The analysis here is of England, Wales and Scotland, as in the rest of the book. The substantial differences between the education systems of England/Wales and Scotland are discussed by McPherson and Raab (1988, pp. 29–52). LEAs refer throughout the book to Local Education Authorities.
2. The 1950s and 1960s were "*the golden age of teacher autonomy*" with respect to the curriculum (Lawson, 1982), in which an "*ideology of teacher professionalism*" (Broadfoot, 1980) became dominant in education to the exclusion of other interests. These professional interests assisted in the creation of the "secret garden" of the curriculum although, as we have seen, these interests were constrained by and interacted with those of the examining bodies. In extreme cases this led to "anti-vocationalism" which opposes business involvement in schooling. This has reinforced an artificial separation of general education from vocational education and training (Rae, 1989).
3. See e.g. Bostok and Smith (1990) and comments by Daniel Silverstone, Deputy Director of Education in Hackney, quoted in *TES*, 29 March 1991; note earlier appraisals by Ball (1985) and Welton and Evans (1986).
4. TVEL – Thames Valley Enterprise Ltd (1990).
5. LEAs pay a fee in order to become part of the SCIP network and to use the name.
6. Confidential interview comments from a variety of business leaders.
7. Hinckley *et al.* (1987); although it is argued that even work experience needs a tightening up of monitoring (IPM (1984b), Bennett (1992)).
8. Interview comments from Cay Stratton, April 1989.
9. We are grateful to the TA for allowing access to all first round bids for Compact funding. Our comments are drawn from these and from case study interviews.
10. Source: Department of Employment statistics.
11. It is enlightening to note in this connection that there is evidence of closer integration of TVEI with EBPs in Scotland where TVEI statements have often provided the basis of the EBP vision. A key factor leading to this appears to have been the late start of TVEI compared to England which has facilitated the closer integration of the two: based on interview comments and Raffe (1989), Black *et al.* (1988) and Bell *et al.* (1988).
12. See Bennett *et al.* (1989c), Bennett (1992); a similar but different emphasis is given by Cleverdon (1988).

8. *TRAINING*

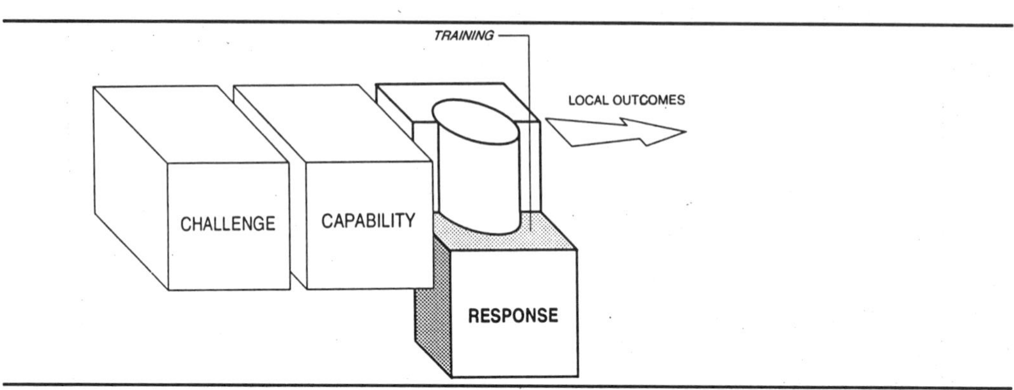

The training response

Britain's training response to economic challenges has been woefully inadequate. The result has been a series of long-term gaps: of a national vision for training; a strategy to implement it; and a delivery structure that can be relied on to provide it.

The late 1970s and 1980s have seen some notable advances in overcoming these problems. There has been continual modification of training programmes aimed at both the youth and adult age groups, major changes to organisation and delivery institutions, and a serious attempt to improve the link between training and the other fields of economic activity. But perhaps the most significant development at the start of the 1990s has been the recognition, by all main agents, that training is a major problem for Britain that has to be tackled.

Training policy is a major aspect of a more general concern with human resources. The recent debates in Britain have at last recognised that human resources are one of the key elements in economic development, and one of the areas of greatest deficiency is Britain's capability to respond: the CBI (1989a, p. 16) has referred to this as "*the key to competitiveness*". The view is widely shared (see e.g. Daly, 1986; Prais, 1987; Finegold and Soskice, 1988; Keep and Mayhew, 1988; Dore and Sako, 1989; Cassels, 1990; CBI/Manpower, 1990; NEDO, 1991). In this chapter we assess how far the developments that have occurred will satisfy the requirements of the future. Our discussion traces developments as follows:

- Recognising malaise;
- Searching for national solutions;
- Stimulating local business involvement;
- Towards local integration in a national framework: Training and Enterprise Councils (TECs);

- New Foundations: National Vocational Qualifications (NVQs) and Investors in People (IIP);
- Filling the gaps.

Recognising malaise

Numerous reports over the years have stressed Britain's unfavourable training position. One of the most influential has been *Competence and Competition*. This compared the British position with that in the USA, West Germany and Japan and found that the UK faced *"deep-rooted problems"* and was *"in danger of falling further behind"* (NEDO/MSC, 1984, p. 5). As we have seen in Chapters 3 and 4, fewer Britons stay in full-time education or receive training, and more receive lower qualifications, than any major economic competitor. The Government's White Papers of 1988 and 1991 identified lack of training in Britain's workforce as a key barrier to economic growth.

Training is a field in which difficulties arising from fragmentation, competition and gaps between supply and demand have been major constraints on developing capability. The origin of these difficulties are to be found among both of the major actors involved in the training process:

- Business;
- Public and private providers.

The structure of relationships between supply and demand is shown in Figure 8.1. We look at each element below.

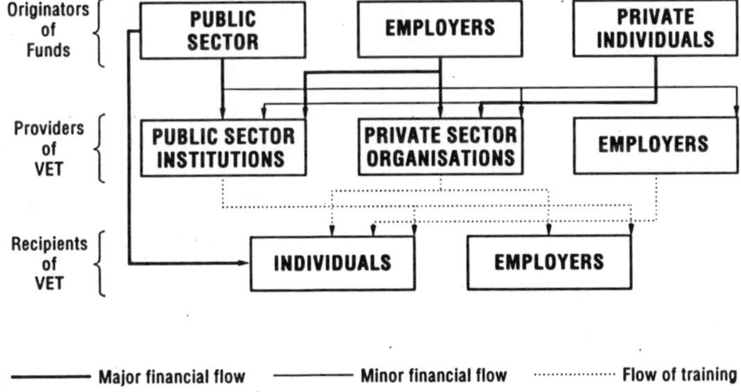

Figure 8.1 Demand and supply relations in training (after MSC, 1987)

Business

Despite the centrality of skills to their supply-side requirements, and despite spending around £18 billion on training in 1987 (CBI, 1991a, p. 17), most businesses have failed to recognise its importance. The report, *A Challenge to Complacency* (MSC, 1985) had a major impact on the business community when it appeared in 1985. This report found that whilst most companies agreed that Britain did not train its workforce to the same high levels as other nations, they tended to think that their own training policy was adequate. Few businesses thought training was sufficiently important to warrant its inclusion as an integral part of corporate strategy, and indeed many saw expenditure on training as an overhead to be minimised rather than an investment in future productivity. Few business managers recognised the links between training and competitiveness. As a result, little attention was devoted to the consideration of training needs. The report was damning of the complacent attitudes it found amongst businesses. Factors such as "poaching" and uncertainties over future economic trends were criticised as *"post hoc rationalisations"* which *"reinforce already negative attitudes to training"* (ibid, p. 4). In short, the problem was system-wide. Businesses have failed to take responsibility for their own training. Government intervention through Industrial Training Boards and provision though colleges simply reinforced the tendency to believe that training was someone else's responsibility.

There have been improvements from this very poor baseline of the mid-1980s. In the 5 years up to 1989 the number of employees receiving training rose by one half (CBI, 1989a, p. 17), and between 1984 and 1990 the number of employees receiving training from employers almost doubled. However, in 1987 52% of the workforce still received no training (in certain sectors the figure was much higher, e.g. 67% in manufacturing, TA, 1989a), less than 1 in 3 businesses had a training plan or training budget, and only 1 in 10 had formal training targets for their whole workforce. Thus change has been slow, and 1991–2 has seen the recession affecting businesses' training budgets (Industrial Society Survey (reported in *Financial Times*, 18 March 1991)).

Providers

Reinforcing sluggish attitudes to training amongst businesses has been a training system characterised by confusion and ad hocery. *The Challenge to Complacency* Report (p. 5) identified a clear need *"to make it easier for companies to define, and obtain from external providers, the training they require"*. Training has traditionally been provided through three main channels: private training providers; directly by industry and commerce; and by the public sector (primarily colleges of further education) (see Figure 8.1). The key difficulty for users of this system is not simply the complexity of providers but the irrationality and confusion of the overarching system of qualifications. Routes into, through and out of further education (FE) are extremely difficult to untangle for employers and students alike. The field has been referred to as an "alphabet soup" by more than one commentator. We deal with the private and public sectors in turn.

(i) Private provision

The contribution of the private sector to training is considerable, but is characterised by enormous variety. In a survey carried out in the 1970s, Williams and Woodhall (1979) found the independent FE sector to be *"... diverse and volatile ... with a great heterogeneity of establishments in terms of size, standards and types of course"* (p. 100). It was responsible for a *"significant proportion"* of all Vocational Education and Training (VET) and filled some important gaps in public provision, especially in the area of correspondence and short, intensive courses. This situation has not radically altered. Indeed, as Cantor (1989, p. 141) points out, private providers received a fillip from the Youth Training Scheme, through which many received Approved Training Organisation status as Managing Agents.

Our own work shows that private training providers have become important actors in a number of localities by acting as hosts for initiatives such as Local Employer Networks (LENs) (see Bennett *et al.*, 1990a), and the DTI's Enterprise and Education Advisers and Teacher Placement Organisers. Private providers can range from very small secretarial colleges to the Group Training Associations which exist in a number of areas through local employer subscription to cater for local training needs.

Variations in the quality of provision provided by private trainers has been a cause for concern, especially given the activities of some unscrupulous providers, and there are only a handful of voluntary accreditation bodies covering a minority of independent providers. Despite this variable quality, the private sector has important lessons for public provision with respect to flexibility and the cost advantages to consumers of tailor-made courses (see Williams and Woodhall, 1979; Birch, 1988; Müller and Funnell, 1991; Funnell and Müller, 1991).

Apart from provision through the private colleges and providers, many companies provide their own training. In some localities, key local employers in effect provide a training service for other businesses. For example, ICI fulfills this function on Teesside, training employees who then pass on to be employed by other businesses, many of which are suppliers to ICI. Other companies have training schemes which have a national reputation, for example, Marks and Spencer. Involvement in training varies substantially between sectors. In the distribution sector for example, companies are working hard to reverse a poor reputation. Involvement also varies by size of company: small companies find it difficult to plan forward – managing directors spend most of their time "fire-fighting" and small firms are more vulnerable than other businesses to minor fluctuations in the market which affect their training needs.

An important source of quasi-private provision has been through the Industry Training Boards (ITBs). Twenty-three ITBs were set up in 1964 to cover the key industrial sectors which then collectively employed more than half the country's workforce. Businesses had to pay a levy to their respective ITB which was then supposed to cater for training their workforce. Unfortunately, the system had major shortcomings and a number of the ITBs signally failed to provide for the needs of their industries, leading to the closure of all but seven of them in 1983. In place of these ITBs, no fewer than 120 voluntary training associations came into being. These have shown varying success in catering for their sectors, notable being the British Printing Industries Federation Training Organisation (see Cantor, 1989, p. 145). The remaining ITBs were placed on a voluntary footing following the publication of the 1988 White Paper *Employment for the 1990s* and all but two quickly closed. The remaining two ITBs, for the construction sector and the engineering industry, had strong pressure from their members to continue (CBI, 1989b, p. 17). However, both have had some difficulties in continuing.

(ii) Public provision

Recognition of the need for a national public policy on training is a relatively recent phenomenon. The need for a comprehensive approach to the training needs of the economy led to the formation only in 1974 of the MSC. However, no thoroughgoing attempts to ensure that Britain's workforce is adequately trained occurred until the 1980s. As a result, the provision of training in the public sector has been left to local authorities through their colleges of FE. FE colleges provide a significant source of training provision through what is known as work-related further education or WRFE (previously known as work-related non-advanced further education or WRNAFE). FE faces a number of problems in responding to business needs.

One of the main difficulties for FE colleges stems from their tradition of seeing themselves *"as offering youngsters a mixed diet of education and training"* (Cantor, 1989, p. 147). As a consequence they have seen themselves providing a service to the local community. This has not always been fully consonant with the need to provide local businesses with trained employees. The tensions between having to maintain these two positions simultaneously can be acute. During the 1980s, FE colleges have arguably moved along the education/training spectrum towards training. This was closely linked to the growing influence of the Training Agency with its stress on vocationally-related courses. In some colleges, TA-funded schemes accounted for up to 40% of revenues in 1989 (Cantor, 1989, p. 125). Despite these developments, the educational emphasis of FE has contributed to a culture which is not traditionally amenable to being responsive to the needs of business. As a result, colleges have a very varied record, tending to see themselves as *providing* a service rather than having to *market* their services to their clients – businesses and trainees.

Sitting uncomfortably on the divide between school and work, FE colleges are usually expected to provide a whole range of courses from advanced academic ones to basic literacy and numeracy courses, and general community support. The problems this approach engenders were identified in *A Challenge to Complacency* (MSC, 1985, p. 6) as a key focus of concern: colleges have traditionally been funded and managed on broadly similar lines to schools and this *"acts as a positive disincentive for them to be responsive"*. Patterns of resourcing have been based to varying degrees on student numbers and the rolling forward from one year to the next of existing expenditures and staff-student ratios. Like schools, FE colleges are rigid structures consisting of resources and teaching staff who cannot be readily switched from one use to another. This is not such a problem for schools where pupil intake is more or less guaranteed, and the parameters of the curriculum do not change as rapidly. But neither of these is true of FE. FE colleges require sometimes massive and rapid shifts between subject areas in order to be capable of responding to employers.

These cultural and organisational rigidities have made it difficult for FE colleges to adapt to the rapidly changing economic conditions of the late 1970s and 1980s in terms of the types of businesses they cater for and the types of skills they must teach. Thus, for example, the traditional emphasis of the colleges on engineering and apprenticeships has had to be replaced with a greater concern for the service industries and shorter one-off courses. Figure 8.2 shows changes in the structure of courses between 1975 and 1985. This shows quite plainly the continued dominance of engineering courses and the traditional examined subjects throughout the period. Although there has been significant growth of enrolments in the professions, business and management, the proportion of courses accounted for by this sector fails to reflect its importance to the economy. Also notable is the limited growth in the number of enrolments in the hotel and catering sector.

Despite these mismatches, the education sector has been largely content with its ability to respond to changing demands. In 1985/6 HMI concluded that most colleges *"appeared to have managed relatively successfully the challenging task of changing the size and composition of the teaching force in line with the changing pattern of course demand"* (DES, 1986, p. 54). The 1987 HMI report *NAFE in Practice* found that 95% of the employers it surveyed felt college provision was satisfactory or better (DES, 1987, p. 60). More

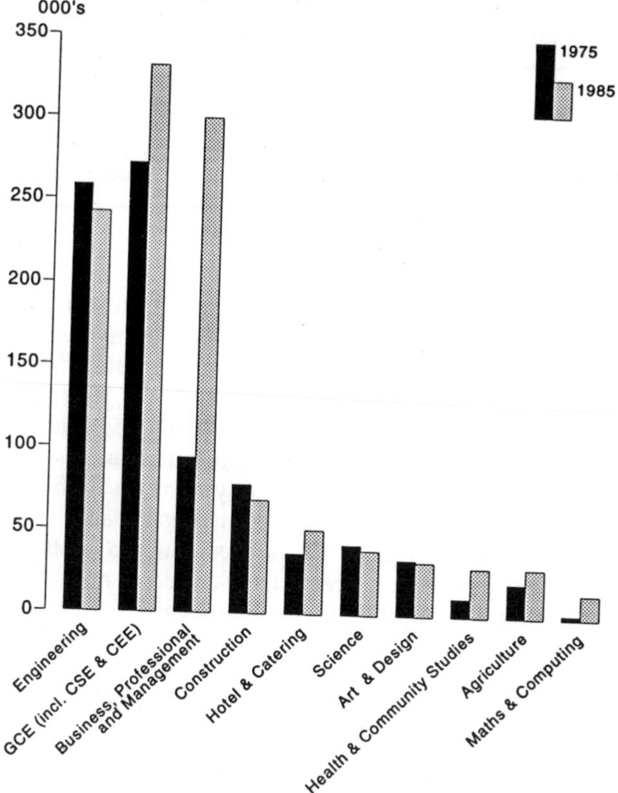

Figure 8.2 Change in Further Education enrolments by subject group in England and Wales between 1975 and 1985

Source: DES / Welsh Office (1987) *Managing Colleges Efficiently*, p.6

generally, NAFE was judged to be *"a flexible and responsive service"*. Yet in important ways those attitudes are analogous to the complacency amongst the business community already noted. For example, the survey of employers in *NAFE in Practice* was only of those employers already with college links. They presumably would not have maintained such links if they felt them to be unsatisfactory. As a result, the HMI assessments miss the mass of employers who have no links with colleges, i.e. they fail to address the system-wide failure of a gap in training culture.

In addition to confusion of purposes, FE colleges share with schools a post-war tradition of local autonomy. This has led to a huge diversity of provision. Important indicators of the nature of this variation can be derived from gross expenditure per full-time equivalent (FTE) student (see Table 8.1). The variations in provision are very large in FE. They are much larger than for secondary education, and are larger in London and the metropolitan areas than elsewhere. The autonomy allowed to LEAs under the 1944 Education Act has led to much greater diversity in FE because of the lack of norms regarding appropriate staffing levels, modes of delivery, etc.

The wide variation is due to differences in both the type of courses on offer to students and the types and structures of colleges used to deliver FE. It rarely appears to

Table 8.1 Gross expenditure per FTE FE student in England and Wales, 1988–9 (estimates in £)

	Mean	Standard Deviation	Inter-quartile range
London Boroughs	2,819	1,056	2,267–2,976
Metropolitan Districts	2,385	554	2,003–2,696
Non-Metropolitan Counties	2,735	388	2,453–2,996

Source: CIPFA Education Estimates, 1988–9

relate to different local needs. For example, Table 8.1 shows that, contrary to usual expectations, there is greater expenditure per student on average in the shire counties than in metropolitan districts where needs are usually greater. These relationships have changed considerably over time. Comparing the data for 1988/9 with that for 1982/3 reveals significant shifts in student numbers whilst expenditure per capita has remained nearly constant. There have been important changes in enrolments due to demographic decline, and changes in unemployment and job opportunities without commensurate adjustments in expenditure and the associated structures of provision. Significant shifts in the rank order of LEAs according to costs per student have occurred at different rates, in different directions in different authorities. Changes to FTEs represent changes both in the number of enrolments and the type of enrolment (full- or part-time). Overall, the largest increase in rolls has been in the metropolitan districts – especially in NAFE (see Table 8.2). As a result, by the end of the 1980s, although an authority like Birmingham was spending at comparatively low levels per student, it was catering for a large number of students relative to the size of its population.

Table 8.2 Percentage changes in number of NAFE students (FTE) per capita between 1982/83 and 1988/89

	Mean (%)	Interquartile range (%)
London Boroughs	13	–8 to +23
Metropolitan Districts	24	–5 to +38
Non-Metropolitan Counties	12	+1 to +24

Source: CIPFA *Education Estimates*, relevant years

But student numbers are only one factor affecting variability. Figure 8.3 shows the proportion, and change in proportion of, FTE NAFE students on full-time courses. The pattern reveals important differences between ostensibly similar and often neighbouring authorities. The patterns are unrelated to broad factors such as local socio-economic conditions. Instead, they point to the operation of factors connected to individual college autonomy, LEA traditions in FE, variations in employment opportunities, alternative sources of training and the educational attainment of local populations.

Our case studies show that different colleges and LEAs have exhibited different capacities to change. In general, there has been a lag between changes in the industrial structure of an area and corresponding adaptations of college structure and curricula. By the late 1980s only some of the more advanced LEAs in FE – Cleveland, for example – had begun to move towards the allocation of resources to colleges on the basis of unit costs rather than past patterns in advance of government legislation. However, even by

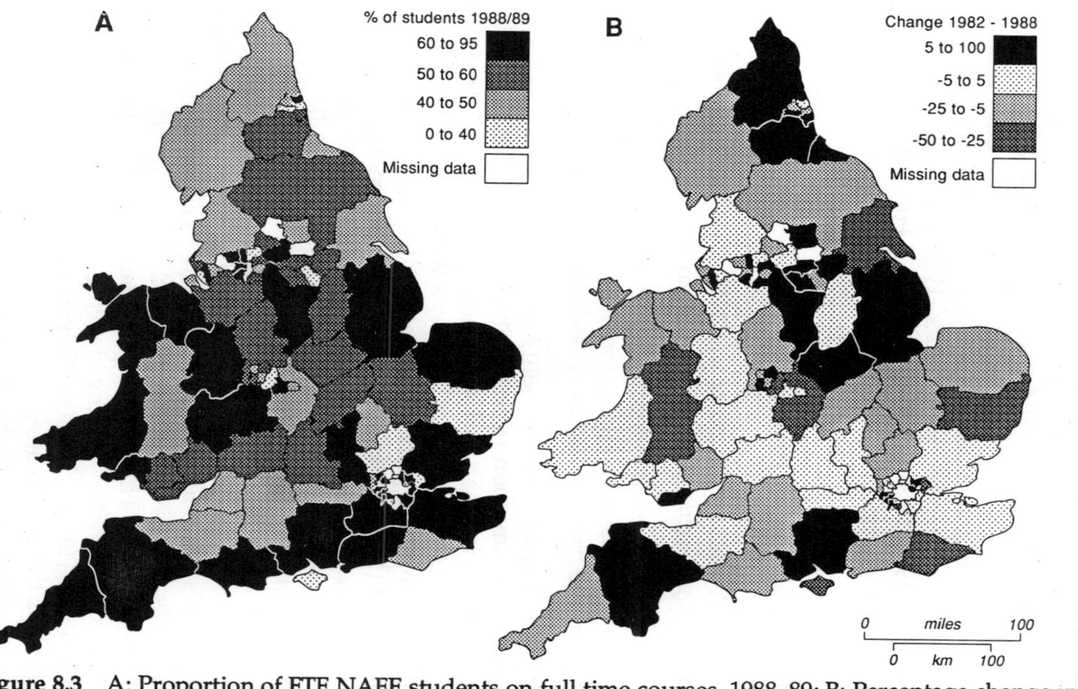

Figure 8.3 A: Proportion of FTE NAFE students on full time courses, 1988–89; B: Percentage change in proportion of FTE NAFE students on full time courses, 1982/83–1988/89

Sources: CIPFA estimates, 1982/83 and 1988/89

1991 only 44% of FE courses were judged relevant by employers, with a further 25% rated as partly relevant (DE, *Skills and Enterprise Briefing*, 2/91, August 1991).

The speed with which colleges have reacted to change usually depends crucially upon the role of the Principal. Time and again we came across instances where colleges moved from out-dated curricula to a much more flexible system only after a change of Principal. The important role of the individual has been confirmed as important by a recent HMI report on engineering courses in FE which found that *"in most colleges, heads of department play the major role in creating and maintaining links with industry"* (DES, 1988, p. 11). Our own findings confirm this role for the departmental head but also the need for a responsive Principal if the practice of "good" departments is to spread throughout a college.

It is clear that the FE colleges have suffered from confusion of purpose as a result of varying signals from government, LEAs and Principals, compounded by the effect of the autonomy of teachers. As a result, they were not readily able to cope with the call for enhancement of publicly-provided training that developed rapidly in the 1980s. Efforts to increase their efficiency, on the one hand, and their orientation to employer needs, on the other hand, have become the main thrust of the 1991 Education White Paper and other wider debates (see e.g. Jones, 1985; DES, 1987; FEU, 1987; Birch, 1988; FESC, 1989; Gleeson, 1989; Burke, 1990; Müller and Funnell, 1991; Funnell and Müller, 1991).

Searching for national solutions

Throughout the 1970s and for much of the 1980s, attempts to solve Britain's training problems were distinguished by two main features:

i) They were national rather than local;
ii) They centred on national training *programmes*, rather than on tackling the *institutional* deficiencies of the training *system* of both public and private provision.

Figure 8.4 shows the chief developments in this period. The establishment of the Manpower Services Commission (MSC) in 1974 marked the beginning of attempts to introduce a comprehensive, national approach to training needs. However, the MSC suffered from a number of deficiencies. Firstly, it was conceived in the corporatist mode of government intervention. It proved to be an inadequate tool for (a) responding to the needs of business and (b) for levering change amongst training providers.

Despite the existence of Local Area Manpower Boards (LAMBs), the MSC was highly centralised, with little real autonomy in local areas. As a result, it proved to be a poor mechanism for transmitting the correct signals from businesses to providers. Instead, the solution to deficiencies in training were mainly sought through government expenditure on national training programmes administered by the large bureaucracy of the MSC. The early 1980s saw major programme changes with the development of the Youth Opportunities Programme (YOPs), Youth Training Scheme (YTS) and subsequent Youth Training (YT). The area of adult retraining had to wait longer for major change, which came in 1988 with the development of the ambitious Employment Training (ET) scheme. The Job Training Scheme (JTS) of 1987 came in for severe criticism on the grounds that it was attempting to provide business with cheap labour and proved extremely unpopular with the unemployed. Other retraining schemes include

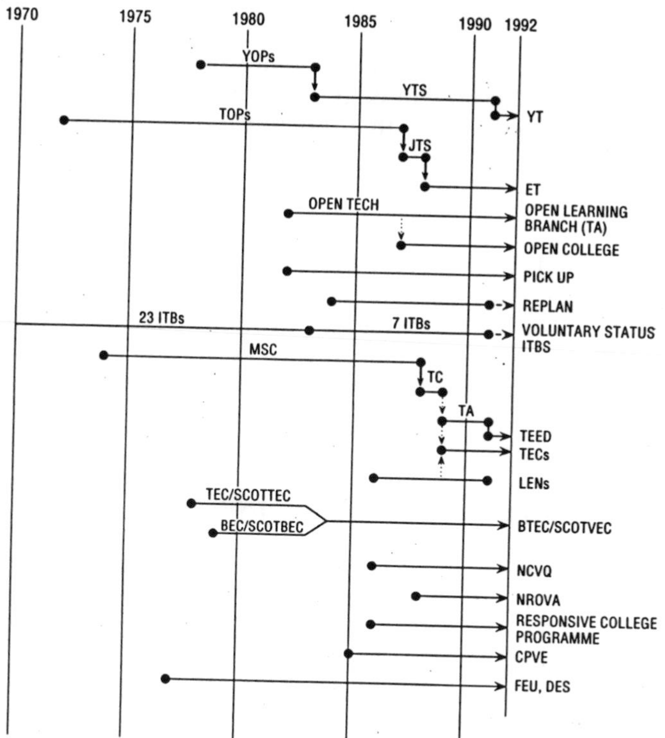

Figure 8.4 Training programmes and organisations, 1970–1992

the Open Tech, which became the Open Learning Branch of the MSC, experiences from which fed into the formation of the Open College, and the DES's PICKUP and REPLAN schemes.

We cannot discuss the YT and ET national programmes in detail. However, some comments are necessary because they are important to the argument we are presenting. First, it is clear that the structure of YTS was coloured by the fact that it was initially conceived as a reaction to the sudden large rise in youth unemployment of the early 1980s and, in the aftermath of the riots of 1981, was also seen as a means for keeping the young occupied in order to avoid major social unrest. However, there was also a wider strategy, laid out in the 1981 White Paper *A New Training Initiative: a programme for action*, which aimed at providing for all young people under the age of 18 who did not enter full-time education, a period of planned work experience and related education and training. The original 1-year YTS was eventually replaced by a 2-year version, and YTS has had the effect of bringing about a *de facto* raising of the school/college leaving age to 18 for those young people not going directly into jobs or going on to "A" levels.

Nonetheless, despite undoubted improvements in its track-record over time, YTS suffered from having no clear end-point for most of its trainees and failed to prevent the emergence of skill shortages in the late 1980s. These problems were due in part to inherent problems within YTS, in particular its *national* nature which limited local flexibility. But it is also true that, however good YTS might have become, it always had to operate in an *institutional* framework which was seriously unresponsive to economic needs: in this context it was bound to underachieve. It was part of the perverse policy syndrome. The chief problems were as follows:

- The system was not conducive to local flexibility and did not reflect business needs at the *local* level; whilst the system might ensure a general matching of training to business needs at national level, this did not ensure a match locally, where it matters;
- The traditional system of qualifications made it difficult to define a national minimum target for trainees.

Recognition of these problems led, in the first instance, to attempts to stimulate greater responsiveness amongst public sector training providers through the internal reform of local FE provision. This has been followed by attempts to stimulate increased business involvement through new bodies, culminating in the advent of TECs and LECs, along with the major reform of the system of vocational qualifications. We look at each in turn.

Stimulating responsiveness in local FE provision

The first major attempt to improve the provision of FE by local colleges occurred in 1985 when central government transferred 16% of local authorities' grant for work-related NAFE purposes from the DES Education Block Grant to the MSC. LEAs' receipt of this finance now depended on completion of an annual, rolling 3-year NAFE plan which had to satisfy the MSC. A key component of the plan concerned the responsiveness of provision to business needs.

NAFE plans were a new departure for many local authorities: few authorities, and few colleges, planned their provision of FE and some LEAs had no systematic idea about their provision at all. NAFE planning instituted a whole new process of consultation for local authorities, and in many cases brought employers into the procedure. Wicks (1990, p.267) found that 44% of NAFE Plan committees included individual employers or employers' representatives; 31% included Chamber of Commerce members. Despite initial fears of centralisation, many LEAs came to welcome the opportunity to plan provision presented by the MSC and extended the annual review to the whole of FE. DES (1987, p. 7) commented: *"The Work-Related NAFE initiative has begun to have beneficial effects, and in many LEAs the need to construct a development plan is helping to direct resources more effectively"*. Around the same time as NAFE planning was being introduced, various attempts were being made to encourage colleges themselves to be more responsive. DES Education Support Grants supported the College Employer Links Project, whilst the MSC funded the Responsive College Project (now Programme) as a pilot in 10 LEAs. Two major reports of the mid-80s (Audit Commission, 1985; DES / Welsh Office, 1987) also stressed the centrality of improving the effectiveness and efficiency of the management of college courses.

Notwithstanding these developments, the strongest influence on tailoring college provision to employers' needs was arguably YTS. YTS came to account for an important part of college provision, bringing about an increased role for colleges in training and reversing a long-term decline in part-time day release courses (DES, 1987, p. 7). No less than 42% of YTS trainees attended FE colleges for their off-the-job training by the end of 1986 (DES, 1988, p. 1). At the same time, however, YTS also seemed to highlight the inadequacy of colleges' ability to respond rapidly to change. Although HMI found colleges to be *"responding effectively"* to managing agents and trainees' needs, liaison between agents and staff was *"not well established"* and many teachers had *"little or outdated industrial experience"* (*ibid*, pp. 7–8). The best results were achieved where college work was most closely related to work experience (ibid, p. 4).

Ironically, all these developments were leading colleges towards greater autonomy and away from the LEA-level of planning which was embodied in the MSC work-related NAFE reforms. There was much support for giving colleges greater autonomy and the 1988 Education Reform Act gave colleges new responsibilities over budgets and staffing. These responsibilities were granted to new governing bodies which were now to include an increased representation of business interests. In 1991, the Education White Paper announced that college autonomy would be further increased, with colleges to be centrally funded from April 1993, rather than LEA-funded. These changes will probably encourage greater local flexibility and may well lead to greater responsiveness to business needs, especially if TECs and LECs are given major responsibility for funding FE colleges rather than using a central funding council under the auspices of the DES. This is an area which is not yet resolved and over which considerable tension has developed.

Stimulating local business involvement

Apart from these attempts to change the shape of training by stimulating the education sector, central government has also sought to encourage business involvement more directly. The aim has been to allow business directly to register its skill requirements as a means of better linking demand and supply for training. This approach has led to the most radical change in the field of training – the introduction of TECs – and it is for this reason that our analysis now concentrates in this area.

The search for a business vehicle

The private sector emerged as an increasingly important actor in training provision during the 1980s. As we have noted already, YTS and ET were provided through a network of managing agents (separate managers and agents in the case of ET), many of whom were in the private sector. Yet what was clearly required was a means of articulating the voice of business *as a whole* which was independent of the interests of the training provider. The problem for Britain is that a national tradition of strong business organisations does not exist in a way comparable to, say, Germany and France. Until TECs, the nearest Britain comes to these countries' patterns is through Chambers of Commerce.

British Chambers became increasingly important actors in training in the 1980s and are involved in a broad range of activities including:

- The provision of separate training centres;
- The provision of separate training subsidiaries;
- Acting as managing agents or ATOs for YTS and/or ET;
- Restart;
- Jobclub;
- Hosting Local Employer Networks.

The degree of Chamber involvement is highly variable. Chapter 6 has shown quite clearly that there are key groups of lead Chambers, with Figures 5.11 and 6.6 showing that the coverage of Chambers is highly variable both in terms of whether a Chamber exists and the range of its activities. Strong Chambers tend to be present in the traditional industrial areas of Britain and are not always present in areas where current needs are highest.

As a result Chambers have not been able to host all *national* training activities because of their uneven geographical coverage. Added to this is the problem that Chambers articulate their members' needs for training at the same time that they provide training, which can lead to a conflict of interests. There is also the issue of membership itself. Without a statutory status, Chambers have found it particularly difficult to attract members from small local companies. Despite these aspects, Chambers have performed a key role in the development of training and are the largest single body involved in YTS in the country.

The LENs initiative

The notion that Chambers or similar business bodies might provide *systematic* employer involvement in VET at local level led in 1985–6 to a Collaborative Project between the Association of British Chambers of Commerce (ABCC), the CBI and the MSC (see MSC/ABCC, 1986). This project came in the wake of the 1984 White Paper *Training for Jobs* (HM Government, 1984) which announced the introduction of Professional Industrial and Commercial Updating (PICKUP), Technical and Vocational Education Initiative (TVEI), NAFE Plans and the further development of the MSC's adult training strategy. It was clear that, to be successful, each of these programmes required the active involvement of employers in VET at the local level and that new mechanisms were required to achieve this involvement; exhortation to employers and calls to LEAs were not in themselves sufficient to achieve the required system-wide change. The Collaborative Project concluded that Chambers should be the focal point, information centre, and major source of influence on both employer attitudes and providers in the field of training.

Whilst demonstrating the potential role of host bodies for the new initiatives, it was clear that because of their uneven geographical coverage and variable track record – and in the absence of a major constituency pressing for the introduction of public law status – Chambers alone could not provide the answer. Nor could the CBI fill the gap. Although the CBI is an effective national lobby, it has little local presence. Indeed, in the early 1980s a group of CBI member companies in the aerospace and motor industries had pressed central government to establish Local Employer Forums on the lines of German Chambers of Commerce.

Building on these developments, a joint ABCC/CBI/MSC Planning Group was formed which launched the LENs initiative in October 1986. The first LENs appeared in April 1987. The LENs initiative proved to be important in gathering experience on local employer bodies and hence we deal with it in some depth.

The objectives of the LENs initiative were broad and ambitious. They sought to bring together into a closer relation the provision of VET and employers' needs. This was to be achieved through three main objectives:

i) Collecting and interpreting local labour market information;
ii) Representing employers in the local planning of vocational education and training (such as Governors, Liaison Groups, NAFE Planning committees, Area Manpower Boards, Education Committees, etc.);

iii) Providing consultancy and advice to employers on training and to Area Manpower Boards.

In addition, LENs could also serve to strengthen school-business links such as TVEI, encourage the participation of employers in YTS (and subsequently ET), support local NVQ requirements, contribute to teacher-training, offer careers and placement advice, publicise skill needs, and help local school and college curriculum development (LEN, 1987, p. 7). To these aims was later added a coordinative role: to use LENs to seek a cooperative framework of links between local actors and between projects, programmes and initiatives (*Network Memo*, 1988, p. 14). The launch document *A Foundation for the Future*, summarised the tasks as *consulting* employers on needs, *representing* employers in decisions on provision, and *providing* advice to employers. Where necessary, they should also "consider whether or not the Networks should promote change in any one of these areas (LEN, 1987, p. 7). To some extent a shift of emphasis then occurred since, by 1988, the aims had become more focused on being involved chiefly in the planning and delivery of local vocational education and training (Field, 1988). The early breadth of objectives thus obscured the central focus which was intended to be on NAFE plans.

The objectives were ambitious enough in themselves. They appear very ambitious when viewed in the context of the funds that were made available. There was initial funding of £3.6m from the MSC. But this was to be spread over 132 LENs in England, Scotland and Wales: it was intended that there should be at least one LEN per LEA. The resources amounted to no more than £20,000 for each LEN, with one or two exceptions for special cases, for the first year of operation. This was enough to employ a "pair of hands" (the Network Manager) and not much more. The first year was followed, at a late stage, by a second year of funding of £10,000 per LEN. Subsequently, LENs were asked to submit bids for Local Development Projects (LDPs) of which 62 were in existence by July 1989. Although targeted on specific objectives, the LDPs effectively provided further support, although clearly not every LEN could be successful in its bid. The political objective was that LENs should quickly become self-funding. Initially, the MSC intended this to occur after just 1 year of pump-priming. This proved wholly unrealistic, however, such that the second year and LDP support were required for them to continue. Nevertheless, the political objective remained that they should be self-financing. This proved to be a very challenging target.

A key part of the LENs initiative was to use "base organisations" as hosts for the programme. By this method it was hoped to make the resources go further by using existing organisations, expertise and networks of employer relations with education and training. Base organisations could be Chambers of Commerce, Training Associations, Enterprise Agencies, or even individual businesses. Economies were sought through such organisations providing linkages to existing initiatives, premises, providing and appointing a governing body, engaging and supervising the Network Manager and underwriting the LEN at least for its initial period. However, it was hoped that a shift in responsibility would occur over time with the Governing Body of the LEN establishing a separate identity from the host.

A tension was thus inbuilt into the LENs programme from the outset. It was given an existing organisation as a host and relied on the expertise and a subsidy, or economy of resources, from the host to make it viable. But at the same time the LEN had to develop a separate identity of its own or it had to satisfy its separate aims within the context of the host organisation. Clearly this could be successfully achieved only if one of two conditions was met: either additional resources for self-financing had to be found to allow it to become independent, or the aims of the host organisation had to be very close to those of the LEN initiative (or amenable to change to accommodate the independent aims of the LEN). This was true whether the base was a long-established organisation or a relatively new one. Now, since self-financing proved extremely difficult to achieve, the most successful LENs were those which were supported by sympathetic or adaptable base organisations. Towler (1989, p. 92) estimates that about 20% of LENs were fully effective in these terms, 20% were unlikely ever to be successful and roughly 60% were in between.

The original aim of establishing approximately 130 LENs was given a strong political priority with a fast start-up. By the summer of 1987 the first 50 were under way. By September 1988 120 were in existence of which only two (Northampton and Southend) had ceased to exist by the summer of 1989. The coverage of Britain was thus nearly total, with only 11 gaps existing. In terms of coverage, therefore, LENs quickly achieved the major part of their goal.

However, LENs ultimately came to an inauspicious end, being taken over, or fading from the scene, with the advent of TECs. The important lessons of LENs for subsequent developments are now considered.

Assessment of the LENs initiative[1]

LENs exhibited a number of characteristics which affected their role in their local economies. We deal here with those features pertinent to our argument: the role of hosts; the extent of employer involvement; and the type of employers involved.

(i) The use of hosts

Although, on the face of it, the use of hosts had much to commend it, there were problems in relying on existing local capacity. Table 8.3 shows that although Chambers acted as hosts in about 60% of cases, there was also a heavy reliance on a diverse range of other bodies. Many of these hosts have rather specific purposes and do not offer the potential of Chambers for seeking or representing more general employer interests. Because of the need for local flexibility, LENs were never given much advice on how to combine the "basic" tasks of consultation, representation and advice with a set of "optional" tasks *"in the right 'mix' for their own areas"* (LEN, 1987, p. 10). But for the reasons stated above, it was important that the objectives of LENs ran with the grain of the host's objectives to ensure success. As a result, some host bodies seized on the opportunity presented by this lack of guidance to incorporate a LEN into their existing activities and to push forward their own training agenda. For others, however – those without clear vision or set of priorities – it was never obvious how to integrate activities with their LEN. As a result, a number of LEN managers were left looking for a role in a confused local milieu.

There was also the problem of accessibility to employers. British Chambers and other base organisations all lacked a means of linking their members to the initiative. Links generally only worked if local employers were already involved. Thus the ability to extend and diffuse training objectives among employers, and improve employer links to trainers and educationalists, which were key objectives of LENs, could not easily be

Table 8.3 LEN base organisations

Chambers, employers' assocations, employer networds (free-standing)	66
Training agencies, trusts, associations, groups and private providers	17
Enterprise agencies or trusts	10
Private businesses	10
Local authorities (Enfield and Bexley)	2
Management and business centres	2
Others (including new town DC and UDCs)	3
Total	110

Source: Original analysis of Network Project Directory, April 1989

achieved through many base organisations. As a result, the use of host organisations is seen, in retrospect, as a design fault that both prevented employer skill demands being strong enough, and created an initial false sense of security. In the event, the promises of support by many hosts also could not be delivered because of their lack of resources or their thin penetration of the employers in their areas.

The problem of accessing employers was exacerbated by the large variation in the number of employers covered by the LENs in different areas. From a sample of 48 LENs, the size ranged from 1,121 employers in Hexham to 36,000 for Bristol / Avon. See Table 8.4.

The smaller LENs, in terms of the number of their employers, tended to be in dispersed industrial areas and small free-standing central place towns: for example Peterborough, Chesterfield, Rochdale, St Helens, Hexham, North West Wales, South Leicestershire and North Hampshire. The largest LENs in the sample covered the City, Warwickshire and Central Scotland. This brings out the range of geographical variations of different areas discussed further in Chapters 10–14.

Table 8.4 Numbers of employers in LENs areas (from a sample of 48 LENs)

Number of employers in LEN area	Proportion of sample LENs (%)
(min: 1,121)	
0–4,999	27.1
5,000–9,999	20.8
10,000–14,999	33.3
15,000–19,999	10.4
20,000–25,000	2.1
over 25,000	4.2
(max: 37,500)	

The variation in size of LENs, together with variations in the form of the client group of trainees/courses that a LEN was supposed to serve, raise questions about the decision to adopt relatively uniform funding. Although there were differences between some LENs in level of funding (for example, Manchester received much more than average) most LENs received very similar funding irrespective of size differences. The administrative boundaries of LEAs dictated the level of resources and these did not necessarily relate to the needs of the local industrial base.

(ii) Employer involvement

Although LENs were supposed to represent the views of their respective business communities, they generally did not achieve a representation of different types of industry according to their actual importance in the economy. Table 8.5 shows the dominance of manufacturing companies on LEN governing bodies: they accounted for over 55% of employers, with over one-quarter of all members being from the metals and engineering sector. Of the service industries, banking, insurance and ancillary business services together accounted for only 14%, whilst there was a manifest under-representation of retailing and leisure industries, with only 9.1% membership.

In terms of firm size, LENs also tended to give the strongest representation to large firms employing 200 or more staff; 66% of governing body members came from these companies. (See Table 8.6). Greatly under-represented were small firms employing less than 20 employees, which accounted for just 7% of board members. As another indicator of size, analysis of whether companies appeared in the *Times 1000* classification by turnover indicated that 25% of LENs governing body members came from these firms, confirming the importance of very large companies to the LENs initiative.

LENs were a new venture which sought to stimulate employer involvement from a wider base than previous community initiatives. To ascertain the level of prior involvement or interest in public-private partnership activities, we carried out an analysis of

Table 8.5 Sectors of companies represented on LEN governing committees: percentage members by simplified SIC sector

Extractive industries and primary processing		4.5
Construction		4.0
Chemicals	manufacturing	6.8
Metals and engineering	manufacturing	26.7
Food and drink	manufacturing	7.4
Timber, paper and rubber	manufacturing	5.7
Other manufacturing	manufacturing	8.5
Wholesaling and retailing		5.7
Hotels, catering, cultural and recreational		3.4
Transport and communications		5.7
Banking, insurance and ancillary		7.4
Business services and other		6.8
Law, accountancy and advertising		4.5
Utilities		2.3
Other services		0.6

Source: Sample of 16 LENs with 194 employers in case study areas

Table 8.6 LENs sample by employer size, sector, "Times 1000" listing and BiTC membership

Number of employees	Samples as % of total	% in Times 1000	% BiC membership	% manufacturing /construction	% service
1–19	7	0	0	1.9	5.0
20–199	26	1	1	15.7	8.2
>200	66	27	22	40.3	24.5
Sample size	191	163	163	–	–

Business in the Community (BiTC) membership of LEN governing bodies. This revealed that no less than 20% of LEN governing body companies were BiTC members. This is remarkably high given that the national membership of BiTC and ScotBiC was fewer than 500 at the time of analysis (see Table 8.6).

There is a strong interrelationship between employer size, *Times 1000* listing and BiTC membership in the governing bodies of LENs. As shown in Table 8.6, the smallest companies that did find a place on LENs tended to come from the service rather than the manufacturing sector.

These findings highlight that the LENs initiative tended to involve large companies, a significant proportion of which were also members of BiTC and thus were already committed to the broad concept of closer links with the public sector. Apart from the low representation of small firms and the service sector, small manufacturing companies also seem to have proved hard to involve in LENs.

LENs also included other business organisations on their governing bodies. Table 8.7 reveals that, although the involvement of organisations on LENs was not directly sought other than as hosts, most LENs contained a representative from the main local employer body, and a fairly high proportion of LENs also included representatives from other local business organisations. Despite the policy desire to avoid specific organisations, the wide variety of organisations represented on LEN committees seems to reflect local circumstances; i.e. it represented an attempt to include important local forms of business organisation and to accommodate a sensitivity to local politics. The very poor representation of local authorities, despite their role as large employers, often the single largest employer in a locality, reflects the political decision to concentrate LEN strategy on private sector businesses. The further danger of including local authorities, from a central government perspective, was that, even when they were willing to serve, it was very difficult to ensure they acted simply as employers with a consumer interest, rather than as producers or as centres to exercise political power. Local government has had this continuing conflict of interest, that it is simultaneously a consumer *and* a producer of VET (albeit through different departments) and this position has weakened its negotiating stance both with LENs and TECs.

Towards local integration in a national framework: TECs

The use of host bodies for the achievement of the aims of the LEN initiative raised important questions about the best means of bringing about employer involvement in

Table 8.7 LEN committee membership: number and proportion of LENs which contain at least one member from different sources (from a sample of 52 LENs as at April 1989) (includes co-opted members)

	No. of LENs	%
Business	52	100
Employer bodies	42	81
Enterprise agencies	15	29
Other	20	38
Training bodies	20	38
Local authorities	12	23
Industry Matters and UBI	7	13
Voluntary sector	2	4

training. By 1988 LENs had become part of a continuous process of change and suffered from becoming to some extent isolated from other major developments. In December 1988, the White Paper *Employment for the 1990s* (HM Government, 1988) appeared, announcing the intention to create Training and Enterprise Councils. TECs were to be new free-standing bodies which would *"plan and deliver training and promote and support the development of small businesses and self-employment within their area"*. By rejecting hosts, the TECs initiative took on the far more ambitious task of creating, *de novo*, a structure that would bring all areas up to a similar capability with respect to tailoring provision to employer needs.

In this section we present an assessment of the early phases of TEC/LEC development. We draw on the more detailed work in Bennett *et al.* (1993):

- The establishment of the TEC/LEC organisation;
- The changing environment for TECs and LECs, particularly in the area of vocational qualifications.

The organisation of the TEC/LEC network

At its conception, it was intended that a TEC/LEC network would come into being somewhat spontaneously. Groups of local business leaders, guided and assisted to varying degrees by the Training Agency, would come together to propose TECs for their local areas. TEC boundaries would thus not be pre-determined by any existing administrative boundary, but would, rather, be constituted according to the shape of local labour markets as perceived by business itself. This was an essential element of the Government's desire that TECs and LECs would be determined by business needs.

In practice, this has not worked out as intended. This is not surprising, given that a new business organisation was being created. The main dimensions which we analyse below are: geography, local representation, local flexibility, targets, budgets and interfacing.

Geography: meeting business needs or conforming to existing patterns?

Defining the geography of TECs and LECs proved to be a difficult task. Although intended to be spontaneous, most TEC boundaries follow existing shire county or metropolitan district authority boundaries. This appears to reflect the demand by TEED to relate TECs to the areas covered by LEAs. These boundaries seldom show a consonance with actual labour market boundaries and this has created considerable difficulties by fragmenting important labour markets between TECs, particularly in the metropolitan areas and London.

Our research suggests that the constitution of local TEC networks, particularly in urban areas, owes as much to local politics, personalities and "empire building" as to satisfying the "rational" needs of some putative business community. Local politics could involve competition between all the different local interests. But particularly important were:

- Competition between business communities or rural groups of business leaders, e.g. in splitting Nottinghamshire and Derbyshire; in retaining many small areas as with Oldham, Rochdale, and most of London;

- Competition between established business interests and Local Training Agency staff involved in setting up TECs. In a number of cases, it is known that local TA offices were important in forging the shape of TEC boundaries. In London, for example, the TA was active in arbitrating over initial boundary problems, such as the allocation of Wandsworth and Camden. Their decisions were not necessarily in agreement with local business leaders' wishes. Elsewhere, as in London, local TA area office boundaries are known to have been important in determining TEC boundaries. It also proved particularly difficult for TECs to cover areas across a TA region boundary;
- Competition between local authorities. This is, perhaps, surprising given the Government's determination to distance TECs from local authority influence. But it is clear that, in a number of areas, it is the local authority boundary which has essentially defined "place". Rival authorities, often of the same political colour, have made it clear in a number of cases that a TEC embracing more than one authority would be unacceptable. This seems to have been significant in Greater Manchester and it was pressed on the TA by many London boroughs;

The resulting pattern of TECs is thus the outcome of "behind-the-scenes" processes and it is unlikely that the boundaries will all stand the test of time.

In Scotland, there was a more central determination of LEC boundaries. Although there were considerable tensions in both Highlands and Islands Enterprise (HIE) and Scottish Enterprise (SE) areas, the pattern of LECs was agreed at the outset; the pattern did not "emerge" slowly over time as it did for TECs. As a result, the element of "first-come-first-served" which shaped the pattern of TECs is not as prevalent in Scotland.

Representation of local interests

TECs are managed as companies limited by guarantee with a Board usually of 15 members. The Government has determined that two-thirds of these should be drawn from the private sector and one-third from all other interests: public sector employers, local authorities, unions and the voluntary sector.

Most TECs have not experienced difficulties in finding representatives from local authorities to sit on their boards. Rather, they have had difficulty fitting the number of potential candidates to the small number of places available, particularly for TECs covering a large number of local authorities. In most cases chief executives and chief education officers have found a place, less commonly a local councillor. Only a small number of unions have found a place. However, the voluntary sector has proved more difficult to involve. Our work in west London (Bennett *et al.*, 1990b) demonstrates the difficulties inherent in finding voluntary sector representatives that can play a wider support role to bodies like TECs.

The representation of business interests has also created difficulties. Although TEC board members are, theoretically, not supposed to be "representatives" other than of the general business community, finding a means of articulating the views of all types of business has emerged as an important difficulty for TECs. To achieve this, many have adopted sub-structures based on industrial sectors or geography to ensure the adequate representation of differing business needs. However, many have been aware of the need for "representatives" on their main boards. In order to assess this, we have analysed the company and other origins of 275 board members on a sample of 33 TECs. Table 8.8 shows that, even more so than LENs (see Table 8.5), TEC boards over-represent the manufacturing sector, which alone accounts for 61% of board seats, and consequently under-represent the service sector. Banking, insurance, and business services are especially poorly represented, compared to our LEN results. In terms of firm size, our results show, once again, a major over-representation of large companies: companies of 200 or more employees account for 77% of board seats, whilst 30% of all board members appear in the *Times 1000* listing. Only 4% of board members came from companies employing fewer than 20 people. TEC boards thus under-represent small-sized and service companies even more than LENs did. In terms of previous commitment to public-private collaboration, the analysis shows that 20% of board members are members of BiTC (the same proportion as for LENs). Thus, an important core of members came from companies already involved in broadly the same type of initiatives entailed in TECs and our case studies suggest that many had been involved in LENs.

Local flexibility vs. national needs

Although they initially have responsibility for the national YT and ET schemes, TECs are moving towards increasing flexibility in their ability to tailor local training to business needs. Debate has surrounded the extent to which TECs should be given autonomy in these matters. The CBI (1989b, p. 13) pointed out, early on, that senior business leaders *"do not see themselves acting as rubber stamps for the delivery of existing programmes"*. The CBI felt that it was important that TECs should have *"both extensive scope to adapt national programmes to meet local needs and sizeable discretionary budgets"* (ibid). They went on to criticise the Government's proposals to allow the "average" TEC only 1.5% of its total publicly funded budget to go towards its discretionary Local Initiative Fund (LIF). It argued that the LIF needed to be at least 10% of the total grant to allow sufficient management flexibility to attract top business leaders and to enable each TEC to develop its own mission.

Table 8.8 TEC board members' companies by aggregate SIC sectors

SIC sector		%
Extractive industries and primary processing		4.4
Construction		7.6
Chemicals	manufacturing	9.1
Metals and engineering	manufacturing	24.0
Food and drink	manufacturing	7.3
Timber, paper, rubber	manufacturing	5.5
Other manufacturing	manufacturing	14.9
Wholesaling and retailing		5.8
Hotels, catering, cultural and recreational		2.5
Transport and communications		4.0
Banking, insurance and ancillary		6.5
Business services and other		2.9
Law, accountancy and advertising		1.5
Utilities		2.2
Other services		1.8
Total		100.0

Source: original analysis from 33 TEC development bids of early TECs in 1990

The issue remains one of balancing the need for local flexibility with the need to satisfy national training needs. Aside from the issues surrounding the LIF, what discretion ought to be granted to TECs in the area of the national training programmes? More specifically, what is to be the fate of national training providers under the new arrangements? There is a danger that Britain's training system might become too decentralised. Some business sectors clearly require national schemes. The CBI (1989a, p. 9) pointed to the *"overwhelming majority"* of members in the construction industry and the construction sector of the engineering industry who wanted their ITBs to continue. Some major national companies and national training providers have also been concerned to emphasise the importance of nationally-uniform provision. These businesses and providers worked through the TA's Large Contractors Unit and Large Companies Unit (LCU) for YTS and ET respectively, before the conception of TECs. These units provided a means by which they could ensure uniform provision for their trainees without negotiating with individual TA Area Offices. The two LCUs have since been replaced by the TECs and National Providers Unit (TNPU), which by 1992 is expected to be wound up.

TNPU was intended to fulfil a similar function to the two LCUs, with the crucial difference that TECs had the *choice* of using it. Hence, it was envisaged that TECs might hold some contacts with providers directly and others through the TNPU. However, in practice it was clear that by 1991 the TNPU had become little more than a "post-box" for contracts. There was no TNPU contract for national providers: they had to contract directly with TECs. This imposes a large administrative burden on national providers. At the start of 1991 the situation was exacerbated by the fact that many TECs were still deciding whether to use national providers at all when the point was passed at which providers had to issue statutory redundancy warnings to their staff. Many were talking openly of the destruction of a national training infrastructure for the sake of local flexibility. In the event many large national providers have withdrawn from YT, e.g. B&Q, and Dixons.

The problem for TECs is that in terms of operational efficiency, it is clearly better for them to use as few providers as possible. At the same time, it is also in TECs' interest to generate competition amongst providers in order to drive down the unit cost of training places at a given level of quality in order to maximise operational surpluses. It is also in TEC's interest to dictate the terms of their contracts rather than to be bound by one held by the TNPU and dictated by a national provider. All these factors have militated against TEC's using national providers.

Targets and budgets

1991 and 1992 saw significant cuts in funds for YT and ET; 1993 is seeing threats of further cuts of up to 30%. Not surprisingly, this has caused consternation amongst business leaders, though in one sense it probably gives them an appropriate introduction to the instability of the public sector. The question of budgets raises two main issues.

Firstly, cuts raised the spectre of TECs being forced back into their core programmes. Although the LIF remained untouched by the cuts, the administrative problems caused by budgetary uncertainties are likely to make TECs act warily because of fear of further cuts. They are also likely to reduce the amount of time staff have for innovative schemes because they are busy coping with the problems caused by spending constraints. In short, cuts are not conducive to encouraging innovation on the part of TECs. Cuts discourage TECs from broadening their remit beyond what they *have* to do.

Secondly, the cuts focused the minds of TEC staff on the question of what it is they are supposed to be doing. Some restorations of part of TEC spending have been related to increases in unemployment. This has made chief executives wonder if they were supposed to be responding to *unemployment* targets or the *economic development* targets for training into employment which was the key thrust of the TEC prospectus. If they are to be concerned with some form of welfare relief this creates some tensions with their other roles in developing employer commitment to training. The two can be incompatible.

Interfacing between TECs

The way TECs have been conceived means that interfacing with other TECs and other organisations will become an important concern. Interactions with other TECs will be most significant in metropolitan areas. It is in these areas that there will be substantial cross-border flows of individuals for both jobs and training. There are already important instances in most urban areas of competition for students between FE colleges in different LEAs. With TECs, this will, of course, become competition between TECs. Once trained, it has been common for employees to move outside the LEA in which they received their training. This was not a major concern for LEAs. But for TECs, it raises the problem that groups of employers in TECs end up training workers for other groups of employers in other TECs: the poaching problem is shifted to a different geographical level. These issues clearly raise important questions about who pays for training and how TEC budgets are determined.

Emphases of TEC/LEC programmes

The TECs/LECs are the newest local actor and their programme activities are thus difficult to assess. The results of early surveys (Bennett *et al.*, 1993; see also Bennett *et al.*, 1989a, 1990a, 1991a; CLES, 1990) indicate the following major conclusions. *First*, there is a considerable tension between the declared focus of TECs on training in employment and their training funding which is largely focused on programmes for the unemployed. The relatively poor record of employer-provided training in Britain has been long recognised. The Government set one key objective of the employer-led TECs to be to lever reluctant employers and employees into action to enhance training in employment. However, as TECs have got underway there has been a significant shift in government rhetoric which is reflected in the performance requirements that are now in TEC corporate plans and contracts. A much greater emphasis is now being placed on youth training for 16–19 year olds, the short-term unemployed, the easy-to-train elements of the long-term unemployed and women returners.[2]

Second, this changing focus has been particularly affected by the recession of 1990–2. TECs and LECs were conceived in relatively prosperous times, but born during a recession. Despite evidence that companies' training budgets were holding up better than they had in the recession of the early 1980s (Industrial Society survey, *Financial Times*, 18 March 1991), TEC and LEC success may well come to depend on the health of the economy if it is to lever employers and change the emphasis of programmes from alleviating unemployment to building on the success of employees in employment.

Between individual TECs there are considerable differences in emphasis. Those in high unemployment areas have naturally focused more on the unemployed. But TECs in areas of low unemployment see their objectives more in enhancing training for those in employment, as well as filling skill shortages expected to emerge in the next 5 years. These TECs naturally look mainly to the easier-to-train unemployed. This emphasis has continued despite the recession and increased unemployment in 1990–2, i.e. the recession has been seen as a short-term hold on a continuing trend of emerging skills shortages in the long-term. Another phenomena has been the pressure to "cream" within the unemployed. Performance targets placed by government on the TECs are tending to emphasise programmes with high levels of qualifications obtained or high levels of placements in jobs. This is tending to focus participation on those that are easiest to train and place, and who might have been placed anyway, leaving the difficult-to-train behind. There are obvious benefits for TECs to place most emphasis in their programmes on the 16–19 group and short-term unemployed, with much less attention on the long-term unemployed except in skill shortage areas such as London and the South-East.

A *third* area of tension has been how TECs relate to other enterprise bodies. Many early TECs took the rather "macho" approach, in the words of one TA senior commentator, that they could do everything themselves. They were encouraged in this outlook by the TEC launch and prospectus which hardly mentioned other agents – such as Chambers of Commerce, LENs, local authorities or enterprise agencies. In many ways the Government may have been deceived by their own rhetoric into believing that TECs could take this lead everywhere. But later cuts in funding and the need to use other agents to make realistic developments in enterprise policy has subsequently led to a more realistic approach. There have also been strong questions raised as to whether it was a sensible policy for TECs to seek to replace, using public money, private sector bodies such as Chambers, or effective public-private partnership bodies like enterprise agencies. A more realistic approach has developed "on the ground" following an accord developed between the Chambers, TECs and enterprise agencies at Sunningdale in September 1991 and a subsequent announcement of an accord between the DE and DTI (see *Financial Times*, 16 November 1991 and DE Press Release). The open question, however, is whether politicians and/or civil service departments are sufficiently committed to allow these accords to develop into a self-sustaining structure in each area.

A *fourth* problem has been how TECs should balance their emphasis of activities given restructured (and diminishing) funds. In the fields of training they are key players and control most of the public money available. Hence TECs should be able to deliver major changes to the system. However, in the fields of education and enterprise, discussed in earlier chapters, their budget and activity is only one among many. Hence to be successful they will have to work with other agents in partnership. But this requires time and patience, and may be accompanied by frustration.

The TECs/LECs present a fascinating development and are a precedent for decentralisation to private sector-led bodies that may be followed for other central government programmes. Important issues that they are wrestling with in their early stages are (i) how to deal with areas of cross-border flows and coordination that occur, especially in London and other conurbations, (ii) how overlaps with other business organisations are to be dealt with, (iii) how effectively they will be able to lever contractors for training and enterprise services in their areas on a restricted budget, and (iv) how their outputs can be assured to meet the needs of stimulating a system-wide change. We turn to these questions below.

New foundations: NVQs and IIP

The introduction of NVQs

The intention of TECs is that they become regulators of local training markets (Main, 1989; CBI, 1989a). But clearly a national framework is required to prevent an "over-localisation" of training. As we saw at the start of this chapter, the traditional pattern of FE courses and qualifications has been an extremely complex "alphabet soup". Adding further geographical variability to this pattern would simply make matters worse. In this context, the rationalisation of qualifications through the National Council for Vocational Qualifications (NCVQ) is critical. Established in 1986, the NCVQ is dedicated to devising a national framework for qualifications. It has so far established four Levels of National Vocational Qualifications (NVQs) into which most of the awards offered by the major existing examining bodies – BTEC, CGLI and the RSA – are fitted. There are plans to expand the levels to 5 to include degree level and professional training.

The NCVQ does no examining itself but accredits other organisations' qualifications so that they may count towards a particular Level. "Lead industry bodies", based on the main industrial sectors, have been established to ensure the input of business needs into this process. In addition there is also a system in which individuals may accumulate transferable "credits" towards the achievement of different NVQ Levels. To this end the National Record of Vocational Achievement (NROVA) has been introduced. This will be given to individuals who can accumulate credits, not only through traditional courses, but also through the assessment of work-based competences. There will thus be a multiplicity of different pathways to reach the same target.[3]

The development of NVQs has not proceeded without difficulties, however. Until mid-1991, the NCVQ had used "conditional accreditation" virtually to rubber-stamp most existing qualifications as NVQs (see HMI, 1991). As a result, there has been little control over quality, with resulting criticisms of equivalence, particularly between craft and engineering skills, on the one hand, and clerical, catering or retail skills on the other hand. Now, however, qualifications have to meet the NCVQ's criteria before they qualify for NVQ status and this should improve quality standards in the longer term. There were also doubts in the initial years over the breadth of accredited courses: the input of lead industry bodies in particular has been criticised for producing too narrow curricula that neglect broader, basic educational requirements. But 1991 saw a new commitment to including in the curriculum blocks of time dedicated to developing broader understanding as well as job-specific skills. The NCVQ may also embark on an attempt to sort out the tangle of qualifications by licensing only those bodies it deems necessary and of sufficient quality to award NVQs.

A further difficulty is that of equivalence between the NVQ and more traditional academic qualifications. This applies both to the NVQ – "A" level relationship and to subsequent qualifications such as BTEC and HE degrees. It has been difficult to get the educational establishment to accept the notion of equivalence because of the superior status traditionally accorded to wholly academic subjects. For example, a NVQ consultative document released in November 1991 placed one NVQ level 3 equivalent to 2 "A" levels at grade E. The CBI has criticised this as severely eroding the standard of NVQs, and has asserted that in the workplace one NVQ 3 is preferable to two "A" levels because of its greater breadth of study (quoted in *THES*, 9 November 1989, p. 3). Similar problems affect the details of credit accumulation and transfer into higher education. To succeed, therefore, NCVQ will have to fight a long and tenacious battle with educationalists to establish acceptance of formal equivalence. But the battles will be even greater amongst young people and parents, as well as among many employers, in order to convince them that NVQs are not a second class route.

Equivalence of NVQ to European standards needs also to be achieved. At present no formal equivalence is accepted and the level of NVQ 1 would not even merit consideration in Germany. Discussions are well advanced in seeking EC equivalence, but there are major stumbling blocks in achieving it mainly deriving from (i) the complexity of the programmes, and (ii) the lower standards set in some of the clerical, catering and retail skills areas.

The NVQ framework provides a major step forward for Britain. It is a means by which TECs can have local flexibility in the types of courses they provide whilst ensuring that these courses count towards nationally recognised qualifications. NVQs also overcome one of the major problems with the national YTS – that there were no national targets.

The definition of national training targets has, however, also been controversial. Initially proposed by Norman Fowler in 1989, his successor as Secretary of State for Employment, Michael Howard, initially sought to remove the governmental commitment to targets, purportedly because he believed that they could not be met. Subsequently the national targets have been reasserted in a CBI (1991a) document supported by government and most other key agents including TECs, the TUC, ABCC, etc. The new targets launched by Michael Howard can be summarised as follows:

For young people:

- By 1997 at least 80% of the 16–19 age group should gain NVQ level 2 (equivalent to 4 GCSE grades A–C) in their foundation year of education or training (normally by age 17). They will also have a *right* to structured training, work experience or education leading to NVQ level 3 (in 1990 45% of young people achieved NVQ level 2);
- By the year 2000 at least 50% of 16–19 year olds will gain NVQ level 3 or its equivalent (in 1990 30% of 16–18 year olds achieved NVQ level 3).

For employers:

- By 1996 all employers should take part in training or developmental activities as the norm, with at least 50% of the employed workforce aiming for qualifications or modules leading to NVQ;
- By the year 2000 50% of the employed workforce should be qualified at least at NVQ level 3 (in 1990 33% of the employed workforce have NVQ level 3 or its equivalent);
- By 1996 at least 50% of medium and large companies (over 200 employees) should qualify as *Investors in People* (IIP) assured by TECs/LECs (q.v. below).

These targets are demanding. They are easier to achieve for younger people than for the existing workforce. However, the existing workforce has to be a prime target since 90% of those who will be in work in the year 2000 are already in work (q.v. Chapters 2 and 3). Nevertheless large doubts remain as to whether TECs and LECs will have enough leverage to achieve the targets for those in employment. This leads our discussion to the issues of training credits and the Investors in People initiative.

Training credits and careers advice

By clarifying the system of vocational qualifications, NVQ opens the way for the introduction of a credit or voucher system. The introduction of this system was placed firmly on the agenda by the CBI (1989a). The credit system which has been adopted for TECs ensures that every 16-year old receives a voucher of a certain value which permits them to purchase education or training to approved standards of NVQs or its equivalent (at least at NVQ level 2). The value of the credits ranges from approximately £500 to £5,000. It is paid through the TEC. Not only does this produce flexibility and competition among training providers, but it also allows central government to modify YT. Such a strategy clearly fits snugly with the government's wider approach to public services. Credits were piloted in 11 TECs/LECs from April 1991, with extension to 9 further TECs/LECs in late 1991[4]. It is intended that they are extended to the rest of the country. They were a prominent part of the Government's 1991 Education White Paper proposals.

Training credits are designed to form an essential link between the training supplier and individual trainee. Whilst TECs, NVQs and IIP tackle the problem of getting employer demands for skills into the training system, the supply of skills through the take-up of different courses by young people has been a more stubborn problem.

The aim of the credit is to shift responsibility for making decisions on training to the school leaver. But this choice will take place in a framework of training opportunities defined either by employers themselves, who will receive the credit to help them bear the costs of training their employee, or through the TECs who define the range of courses they contract for delivery. Young people not going into a job may be able to use the voucher as a living allowance whilst undertaking a YT course.

The pattern of credits varied at its outset as it was developed first through pilots. The long-term general shape of credits will depend upon the implementation of the Government's 1991 Education White Paper. But some indications are already clear. *First,* the Government seems prepared to accept considerable variability in the costs of training, even if in some cases this cost is very high, e.g. for advanced engineering skills. This is indeed essential if credits are genuinely to tackle the problems of skilling rather than offering a palliative to unemployment.

Second, the Government is on record as giving a commitment to offering credits to all as a *right*. This has occasioned extreme scepticism among many commentators in disbelief that the Treasury will, in fact, allow this expansion in public spending to occur (e.g. Corney, 1991; Ashby, 1991). The Government's hope is that the long-term costs will be contained by efficiency gains in reducing surplus course provision in FE and by increasing employer participation. The long-term commitment has yet to be tested and will fall across the life of at least two parliaments.

Third, the Government has accepted considerable variation in the nature of credit systems in different TEC areas. This appears to be not just a means of gaining experience in early credit pilots, but a genuine acceptance that different labour market conditions require different approaches. This is particularly marked between tight labour markets and those with long-term high unemployment levels. The early results show considerable variety around the common pattern. For example, in Kent and Birmingham, only those people entering certain skill shortage areas will get a credit. In Bradford, Devon and Cornwall, and Grampian the balance of skill needs is being achieved by variations in credit values (*Employment Gazette,* May 1991, pp. 248–9).

The developments of the White Paper envisage that these lessons will lead to a generally low level of credit, or withholding of credits in some low skill sectors. This will be achieved through the three mechanisms of NVQ, IIP and TEC decisions. The level of credits is expected to vary across skills in each place, and to vary between places depending upon relative costs and demand. Thus credits will be *generally* available at a low level (of a living allowance whilst on YT of £29.50 per week in late 1991), as well as selectively available to different skill groups at different prices. The concept of *right* to credits therefore is strongly tempered by steering of provision and financial incentives to both young people and employers. It is an open question whether this approach can be sustained against vigorous lobbying from disadvantaged industry groups and against Labour Party philosophy of seeking equity.

A *fourth* issue relates to the role of information and advice. To make sensible choices, young people need not only financial incentives that steer them to areas of relative skills demand, they also need to make sound judgements of their own potential and capability. The provision of information and advice has not yet yielded clear-cut solutions. TECs have sought a variety of approaches. Northumberland and Hertfordshire have attempted to improve schools-based careers libraries and advice, many TEC pilots have introduced free telephone helplines, Birmingham has developed 15 sector Compacts to deliver advice and tailor credits (following its long-term sectoral approach: see Chapter 11), and many pilot TECs have enhanced the careers service and have developed individual Action Plans.

At the centre of this dilemma on how to provide information and advice is the role of the Careers Service, the balance of LEA compared to individual school-based systems, and the broader relation between education development pre-16 and the world of work (through EBPs, Compacts, work experience and other mechanisms discussed in Chapter 7). In mid 1990 an enquiry was set up by the DE into the Careers Service. This resulted in radical proposals for reform including the channelling of its funds through the TECs/LECs. The DE has been responsible for only part of Careers Service funding and met a strong defence from the DES. The result has so far been something of a stalemate. The TECs/LECs are developing their own initiatives related to credits which will in some cases strengthen and in other cases by-pass the Careers Service. The White Paper (DES/DE/WO, 1991) affirmed support for the existing Careers Service, but called for improvement in the quality of its services and closer relations to employers through TECs. It envisaged one of three possibilities: (i) LEAs and TECs working jointly on the Careers Service in partnership through EBPs, (ii) legislation to open up the Careers Service to contracting out from LEAs, and (iii) being run by TECs.

In the short-term, option (i) has become the favoured route. In November 1991 the Employment Secretary set out plans for Employment Department funds to be based on *Careers Service Partnerships* between local authorities and TECs. This was the outcome of lengthy discussions with local authorities and TECs and reflects a slowdown of reform in the face of both DES and LEA resistance and a change in approach in the pre-election run-up. Careers Service Partnerships required the Careers Service to bid for its DE funds but left its main DES funding intact. It is likely, therefore, to affect LEAs very differently depending on their depth of organisational commitment to Careers Service development. Following our assessments of EBPs in Chapter 7, we would expect these changes to act as "bolt-ons" to existing LEA Careers Service structures, rather than deeply imbuing the required changes in the range, approach to delivery, and quality of advice available to young people.

The resolution of the problem of delivery of careers advice is a crucial one which impinges strongly on mainstream pre-16 education. Following our discussion of Chapter 7, we conclude that the key requirements are: (i) better tuning of the national curriculum to the world of work through more positive development of work experience and related projects, (ii) founded on deeper and more effective partnerships between school pupils and employers, (iii) a strong role for employer bodies in these partnerships which (iv) we conclude can only be achieved by bodies that have greater representational legitimacy in the business community than TECs/LECs. We develop this further in Chapter 15.

Investors in People (IIP)

IIP is intended to be a system of accreditation and quality control of employer based training. It will act as a kind of *kitemark*. It is anticipated that TECs will combine IIP with the leverage of their funds and credits to support trainees only in IIP accredited companies. This is the main mechanism that it is hoped will spread a training culture to smaller firms. If the proposal, to use a training levy with IIP companies exempt, were to be implemented then this leverage would become more compelling. It is also argued that the demographic downturn (see Figure 3.9) will affect the labour market so that companies seeking to recruit will have no choice but to meet IIP standards if they wish to be attractive to young people.

IIP involves (CBI, 1991b):

- A business making a public commitment at senior level to develop all employees to achieve business objectives using a written but flexible plan specifying how needs will be assessed and met; this will be communicated to employees showing how they can contribute to success, involving employee representatives and unions where appropriate;
- The business regularly reviews the training and development needs of its employees through its business planning linked, where appropriate, to NVQ;
- The business develops its training commitment from recruitment of an employee throughout their career;
- The business evaluates its training investment at all levels against its goals and targets in order to improve future effectiveness.

The IIP initiative is closely coupled with NVQ targets. These two forces, combined with training credits and TECs/LECs could potentially change the training system. Also significant is the attempt to link IIP to the Management Charter Initiative (MCI).

MCI was an outcome of the MSC/NEDC/BIM report (1989) (the "Handy Report") and the Constable and McCormick (1987) Report. These argued that Britain was lagging behind other countries in its general level of management education (see Chapter 4). However, it has only been more recently realised that management education is also a crucial mechanism for attaining targets in work-based learning to complement the development of NVQ, adult career development and the leadership of bodies like TECs. The crucial gap in training that Britain has found it difficult to fill is the training of the trainers in the workplace. This requires some equivalent of the German Meister in supervisory skill areas.

MCI has been an attempt to fill this gap. It was developed jointly by CBI, British Institute of Management (BIM) and Foundation for Management Education (FME) through the Charter for Management Education (CMED). It has primarily focused on three elements: (i) developing a Code of Practice, available since July 1989, (ii) building networks of the employers and providers of educational support who adopted the Code of Practice, and (iii) developing an improved structure of management qualifications, including recognition of prior learning (TA/DHS, 1989; CMED, 1988; Reid, 1989). Whilst useful in themselves, these focuses are clearly on formal management qualifications rather than management training as a support for work-based training.

The development of IIP and MCI are major developments, which, if implemented in a sustained way, have a real chance of engineering many of the required system-wide changes. The difficulties in the way of the new system are, however, numerous.

First is the problem of how effective the training will be. Although nominally set at an NVQ standard, many companies will use their own systems with formal equivalence to NVQ, but which may not be at a genuinely comparable standard. This is made more likely given the doubts about true equivalence within NVQ itself.

Second is the problem of how assessment will be undertaken. The use of BS 5750 was originally envisaged to tackle management training standards. This would be applied to effective management systems, which would include trainer training. IIP, however, is more concerned to demonstrate a commitment to a learning culture rather than effective training management. There is thus a confusion of purpose and capacity in IIP. Uncertainty also surrounds its implementation. It is an important question as to whether TECs are appropriate for this purpose. There certainly must be doubts as to how rapidly such a system can develop. It has taken over 15 years for BS 5750 to be established as a manufacturing standard.

Third is the problem of take-up. The ability of TECs to exert strong pressures through the use of public money for trainees, training credits and NVQs, all lie some years in the future. In the meantime, take-up of IIP has been very slow, only 60 companies accredited in the first year. The future will rely on good will and exhortation: not a guaranteed recipe for success in diffusing the training culture to smaller firms given the systems failures we have noted.

Fourth is the question of sustainability. It will require two parliaments fully to implement the proposals. Against a background of cuts in funding of TEC programmes (cuts in BGT are particularly important to IIP) and the major reforms of programmes likely under each new government, doubts remain as to the long-term commitment that will be achieved.

Fifth is the absence of a well developed route for trainer-training. Although possible within NVQ, MCI, and IIP, none of these are specifically designed for the purpose of enhancing the quality of training managers and supervisors in the workplace. They are largely outside NVQ, beginning to be addressed by MCI, and whilst crucial to IIP have not yet found a formal place within its system. This gap is possible to fill, but needs a deeper and better financed approach. This partly explains the reluctance of many TECs to take up IIP and MCI (see Bennett *et al.*, 1993).

Filling the gaps

The evolution of training in Britain in the period since 1985 has gone a very long way to putting in place the system-wide reform that we have argued is required. In a very real sense the foundations of a quality system have been laid. Thus a major leap forward has been made. The question we now must ask, however, is how far this system can be achieved. We identify the following problems that still have to be overcome:

- *Stability*. The system of NVQ and IIP cannot be fully implemented until 1996. The timetable for GNVQ is even slower. This covers not only the lifetime of the new government from 1992, but also the life of two further parliaments. History shows the dramatic effects of changes in governments. The stability needed to implement the NVQ-IIP system will require an alertness of the key agents to keep each new government on the path of progressive development;

- *The development of TECs and LECs.* Whilst business-led, there is a tension over their long-term stability. First, there is the problem of TEC Boards' full control over staff and programmes; second, there is the issue of how representative TECs/LECs can ever be of their business communities;
- *Credits.* These require the continued commitment of government to young people's entitlement. There is a continuing conflict between the concept of entitlement and the Treasury's view that if employers want their staff to be qualified then they should pay for them;
- *Diffusion of training culture.* There is a major problem of developing training down the size spectrum to smaller and medium-sized businesses. The leverage of the IIP kitemark and the diminishing public money of the TECs is unlikely to persuade many smaller firms unless labour supply is very tight. The alternative of the leverage of a training levy will be greater, but presents genuine difficulties for many small firms that cannot readily offer their own training tracks, or may find it inappropriate to their needs. There is a gap between thinking on training and thinking on enterprise development. The absence of a link between the needs of training, on the one hand, and the needs of business support in a wider sense, through the stages of foundation, development and growth, on the other hand, is a key gap in the case of smaller firms. Without a proper link and mechanism of transmission to small businesses, TECs/LECs are handicapped;
- *Trainer training.* Whilst all the developments will stimulate the development of management and supervision training within firms, this has at present no proper organisational base within the institutional network and it is not built into the system of NVQs. There is thus no equivalent of the German meister. Although there are some outstanding examples of the implementation of MCI in large companies, even the most fervent supporters of MCI recognise that it is not yet an adequate system for transmitting the stimulus required for trainer training;
- *IIP quality control.* This is itself open to a number of challenges. Whilst too early to judge fully, it is clear that its development has been slow to take off and has little prospect of diffusing rapidly or deeply among businesses. There is also a danger that IIP aims at the wrong target and that it is too internally controlled through the Department of Employment and TECs. Although the NTTF and TEC Boards are concerned to specify high quality standards, these standards are more concerned with diffusion of training culture rather than effective training management;
- *Equivalence of status.* Transferability of NVQs, particularly between GNVQ and "A" levels will take a long time to establish and will need strong employer leverage if it is to overcome deep-seated parental, employer and other prejudices against the vocational route;
- *Careers advice.* There remains a problem of linking vocational development post-16 to a better information service to young people. The reform of the Careers Service and school-based careers guidance is still a political football; the full implementation of a national Record of Achievement is still in its infancy; and the development in schools of vocational education, business links and work experience hangs in the balance pending the evolution of the national curriculum (as discussed in Chapter 7). Section 24 of the Education Reform Act can be used as a strong lever to make NVQs and business involvement a common currency after 1993. But there has to be considerable doubt that this will be fully achieved.

This assessment is not intended to be negative. On the contrary, the foundations of a strong system have now been established that could allow Britain at last to achieve a world class standard in training – a goal that has eluded the country since at least the 1870s. However, it is essential to identify the problems that remain to be overcome. We develop the arguments further in Chapter 15. Britain must learn to emulate German or Japanese practice of continuing to develop systems rather than throw them away with each change in minister or new government. To succeed, the strategy that has been developed must be implemented in a sustained and committed way for a period of at least 10 or 15 years before the attitudes of employers, employees, trainers, educationalists and parents have developed sufficiently to assure a self-sustaining momentum.

Footnotes: Chapter 8

1. This discussion is a summary of that available at greater length in Bennett *et al.* (1990a) and is based on a complete study of all LENs, supplemented by more detailed analysis of a representative sample of 52 LENs (43%). We are grateful for the support of the Training Agency for access to some of these data.

2. Even though the balance in favour of training in employment is still advocated (see HM Government, 1992; DE, 1991, *A Strategy for Skills*).

3. Arrangements for Scotland follow similar principles for Scottish Vocational Educational Certificates: we use, in general, the English terms.

4. The April 1991 pilots were Birmingham, Bradford, Devon and Cornwall, Grampian, Hertfordshire, Kent, N.E. Wales, Northumberland, S. and E. Cheshire, S. London and Suffolk. The further 9 TEC pilots announced in December 1991 were Calderdale and Kirklees, Isle of Wight, Merseyside, Northampton, South Thames, Stafford, Mid Glamorgan, Caithness and Sutherland, and Dunbartonshire.

PART III

The Local Dimension: Horizontal Integration

9. *LOCAL NETWORKS*

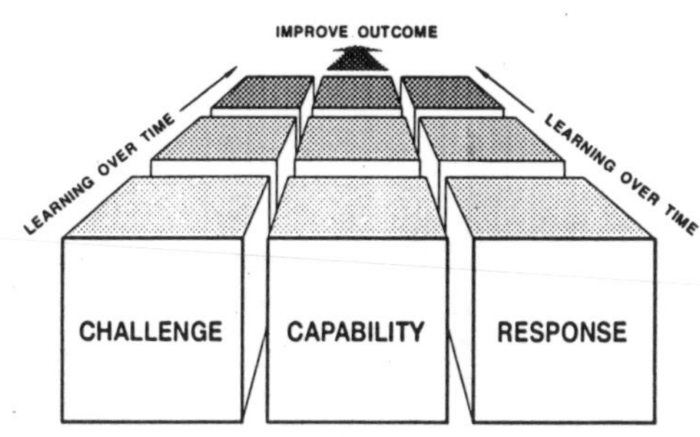

Developing integration

In this chapter we introduce the key themes of Part 3 of this book. These cover the *horizontal* integration of vertical programmes at a local level. This discussion complements the national level debate outlined in Part 1, and the analysis of each main programme field of enterprise, education and training in Part 2 of this book.

In each part of our previous analysis we have identified a national problem of "systems failure". We have argued that this arises from the tension between national and local, frictions between public and private, and the influence of the contrasted cultures and 'histories' of different institutions, particularly between producers and clients. These gaps have been argued to be placing major constraints on Britain's economic progress. The conclusion has been that *the major barrier to improving Britain's competitiveness has been an absence of INTEGRATION to achieve strategic economic goals.*

In this chapter we examine the *local* problems of integration. We establish a framework for the assessment of the wide variety of attempts to achieve integration that have been developed in different local contexts. Our argument throughout has been that improving national capability requires a *local* client-focused vision; that a client-focus requires a localised *responsiveness* that is fitted to the needs of the local economy; and hence that local responsiveness, as "fitness for purpose", will require major contrasts of fit between places depending upon the nature of the local economy, its institutional structure, and its geography.

In the discussion so far we have evidence of constraints on Britain's economic capability. In general, we have argued that there are significant deficiencies in the programmes, and agents providing programmes, which are characterised by: fragmentation; overlaps; gaps; complexity; and poor focusing. These constraints operate across each field of activity, as shown in Part 2 of this book. In Part 3 we demonstrate the constraints on capability at a local level. We also describe developments that have occurred which are seeking to achieve integration.

We develop the concept of fitness for purpose below through discussion of 5 main elements:

- Local capability;
- The importance of local networks;
- How local networks work;
- From networks to partnership;
- Developing a learning process.

Local capability

What makes one place more economically successful than another? We have already introduced this question in Chapter 6 as an issue concerning the local factors supporting or inhibiting enterprise development. A wide range of factors have been identified which influence how fertile the local environment is to enterprise. These are summarised in Figure 6.3. Here we turn to how these factors translate into a total environment that is locally favourable or inhibitive to economic development.

Considerable analysis of this issue in the US, as well as Europe and Britain, now allows a good understanding of the key local environmental conditions required. In general, the most progressive and innovative environments are those with company headquarters, not branch plants; with a strong presence of small firms, or strongly decentralised large firms; with facilitative conditions for internal and external flexibility in production, marketing and subcontracting; and a supportive local institutional environment.[1]

These findings are reinforced by conclusions on the nature of entrepreneurism. Generally there seems to be no strong evidence of special types of entrepreneurial motives – although motivation is necessary, entrepreneurs and entrepreneurial environments are not separate from the rest of the economy.[2] Rather, the determinants of entrepreneurism and local innovative capacity appear more to be related to (i) exposure to opportunities, and (ii) access to resources and the required factor inputs – particularly human capital. Both factors have a preeminently local dimension.

Exposure to opportunities is a locally fixed variable for most enterprises. Opportunities arise from the economic and wider "social networks" of the individuals who make up the business managers (whether large or small). Similarly, the support environment for survival also depends on local contact networks. Survival rates can be radically improved by the networks of support available, and networks of information that link businesses to markets and niches of economic opportunity. Recent sociological studies have demonstrated how these networks extend much more widely than social position / class conceptions, to broader local determinants of information on available market opportunities (e.g. Aldrich and Zimmer, 1986). A critical policy question, therefore, is how to stimulate such networks to work better in order to allow wider and more rapid entry and improve the chances of business survival.

Access to resources is a second key determinant of the innovativeness of an environment. This appears to apply equally to the effect on the entrepreneur, the family's resource, ethnic minority support (Curran, 1986), and to broader neighbourhood contexts (Mason, 1989; Binks and Jennings, 1986), which show that survival rates and start-up rates of businesses are all strongly related to the easy availability of the required factor inputs.

The combination of the two influences, of exposure to opportunities and access to resources, has led to the identification of differences in local environment for different types of firm by size or sector. For example, Hickman (1981, p. 7) concludes that "*the best regions for growth for certain types of firms are not best for other types of firms. Regions rich in start-ups are not the same as regions with strong expansion growth ... regions fall into different typologies, each relying for economic development on a different economic mix ... providing a natural "fertile soil" for different types of firm.*" This leads to the natural policy conclusion that it is necessary both to understand the texture of the local fabric, and to identify the key points where enhancement is required.

One of the few empirical analyses that attempts to generalise across the many related factors that affect innovative environments in Britain is that of Moyes and Westhead (1990). Their results, shown in Figure 9.1, draw out the strong differences between the innovativeness of the rural and south-east parts of Britain, compared to the low innovativeness of Scotland's central valley, North-East England, South Wales valleys and the Staffordshire–South Yorkshire–East Midlands triangle.[3]

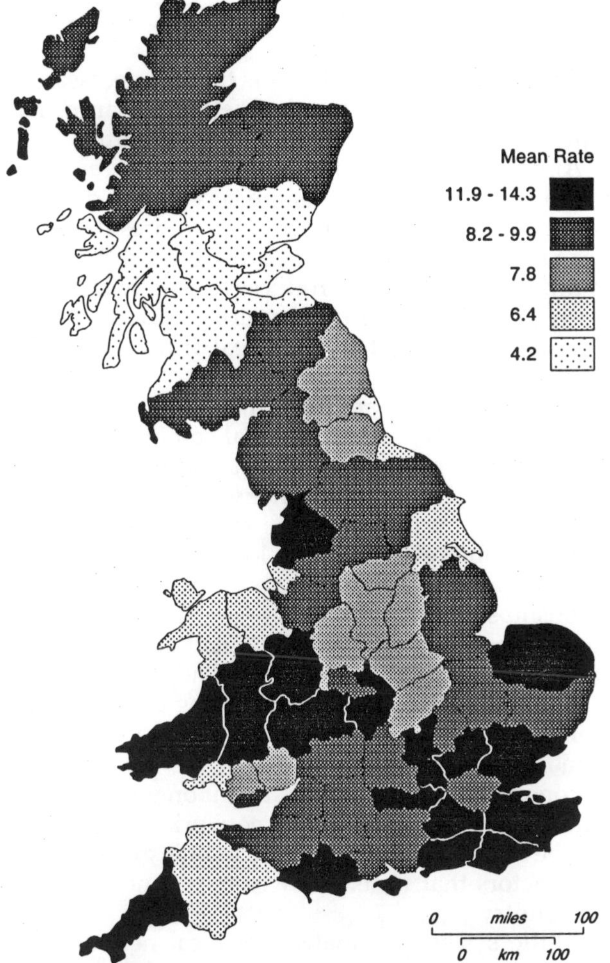

Figure 9.1 Relative strength of local environments for innovation in Britain. The scores measure the mean rate of new firm VAT registrations related to the sum of a large range of local factors derived from principal component scores
Source: from Moyes and Westhead, 1990, Figure 5

The policy question that derives from these differences is, first, how to facilitate innovation and entrepreneurism in contexts where it is not thriving spontaneously, and second, how to enhance development even in those contexts where the rate of innovation at present appears healthy.

The common factor in the studies of exposure to opportunities and access to resources is the operation of effective networks. In areas with strong spontaneous development there is usually a tradition of supportive social and economic networks stimulating both enterprise and resource supply across all necessary production requirements. The policy question then turns on how to enhance local networks. In the rest of the discussion in this chapter we analyse, in turn, the characteristics of local networks, how they can be enhanced by learning, and the role of government in their development.

The importance of local networks

Networks are the links of producers and clients that are necessary to assure an economic capability and responsiveness. Networks seek to enhance market allocation decisions: in economic terms they facilitate the externalities of decisions becoming internalised (see Appendix 1). Networks mean that key agents have to work more closely together, and that business clients are serviced at different times by different producers. To assure a quality system, however, requires that a *"throughness"* must be developed with, as far as possible, the client being guided through the service structure often without the differences between producers being "visible", and certainly without differences between producers causing barriers of access to services. Networks are therefore a major element in achieving local integration as well as enhancing innovation.

Networks for economic services are fundamentally local affairs. They depend upon the way in which businesses are served by local community and business leaders and elites, the way in which local networks perform, and how participation takes place at a local level. However, the character of local networks, their leadership and elites, is also fundamentally determined by the economic structure and layout of their economies which itself depends on the relation of the local economy to the national and global economic system. As a result, different types of area possess very different types of networks of relationships. For example, there are strong contrasts between older and newer industrial areas; between areas concentrated on urban settlements and those in more dispersed urban or rural areas; and so on. These contrasts are analysed at length for each area in the whole of Britain in the following chapters.

The contrasts of networks between areas create very different possibilities for development. In some areas networks allow a strong positive lead to be taken which allows the rapid economic change and adjustment on which service quality is founded. In other areas, the absence of an effective network, or a network tuned to bygone circumstances, can be a strong inhibition to economic growth. Local networks are thus strong supply side factors that raise or lower the economic growth potential for different parts of the country.

There has been little systematic analysis of local networks in Britain that is at a sufficient geographical scale or has the required focus for our discussion here. However, there are some recent studies that are informative of the broad patterns that arise in different circumstances. We first outline these and in Chapter 10 show how they can be applied to different contexts.

In discussing networks we make an important distinction between two sets of agents:

- Leaders and local elites; and
- Citizens, participants and implementors.

We develop the concept of learning and animation required to make networks perform effectively. But there is different learning required by different agents in different places – sometimes among local leaders, sometimes among participants, often among both. In Chapter 4 we have commented on the changing origins and roles being played by Britain's managers, elites and leaders. In the following discussion we show how these roles require development at the local level.

Considerable research has gone into the analysis of networks and power structures in local economies from the point of view of political and social participation. However, there have been far fewer analyses of how local economies are affected by participation. Some early studies have demonstrated the importance of local business elites and their networks (Lammers, 1967; Heller, 1973; Dahl, 1961; a more recent review shows how little use is made of network concepts in the literature (Friedland, 1982, Chapter 2)). However, for recent analysis for Britain we are reliant almost exclusively on the work of Geraint Parry *et al.* (1992) and the new materials generated in this book.

Parry has analysed participation networks in 6 highly varied localities in Britain[4] from which more general conclusions can be cautiously drawn. Parry has found considerable consistency in the factors affecting participation levels in each locality. This accords with other participation studies (particularly Verba and Nie, 1972; Verba, Nie and Kim, 1978). The variation in participation between areas, when the effect of social composition and level of resources are controlled for, leaves a significant difference in community effects that appears to be attached to place as such. The conclusion is that some places are simply much more communitarian than others. In Parry's sample it was the rural and fringe metropolitan areas that have lowest levels of community activity; and the industrial towns and London neighbourhood that had the highest levels of community activity.

Parry also analysed the way in which local leaders relate to wider local community values. Parry found a very strong association between the agendas of local citizens and local leaders. He further concluded that this strong leader-citizen concurrence on almost all issues gives every appearance that citizens affect the leaders, and vice-versa, even if only a small minority of citizens are actually active in most economic and political decisions. This indicated a very low level of autonomy of elites, contrary to the expectations of many previous writers (e.g. Nordlinger, 1981; Gurr and King, 1987). However, local business leaders were the group most significantly differing in their agenda from local citizens: they had a 65% concurrence on the key issues identified locally, compared to 78% for elected council members. And economic issues (particularly unemployment) were the areas which had least concurrence in level between elite and citizens: "the elite established unemployment as an issue quite independently of the actually expressed priorities of citizens" (Parry *et al.*, 1992, p. 387).

Parry's findings have profound implications for our argument. They are suggestive of three important possibilities. First, that there is a gap between, on the one hand, the business leadership and economic objectives of localities, and on the other hand, the citizen view of what are the important issues. This confirms our observation of Britain's economic "system failure", but now on the basis of generalisations across varied localities derived from individual interview records. It is suggestive that citizens poorly perceive the economic needs of their own livelihood based on the requirements of the economy of their locality as a whole.

Second, Parry's findings suggest that whilst local political leaders are most in tune with citizen views, they are distant from action on economic issues. This implies that the main, or often sole, source of leadership on the local *economy* are business leaders who appear to be the least able to mobilise citizen support. This further implies a strategic gap between those agents who have economic capability but little local power, and those agents who have local power both to mobilise and to respond to citizens but have few economic objectives. Of course low levels of participation do not necessarily mean low levels of total power, since businesses control jobs and investment (see also Dahl, 1961; Friedland, 1982; Form and Miller, 1960; Freeman *et al.*, 1963). But Parry's results confirm the need we have argued to link actors together to encourage a wider sharing of economic objectives among the non-business leaders and agents in the community.

A third implication of Parry's findings derives from the differences in participation between areas, both for citizens and leaders. In general rural and fringe metropolitan areas have the lowest levels of community activity and concurrence among the leaders on the key issues, whilst small industrial towns and the London neighbourhood of Stockwell had both the highest activity and concurrence on issues. These suggestions from Parry's study are directly in line with the conclusions on the networking capability in different parts of Britain which we outline below.

How local networks work

Turning to how local networks actually work, there have been very few analyses that lead to an operational method that allows generalisations to be drawn across the whole country. We follow an approach here of outlining a number of models of networks which we then use to compare areas. The main models we employ are shown in Figure 9.2. The networks we observe in many areas are fragmented between individual programmes. This produces the outcome shown in Figure 9.2A. This has an absence of a network, as such, linking actors.

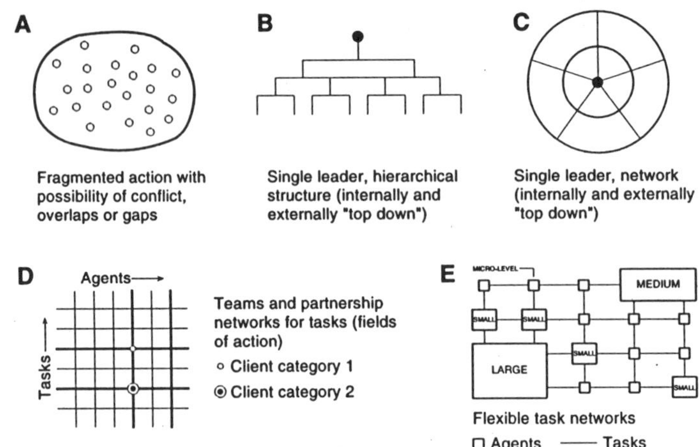

Figure 9.2 Networks of relations between agents at a local level

A different type of fragmentation arises from the traditional hierarchical "line management" structures shown in Figure 9.2B. This has a strongly developed vertical division between programmes and usually many tiers of administration. It is the structure characterising most civil service offices and is the traditional structure in many large companies. It is associated with the hierarchical business planning models originated by Taylor (1911), Gulick and Urwick (1933), and is sometimes referred to as Taylorism. This approach leads to fragmentation through "top down" planning. It often seems that central government prefers a model such as 9.2B. This fits with the civil service's own structure and fits to its programmatic approach and needs for accountability. The combination of models A and B is largely responsible for the "patchwork quilt" of local programmes observed by the Audit Commission (1989) and reviewed in Chapter 5.

Attempts to improve the capability of local networks have usually focused on two alternative models. One is shown in Figure 9.2C. This is strongly focal on a single central point, with line structures outward, but complex cross-linkages between programme lines. This approach has been attempted in a number of corporate management initiatives in both businesses and government bodies (particularly local authorities). It focuses on strong central leadership, and may be combined with strong moves to decentralise so as to "empower" points of decentralised control. This is very much how Urban Development Corporations (UDCs) and Training and Enterprise Councils (TECs) were conceived: to become the key strategic leaders and power brokers in the local economy developing a network of interlinkages and subcontracted relationships with other actors and networks as part of the process of animation. The empowerment concept derives largely from the USA where it has been used to shift welfare state and other public programmes to approaches that focus on the role of individual incentives – empowering clients rather than producers (see e.g. Peters, 1990; *The Economist*, 24 November 1990, pp. 45–6, "A banner with a strong device: empowerment"). That this American empowerment debate has been influential on the thinking behind TECs is clear from Cay Stratton's (1989) comment: *The TEC must be about empowering individuals and neighbourhoods ... It must do things with people, not to them or for them. And the TEC can achieve these ends only if it retains its position as both a strategic body ... and as an open, accessible, forward-looking institution.*

The danger in model 9.2C is that too much depends on central coordination. It can become heavily "top down", which may undermine broader networking and local initiative. It can also become highly over-bureaucratised. In the case of TECs, there is evidence that it can become subverted by the line structures deriving from the former civil service and by the pressures coming from numerous separated but vertically integrated central government and other programmes (see Bennett *et al.*, 1993).

In most places "top down" models, like Figures 9.2B and 9.2C, are in any case unrealistic and unachievable. Instead networking has to be more flexible, tailored to each category of client need, and to each agency role. Indeed the concept of client focus and "throughness" cannot be addressed by "top down" planning models alone. One approach that allows more "bottom up" networking is shown in Figure 9.2D. This seeks to demonstrate the way in which programmatic tasks and agents can be combined to meet the particular needs of groups of clients on a client-group by client-group basis. Each category of client has a separately tasked structure of support that cuts across the different programmes and agents, but links them into a specific network of programme delivery.

The models A-D in Figure 9.2, and the concepts that lie behind them, are a development of the organisational models developed in management science (see e.g. Drucker, 1985, 1989; Handy, 1985). In Charles Handy's models, for example, Figure 9.1A is an individual/"person" culture, B is a "role" culture, C is a "club" culture and D is a "task" culture. Commenting on the task model Handy suggests that it can respond in a less individualistic way than top down "clubs", and more speedily and flexibly than "role" models. Ideally the task model allows each task to draw on the agents, talents and resources it requires, each task can be approached differently, and it is well suited to looking forward, and to problem-solving. It is also more rewarding to competent people or organisations. Its drawback is that it is time-consuming, cannot be easily routinised, and thus requires largest time inputs from the most competent people in leadership positions. It also tends to delegate a lot of discretion and budget to task leaders and, therefore, requires that they have the competence to employ that discretion.

Even the most superficial appraisal of these management models makes it obvious that the task model D offers considerable opportunities for achieving local integration, innovation in methods of linking agents together, and the demonstrable improvement in overall quality that can be achieved from linking programmes. Hence it is an important model to pursue in stimulating action and animating partnership at a local level.

However, the task model requires strong external support and coordination in order to stimulate tasking – this usually does not happen autonomously in a local economy. The task model is also least well-suited to guaranteeing quality in routine and more repetitive tasks. And it has major drawbacks for application to situations of "systems failure" where task leaders may not be available with the necessary level of competence. The task model is best suited to *strategic* development in local economies where the key actors are highly competent and consensus on roles can be achieved.

Recognition of these limitations leads us to propose a new and rather different model, shown in Figure 9.2E. This model is stimulated by the concepts of flexible organisation now being evolved in most leading businesses (see Chapters 2 and 6). *Flexible structures* do not have rigid relations between agents, but a changing and evolving network of contracting and subcontracting. Births and deaths of initiatives are thus easier, and this allows more rapid innovation and entry of new ideas by readier creation of new initiatives and faster and less painful removal of inefficient activities. This is a *responsive* local structure. The same structure increasingly characterises the internal structures of management of firms, with less rigid distinctions between managers and workers and greater incentives for individuals to perform in a wider variety of different environments.

Flexible structures provide the capacity to be responsive. In this sense they incorporate the task model 9.2D. However, there must also be strong points holding the networks together, animating them, and frequently resourcing them. In a business these strong points are the core staff and management team. In a local economy there is no counterpart of a single core, because there are usually many important key actors. There are, instead, multiple cores, of different size and effectiveness. The large and significant core agents are the critical elements, both of cement and animation, that keep these networks together.

To be effective these networks must ensure that (i) smaller agents are linked to the tasks developed in the cores. This can usually be achieved by contracting and subcontracting. Tasking will be fairly straightforward since the large core agents have enough power or resources to ensure compliance. In addition, (ii) the core agents must link with each other to achieve a common strategy for the benefit of the area. This means that an integrated network is achieved, rather than a group of fragmented initiatives, each looking to the goals of different core actors. Finally, (iii) each core actor must look to its own internal organisation to ensure that each of its own departments or subunits is relating both to the core's corporate objectives and to the wider collective goals of the area as a whole. This is particularly problematic within large bodies and public sector bodies, such as local authorities and TECs. The difficulty of internal focus arises because such organisations often have multiple objectives (e.g. social and economic, different departmental priorities) which conflict with each other. They are also prone to bureaucratic capture and labour relations agreements that divert or frustrate core objectives.

The large and most significant core actors around which the networks are built are usually:

- The local authorities;
- The chief local business bodies – usually Chambers of Commerce, sometimes enterprise agencies;
- The TECs/LECs;
- The large local firms.

The smaller actors in the network are very numerous and vary a great deal between places. They are usually composed of:

- Small and medium sized firms;
- Enterprise agencies;
- A variety of employer groups;
- Trade unions;
- Central government bodies (UDCs, CATs, TFs, etc.);
- Central government initiatives (LENs, Compacts, EBPs, EEAs, etc.);
- Voluntary and community bodies;
- Training providers.

In this list "smallness" does not refer necessarily to the total size of an agent, but to their specific role or power to influence economic development.

In many areas the roles of core and smaller agents may reverse. Some areas do not have significant large employers or major Chambers of Commerce; in some areas the local authorities or TECs/LECs may be small or ineffective relative to the geographical span of the local economy and labour market. As we argue in Chapters 10–14, the relative absence of core agents, in terms of size or effectiveness, is a particular problem in fringe metropolitan and many rural areas. Additionally, a problem may arise that the core agents in one part of the local economy are not matched by strong core agents in other parts of the economy. This may affect sector coverage (e.g. different relative strengths between business organisations, local government, community bodies, and the enterprise sector) or geographical coverage (strong presence of core agents in some parts of the local economy but not in others). This affects almost all areas, but is a particular problem in dispersed industrial areas and in rural areas. We analyse these different types of networks in later chapters.

As a result of these area differences, enhancement of local networks will usually require a blending of different approaches in different places. This blending will often require different structures at the level of key management/leadership than at the more operational level. Thus there must be different networks in different places, for different programmes, depending upon the competences available. This can also be interpreted as the background for developing evolution and learning, as introduced below.

From networks to partnership

Networks are the essential means for linking one group of agents to others whom they affect. Networks are the mechanism for exchange of information and services in support of business development. But the network concept alone does not fully capture what we believe is required to overcome the problems of Britain's economic system failure. In addition, there is required the commitment of the agents to work fully together. This means:

i) Accepting long-term structures that work towards sustained commitment to change and achievement of quality;
ii) Accepting an active commitment to changing the internal operations of each agent, and helping other agents also to change to achieve an improved system overall.

Hence networking alone is largely passive, what is required by the two requirements listed here is the development of a system-wide change to *partnership*.

Partnerships are based on firm agreements by agents to work together. They extend far beyond network flows of information, to offer a system that ensures that the problem, or the client, is fully addressed. Partnerships can range from agreements between actors to work together towards a common end, to agreements which form a legal contract through which specific targets for performance are defined by the contracting parties. Over this range of possibilities the parties may act as relatively equal partners, but frequently the partnership is not equal: it is more important to one party than to others, or performance is mandated or coerced by one party on another (frequently through financial powers).

Recognising that there may be inequalities in partnerships is an important prerequisite to tackling the problem of systems failure. We have seen, in our earlier discussion, that a major part of Britain's systemic problem is the failure by many key agents to address economic *as well as* specific programme targets. Sometimes inequalities must be built into partnerships to ensure that economic objectives are sought and achieved by agents, along with their other objectives. This is particularly true of education and training which have the obvious problems of balancing economic with more general cultural and human requirements. But it is also true of government policy in the field of enterprise development which has often diverted from sustained commitment to business towards palliatives for the unemployed. We have also seen how, in Parry's studies of local participation, business interests are relatively marginalised and isolated from citizen and political agendas.

In our concept of economic development partnerships there will be senior and junior partners, there will be leaders and animators, and those that are key participants and implementors of programmes (see also Bennett and Krebs, 1991, Chapter 7; Fosler and Berger, 1982; Cowie, 1985; Petersen, 1981; Parkinson and Judd, 1990; Logan and Molotch, 1987). This concept is quite different from the concepts of local "coalitions", "local cooperation", or "local governance" (e.g. Cawson, 1985; King, 1985; Harding, 1990, 1991; Lever and Moore, 1986).

Partnerships are thus an attempt at focusing or improving situations in which local systems supporting the market would otherwise fail. Remedying market failure in the field of economic development, unlike policy for social or welfare services, cannot be a purely government-led activity. Economic development is concerned with wealth creation and business investment: it is fundamentally a business-led activity. Thus the system problem of market failure in business' needs must be treated as a programme to enhance the business environment among the actions of other public and private agents. The precise mix, however, is difficult to determine *a priori*; and it will differ significantly between areas and programmes. The partnership concept captures the need to bring agents together in the most appropriate roles in each different context to achieve the developments required.

In the discussions of each field of activity in Chapters 6–8 it appears that firmly-based partnerships are more successful than loose relationships, e.g. in the development of strategic partnerships between businesses, as well as Compacts or TECs. Written or contractual agreements appear frequently to provide the sharp focus on goals by each party which helps in turn to focus on improving performance targets.

There is no one recipe for partnership that is likely to ensure success. Overcoming systems failure requires blending of different approaches to different problems in different situations. But partnerships for economic development should not be single-purpose or fragmented. Quite the contrary. We have identified the need to integrate into flexible network structures across the fields of human resource strategies, enterprise and business growth programmes, and physical redevelopment. Thus partnerships must ensure both *horizontal integration* between agents in different programmes and *vertical coordination* to ensure that each programme is focused on its outcomes in order to achieve a quality solution. The flexible network structure we have proposed for partnership development (see Figure 9.2E) focuses on bringing together two key aspects: the *development process* (i.e. links) and its *animation* (i.e. strong points or core actors). Partnership is the means of matching agents with roles in order to achieve this link.

To achieve success, the development process must interlink with its animation at all levels. This is the structure of the flexible network structure we introduced earlier, but with an animation and coordination process. At each stage in the development process the appropriate agents are involved in the most effective relationships with clearly defined roles and performance targets. Similarly, each aspect of animation involves each stage of the development process:[5] from identification of the problems, through the enhancing the fields of action that are possible, down to the activities and projects that seek to achieve specific outcomes. This process can be developed in part through learning, which we introduce next.

Developing a learning process

In situations of systems failure, developments do not easily occur spontaneously, or if they do their effects are not absorbed spontaneously by other agents. Indeed, definitionally, systems failure suggests that some agents have radically to develop and evolve. This requires a learning process to be initiated and followed through steadfastly.

The flexible networking model (Figure 9.2E) requires key "anchor points" of development by the chief actors in a local economy. They are the first targets for learning. Beyond them, the complex webs of contractors and sub-contractors can usually be levered into change by the chief actors. Various approaches have been attempted to stimulate or even lever the development learning among the core agents in local areas. The most influential have been the large scale development agencies developed by the former Scottish Development Agency (SDA) and Highlands and Islands Development Board (HIDB) in Scotland, Welsh Development Agency (WDA) in Wales and IDB/LEDU in N. Ireland. Smaller more localised development agencies have been stimulated by both local government (e.g. Sheffield's Department of Employment and Economic Development (DEED)) and central government, eg.. UDCs, CATs, TFs. Most of the smaller agencies have been less successful for general area development, although they have each scored notable achievements for some programmes. There have also been a number of private-led, or mixed public-private activities associated with the Phoenix Initiative and BiTC Business Leadership Teams (for a review see Bennett and Krebs, 1991).

Generally, the large scale development agencies have achieved most, have been most effective, and have been able to move most rapidly. This is particularly true of the SDA/HIDB and IDB/LEDU. But the dilemma has been that they have not always been able to stimulate change among the key local agents and in all programme fields. Hence, the "ownership" of change has been externalised and its continuation often depends on the maintenance of external support. TECs/LECs have sought to overcome this dilemma by setting up a stronger local board and providing an externally supported local staff on a nationwide basis. However, "ownership" by the board is proving inadequate from two points of view (see Bennett *et al.*, 1993; these problems are discussed at greater length in Chapter 15): first, it is often still too remote from many parts of the local community, although much depends on how the TEC/LEC Board chooses to develop bridges and links; second, it often has too weak a business lead because the Board is a part-time body which often constitutes an isolated group of individuals who cannot speak for or commit the wider local business base, and often cannot fully control its full-time civil service staff who may pursue a variety of other often historical objectives.

To achieve a long-term change that reverses the systems problem the talent and energy of the people and key organisations anchored in the local community must be harnessed. Local people and key agents must not be either demoralised and marginalised or merely left to maintain accustomed practices separated from the economic development process. Instead they should be fully involved, particularly at the outset, in the development of strategy and its implementation. Only by building with and into local communities can a motivation for change and economic development become a self-sustaining momentum for the long term.

The learning process that has been developed in Britain to date demonstrates that there is a form of generalised *mechanism* for sustaining and leading change. This mechanism can be summarised as a stage-wise process[5]:

- Establish a leadership team of the key agents in the local economy with strong external expertise to fill any gaps;
- Take stock of problems, strengths and weaknesses in the local economy; search out the gaps and business opportunities; assess the competition; think strategically;
- Form and "sell" a long-term vision of the community to the wider network of agents as a basis for action;
- Build a firm foundation: a partnership that adds the value of collective action to individual activities;
- Get action underway and demonstrate change through 'flagship' projects that symbolise change and inspire confidence;
- Build on successes and spread the vision: keep everyone involved and develop local "ownership" along the way;
- Ensure quality: that outcomes are really improved, and aim for the long-term – only the best will do;
- Spread motivation: build the capacity for self-help and self-sustaining future development through an enduring flexible network.

This mechanism seeks to give confidence to an area that change will occur – that commercial returns can be achieved, that jobs can be created, and that the entire community can benefit. The mechanism is not a model but a flexible framework that can be developed for different local contexts. Its main focus is on the areas where networks presently fail to deliver the system outputs required by the economy. It is an action-orientated approach.

We can capture the learning process as the need to shift from reactive to proactive modes of behaviour. Figure 9.3 shows this shift in terms of the simple criteria of flexible and task models versus role models of organisation. This covers perception and response to change, as well as the local scope to develop a "bottom up" capacity. Much of what we have seen in Chapters 6–8 has suggested that local agents are often reactive, and dependent, rather than coherently focused. This results in the "patchwork quilt" of independent action we have observed.

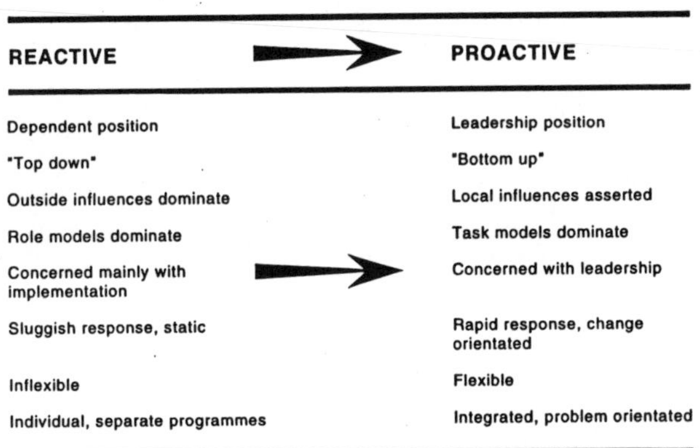

REACTIVE	→	PROACTIVE
Dependent position		Leadership position
"Top down"		"Bottom up"
Outside influences dominate		Local influences asserted
Role models dominate		Task models dominate
Concerned mainly with implementation	→	Concerned with leadership
Sluggish response, static		Rapid response, change orientated
Inflexible		Flexible
Individual, separate programmes		Integrated, problem orientated

Figure 9.3 The development of learning: moving from reactive to proactive

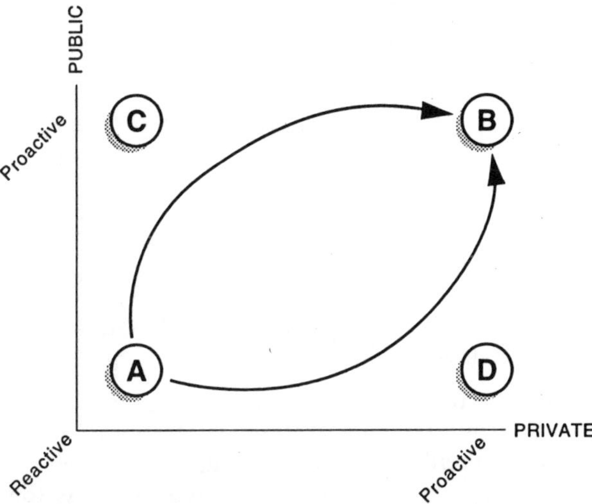

Figure 9.4 Forms of public-private collaboration and "partnership" related to extent of reactiveness or proactiveness, and change over time

In our analysis of the development of the learning process in different local contexts in the following chapters we focus particular attention on where agents in the local economy are placed on the scale of reactive/proactiveness. One key dimension of comparison is between the outcomes associated with different *mixes* of public and private collaboration – the "partnership" process. We exhibit in Figure 9.4 some of the possible comparative positions. Generally we believe that all local economies should develop the capability to be at point B. This maximises their responsiveness, flexibility and client focus to respond to challenges that will confront their economies in the future. However, we have seldom found, in our study areas, the passage from A towards B to be a very direct one. Quite often there is movement along the axis from A to C where public agencies or public sector resources are necessary to provide the vision and leadership to lever change. In other cases movement is from A to D, with private sector leverage by major companies, property developers, TECs/LECs, and Chambers of Commerce providing the vision, resources and leadership that stimulates change. The following is a simple typology of the different situations shown in Figure 9.4.

A. *"Dependent"*
- "Branch plant" economy
- Major declining sectors
- High unemployment
- Little visible sign of activity
- Fragmentation, apathy or conflict between sectors

B. *"Proactive"*
- Strong local employer base
- Major growth sectors
- Low unemployment
- Many visible signs of activity
- Integration and partnership between sectors

C. *Public leverage*
- Weak employer base, often with large public employment sector
- Growth in public employment or leverage
- Unemployment beginning to be addressed
- Some signs of independent activity
- Specific partnerships led by local authority, UDC or SDA/WDA, etc.

D. *Private leverage*
- Strong employer base
- Major growth sectors
- Unemployment being addressed
- Some signs of independent activity
- Collective action by business (e.g. Chambers of Commerce, enterprise agencies) or large local companies (such as ICI, BSC, NCB, Marks & Spencer)

Models C and D may be useful learning stages on the way to the full integration and proactive participation of all agents in the local economy, public and private. It may also be the case that different sectors, areas or agents may be pursuing different paths from each other at any given time. The proactive model is the end-point of flexible networking and tasking, our model shown in Figure 9.2E.

Research developed in the following chapters, as well as in the wider context of local organisational development in the EC-12, shows that this learning often goes through a series of distinct stages to reach this endpoint. Recognition of the existence of these stages, and the need to develop a learning process in this way, is important to understanding how mechanisms and vehicles for change can be developed at local level. It can, for example, be used to transfer experience between programmes, or between areas. This learning process, shown in Figure 9.5, can be summarised as follows (see e.g. Bennett, 1989a, 1990b; Martinos, 1989; Business in the Cities and Bennett, 1990):

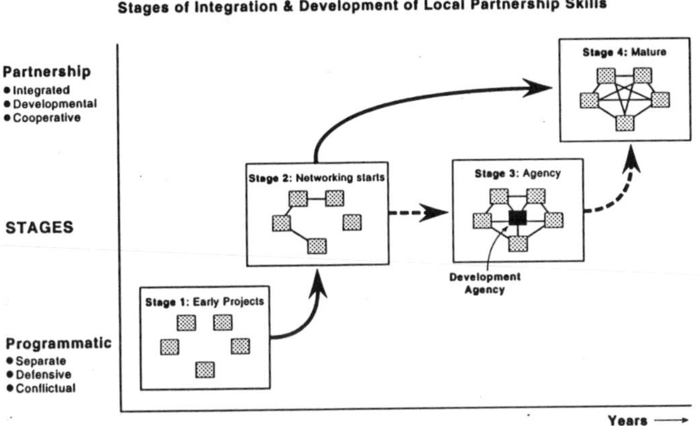

Figure 9.5 The learning process of network development in each area
Source: based on the research reviewed in Chapters 10–14 and Bennett, 1989a.

Stage 1 of learning is concerned with *acquiring the know-how of development*. This is largely *methodological*, covering how to do things, and *foundational*, not aiming at high-level innovation, but at the application of established and proven approaches. The emphasis is usually on developing experience in how to initiate projects and do things, perhaps through experimentation and demonstration, e.g. "flagships". Often a high level of public support is required.

Stage 2 is the start of proper networking, in which *the know-how of development* is used. From Stage 1 there should be a core of local people and institutions with experience in stimulating and facilitating economic projects. These agents can improve their effectiveness and enhance their targeting of programmes by linking together. Public sector funds are usually still a critical ingredient to success at this stage, but more autonomous support is developing and a stronger client focus is emerging. Arguably this is the point that TECs have now reached.

Stage 3 is an intermediate stage where considerable capacity has been developed, but where a *development agency* with an expertise, autonomy and leadership capacity is required to put larger networks together. A development agency is additional and, to some extent, external to the main local agents and is a force that focuses on bringing things together on a large scale. This is the model used by the former SDA and now employed by LECs. Where the development agency is relatively small, its success will depend on leverage and cooperation with other agents (as with UDCs, CATs and TFs).

Stage 4 is that of a mature network of cooperation between all key agents. This is a basis for locally *self-sustaining development* capability with a "critical mass" of agents and initiatives. Most actions will have now become self-sustaining and will focus on clients and quality.

Generally these stages of learning can be seen as moving local agents from a reactive posture, which accepts the influence of external agents, central government, and the world market, to a positive proactive posture, which grasps opportunities and develops the capability to respond now and in the future (see Figure 9.3).

The concept of learning to generate a proactive capacity shown in Figure 9.5 depicts networks between actors developing during the learning process. This pattern of emerging networks over time is confirmed in later chapters. Of course this figure presents a simplified picture. In reality, the precise timing of actions will depend on various factors, including the availability of resources and the preparedness of the local and external agents. Different programmes and fields of action will also develop at different paces. But the concept of learning stages does focus on the need to develop the capability that is the basis for self-sustained development of local economies.

Interpreting learning experiences

The rest of Part III of this book presents detailed materials for a number of places in Britain. It describes the key aspects of their institutional environment, their networks, the learning they have developed, and the gaps that remain to be filled. From this material it is possible to derive an overview for Britain as a whole of the extent to which local capability is being developed to yield the quality of client-focused support that must be sought. Clearly, given the number of different contexts that exist in Britain, and the marked variation between them, we would not wish to claim that our assessment is complete. However, we do believe it gives the best-informed overview yet available of the extent to which a local capability is being developed across the country in those fields that have most immediate importance to Britain's economic progress.

The chapters that follow avoid case studies in the conventional sense. Instead, we provide a framework of analysis for assessing the varying dimensions of the local context (in Chapter 10). Then in Chapters 11–14 we focus on four types of area which possess different conjunctions of circumstances and institutions:

- Large cities (Chapter 11);
- Fringe metropolitan areas (Chapter 12);
- Dispersed industrial areas (Chapter 13);
- Central places and rural areas (Chapter 14).

These chapters are based on a series of semi-structured interviews carried out both with national bodies and in a wide variety of areas mainly in 1988–90, but continuing until 1992. This has been an important formative period for the development of the learning process that is dramatically enhancing local capability in many places. This period also covered one in which various experimental initiatives were developed – such as LENs, Compacts, small firms support, BLTs, and new statutory powers for local authority economic development. In addition, from 1989 the development of the major new government initiative of TECs and LECs began strongly to influence local responses, as also did the Chambers of Commerce National Development Strategy.

The local assessments undertaken, therefore, allow some commentary on longitudinal development, but we place greatest emphasis on comparing areas in terms of context, institutions, and requirements. The assessments are mostly based on so-called "elite" interviews with the key actors in the local community – in business, the public sector, voluntary groups (where appropriate) and other key agents. By focusing on key animators of local change a detailed assessment of the extent of local integration is provided, and interviews that used "triangulation" between agents allow their responses to be cross-checked against each other. Triangulation was an important process, because of the subjective nature of most of the material being assessed, and because it was a safeguard against being misled by the varying emphases of different local agents. A further safeguard on the quality of the generalisations drawn is the scale of the interviews undertaken. Over 200 interviews were undertaken in 11 areas, and over 100 further interviews with national or regional bodies. A number of interviews were follow-ups to earlier interviews; in a considerable number of cases there were multiple follow-ups allowing an intense knowledge of the chief study areas to be developed. The details of this strategy are given in the Appendix.

Footnotes: Chapter 9

1. See the UK research of e.g. Oakey et al. (1980), Boddy et al. (1986), Hall et al. (1987), Sweeney (1987), Rubery et al.(1987), Atkinson (1985), IMS (1986), Amin and Goddard (1986), Breheny et al. (1988); see also the references in Chapter 6.
2. See the empirical analyses of entrepreneurial entry by Bannock (1981), Casson (1982), Geroski and Schwalback (1990), Evans and Leighton (1989), Blanchflower and Meyer (1990), Cable and Schwalback (1990).
3. Moyes and Westhead's analysis is based on a principle component analysis followed by a cluster analysis. The dependent variable was new firm VAT registrations 1980–83. The five main components identified were: (i) services and commerce, (ii) personal wealth and attainment, (iii) SMEs base and high self employment, (iv) low unemployment levels, (v) high rate of increase in unemployment. Westhead and Moyes' (1991) later research updates these results, but does not significantly change the pattern of conclusions.
4. Sevenoaks, Stockwell, Spotland (Rochdale), Machars (Dumfries and Galloway), Oswestry and Penrhiwceiber (Welsh mining valley).
5. Based on Business in the Cities and Bennett (1990, pp. 26–29) which also outlines a series of action steps.

10. *DIMENSIONS OF LOCAL CAPABILITY*

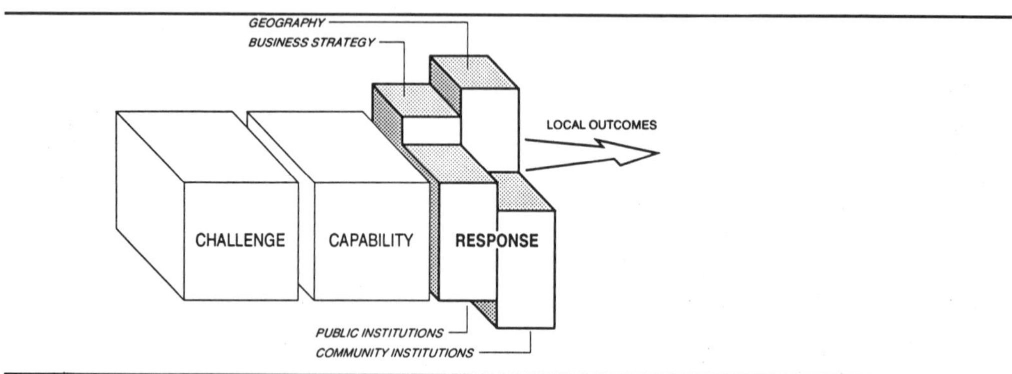

Agents for change

We have argued throughout our discussion that the sequence, CHALLENGE – CAPABILITY – RESPONSE, has to be built from the institutional structure of each place. In this chapter we appraise the dimensions that underpin the scope for local agents to provide that capability, or to change and adapt. We also identify the gaps and opportunities that have to be filled and the learning that is required in order to produce an effective and flexible local partnership network.

We focus our discussion on the relation between local businesses, local business organisations, local government and local community bodies. In each case we are looking for the dimensions that underpin an area's position on the scale of reactive-proactive (Figure 9.5) in order to assess the points at which animation and stimulus may overcome system gaps. There are, in general, four types of situation that may commonly occur (see Figure 10.1):

A. All local core agents strong – STRONG CAPABILITY
B. Local business agents strong, local government and community weak – SYSTEM GAPS
C. Local business agents weak, local government and community strong – SYSTEM GAPS
D. All local core agents weak – WEAK CAPABILITY

These different situations do not arise by chance. In the discussion below we analyse the different elements that lead to these different situations. We focus on the following four key dimensions of local capability development:

- Geography and settlement structure;
- Local business structure (economic linkage, concentration and dispersion, firm size and structure, sector, and business organisations);

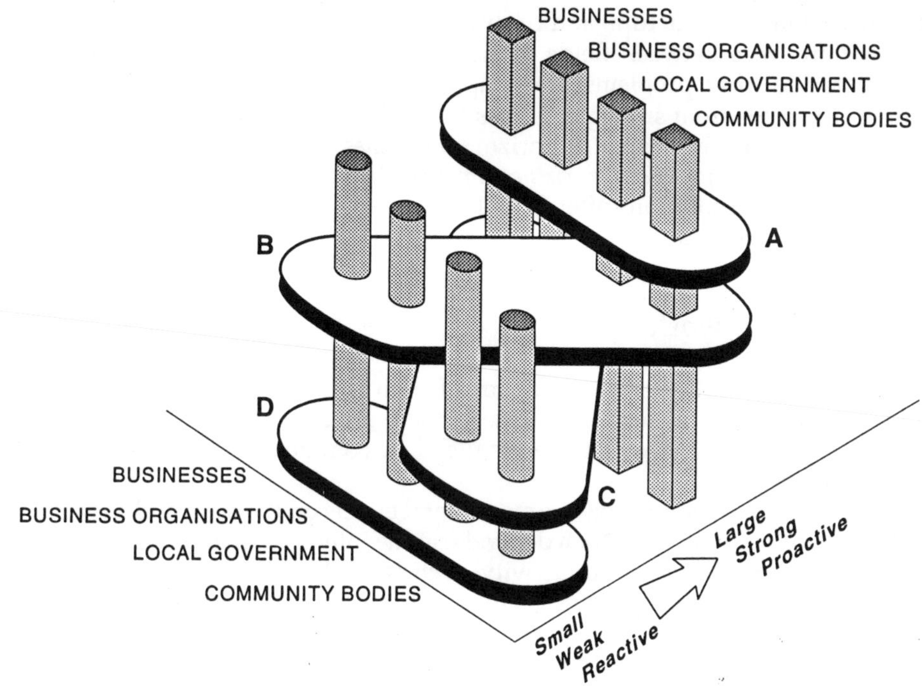

Figure 10.1 Local agents in relation to their scale, strength and type of activity

- Public institutions (local government and development agencies);
- Local community institutions (social character and politics, local values, voluntary organisations and community groups).

Each of these dimensions tends to interrelate with each other. Each is discussed in turn below and the major contrasts between areas are appraised.

In the focus on the capability of agents and their capacity to change, it is important also to distinguish the extent to which it is possible for agents to change. We distinguish two different types of factors:

- *Structural factors*: those which are extremely difficult to change in the short to medium term through government or other action. Although they might be changed in the long term, they are often very resistant or impervious to change;
- *Contingent factors*: those that are amenable in the short term to change by government or other agents. However, the length of time required to effect change can vary considerably.

The links between contingent and structural factors are often crucial to determining the success of a local initiative. For example, the presence of a Chamber of Commerce or a TEC/LEC is no guarantee of the involvement of an effectively organised business community that offers a local capability. Other factors, particularly the nature of the local businesses themselves, as well as the quality of personnel and the appropriateness of vision that is pursued, will also be central in determining the capability of a Chamber or a TEC.

The nature and mix of structural and contingent factors will, of course, vary between areas and within areas between fields of action. It is critical to local capability that initiatives to tackle local problems are adapted to the way in which these factors interact to produce coherent strategies across the different vertical fields of activity. In this chapter we explore the scope for horizontal synthesis by analysis of those factors which *affect the potential for effective partnership formation* at a local level. The chapters that follow examine the solutions offered to the problems faced in the different types of area that we have identified.

Geography and networks

The geography of a locality is an amalgam of each dimension of its economy and society. However, as well as local uniqueness, there are also a variety of elements in common between places. Many of the elements in common derive from an area's settlement structure.

Differing settlement structures have fundamental effects on the form and capacity for development of local initiatives. Much depends on the interrelation of settlement layout with the spaces covered by economic activity, such as market and commuter flows, and the local government administrative structure. Figure 10.2 shows different matches of activity spaces with administrative spaces. Most facilitative for effective networks is a close matching of the economic activity space with local government boundaries. This is a "truly-bounded" situation. Coterminosity encourages a high level of participation of individuals in political and other decisions, a relation to a natural "sense of local community", and a ready relation of economic actors in the private sector with public sector employers and local government.

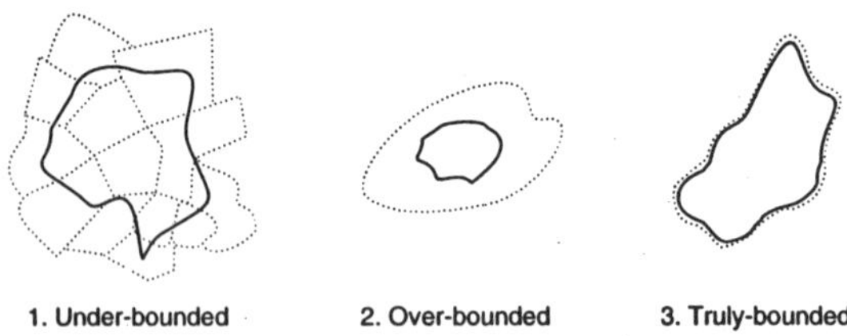

Figure 10.2 Forms of bounding of administrative space in relation to economic space
Key: administrative space (dotted lines); economic activity space (solid lines) (after Bennett, 1989c)

More commonly, however, activity spaces and governmental structures are not coterminous. "Under-bounding" occurs when the economic activity space spans many administrative boundaries. This occurs in most metropolitan areas, in London, and in many non-metropolitan counties. The result is confusion to lines of local political participation and accountability, a "spillover" of interests resulting in tensions between local representative structures for separate boroughs or districts, and tensions between the economic actors who have broad objectives and local government actors who have narrower ones.

In contrast, "over-bounding" occurs when the economic activity space is very small compared to large local government units. This arises in many rural areas where over-large non-metropolitan counties / Scottish regions greatly exceed the chief area of economic focus. For many large cities in rural areas, their main sphere of influence (e.g. the travel-to-work area) is significantly smaller than the administrative country / Scottish region, e.g. for Leicester, Nottingham, York, Northampton, Southampton–Portsmouth, Plymouth. It also affects many smaller, often older county towns, e.g. Shrewsbury, Perth, Dumfries, Ayr, Exeter, Winchester. It is a major phenomenon in low density rural areas which may have a large number of such small towns, e.g. N. Yorkshire, Lincolnshire, N. Devon, Cornwall, N. Wales, Dyfed, and most of the Scottish Highlands. The frequent result is a tension between the objectives of the smaller towns and the broader, often less economic, objectives pursued by the larger administrative areas.

We can relate the size and boundedness of geographical areas and agents to our assessment of capacity, shown in Figure 10.1. In general, geographical small areas give a coverage which is partial, patchy and leaves gaps where no agent is able to attain critical mass and a full capability. This is to be contrasted with large geographical units that can give wide coverage and attain a critical mass that provides the possibility for a true capability. Size is used in both an absolute and a relative sense. Absolute size is important to attaining a critical mass that can achieve a true local capacity. Relative size is also important since size in some areas (e.g. the Highlands and Islands) may be sufficient, whereas it would be too small in other areas. There are four types of geographical situation related to the local key agents (see Figure 10.1):

A. All local core agents cover whole area and attain critical mass;
B. Local business agents cover whole area and attain critical mass, but local government and community bodies are small and have gaps in coverage;
C. Local business agents are small and have gaps in coverage, but local government and community covers whole area and is strong;
D. All core agents are small and incomplete in geographical coverage.

Generalising across these different situations, and clearly subject to a high level of local variability, we have found that there are four main and distinct types of settlement structure that affect the nature of local capability:

- Large cities and metropolitan cores;
- Metropolitan fringe areas;
- Dispersed industrial areas;
- Central place and rural areas.

Large cities

Of these four types it is perhaps the large cities which are most often facilitative of coherent integrated action. There are a number of reasons for this. The cores of Britain's major conurbations and free-standing cities often have well-developed senses of identity and are sometimes close to true-bounding. If not truly-bounded, they are underbounded and the core city is able to exert a dominant influence. Thus, there is a ready focus for partnership activity and a ready motive for overcoming local disputes in the interest of the greater good of "the city". Not unrelated to this is the fact that the economic and social problems which have been the stimulus for most partnership activity are often most acute and most visible in the larger cities. In many cases the scale of the problems faced by these cities are so great that they have been sufficient to overcome disagreements among local actors. Apart from these forces, the geographical compactness and social and economic integration of the larger cities encourage regular interactions between key players. In the free-standing cities, actor networks can be clearly defined and are often much simpler than elsewhere; they can, indeed, resemble a 'club' in which everyone appears to know everyone else and in which there is much informal as well as formal contact. This is not necessarily true of the metropolitan fringes. Networks here tend to be complex and extended. However, in the largest cities there is the potential for a hierarchical structure of networks to come into play.

Metropolitan fringes

None of these factors which encourage partnership activity hold for metropolitan fringes and central place networks. These areas face different problems. In the metropolitan fringes, a number of factors militate against effective integration. They are characterised by small industrial and large residential base, weak senses of local identity and, in more prosperous suburban areas, few major problems to focus attention. They are radically under-bounded with most economic influences external to the area. The result is that people do not have to work together. Local business tends to be disorganised – suburban Chambers of Commerce in London and the metropolitan conurbations are generally weaker or limited in scale (in the small to medium size category), of generally poorer leadership and inadequate *critical mass*. High commuter flows mean that many metropolitan fringes are dormitory suburbs with local inhabitants living and working in different areas: as a result, the loyalty to locality is weak. Where metropolitan fringes do have the stimulus to partnership provided by major problems, as in the outer housing estates of cities such as Glasgow or Dundee, the problem of a lack of an indigenous business community to provide a basis for regeneration again proves to be a serious handicap.

Central places and rural areas

"Central place" cities refer to the settlement structures of large parts of rural or county Britain. A number of important areas are focused on their county towns, Nottinghamshire on Nottingham, Leicestershire on Leicester, Derbyshire on Derby, North Somerset and Avon on Bristol, etc. The major difficulty for these areas is that, whilst there is a clear rationale for partnership activity in the county towns or cities, and local networks of actors are quite capable of providing the basis for this activity, this is usually not true of the more rural hinterlands. These areas are usually over-bounded. The problems faced by the cities and their network of institutions are often quite different to the problems and institutions in the more rural areas. This has emerged most strongly for those cities – Nottingham, Derby and Leicester among them – which have active Chambers of Commerce which in the past have *not* been able to extend their spheres of influence as far as they would wish into their county hinterlands. This has had important consequences for the business networks which have provided the basis for subsequent Chamber or TEC development. Thus Nottinghamshire and Derbyshire are both covered by two TECs, reflecting local economic cleavages, conflicts in business networks, and problems for the Derbyshire and Nottinghamshire Chambers of extending their activities fully into the north of their counties. Cleavages such as these can go back many decades and are deep-rooted. They also relate to the over-bounding of local government boundaries in the cases of Nottinghamshire and Derbyshire. In the case of Hereford and Worcester, or Peterborough and Cambridge, long-standing tensions between the areas exist from former local government structures.

Dispersed industrial areas

These cover a large part of the country. They have a number of small and medium-sized cities and towns but lack a dominant focal point. Each settlement usually has the capability to forge a significant and coherent body of initiatives, but there are usually strong differences between places and the effect of a threshold size beyond which none can proceed without collaboration. Generally there is strong local parochial sense in each community, but this can work both positively and negatively. Each settlement may be close to true bounding, but as an economy as a whole, the area is underbounded since the economic activity space is considerably wider than the administrative space. Each settlement may have strong local institutions of Chamber, TEC, district level local authority, and community groups. This local strength offers enormous advantages to coherence. But it also offers constraints on development since the strong local bonds can prevent the larger economic problem being perceived. Cooperation between towns in these areas has been historically weak and there has been a laudable sense of wanting to go it alone. More recently, however, there has emerged growing cooperation to work towards larger goals, e.g. in Teesside, North-East Lancashire and South Yorkshire.

London is a special case which requires separate discussion. Although it exhibits many features of large cities and their fringes, particularly under-bounding, it has some key characteristics which place it in a unique position. First, London's core contains most of the largest national and international companies in the UK. Their networks are of national rather than local importance. Most major London businesses, as a result, do not see a clear local responsibility to London itself (although there are some exceptions to this). Second, central London's businesses are dominated by financial services, tourism and retailing which are sectors that generally have had a lower tradition of involvement in local affairs. Third, there are enormous flows of workers from the suburbs into the central core, which undermines the source of employer-employee relationships, i.e. economic under-bounding is extreme. Fourth, and related to these factors, London constitutes a huge and integrated labour market with few focal and identifiable sub-markets (Heathrow and Croydon are exceptions). Fifth, rapid economic growth in the rest of the South East has attracted an increasing set of flows of reverse commuting and economic linkage outward as well as inward. As a result, there is a high degree of economic interlinkage and flux into, across and outside London which is not found to the same extent in other metropolitan areas. This means that its problems require to be tackled on a London-wide or even South East scale, as well as in more local contexts. Given its size, this presents a formidable challenge.

The national pattern

To focus the discussion, Figure 10.3 displays a map of Britain classifying areas by the form of settlement character related to economic and administrative boundaries.[1] From this map it can be seen that the core city areas sit as potential regional foci, surrounded by fragmented metropolitan fringes. Beyond these are central place cities, defined largely by their main travel-to-work areas (TTWAs), that sit as islands within more dispersed rural areas. The dispersed industrial areas sit as "adjoints" to the system as a whole, often as larger settlements in the fringe metropolitan areas that have grown up to a greater status.

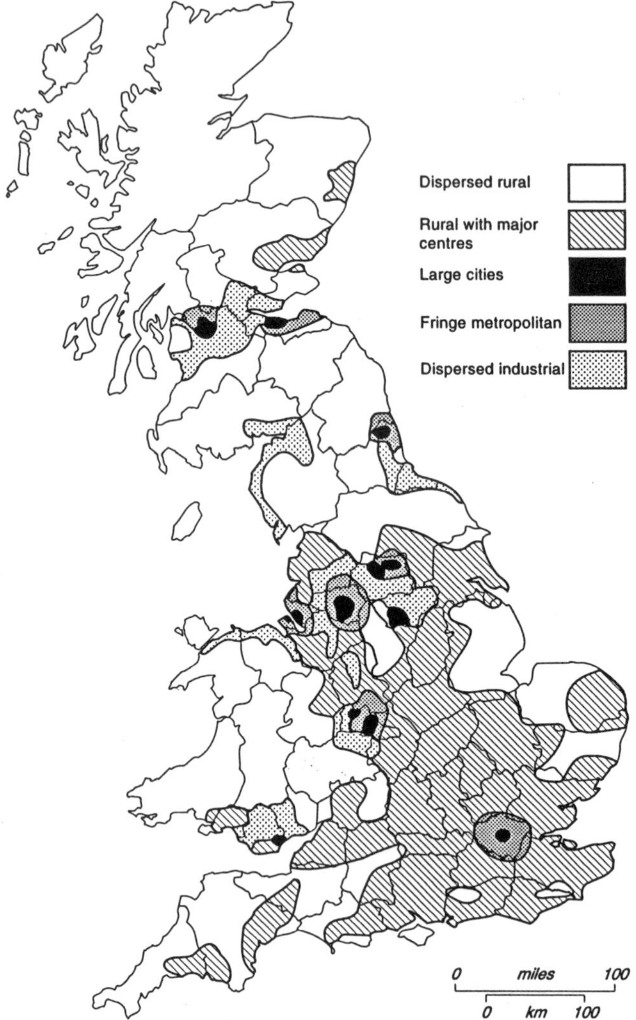

Figure 10.3 Britain and its settlement geography

Whilst this map can only be used as an approximation to describe the wide and complex array of local communities that exist, it provides an important means of unravelling the local economic networks which we use as a focus to our discussion in Chapters 11 to 14. The capability of each area can be related to our dimensions of proactive – reactiveness, and geographical scale (Figure 10.1). Our four types of area in general straddle different parts of each scale, but Figure 10.4 shows some of the generalisations that can be drawn. In terms of this classification, Table 10.1 shows the approximate number and proportion of businesses in each type of area. The very large number and scale of areas falling into the central place, rural and fringe metropolitan groups exhibits the focus for some of the main system problems.

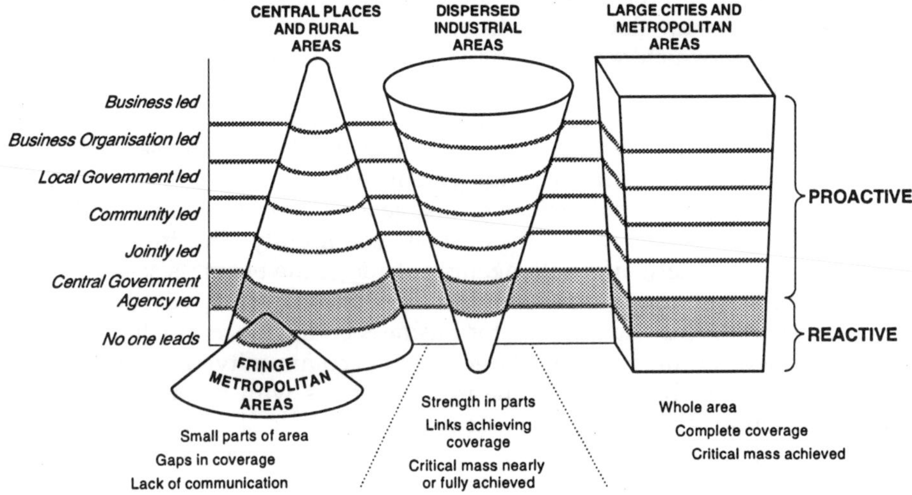

Figure 10.4 Local agents in relation to types of area and scale of activity that can potentially be achieved

Table 10.1 Businesses and population in relation to the economic networks of different areas in Britain

Area	No. of business units (000s)	Business units as % of UK
Core cities	219	19.5
Fringe metropolitan	144	12.8
Dispersed industrial	94	8.4
Central place cities / rural	465	39.3
Dispersed rural areas	225	20.0

Sources: Business Units, Census of Employment 1987 special tabulations

Local business structure

The structure and organisation of businesses, separately, and through organisations is a crucial dimension affecting local capability. Here we examine:

- Economic linkage;
- Size of business community;
- Concentration and dispersion;
- Firm size and structure;
- Sector;
- Business organisations.

Local economic linkage. The degree of local economic linkage between businesses is a strong influence on the scope for integrated local development. Although the forces of economic change are arguably towards the *disintegration* of local linkages and the reformation of inter-dependencies on a much larger national and even global scale, there are still many examples in Britain of fairly high degrees of local self-containment. This may arise, as in the case of Teesside, from the dominance of large companies over local suppliers: although the two large local firms, ICI and BSC, are integrated within the world economy, many local small to medium-sized companies are highly dependent on ICI and BSC which are the dominant players in the local economy. But close economic interlinkage can also arise in large cities such as Sheffield, where there are important links between local medium-sized firms. In small rural centres local interlinkage may reach extremely high levels of interdependence because of their relative physical isolation from other major employment centres.

The effect of strong local economic interlinkage is to increase the likelihood of shared purpose and common goals within the business community. This increases the potential cohesion of wider networks with agents outside of the business sector.

Size of business community is very important. First, size offers a capacity to deliver a critical mass of resources and support for business bodies, such as Chambers of Commerce (see Bennett, 1991a). Second, a large business community, *ceteribus paribus*, tends to carry more weight than a small one in interactions with other actors outside the business community. Third, there appears to be a threshold size for successful business involvement in partnership activities. The larger the business community the more likely it is that an effective business leader, group of leaders, or organisation such as a Chamber of Commerce, will emerge to champion business interests. Moreover, there is a danger that without a large business community upon which to draw, the same small group of businesses will be called upon time after time for partnership activities with the result that their resources and resolve may be sapped.

Concentration is closely related to both size and economic interlinkage. It occurs when a large number of businesses are closely linked in a locality. This usually offers the greatest potential for successful intervention in the vertical fields of action. Concentration facilitates ease of interactions, especially face-to-face meetings. Concentration often arises because of a need for economic interlinkage and this strengthens the base for integration with other non-business agents.

Dispersion is often characteristic of communities with small-sized businesses, particularly in rural areas. Communication over long distances militates against the formation of successful business "constituencies". This often arises over whole county areas, partly because of the lack of informal, day-to-day or face-to-face meetings but also because of the lower likelihood of shared experiences. An attempt to overcome this feature is evident in the area board structures adopted by many rural TECs. But dispersion and size can also be problems on the fringes of the major conurbations. These more suburban areas have relatively small local industrial bases with heavy commuter flows out to urban cores. In this context the boundaries of 'logical' local labour markets are difficult or impossible to draw and, in their absence, attempts have been made to build partnerships on the basis of local authority boundaries. This has often exacerbated the problems of dispersion and size because they are not related to meaningful labour markets. We return to this point below.

Firm size and structure. Internal company organisation often affects both the *propensity* for business involvement in partnerships and the *nature* of that involvement. Company structures also affect the capability of local businesses to act as *communities*. These differences strongly interrelate with firm size. Broadly, we can isolate three typical categories of firm structure:

- *The small, owner-manager firm.* These firms have a low propensity to become involved in partnership activity firstly because of a lack of spare employee capacity to take part in anything outside of the direct task of running a business; and secondly, because many (or most) small businesses have less control over their market and have to spend most of their time 'fire-fighting', coping with exogenous crises.
- *The local, medium-sized firm.* These firms exhibit perhaps the greatest potential for successful partnership involvement. Often stemming from long-established, family concerns, these firms are often sufficiently stable and sufficiently large to support activities which can bring long-term benefits. The rooting of these companies in their local communities means their dependence on the local economy is high and, aside from any altruistic social concerns, provides a motivation for involvement in partnership activities. Such firms also often have great resources of skills and long-standing personal networks among their chief executives or chairmen. They can provide genuinely local business leadership, but much depends on the quality and vision of the business leaders. These businesses can also be some of the most resistant to change.
- *The large national or multi-national company.* The involvement of these companies is affected by their branch structures. It is through their branches (either branch plants, offices or retail outlets) that these companies have an interest in local economies. These branches can be few in number, as in the case of ICI, British Aerospace, Wellcome or BP for example, or constitute an extensive network, as in the case of banks and large retail concerns. In either case large companies tend to have to rely for local involvement on local managers or line managers. Through this reliance, large company intervention depends upon the extent of discretion allowed to the local manager and the company's policy. Where companies have not drawn up policies for involvement in partnership activities, managers tend to be reactive to local requests for action, may often be negative, and tend to respond on an 'as and when' basis. Their first concern is naturally to carry out the job for which they are employed; local partnership activities are fitted in where possible. Where companies have produced policies with respect to partnerships, these dictate the nature of local activity. Their effect, however, is not necessarily substantial. Company policies will not shift managers to proactive positions, if they are bland statements of general community commitment. They can have major impact, however, when the policy is backed up by clear incentives and career development. The extent of local manager discretion over policies is also important. This varies considerably from firm to firm. So too do the resources available for action. Local managers typically have only limited funds; for major interventions they have to refer decisions 'upwards' in their companies. These factors considerably restrict managers' ability to respond promptly and positively to events. This stands in contrast to the chief executive of a local firm who has the ability to make rapid, high-level commitments.

Despite the constraints on large companies, there is a growing number of examples of large companies providing vital resources for localities. Often most successful have been secondment programmes. The best of these are closely tied to the parent firm's staff development schemes and the support provides high-quality goal-oriented managers for periods of 1, 2 or 3 years to run initiatives; the secondments are closely monitored to ensure that targets are met; and there is close feedback between the sponsor and the host body. It is generally accepted that the best secondees are mid-career managers who use the secondment as a positive career step, and who will return to their companies after the placement. This represents a major advance on past tendencies to use secondments as a means of shuffling out "awkward" or pre-retirement personnel. Secondments by Marks and Spencer have been crucial to the successful development of Compact schemes in the case of Merseyside and Mid Glamorgan.

Where different types of firm predominate in a locality, the response of the business community to integrated development will vary considerably. Large parts of the suburban fringes of the major conurbations are dominated by small firms and branches of large companies which, for the reasons discussed above, are restricted in their ability to take part in partnership activities. In areas such as these, a Chamber of Commerce may be critical as a coordinator of business involvement. In other areas, a few key local firms with local chief executives may be able to provide a level of leadership capacity, as in Dundee, Oldham, Rochdale or Blackburn. Their effectiveness varies and depends on their capacity to lever other agents into action. Where no Chamber or other local agent exists, a lack of leadership characterises these fringe metropolitan areas, e.g. in West London. There are also instances where large international and national companies have taken an effective lead, as in Teesside and East London for example. Where large companies have been strong forces in local leadership the crucial factor has been the seniority of local management and their ability to make executive decisions. In contrast, even in major centres such as Manchester, the presence of a large number of regional headquarters of large companies has tended to affect adversely the integration and capability of the business community, whilst in Mid Glamorgan many important national companies have held back from taking leading local positions. In London, where the national headquarters of so many companies are to be found, unique patterns of networking have come into being which often lack strong local presence. London is discussed in detail later.

Sector. Apart from internal firm structure, the other chief characteristic of companies which affects capability is their *sector*. The effect of sector is complex. Different industrial sectors have different requirements of education, training, enterprise and physical development, different means of satisfying those requirements and hence different traditions of involvement in their local business communities. The potential for partnership involvement of a particular sector will vary between the fields of action. To illustrate the complexities involved we shall take an example from training.

A number of manufacturing sectors have an established tradition of collaborative action to address their needs in training, very successfully in the case of engineering for example, less successful for construction. By contrast the rapidly expanding retail sector has no such tradition; on the contrary, until recently, they have had a long-standing reputation for poor training. The degree of integrated business action in training by different sectors is closely related to the type and level of skills required by the industries. Hence, whilst engineering had specific and higher level skill requirements, the retail sector on the whole has required lower and more general skills. Retailing has thus been able to rely heavily on general education and school leavers, whilst engineering has had to collaborate with providers to develop training programmes. In addition, whilst the retail sector consists of a large base of very small employers as well as the well-known national enterprises, the engineering sector embraces firms with a more even spread across the entire range of sizes and organisation.

As a result, retail training has either not occurred at all, as in the case of most small shops, or has been provided in-house by the national chains. In engineering, collective action by the small and medium-sized firms, in particular, has been essential: first, because specialist courses must be provided, and second, because these firms are too small to provide proper training themselves.

It is clear from this example how the particular interests of firms in different sectors condition their responses. It is, therefore, difficult to generalise about the potential for integrated action by each sector across different fields of activity. However, it is clear that, compared to manufacturing, the most rapidly developing sectors of recent years – retailing and finance – usually have much a weaker tradition of active participation in local activities or involvement in local business organisations such as Chambers of Commerce. Retailers have also tended to be members of Chambers of Trade which have not sought to develop local business services to the extent that have Chambers of Commerce.

Business organisations. A key factor affecting local capacity for integration is the presence or absence of an effective business organisation. Until very recently the only body concerned with integrated development was the Chamber of Commerce (Chambers of Trade have usually played only a very limited economic role and provide few services to business). But, as described in Chapters 6–9, the 1980s have seen attempts to stimulate a number of new forms of business organisation in different fields of activity; for example, enterprise agencies, BLTs, EBPs, and most recently TECs and LECs. These new bodies have filled important gaps in key areas. But integrated business action *across* fields and in all areas is still awaited.

As a result it has traditionally been Chambers of Commerce that have been the key local force for integration. They have acted as major hosts for LENs (in 55% of cases) and have been the most important signatories to Compact contracts (67% of first round cases). Chambers have been the only bodies able to offer the potential to perform a general function of representation for their business subscribers across sectors and in all fields and with a very broad national coverage.

Despite the important contribution that Chambers have made, they have varied widely in their willingness and ability to mobilise the resources of the business community into effective action and also in their style of operation. The largest and most powerful Chambers are key players in integrated local development. Many have been important in setting up TECs and LECs and have been major leaders in their areas. Others have been less effective. As shown by Bennett (1991a), in 1990 perhaps 30 Chambers were really effective organisations. The key factors in determining their capability is their size and resources, and the quality of their presidents, chief executives and staff. Where Chambers have not been effective is where they are too small to be major players, or where they have failed to keep pace with new developments because of lacklustre leadership and parochial vision, which has sought to maintain them as old style 'luncheon clubs'. However, since the development of the National Strategy by Chambers (ABCC, 1990) the Chamber network has been steadily developing a stronger and more reliable capacity aiming at a quality standard across the whole country.

More recently, TECs and LECs have provided a significant supplementary or alternative business-led body to that of Chambers. They have the advantage that they have been set up in every area and have considerable budgets which can be used as leverage on other agents to encourage integration. Also, although business-led, TEC/LEC Boards do include non-business members from local government, education, unions and other sectors. This offers the scope for them to become major forces for integration in their areas. However, like Chambers, the quality of TECs and LECs varies. Indeed, similar constraints operate which derive from the size of budget, quality of staff and ability of local business leaders. Moreover, it is probably true that in most, but not all, cases the areas with weak Chamber presence also have relatively weak TECs or LECs.

There is also considerable concern about the extent to which TECs/LECs can be forces for integration outside of the fields covered by their main budget, namely training and enterprise.

Different problems apply to UDCs, Task Forces, CATs, and the RDC which are all usually too specific, or too limited, in geographical area, to be effective forces for integration (see Figure 5.4). In general, therefore, the presence and effectiveness of local business organisations is still a variable aspect of local capability. This is one of our key objects for further discussion of future policies in Chapter 15.

Public institutions

The structure of public service delivery in any locality is critical to partnership. A number of different bodies are involved:

- Local government;
- Development agents (such as the Training Agency, UDCs, Task Forces, CATs, RDC, and the Scottish and Welsh Development Agencies).

The precise mix of these organisations – their boundaries and activities – varies between areas and introduces an important variable local condition into partnerships (see Figure 5.4).

Local government

Local government affects partnership both through the location of its boundaries and its structure. The most important general factor is the difference between metropolitan and non-metropolitan areas in the number of tiers providing services. In the metropolitan areas, there is just one tier of local government, the metropolitan districts and London boroughs. In non-metropolitan areas, services are delivered through two tiers of local government, the county councils and the district councils with a very minor role played additionally by the parishes. Thus, whilst the metropolitan districts have responsibility for the vast majority of services (apart from those now in the hands of the residuary bodies), services are split in non-metropolitan areas between two tiers. The greatest difference between urban and rural areas is often the responsibility for secondary and vocational education, which is part of the unitary functions of the district/borough in metropolitan areas, but is held at the upper tier level (county) in non-metropolitan areas.

The way in which these two different sets of boundaries cross-cut the patterns of activity of the business community has an important bearing on the nature of partnership. Local authority boundaries can either reinforce, determine or counteract local economic conditions. Where a single metropolitan authority covers an area coterminous with local business networks the possibility of partnership is likely to be strengthened. The single authority reinforces the sense of local identity and there are no other local government units to weaken its role by dividing responsibilities. In other cases, the local authority may provide the focus in highly fragmented labour markets, particularly where the business community is weak. Examples of local authority initiative are especially common in city fringe areas where local authorities have attempted to establish partnerships, not always successfully, in areas which are defined for purposes of public administration but which make much less sense in terms of business action. This characterises Newham, Richmond-upon-Thames, Sandwell and Tameside.

Where there are discontinuities between business community boundaries and those of local government, the effect can often reduce the potential for effective partnership formation, even if the business community is strong, because the relevance of the local authority is low, or complex discussions and demarcation disputes must be overcome between local authorities. This is most common in city core areas. For example, in Salford, Manchester, Birmingham and inner London, the established business networks span several local authorities. This makes networking problematic and makes more difficult the integration of activities across the core area. Differences in political control between authorities can add to these complications.

The two-tier structure of local government in the non-metropolitan areas raises a set of further problems. In general, it adds to the complexity of local networks. We have already discussed the problems confronted by TECs and Chambers of Commerce in major cities such as Nottingham, Derby, Leicester, Southampton, Portsmouth, Bristol, Cambridge or Dundee, which fall under the jurisdiction of both a district and a county or Scottish region council. In these circumstances the ability to generate a distinctive local image for the city is attenuated because the county/region council also needs to be seen to be acting for its whole area. More importantly, the division of responsibility for services reduces the ability of local government to respond rapidly to developments. Problems of response are exacerbated where the different tiers of government are under different political control.

In certain fields of activity the heterogeneity of the areas covered by the county/region councils can lead to problems. In education, for example, economic and social problems will usually be focused in a small range of places. Similarly, there will be inequalities in the extent to which local business networks exist. These problems particularly characterise dispersed industrial areas such as Lancashire, North Derbyshire, Glamorgan and Strathclyde. But similar, more local, variations occur in all local authorities, even for the small London boroughs. Focusing on problems requires a focusing of responses, but it is often very difficult for a local authority, particularly a county council, to take action in only one part of its area. Moreover, in those fields of activity, such as environment, planning and transport, where there is scope for both the district and county to take action, there is further considerable potential for disagreement and conflict.

Local government internal organisation. Local authorities are not monolithic entities: they exhibit major differences in their mode of internal operation. Sometimes this takes the form of important differences in formal structure. For example, many large county/region education authorities are sub-divided into neighbourhoods and sub-areas with some functions devolved to area officers. This is an increasing trend, primarily because of the advent of legislation to encourage decentralisation of financial, managerial and other responsibilities within LEAs. It can have an important effect on local government's response to partnership activities. For example, a number of LEAs such as Shropshire and West Sussex have area-based rather than county-wide EBPs; and Cambridgeshire has led a pattern of decentralised LMS in schools. Some authorities have adopted an approach to service delivery which attempts to integrate provision across the different policy areas. In some cases this has been sought by decentralising provision to local "neighbourhoods" e.g. as in Tower Hamlets.

Elsewhere, differences between authorities are as much a matter of style, tradition or disposition as they are of formal structures. Some LEAs have a tradition of decentralising responsibilities. This can be especially important in those fields of activity where there is considerable scope for autonomy and hence variation at the point of service delivery, e.g. education and training. Where there is a tradition of decentralisation, partnership notions that imply some type of central structure that seeks coherence and coordination can meet stiff resistance. The renegade head teacher or maverick college principal is part of the currency of local authority tradition, but their independence as often as not may facilitate a more local approach to forming partnership links.

A further dimension of internal local government variation concerns the relation between officers and members. In our main study areas, the capability of local authorities to make strong contributions to integration is normally considerably strengthened where officers are given a relatively high degree of executive authority to act on behalf of their authorities. This seems to have helped Salford in comparison to Manchester, for example, where excessive political intervention has normally been a constraint on action and has hindered local government's ability to integrate and respond quickly and positively to approaches from business. There is a similar contrast to be drawn between the officer autonomy in most outer London boroughs and the high level of intervention in most inner London boroughs. Of course, problems can arise in other cases where autonomy has been allowed to develop but is not complemented by a quality of officer leadership that allows integration to develop. A number of our study areas evidence the effect of lack of officer vision on the development of local capability, particularly in the field of education.

In emphasising the benefits of officer autonomy, therefore, it is important to stress two things. One is that monitoring of effectiveness is required. Second, it is important to the democratic process that authority is *granted* by the members and not *assumed* or *taken* by the officers: sound links to members are essential to ensure that officers follow strategies that are locally legitimated.

Development Agencies

UDCs have been one of the most important catalysts to economic change and network formation in those ten urban areas in England and Wales where they exist. UDCs are key actors in physical development. However, as the London Docklands Development Corporation (LDDC) has demonstrated, UDCs concentrate exclusively on this field of action at their peril. The activities of the LDDC has caused considerable local controversy. The legitimate part of this controversy centres on the need for the local community to gain out of the developments that are stimulated, particularly through increased employment for local people, and not merely to suffer the negative externalities (see HoC, 1988). The other UDCs have learnt from the LDDC experience and most seek to ensure a closer link to education and training so that the local populations can benefit from jobs. Docklands has also now developed close relations with the local authorities to provide training and community facilities (see Chapter 8).

UDCs have a key role to play in partnerships because of the sizeable resource leverage at their disposal, their planning powers that allow rapid decisions to be taken, and the long-term impact they have on the shape of their local economies. They are often not involved to a major extent in partnership *initiation* since they cover only parts of most cities. But their involvement at a later stage is essential since they hold the prospect of bringing about major shifts in local employment patterns and require strong links into the local training and education networks to ensure that the *local* benefits of their activities are maximised.

In Scotland, Wales and Northern Ireland, the development agency role has been played by the wider agencies of SDA, WDA and IDB/LEDU. Of these, the SDA and IDB/LEDU have been the most significant. These agencies have had very important powers that have enabled them to initiate and manage local development using a highly professional approach with high level technical and managerial skills, and new powers that have allowed the development of new structures of inter-organisational and intergovernmental coordination and cooperation, and new links between the public and private sectors. This local structure represents a *de facto* recognition that developing an effective capability to lead or initiate activities in response to the global economic challenge is often beyond the capability of local government or any other single actor acting alone. The development agency approach is proving to be an effective tool for linking local and central actions and we return to it in our concluding chapters. For the present it is sufficient to note that the presence of such bodies has been of major advantage to Scotland, Northern Ireland, and to a lesser extent Wales, in comparison to the more limited powers and geographical coverage of UDCs.

Another source of variation between areas is the variable extent of Urban Programme Authority (UPA) powers, the existence of Task Forces, and CATs, the variable patterns of access to the RDC, and other special programmes and initiatives. The result, to echo the Audit Commission's comment quoted in Chapter 5, is a patchwork quilt of development institutions which vary in their incidence and influence between and within areas.

Community institutions

There is considerable variation in the character of local community institutions, and this can have considerable impact on the capability of localities to respond to economic needs. We discuss below the three key dimensions of:

- Social character and politics;
- Local values;
- Voluntary organisations and community groups.

Within any one place, there will exist several communities at different scales, with different senses of place, and often different political, value or belief systems. Individuals have a variety of community allegiances which exist at different scales and these 'communities' overlap in different ways in different areas. The patterns of participation are usually extremely complex. They relate to places of residence, work, shopping and leisure and define a social and political, as well as an "economic community". This manifests itself in social and political behaviour, and in the patchwork of voluntary organisations and community groups that exist in each place.

Social character and politics

Local social character constitutes one of the key structural factors that must be treated as capable of only slow change in the short to medium-term. It has an important bearing upon local politics because of the clear links between socio-economic composition and voting behaviour. For this reason local political circumstances must also be regarded as relatively fixed in the medium term. Local politics can have a crucial effect on the development of local networks and the possibilities for integration. Up until the Thatcher General Election victory of 1987, a number of urban Labour authorities had pursued an alternative economic strategy to that of central government. This did not embrace the idea of collaboration with local business. In some authorities, most notably perhaps Sheffield, Liverpool and inner London, there was open hostility between local government and the local employers and Chambers. With the 1987 General Election, however, there emerged a 'new realism' amongst most local Labour politicians and a willingness to accommodate to the notion of partnership with the private sector. This was not unrelated to the fact that, whilst local government budgets continued to be cut, central government money was increasingly directed towards schemes that involved a business component. But it also reflected a shift in national politics, particularly in the declared Labour Party policies of industrial collaboration (see e.g. Gyford, 1985; Nicholson, 1988; Travers, 1988).

Politics has also had an important bearing upon partnerships where the boundaries and responsibilities of district and county councils overlap but where the political colour of the councils is different. Even without differences in political party control, there are frequent "doughnuts" where large central places do not fully cooperate with surrounding, more rural, areas. Notable examples are Derbyshire and Leicestershire.

Politics is most likely to be an important local condition where there is either an ideologically committed council or where political control has a tendency to swing between parties from election to election. These are not mutually exclusive. Politicisation in either of these circumstances is likely to have a negative effect on partnership formation. Most successful partnerships have been built on the drive and initiative of officers as well as or independently of local politicians. Officer autonomy, rather than political intervention, seems often to have been an essential local condition for integration. This issue is discussed more fully below.

Local values

Local values have their origins in the social and economic experiences of individuals. Some are more locally-derived than others. In many areas, social and economic processes are tending to break down local networks of interactions and reforming them at larger scales. However, local value systems can prevail through tradition and in many parts of the country new patterns are only now being formed following the disintegration of the old networks during the economic recessions of the 1970s and 1980s. In areas such as Salford there is still a strong local culture related to the homogenous, white, working class community which lived and, until very recently, worked in local manufacturing companies. This milieux encouraged a set of attitudes which has often accorded a low status to the new employment opportunities in the service sector now opening up in neighbouring Manchester. Similarly, until recently, in East London the local traditional low-skilled employment sectors have stimulated a strong bond to small areas with an unwillingness to look for new skills or to travel further for work.

Thus certain aspects of particular value systems can introduce important rigidities into the successful implementation of actions targeted on local problems. This is because many value systems are adapted to social and economic conditions which no longer exist, or are unlikely to be sustained. These can therefore constitute formidable barriers. This is also often a particular difficulty for ethnic communities. However, it would be facile to assert that certain value systems *generally* offer more potential encouragement to economic development than others. Given the relatively slow pace at which changes in values occur, it is better to argue that different communities offer different *positive* potential contributions which need to be tapped. These contributions to the partnership capacity of areas will vary between fields of action.

Different areas have different mixes of values. The most complex interweaving and overlapping of value systems is to be found in urban areas, particularly in the big city cores. It is in these areas that cultural cleavages are often most strongly drawn. Post-war immigration from the New Commonwealth and Pakistan, and more recently of refugees, has led to great cultural diversity in many areas. Many of these ethnic communities feel isolated and marginalised from mainstream British society; they constitute an important challenge to local capacity building. For these groups, local voluntary and community organisations may be far more important.

Voluntary organisations and community groups

Voluntary community action occurs as a result of collective action to fill a need that, often, is not being satisfied either by the market or by local government activity. Different communities have different needs for organised community activity and different capabilities for bringing *effective* community organisation about. These are often overwhelming in their diversity. For example, in Richmond-upon-Thames alone, one of England's smallest local authorities, there are at least 165 voluntary organisations; some larger local authority areas have 600 or 800 organisations. Many of these bodies play a crucial role in providing a point of access to specific groups. Sometimes this access is the only entrée for individuals otherwise marginalised from mainstream society.

In any one locality there is typically a highly diverse collection of community/voluntary organisations with little or no coordination of their needs. Some local authorities have Councils for Voluntary Service in their areas, but these Councils also have a varied record in effective coordination. Local voluntary and community organisations vary considerably in the resources at their disposal and the effectiveness of their organisation. In many localities they provide a critical point of access to disadvantaged sections of the population, especially the ethnic communities. However, accessing community groups is fraught with practical difficulties stemming from their voluntary nature; community organisations are often run from people's homes, have limited resources and time or money, and frequently they can be contacted only out of office hours. In addition, their objectives are often unclear and their potential role with respect to partnership is ambiguous and often difficult to define. Some community groups simply do not have effective organisations to express their clients' needs.

Conclusion

This chapter has focused on the key dimensions that are critical in determining local capability. The following chapters apply this framework to the analysis of four major contexts:

- Large cities and metropolitan cores;
- Metropolitan fringe areas;
- Dispersed older industrial areas;
- Central places and rural areas.

Assessment of local capability in these contexts provides the foundation for our final conclusion on ways forward on policy in Chapter 15.

Footnotes: Chapter 10

1. This map is derived from analysis of the relation between local authority boundaries, settlement structure and TTWAs. It draws on earlier classifications, e.g. Champion and Townsend (1990) but is also significantly different in approach.

11. *LARGE CITIES AND METROPOLITAN CORES*

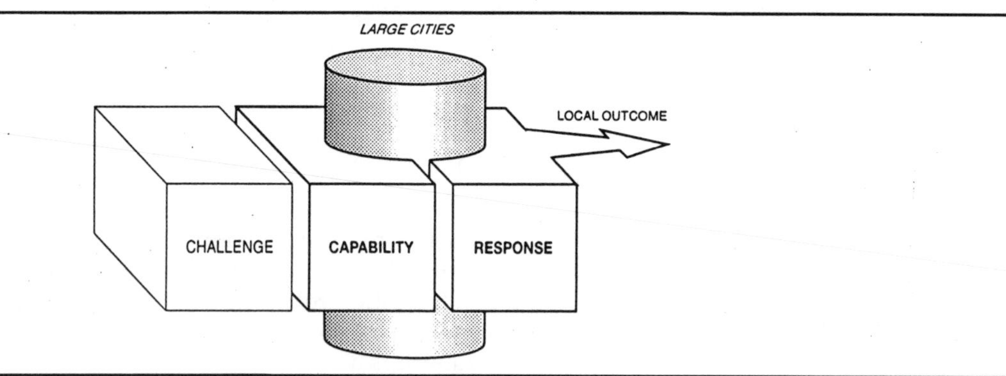

Integration or fragmentation?

In this chapter we examine those areas which have shown perhaps the greatest potential and need for partnership formation – the cores of Britain's large urban centres. Certainly it is these areas which have been in the vanguard of many of the major examples of developing economic capability, both "spontaneous" and "levered". In our discussion, we examine the experience of different forces that work to encourage or discourage local capacity building.

Although large and complex these areas have a common set of characteristics:

- They are important centres, in their own right, of economic, political and administrative power. Although they are in a strict sense "under-bounded", their influence stretches over an area usually much wider than their immediate context. As a result they tend to dominate the metropolitan area or whole regions;
- They are a national transport and economic focus that provides jobs to a much wider area. In extreme cases in central London (Westminster and the City) the ratio of working population may exceed the residential population in a ratio in excess of 10:1;
- Most of the core cities are large local government units with integrated powers (as metropolitan districts). The exception is London which, although having integrated local government powers, has small boroughs and a special, major role of Whitehall that cuts across local government powers;
- As influential centres, they can achieve a great deal but are frequently "hemmed in" by adjacent areas with a more residential character that may be resistant to the needs of the core city business or resent its influence;
- Business organisations are usually the largest and most well-developed in the country covering an area beyond the core city. Their detailed services to businesses outside of the core areas may, however, be thin;

- Businesses frequently have a regional, national or international character. This can often facilitate capacity building by providing a strong local leadership capability. It can also frustrate local capacity building by directing the attention of business leaders away from problems in the local economy;
- These areas, because of their economic power and influence, often offer solutions to the economic problems lying elsewhere. Conversely, the most adversely affected inner cities and Scottish peripheral estates may need support from other more suburban areas;
- There may be extreme areas of disadvantage and social malaise in these areas connected to high long term unemployment, loss of traditional jobs, poor school infrastructure, weak peer support and a paucity of community/voluntary organisations.

The parts of the country with these characteristics represent a significant part of the total economy. They cover approximately 19% of all businesses. They are served by 12 of the largest Chambers of Commerce and 26 TEC/LEC areas. The importance of these areas is in excess of their importance as a proportion of all businesses because they are also the main location of most company headquarters as well as regional business foci. Getting the local development capability of these areas right is thus a priority for the economy as a whole.

The areas chosen for the main focus of our analysis are: Manchester, Birmingham, London and Sheffield. Whilst all possessing certain unique characteristics, these areas share important features that reveal key lessons for the main issue raised by urban cores: achieving an integration over the forces of fragmentation. Among these four cities, Sheffield is different from the others in not being part of a large conurbation. Indeed, one of its most important characteristics is its "free-standing" almost completely "truly-bounded" nature. As we shall show below, this confers on Sheffield a number of advantages not enjoyed by other areas and throws into sharp relief the issue of fragmentation/ integration. It also needs to be said that, although central London shares important features with the other three areas, particularly Manchester, the problems it faces are often of a different order of magnitude; it exhibits some significant *qualitative* differences bearing upon partnership formation as well as *quantitative* differences stemming in part from its social, economic and political context.

There is in our discussion an important conclusion that needs to be clear at the outset. Although the large cities and metropolitan cores that are examined comprise some of the largest and most complex parts of the British economy, the structure of local agents and institutional capability is often dominated by a very limited range of main actors. As we demonstrate below, this has often been one of the main factors in their success. We examine below the central aspects of:

- The limited number of key players;
- Tradition of cooperation and good will;
- Vision, image and flagships;
- Fragmentation and integration.

Limited number of key players

Despite the economic and social complexity of urban core areas, Manchester, Birmingham, Sheffield and, to a lesser extent, London, all have the benefit of a small number of powerful actors. This is most marked in the cases of Birmingham and Sheffield. In both instances strong city councils are matched by powerful Chambers of Commerce which see themselves as playing the leading role in articulating private sector interests in their areas. Such a situation stands in marked contrast to the circumstances described in our examination of fringe city areas where there is a lack of leadership and fragmentation of responsibilities. Figure 11.1 illustrates the position of the two types of area on the "axes of proactiveness" (q.v. Figure 9.4).

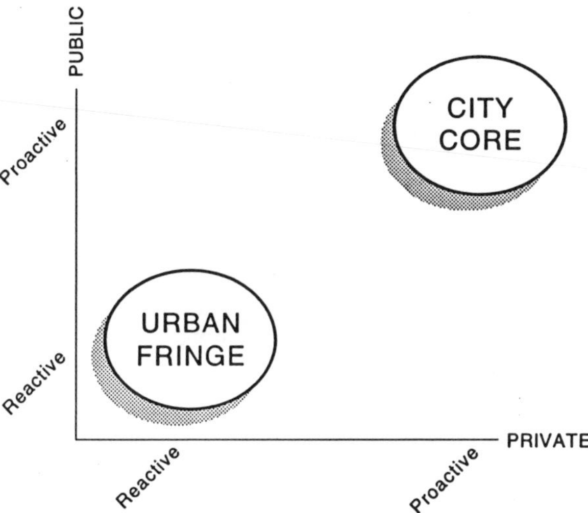

Figure 11.1 Public-private dimensions of capability in core cities and metropolitan fringes

The existence of a small number of key players in such areas is perhaps surprising given the manifest complexity and size of large city networks. As far as *local government* is concerned, authority and power to act on behalf of the locality is conferred in the cases of Birmingham and Sheffield by the single-tier structure and the coincidence of a single local authority boundary with areas which are meaningful in terms of local identity and the economy. In Birmingham the sheer size of the authority confers upon it a powerful position simply because of the resources it can bring to bear in a particular situation. Here too, there is a strong "city fathers" tradition dating back to the municipalism of Joseph Chamberlain in the 19th century.

This laid the foundations for major interventions by the city which are evidenced by the massive redevelopment schemes which still mark the city. It has also ensured a tradition of leadership in the city and high level interactions between the public and private sectors. In Sheffield, though the traditions are very different, the focal geography of the labour market has enabled a small number of key actors to attempt to control events; one commentator likened the city to "a large village". Sheffield City Council is a strongly directed authority. In the first half of the 1980s it was in the vanguard of the development of local socialist alternatives to the policies of the Thatcher administrations. But after about 1986/87 it adopted a more pragmatic, less overtly politicised approach, through no less effective for that. It has tried to stay ahead of government policy and has adopted new structures, in education especially, to serve local needs. Birmingham City Council has adopted a not dissimilar approach. Interviews in the authority revealed the development of a strategy to work with TECs at a very early stage of development. Subsequently, Birmingham TEC's first chief executive was recruited from the local authority economic development department; and indeed some commentators would have criticised the Birmingham TEC in its early days as "subverted by the local authority"!

In Manchester and especially central London local government is more highly fragmented. Both areas have a geographically fragmented local authority structure. Moreover, since all authorities are small, there is no dominant "lead authority" as there is, for example, in Birmingham, Glasgow or Edinburgh. The economic core is split between a number of small local authorities. The recent abolition of the Inner London Education Authority (ILEA) has ensured that this fragmentation runs across all policy fields. The problems for local networks resulting from these structures is increased by the different political compositions of different councils and their attendant attitudes to cooperation and integration, particularly with the private sector. As far as education is concerned, the ramifications of ILEA's abolition have yet to be made fully manifest. ILEA's constituent boroughs are taking responsibility for education for the first time and party politics and local priorities are beginning to intervene to shape relations between the new LEAs, their schools and local business. The abolition of ILEA has provided a new local capacity to address local problems with many new innovations as the boroughs take a lead. This is leading to new possibilities for the boroughs to integrate education with other services – something that was impossible while ILEA existed.

As well as affecting the potential for integration *across* Manchester or London, the partitioning of local government also affects its internal workings. Inner London boroughs have a solid track record of political controversy. The most celebrated examples have been in Brent and Haringey where polarised council views over anti-racism, sex education and social work have led to serious disruption of its education, housing and social services. Those boroughs that are under most insurmountable Labour control have often exhibited the strongest factional in-fighting. This has serious consequences for service management, as evidenced by the Audit Commission (1987), or in reports for some boroughs (see e.g. London Borough of Newham, 1989, and Chapter 12 below).

Having examined the situation in the public sector, what do our case studies reveal about *business organisations* in the urban cores? Ironically, perhaps, such economically complex areas have spawned only one or two key players for business in each locality. In Birmingham and Manchester it is the Chamber of Commerce which has emerged as the leading business organisation. In London, the situation is complicated by the fact that it is difficult for any one organisation to be able to claim to act for business and there is a well-known rivalry between the London Chamber, which is one of the largest Chambers in membership and turnover in the country, and which seeks to represent "Greater London", and more "local" Chambers, which in the case of Westminster is also among the largest in the country. Liaison is not facilitated by the scattering of many very small Chambers around the core. Their boundaries are often indistinct and overlapping, most have few or no staff, and only a few deliver any "services" for their members. Some appear to consist of little more than an answerphone and occasional meetings. In one field visit the "Chamber" was found to consist of an answerphone in a greengrocer's shop! Filling this "local' gap, the London and Westminster Chambers and the London Enterprise Agency (LEntA) have been important in championing the cause of London business and interacting with local government in recent years. In particular, LEntA took the lead, for example, in setting up, with the ILEA, the first British Compact through the formation of the London Education Business Partnership

(LEBP). The current problems of enterprise agencies are illuminating of some of the difficulties faced in London, and are described in Chapter 6.

The Chambers in the other three cases outside London quite clearly see themselves as pivotal. Thus, the Manchester Chamber stated in 1988: "*There is a growing realisation at all levels that urban regeneration is not achieved without partnership between business, local government and national government. The Chamber is uniquely placed to stimulate this collaboration, to provide a focus for the dialogue and to translate agreement into action through our committees of local business leaders.*"

Similarly, Birmingham Chamber stated also in 1988: "*The City and the Chamber intend ... to work together both to build up, and to build on the city's civic pride, particularly in the coming critical years of Birmingham's reemergence as a European city of international stature.*"

Notwithstanding the element of self-publicity in such claims, these Chambers are nevertheless large organisations. Manchester Chamber has some 70 staff and over 2,500 members. Birmingham Chamber occupies large purpose-built offices and employs over 150 people to provide services to its 5,000 members. Both are among the larger training providers in Britain.

Why such dominance has come about is lodged in the history of our oldest urban centres. The history of these Chambers shows that during the Industrial Revolution there was a demonstrable local need for a Chamber voice (Illersic, 1962). The very first meeting of the Birmingham Chamber in 1813 pledged "*to watch over and protect the interests of the commerce and manufactures of the city*". Subsequently the Chambers have grown with their local economies, and are often as complex as the areas they serve.

What are the advantages which can potentially accrue from having only a few key players in a locality? Firstly, with such a situation, interactions are simplified. Responses to external events can be rapid. Agreements on difficult issues can be more readily struck. Collectively, the resources which can be brought to bear on a particular target can be immense. Each player can justifiably claim to represent an important constituency of interest and provide the leadership which flows from it.

These advantages, however, *depend crucially upon their being a vision and agreement between the actors over the means and ends of their activities.* If two equally strong and determined parties have their gun barrels pointing in different directions then the result can be deadlock. This may be a crude description of the situation Sheffield found itself in as late as 1985. A left-wing Labour council spent most of the first half of the 1980s in dispute with local business over the issue of high non-domestic rates and ideologically unable to accept that businesses, which were collapsing in the face of world-wide overproduction of steel, required support from the local authority and control of local tax burdens. In addition, Sheffield has suffered from division between leaders within the business community. Although now progressive, its Chamber has not always been so: an important change occurred with the collapse of local industry in the early 1980s which led to a rebirth of the Chamber with new leadership and personnel. Similarly, a strong resistance to change from the other key business player in Sheffield has also been present – the Cutlers Company. In the face of rapid economic change, organisations – public or private – may not necessarily be equipped at the right time with the leadership or vision needed to act out the roles they need to play to give a true capability to their communities.

A further difficulty which business organisations in large cities face is maintaining contact with members, as well as accessing whole sections of the business community which may not figure in their memberships. In any large organisation it is possible for leaders to become remote from their grass-roots members and it is no different for large

Chambers of Commerce. In business, certain sectors, especially those dominated by small firms, can be especially difficult to access (see Chapter 6). Interviewees in Manchester and Birmingham noted that links within sectors tended to be stronger than those between sectors. This is also true more generally elsewhere. Manchester and Birmingham also have to ensure that their status as *regional* headquarters for a large number of important national companies does not lead to the neglect of the interests of the vast majority of small to medium sized locally-based businesses.

Overcoming these difficulties is not necessarily easy. Interestingly, it was the advent of LENs which gave many Chambers an opportunity to address these issues. The Manchester LEN was set up by the Chamber with a board which was representative of local business organisations. This was seen as a way of enhancing existing networks and was a logical adaptation to the conditions of a large conurbation. However, this conflicted with the approach advocated by the Training Agency (which was funding the scheme) which wanted boards of *"free-standing"* local business people to ensure each LEN keep in touch with employers' interests. As a result, the Manchester LEN was criticised by the TA. In the event, the Manchester Network's structure proved to be unique and very effective. A different solution has been to adopt a sectoral approach. The Birmingham LEN, for example, consisted of 10 sector groups which were given freedom to devise their own training plans. They showed a highly varied pattern of successes.

The Manchester experience exhibits the same conflict between representing local organisations and individual local businesses that has emerged nationally for TECs. Again, the TA has sought independence from "hosts" and other local interests in order to establish a task-oriented development model. Sometimes the independence has been gained by adding a new and not necessarily effective network; in other cases latent conflicts with established networks have inhibited TECs or led to fruitless competition, particularly with Chambers. Effective business networks clearly need special balances to be struck, unique to each area, that can draw on the strengths of local organisations whilst at the same time overcoming their barriers and lack of vision. We return to this as a policy question in Chapter 15.

A final aspect which is raised by the dominance of key players is the possibility of exclusion. Close relationships have the potential to become too comfortable and cosy, too reminiscent of a "club". This can make it difficult for new actors to enter the networks of decision-making. This can be a particular problem for smaller businesses or community groups. But exclusion can also have a positive dimension. In Birmingham, swift and astute action by the Chamber and the local authority prevented the imposition by central government of a UDC on the city and led instead to the development of the Birmingham Heartlands concept in concert between the public and private sectors.

Tradition of cooperation and political will

A tradition of cooperation may often provide either a lubricant to the formation of partnership or a convenient bedrock on which to construct more formal cooperation. But long antecedents do not appear to be as essential as other factors. This is an important message for localities which may feel disadvantaged in central government's drive to forge local partnerships and which do not have an established base. In any case, it is important to note that even the most long-established and effective links between business organisations and local government at senior levels do not date back very far. In Birmingham, such collaboration is commonly said to have been initiated with the decision to build the National Exhibition Centre. However, it is also important to bear in mind that it is often difficult to trace a direct line from particular events to the present day. Often a "myth of origin" is created, not least by the need of many agents to claim "ownership". Partnership development is just as likely to have been episodic and uncertain. As one commentator noted in Birmingham, the Chamber's relationship with the city council had traditionally been "patchy".

Much will also depend on the field of action in question. It is perhaps education which has the longest tradition of attempts to build partnerships. This stems in part from the fact that state education has a devolved structure of "delivery" (the schools) quite unlike any other public service. Schools have enjoyed substantial autonomy throughout the post-war period (see Chapter 7). This has meant that there has been considerable freedom for schools to forge partnerships with local firms. This has led to major variation in the extent and quality of such links, but it has also provided long traditions of cooperation in many areas. This has also meant that local authorities have been more likely to take on partnership-type activities in education than in many other policy areas. Thus, in Sheffield, one commentator dated the LEA's involvement as beginning at least in 1968 when Sheffield piloted the CBI's "Introduction to Industry" scheme. Since then, other initiatives such as Industry Year, work experience, Young Enterprise, etc, have been added in the process of accretion we described in Chapter 7 (see Figure 7.1). Other schemes (the EC's school-to-work scheme for example) have come-and-gone. In Birmingham, school-industry links can be traced back 20 years, according to at least one interviewee. In education it is therefore possible to see a genuine build-up in momentum.

But political will can be just as decisive in bringing high-level partnerships to fruition. Nowhere is this more true than in Sheffield. Until 1986, the public and the private sectors were at loggerheads in the city. The council had set up its Department of Employment and Economic Development (DEED) in 1981 to deliver its programme of "new left" alternatives to central government policy. This centred primarily on "job creation" through "municipal enterprise". Not surprisingly, DEED was a highly politicised operation, and substantially contributed to the antagonism between the council and Sheffield businesses. However, in 1986 there came a realisation of the need to break the deadlock for the greater good of Sheffield. There emerged a willingness to shelve those issues which provided barriers to partnership and to concentrate on issues where agreement was possible (see e.g. Field, 1990). The election of David Blunkett to Parliament as an MP in 1987 removed another barrier since as the former Council Leader he had developed a strong commitment to the "new left" methodology. With the political impediment to cooperation at senior levels removed, Sheffield was able to move rapidly towards partnerships, the lead perhaps being taken by the Education Department which had forged the first EBP outside London in January 1988. Also of significance was the joint commitment of the city, UDC and business community to hold the World Student Games in Sheffield in 1991.

The agreement developed in 1986–7 was masterminded by the "moderate left" on the Council together with the local business leaders, particularly the Chamber and UDC (see Field, 1990; Foley, 1991). It drew together meetings of the leaders of the city including representatives of:

- Industry
- MPs
- Community
- Police
- Health Service
- Fire Service
- Civil Service
- City Council
- Church
- Banks
- Charities
- Professions
- Commerce

They asked, *"what should we do about Sheffield? Two extraordinary conclusions came out of this exercise. The first was that we found that we all had enormous pride in the city. Second we found that we all wanted to do more but did not know what to do"* (Field, 1990, p. 53).

By 1987 it was possible to set up a "Board of Directors" for Sheffield called the Sheffield Economic Regeneration Committee (SERC). This is composed of national government agents, local government, local business, the local community, and the education bodies (schools, further education and higher education). Although this has no authority of itself, it seeks to coordinate actions within the city. The chairman of the Board, Field (1990), claims that the most significant contribution was to set up a *vision* for the city of *Sheffield 2000*. Within this vision a wide range of initiatives then took shape. SERC also formed the basis for Sheffield's response to the TEC initiative: there is a close common membership between the two, and SERC gives the base for a much wider local government and community representation than is possible on the TEC Board. The new attempts to develop partnership have been so successful that DEED has assumed a lower public profile since the mid-1980s with some major movement of staff and loss of political influence. By early 1992 its closure was being discussed.

Vision, image and flagships

Crucial in the forging of political will in Sheffield were both a sense of identity and a vision for the future of Sheffield. Indeed, it was arguably these two factors which were responsible for bringing together the public and the private in the first instance.

The turnaround that has been achieved in Sheffield since 1986 has been built on a citywide integration and vision: of the business-education partnership, the integration of many economic development activities of the TEC, UDC, local authority and other actors together in a coordinated structure; expansion of the role of the Chamber; the institution of a local percentage club for organising business donations; and developments in local banking (Hallamshire Investments) to help free the availability of venture capital. These changes have all been based on careful management of the economic focus, not least through the business leadership of Richard Field (see Field, 1990). There has also been a specific targeting of image (internal and external) of Sheffield as a key object of change. As stated by Field, the holding of the World Student Games in Sheffield in 1991 was one of the key elements of this image-development policy. The objective of image development is coordination of support to business in which all local actors as far as possible speak with complementary voices. This concept of partnership is one of the boldest of area development programmes in Britain. Also important to Sheffield's changes were the speed and depth of collapse of its industry in the early 1980s. This forced a radical rethink in contrast to the "slow attrition" which was more easily but inadequately accommodated elsewhere (e.g. Liverpool or London's East End). In Birmingham a strong sense of identity is also important. But in London and Manchester, the projection of a city image has proved to be much more difficult. The lack of a single body or "lead" body to campaign for these cities has been an important handicap. In this sense Sheffield gains considerable advantage of being a large core city which has almost coterminous boundaries between its economy and its local government. This is almost unique among the large cities in Britain.

Along with a clear image and a clear vision has come a focus on specific projects. Apart from the economic activity and social improvements which they generate in themselves, these projects became important *symbols* for the big cities. As we have seen in Chapter 9, they can become central to the attraction of inward investment and symbolise cooperation and future prosperity. In Birmingham, it is the Heartlands project which has become an umbrella for the integration of initiatives across the whole range of activities. Initially very much concerned with physical redevelopment, Heartlands now includes Compact, along with training schemes. Although less dominated by individual schemes, Sheffield and Manchester also have their major projects, e.g. the sports complexes and Meadowhall development in Sheffield, and Salford Quays and Trafford Park in Manchester. In London, the impact of such a concentration on major projects is less likely to lever change to such a large area, but projects like Stokeley Park, Broadgate, and particularly Canary Wharf and Docklands are redevelopment initiatives which are having major impacts on the local, as well as the whole London economy.

Fragmentation and integration

All the factors described above can be conducive to strong integration within the "large city cores". These integrative forces make for internally strong partnerships. However, until the advent of TECs, the involvement of business was often patchy and depended on historical chance – usually on the existence of a large Chamber or large businesses. Much also depended upon how the patterns of activity of the major business organisations meshed with the network of local authority boundaries and made sense to local businesses. This had the advantage that the situation was fluid and flexible to local needs, but the disadvantage that areas could be left out. The latter is a particular problem for metropolitan fringe areas, as we show in Chapter 12. With TECs, government has had to confront the issue of how to divide the metropolitan areas, bearing in mind the competing demands of voluntary business action and statutory local authority boundaries. The problems they face have been particularly acute in London and Manchester.

In Manchester, the structure of TECs was left largely to a "response mode" to bids. The result has been a fragmented structure of TECs for Greater Manchester and 3 TECs for the county of Cheshire. Partly in response to this experience and its special character, the TA took a stronger lead in London. It appointed a London Employers Group chaired by Allen Sheppard (Chairman of Grand Metropolitan). This Group decided to recommend an approach "which promotes the development of a sound network of TECs in London, and which also combines a mechanism for addressing cross London strategic issues on the one hand, with the harnessing of local drive and commitment on the other" (London Employers Group Report, p. 3). The Group decided against the prescription of boundaries, instead opting for "managing" the TEC development process and "helping" the network to develop (ibid, p. 8). As a result, the boundaries that emerged allowed too many small TECs to develop, left fragmented core cities, and has led to long-term uncertainties (see Figure 11.2).

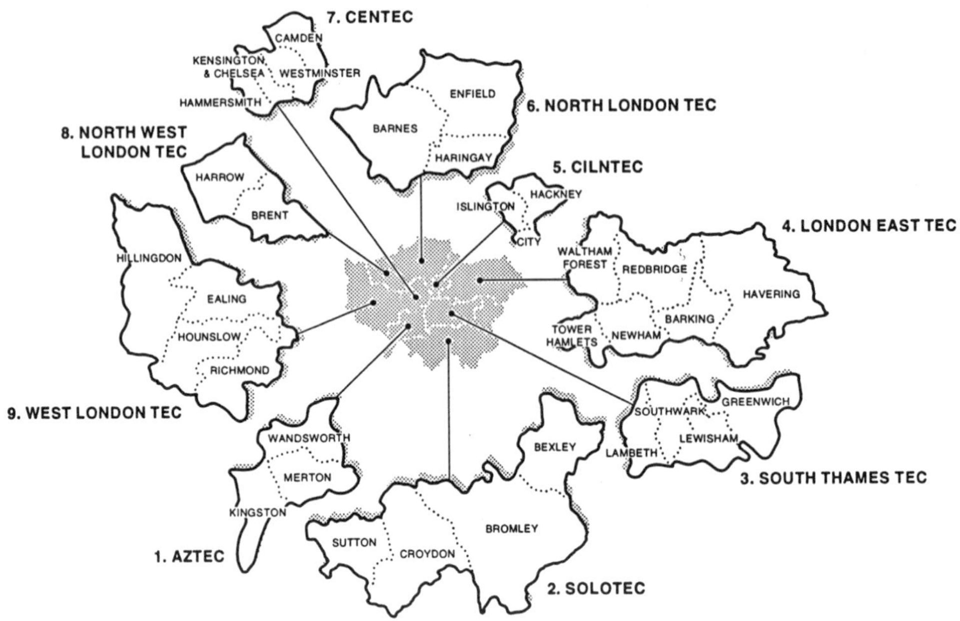

Figure 11.2 The map of London TECs

London presents serious difficulties in the development of integrated business services because of its complex local labour market and lack of coherent business focus. As a result, the London TECs generally have a lower degree of labour market coherence, business focus and often smaller size than TECs in most other urban areas in Britain. The setting up phase was slower and the number of boundary disputes larger than in other areas. The most important boundary problems were on where Camden should be placed; on where Haringey should be placed; on where Wandsworth should be placed; and on whether parts of Surrey, Kent or Essex could be included with London TECs.

In the development of London TEC boundaries three rival concepts developed, and a compromise between these influenced the final outcome. The first concept, primarily promoted by the Training Agency, was the wedge concept. This linked inner and outer areas and had the considerable advantage of developing cooperation between high labour demand and high unemployment areas. East London, North-West London, AZTEC and North London fit this concept. A second concept was political coherence. Many London boroughs found the wedge concept difficult because it brought together Labour and Conservative-controlled areas. The boroughs, therefore, pressed for inner and outer groups. This fits the TECs in South London and South Thames, and, to a lesser extent, CILNTEC. A third concept was local business communities based on major employment centres or the smaller Chambers of Commerce. This tended towards smaller groupings linked to only one or two boroughs. This pressure was important in AZTEC, CENTEC and CILNTEC. Finally, some areas were slow to make any response at all and were difficult to connect into the system. This particularly characterised Waltham Forest.

The large size of the London labour market and its high degree of integration has led the Government to establish, above the 9 local TECs, a higher level body for the whole of the Greater London area. This body is unique in the TEC movement. Termed the

London Strategy Group, this had the purpose of looking at strategic issues that cover more than one TEC area. For example, training for the needs of the tourist and financial services industries has been identified as such a concern (see LEG, 1989). The LSG does not have financial resources. It has not yet proved to be a powerful body and in 1992 looked likely to be abolished, with the result that London still lacks the strategic TECs body recommended by LEG (1989).

London's problems are not distinctive from those of the other conurbations. In Greater Manchester and the West Midlands, there are also multiple overlapping labour markets. And indeed, the pattern of TECs, as it emerged, is not so different for London, Manchester or Birmingham. Despite central government's original attempts not to have TEC boundaries determined by local government boundaries, London's TECs are based on groups of local authorities. In the capital's peculiar circumstances, almost any collection of authorities could be justified. Flows of trainees and workers are so substantial that for many individual business (which may have sites in more than one TEC), the particular TEC with which they are associated will probably prove to be irrelevant since a complex network of inter-TEC agreements (bi-lateral and multi-lateral) will be needed to enable the system to work at all. It was not clear during 1992 that this pattern of inter-TEC cooperation in London was developing at all effectively.

In the other conurbations, it has been easier to acquiesce in a fragmentary approach. Much more so than London, Greater Manchester and the West Midlands consist of groups of towns and cities which are economically and socially distinctive to greater or lesser degrees. The issues have become (i) to what extent the economically dominant cores of these areas can adequately service the neighbouring areas, and (ii) what scale of local organisation is required in order to provide sufficient critical mass to allow a quality service to be provided. Ironically, once again, it is the local authority areas which have dictated the shape of local development. It is the local authority which considerably reinforces the identity and distinctiveness of small towns such as Blackburn, Burnley, Bury, Oldham and Rochdale, and the TEC boundary issue has overwhelmingly focused on which local authorities to allocate to which TEC. In Greater Manchester this has been resolved by allocating Salford, Tameside and Trafford to Manchester and allowing the remaining 6 towns to form 5 other TECs. Almost all of these small TECs have questions of long-term viability and capacity to provide a quality service. This applies also to the smaller TECs in London and the West Midlands.

Lessons

In general, the early relative successes of Britain's metropolitan areas in establishing working partnerships between business and the public sector is undoubtedly due to the synergy which exists between the organisation, the image and the projects adopted in these areas. In this development the core cities have been helped by both their physical size – which has delivered a critical mass of resources and personnel – and by the fact that they were too important to be ignored.

Another key benefit of the core cities has been the unitary structure of local government which has removed the harmful tension present in the non-metropolitan areas; although this works less well in London or Manchester because of the small size of its boroughs.

Despite these benefits, each core city in Britain has major problems of integration. Whilst the cores have secured substantial leadership and major benefits of partnership learning, the rest of the conurbations have often still to find an effective way forward. Considerable jealousies have beset the process. In Glasgow and Edinburgh the tension is chiefly between the large central city and its surrounding fringes. In the West Midlands, Birmingham has been able to act as an effective leader for a considerable area around it, but the Black Country has suffered the disadvantage of a core split between two big players – Walsall and Wolverhampton – that have sought and found little means of practical cooperation. In Manchester and London considerable fragmentation across the whole conurbation is making it difficult for the major leadership required to emerge. Nevertheless in almost all core cities effective networks are now emerging. Given a favourable "environment" and political will, actors in these areas have been able to set about constructing some of the leading examples that are to be found in the UK of working economic development partnerships.

12. *METROPOLITAN FRINGES*

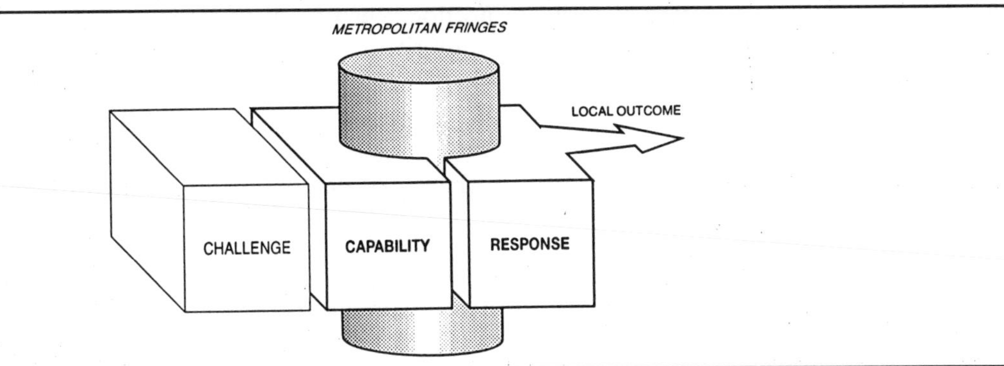

Introduction

Metropolitan fringe areas are within the continuous built-up area of large conurbations, but are peripheral to the main economic and transport focus. There are a large number of such areas in Britain around each of the major conurbations, particularly London, Manchester, Birmingham, Glasgow and Edinburgh.

In this chapter, we show these areas to have common problems in developing a local capacity for leadership and forming partnerships.

The seven common constraints are:

- These areas are radically "under-bounded" (Figure 10.2, q.v.) with their local government powers covering very small geographical areas relative to their economies;
- They have a lack of natural transport or economic focus – definitionally the main centre is nearby, but outside the area;
- There is often considerable resistance or resentment of the influence of the metropolitan cores. This is frequently exacerbated by differences in political party control between core and fringe;
- The local authorities boundaries are usually small in size and have little relation to the economy or labour market. Many of these local authorities embrace a larger number of former smaller local authorities that existed prior to local authority reorganisation in 1965 in London, 1974 in England and Wales, and 1976 in Scotland. This gives to many areas a dispersed pattern of former local government offices. Also local government has usually sought to balance resource allocation decisions to all parts of their areas which has reinforced economic diffuseness;
- There are usually few large firms and a dominance of very small firms mainly serving *local* markets. This leads to a dominance of Chambers of Trade over Chambers of Commerce and a generally weak structure of local business organisation and leadership;

- There is a residential focus with a predominant outflow of journey to work to other areas, or a complex cross-flow, which expresses an integration of the economy into other parts of the metropolitan area. This means that while problems may be evident locally, their solutions may lie elsewhere; conversely, the fringe areas may need to offer solutions to problems located elsewhere in the conurbation;
- Community and voluntary sector identification is usually at a neighbourhood level, a scale very much smaller than the local authority area, resulting in a high degree of fragmentation of local networks.

The strength and relative stability of this disparate and fragmented set of areas suggests that they are not usually proactive. They are thus a key target for capacity building initiatives. But the fact that the problems or potential solutions with which they are confronted lie in other areas presents considerable barriers to the potential for leadership and capacity to be achieved through local efforts alone. Instead, it leads us to a variety of propositions about links across the metropolitan area; the linking of centre and fringe more closely in mutual support programmes; or the need for additional external support in lifting the local capacity.

In this chapter we analyse a series of areas which are examples of the metropolitan fringe phenomenon, and then offer an assessment of possible solutions.

The cycle of fragmentation

There are many metropolitan fringe areas in Britain to which the discussion of this chapter is addressed. They cover approximately 13% of all businesses, of which about one-half are in the London fringe. Each varies subtly, and there are more major contrasts between the London and non-London fringes. They are an important part of Britain's economy and society. We have found these areas to suffer from crucial difficulties in developing a local capacity. Hence, enhancement of the attitudes of people and businesses in these fringes are a major target for raising the capacity and economic performance of Britain as a whole.

From our analysis we believe that metropolitan fringe areas suffer the adverse consequences of a unique range of forces of fragmentation. We suggest that this can be characterised as a cycle that inhibits the process of local capacity building. Causal chains are hard to establish, but we feel confident in asserting that a general cycle of difficulty emerges in metropolitan fringe areas as a result of the coincidence of a set of inhibiting factors and the establishment of a feedback between them. Figure 12.1 attempts to capture what we believe exists. The poor possibility of generating a local vision and, from this, a lack of local leadership stems from the structural features of the metropolitan fringe community and business base. However, the fragmentation which this engenders is exacerbated by processes in the local political sphere which are shaped by, but feed back into, the main process. The cycle of fragmentation of responsibilities is further exacerbated by the uncoordinated nature of central government policies.

The result is a systems failure. Or, to follow our earlier analogy, the different local actors have their guns pointing in different directions. They have different perceptions of what their targets are. Whilst local difficulties may be obvious, how they should be dealt with is a question which, because of a lack of vision and leadership, is rarely tackled other than in a piecemeal fashion. Looking *across* the different

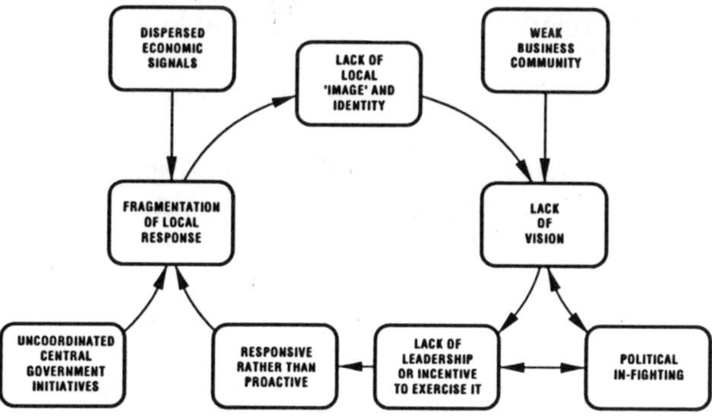

Figure 12.1 The cycle of fragmentation

vertical policy fields, and to the links required to potential solutions that might exist outside of the area, the picture is one of confusion, fragmentation and inability to move forward rapidly and coherently to develop the self-sustaining capacity required.

Integration or fragmentation

The four main areas that inform our analysis are Sandwell in the west Midlands, Salford and some other districts in Greater Manchester; and parts of East and West London (principally focused on Newham and Richmond respectively, but also drawing on research in North Kensington and Waltham Forest). We have also drawn on analyses of *all* TECs/LECs, Chambers, LEN and enterprise agency areas, as discussed in earlier chapters. The choice of our main analysis areas to some extent reflects the problems they share. They are defined according to local government boundaries which are not necessarily meaningful from the point of view of the needs of business, nor frequently, local community or voluntary groups. Such boundaries are not the most appropriate to facilitate partnership formation. For this reason we have not restricted our analysis to the boundaries of local government but use the local authority names as indicators of the general area to which we refer. This is a particular problem in London; and we refer to East and West London rather than the specific local authority areas in which we carried out our research.

Metropolitan fringe areas are within the strong influence of an economically dominant neighbouring urban core. This means they share a number of common features critical to partnerships but also that they possess significant differences. Each area has a strong reliance on small and medium-sized enterprises (SMEs). In the case of Sandwell, approximately 90% of businesses employ less than 50 people. The large local enterprises are not located in the metropolitan fringes, but outside the area in the city core. In most of East and West London this results in a high rate of outflow of residents to work in the centre. This is less pronounced in Salford and Sandwell or some other parts of London such as the Isle of Dogs, North Kensington or Hackney, where there has been a tradition of living and working in the same tightly defined area, e.g. as dock labour, and other traditional unskilled or semi-skilled occupations. These traditional "working class" areas have suffered terribly in the post-war period and many former local jobs have now disappeared. Often this has resulted in entrapment of the former unskilled who have been relatively unwilling or unable to retrain or travel to jobs emerging elsewhere (cf. HoC, 1988). This occurs even when that travel journey is relatively short in distance or time (under 3 miles and less than 30 minutes). Nonetheless, there has been a growing interdependence of the fringe areas with the core city, with other fringes, or even with outer metropolitan areas. This has often allowed a significant rise in incomes and has increased the residential bias. But significant "pockets" of low incomes, and high unemployment, have often been left behind. Frequently, though not exclusively, these are associated with many areas of council housing.

These structures have important consequences for local leadership and image. In London, a major problem for local partnerships is that London's image is one focused on London *as a whole*, supplemented with highly localised "allegiances" to areas smaller than local authorities, e.g. Brixton, Paddington, Isle of Dogs, Twickenham. London is sometimes referred to as a city of "villages". Broad visions at the level of the local authority are hard to develop. Fringe city areas like Salford or the Docklands have some of the longest traditions and the strongest local allegiances. Salford and Docklands make much of their working class roots, back-to-back houses, and in the case of Salford, there is pride in their fame as the backdrop for L.S. Lowry's industrial paintings. However, whether what one local business actor described as its "Coronation Street" image is good or bad for the city in its current position is open to doubt.

Fragmentation of the governmental structure is a major problem. Both Salford and Docklands as *local authority* areas embrace many former districts. Salford contains 5 former districts which were added to the old City of Salford in 1974. Whether Salford has been able to offer a coherent structure and image for all of these areas is questionable. Moreover, Salford lacks a strong or vibrant "city centre" to provide an economic identity for the 1990s. The centre it once possessed on the opposite bank of the River Irwell to Manchester has been a major loser in the restructuring of retail and leisure facilities in the city, although Salford Quays has been a successful and significant development, and some other new property developments are now in train. The case of Docklands is even more complex. It covers parts of five London boroughs (Tower Hamlets, Newham, Southwark, Greenwich and Lewisham) and each of these boroughs contains an even larger number of former London districts existing prior to London government reorganisation in 1965 (see Hebbert, 1991).

This lack of coherence and fragmentation of metropolitan fringes is likely to be increased by current initiatives to decentralise the process of local government service delivery – particularly in the fields of education, housing and social care. Local government is thus in an important, but relatively weak, position to offer leadership in the field of economic development of metropolitan fringes.

The absence of a structured community identity and image also presents broader problems. Areas like Sandwell or Tameside suffer from being caught in the middle of their conurbations. They almost resemble parts that were left over once territory had been allocated to the major cities around them. Sandwell, for example, consists of a collection of 6 townships brought together for administrative convenience. Local people tend to identify with their own local towns within Sandwell, or with Dudley or Walsall, rather than the administrative creation of Sandwell.

Fragmentation of business organisation is also a problem, and is reinforced by the cultural fragmentation and dispersed local economic base of these areas. None of the fringe city areas form strong or meaningful local business communities. No fringe area has therefore provided a strong focus for business organisations. There is no strong

Chamber that covers these areas as its main focal point, for example. Indeed, most Chambers serving these areas are located in city cores. This is particularly true in London. In Salford, numerous commentators have remarked on the broad north-west regional orientation of industry and commerce. Similarly, in Sandwell, businesses are either very local in terms of their markets, or integrated into the West Midlands economy as a whole. More typically, local businesses tend to supply the immediate local market. In London small local Chambers of Commerce and Trade exist in the fringe areas, but only Croydon has grown to be a significant part of the national Chamber network. One such Chamber exists as an answerphone stored behind the cabbages in a greengrocer's shop. At best, they are often little more than luncheon clubs usually between local small shopkeepers, estate agents and solicitors whose business services have failed to get beyond such activities as concern over parking, street signs, or sponsorship of street lights at Christmas. In Salford and Sandwell, autonomous Chambers simply do not exist but are linked to the core city areas of Manchester and Birmingham respectively. These may offer, in part, solutions to the challenges we have identified, and are discussed further below.

The lack of a significant business organisation has important consequences for the local authority. First, in the field of enterprise development, the lack of business actors has left a gap which has been filled by the local authority (very much the case in Sandwell, for example), by enterprise agencies and other actors, or has not been filled at all. Second, during the late 1980s organised business came to play a significant role in obtaining resources from an increasing number of government initiatives (e.g. LENs and Compacts discussed earlier). For local authorities eager to secure new resources in an era of spending constraints, finding a business "partner" or "host" became a major imperative. Failure to do so could be a major handicap, as Sandwell LEA was to find over Compact when its first round bid was rejected. Newham Compact also faced similar problems, and, despite strong support from individual companies, had to set up a limited company as a local business "vehicle", at the request of the Training Agency.

This last factor raises the more general problem of coping with central government initiatives in the metropolitan fringe areas. The diverse, overlapping and normally uncoordinated range of government initiatives has tended to increase rather than diminish the highly fragmented and uncoordinated set of actors and neighbourhood structures in these areas. Local fragmentation meeting up with fragmented governmental initiatives has generally resulted, not surprisingly, in increased competition and confusion. These areas have some of the most fragmented local networks.

The local political structure intervenes to complicate and fragment the picture still further. There are strong contrasts in style but similarity in outcome between "inner" and "outer" fringe areas. Many of the *inner* fringe city areas are dominated by Labour councillors. For example, the 1986 council elections left Newham council in the position of having no non-Labour councillors at all. Similar situations apply in Hackney, Brent, Salford and most of inner fringe Glasgow and Edinburgh. In situations of one party Labour dominance there is usually a strong tendency for factional in-fighting. Ward interests can dominate over those of the locality as a whole. In the worst cases such a political environment can lead to a paralysis in the management of services. This was highlighted in the report on educational standards commissioned by the London Borough of Newham in 1989 which found "substantial mis-management" of services. In such circumstances there are almost insuperable barriers to the possibility of taking effective, targeted action across all fields of activity that can address the enormous problems of areas such as Newham.

In many inner city, Labour-controlled areas there has also been the problem of achieving effective action at all. The Audit Commission (1987), Gyford (1985) and Walker (1983a, 1983b) have characterised this as the problem of breaking out of the cycle of political interference and control by local interest groups for sectional rather than general objectives. This has been a particular issue with respect to dominance of the Labour party by municipal unions in London (see Chapter 4).

The capacity for the development of effective and broad capacity is further inhibited by the jealousy with which local authorities "guard their patch". They are generally unwilling to look beyond their boundaries or to cooperate with other local authorities and other actors. Their tendency instead has been to focus on developing their own strategies and local centres in isolation of the rest of the metropolitan economy. An outstandingly irrational example of this is in Lambeth where a *"new estate of low-density housing occupies the prime development site between Waterloo Bridge and Blackfriars Bridge. ... The area was identified in the GLDP as a 'preferred location for offices' but was zoned in the next year by L.B. Lambeth for housing and industry, with 'future office development to be resisted'. Three miles to the south ... lie the Town Hall and Brixton town centre, where office development is sought. Brixton is the core of Lambeth; Waterloo its northern periphery."* (Hebbert, 1991, p. 206). More generally, Hebbert notes that many London boroughs have attempted to focus their activities on new town halls located in the centre of their areas. Similar patterns characterise other fringe areas.

In "outer" fringe areas, a related but differing set of characteristics have led to similar fragmented outcomes. These are frequently Conservative-controlled areas and generally have a middle and higher-income residential population. They also have multiple former boroughs and have fragmented neighbourhoods. The lack of business base and leadership is often even more extreme with the ratio of local residential to local working population often very high. Richmond and Tameside are essentially residential suburbs with businesses mainly orientated to local residential services. Generally, there is less recognition of the need for coherent action – the "problems" are all perceived to be in other areas.

For education, this creates difficulties of establishing effective business-link programmes and there has often been parental resistance to vocational curricula since children are perceived to be destined for management careers. Similarly, there is often teacher resistance to "eroding" traditional academic excellence both in pre-16 and the post-16 'A' level phase. At the same time, a large proportion of local students may in any case be in private sector schools and thus removed from the direct influence of most government initiatives. Similar problems beset training, which has been generally perceived as a second-level route and may have been poorly funded in FE or adult colleges (although no proper data exist to prove or disprove this feeling). There is also usually a paucity of training providers. The result is a pattern of local provision that often offers less local, parental and peer support to the less able, and the more vocationally inclined.

In the sphere of enterprise, the local culture tends either to emphasise a localised small business emphasis such as shops, traders and local designer services, or is oriented towards larger employers, predominantly in services or administration that are located elsewhere. There are no specific problems that arise from this emphasis, as such. The country, after all needs shopkeepers, managers and good employees. But there are few strengths to draw on here for business growth, and the development of an innovation and R&D base, particularly in manufacturing.

In both "inner" and "outer" fringe areas an associated problem, stemming from the lack of effective and practical political leadership, is that the initiative for change is left to officers further down the administrative hierarchy. This has the effect of allowing patchy responses: some areas have possessed progressive and effective officers, others have not. Largely as a result of chance, different areas have had more or less capacity to act effectively in their contribution to the local economy. Whether or not they have been progressive, officers have had to spend considerable amounts of their time trying to help build a strong political support for change. In education, political lacunae such as this accentuate the tendency, which is part of the tradition of the service, for initiatives to be left to individual schools. This has some advantages. As one key Salford actor put it, there was a belief in the LEA that *"policy comes from practice and sound experience"*. At the same time, we would argue that individual action by schools and other agents tends to rely on chance appearance or disappearance of individuals and is insufficient to achieve a goal of coherence, integration, and long-term, self-sustaining capacity. Each of these characteristics makes difficult the creation of a locally-based and self-sustaining capacity in business support for "outer" fringe areas. Thus, in both "inner" and "outer" fringes a major gap in local capacity is usually evident. We turn below to some possible solutions.

Emerging solutions

The cycle of fragmentation that we have identified places formidable constraints on developments in fringe areas. The key to solutions must lie in breaking into the cycle and in disrupting the negative interactions that feed upon one another. How can this be brought about?

It is clear from our analyses that the cycles we have identified are internal and external to the localities. Overcoming them requires shifting to a different state. This may require major changes, indeed, a quantum "system change" to bring about a *new alignment of actors* conducive to forming an economic development capacity. It is perhaps not surprising that the stimulus for such change should tend to be external, although it will differ across fields of action. In the environment of the 1980s, areas in city fringes were in danger of being left behind in the trend to partnership. For them, it was not simply a question of adapting existing interactions between public and private sector, as it was in the large cities and metropolitan cores, for instance. Rather, networks had to be established *de novo*. In their particular circumstances, the ball inevitably fell into the court of the local authorities, already in place, though not necessarily amenable to, or capable of, change. It also fell to actors in neighbouring areas to extend their influence. These actors had the opportunity to break into the cycle of fragmentation at various points. We discuss, in turn, local government and business organisations.

Local government

Central government policies have been a major stimulus to change in the 1980s. These have made resources available to local actors provided that the initiative they supported was backed by a local business organisation. Most important here have been LENs, TVEI, the DTI Enterprise and Education Initiative and to a lesser extent Compact (given that only UPAs could initially apply). The EBP initiative and TECs have been the main effects in the early 1990s. Although all the resources might certainly be said to be marginal additions to local authority activities, they have nevertheless been significant at a time of financial restraint. It also needs to be borne in mind that many initiatives come from what amounts to the redirection of funds from the previously general and unhypothecated local government grants into targeted initiatives (for example, through the Education Support Grant or Estate Action).

Local authorities have reacted in different ways to central government initiatives of this sort. Salford, described by one observer as *"law-abiding Labour"*, throughout the 1980s showed little public opposition to government schemes compared up to 1987 to Manchester, Sheffield or Newham, for example. However, the "new realism" which emerged amongst Labour authorities after the 1987 general election has brought most Labour authorities into the main government schemes. This has not meant that all political obstacles have been removed, however. Fragmentation is just that: it has not necessarily penetrated Labour councillors ideological objections to many of the schemes, nor done more than adapt the verbal presentation rather than the reality in many cases.

These comments should not be read as suggesting that change has been wholly exogenously created in the city fringes. This would be to deny important local developments. In particular, it is clear that, in many localities, officers were engaged in much "behind-the-scenes" activity in developing local responses to the need for partnership which prefigured central government action. These officers were then able to grasp the opportunity offered by central government initiatives, even if much of this activity was deliberately framed within the constraints and verbal gymnastics of existing local policy in order to avoid a politicisation of the issues. But changes brought about in this way are liable to be slow and small-scale and do not usually bring about a long term or sustained change. They continue to require central government initiatives and money. Only in a few cases by the start of the 1990s had a more self-sustaining base for change occurred by a deeper shift in political ideology or change in senior level officer responsibility in the local authorities.

The lack of broad local leadership has tended to leave compartmentalisation between fields of action. Some of these fields might be highly developed, some little changed since the 1960s. A corollary of this has been that, in different places, different fields of action have been the focus for development of partnerships with the private sector. A particularly clear cut example of this concerns Newham. Newham Compact led the way in forging productive links with businesses at local authority level. Its relationship with one particular company, Rosehaugh-Stanhope, proved particularly catalytic. The lesson here was that it was the meetings over Compact which provided the nucleus for the later development of the London East TEC. In this case, it can be seen that activity in one field of action had the potential for ramifications not only for other fields of action but other *geographical areas* as well. This experience demonstrates that activity that begins in one policy area *requires leaders who can spread the message across other policy areas* if an integrated approach to local economic development is to be achieved.

Business organisation

Developing the business community is a paramount concern for fringe city areas. With the local authority already in place and central government dangling resources before authorities that can demonstrate that they are working in partnership with a local business organisation, officers and members have sought ways of "constructing" a local business voice. However, the scope for local government action is limited. The opportunities for local government intervening in the development of independent Chambers of Commerce are strictly constrained. Even if local authorities were willing to intervene, and this is by no means evident, mobilising moribund fringe city Chambers with their existing *modus operandi* and vested interests is not only a major task, but may frustrate the objectives by using individuals or interest groups that seek to prevent rather than assist economic development. The successful option used in some cases, and generally favoured by local authorities, is to identify key businesses which are willing and able to pull in other businesses. This has been the role played by Stanhope in the Newham Compact. Stanhope had a major local interest in Newham since they were the force behind plans for the redevelopment of the Royal Docks in the south of the borough. Apart from being able to involve their suppliers in Compact, Stanhope exhibited a strong company commitment to community involvement which led to its assuming a more general proselytising role in the area amongst the business community. Stanhope was thus able to provide what is often described as a "gateway facility" to Compact. It was also very willing to recognise the local "community gain" required in a borough such as Newham, and negotiated specific payments and training schemes for Newham residents. A similar example, with a different package of community support, was negotiated by Olympia and York with Tower Hamlets (HoC, 1988). Broader community gain schemes have been important in other "inner" fringe areas through the Phoenix and UDC initiatives, particularly in Salford and Lewisham.

Elsewhere in East and West London, the stimulus of central government largesse has led many local authorities themselves to seek major local employers to work with, for example in Richmond. This also applies to the Salford EBP.

The other main solution to the problem of lack of business organisation involves neighbouring bodies. In both Salford and Sandwell neighbouring Chambers of Commerce had set up branches in the city fringes. In a different way, the London and Westminster Chambers have provided support to other parts of London. These large Chambers have enjoyed something of an ambiguous status, and have not usually been prepared to develop a strong set of local outreach services, prefering instead to concentrate on their main core city sites. The smaller Chambers dependent on the cores have thus had a difficulty in developing independence. The Salford Chamber was set up in February 1987 as a section of the Manchester Chamber. Sandwell Chamber was founded in 1985 and, as well as offering a range of business information services, itself provides "access to the wider facilities of Birmingham Chamber" (Sandwell TEC Application for Development Funding, 1990). Both Chambers are responses by the neighbouring large Chambers to the perceived business needs in these fringe city areas. But there is also a significant element of expansionism by the large Chambers to extend their membership and attain significant economies of scale. In the case of the West Midlands, Sandwell was a very obvious gap in the pattern of Chamber boundaries, sandwiched between Birmingham, Dudley and Walsall. Birmingham's move to set up a branch in Sandwell was seen by many observes as an extension of its influence to preempt the Walsall Chamber. Walsall already had a training centre in Sandwell, but it was seen by at least one local actor as the "great white whale" of the West Midlands, given its tendency to pop up all over the place! Dudley Chamber also had had designs on Sandwell and had been in competition with Sandwell Chamber over the LEN (in the event it was the Sandwell Training Association which secured the role of LEN host).

In Manchester, the Salford Chamber can be seen as an example of fringe and big city integration. The establishment of the Salford Chamber was seen as meeting a local need but also as crucial for preventing fragmentation in the city. It must also be said that

Salford Chamber has a symbolic function which is just as important as the practical ones. There are long-standing rivalries between the people of Salford and Mancunians and, today, between the two local authorities. It is arguably these considerations rather than strict economic rationality which dictated a separate Salford Chamber section. Apart from the area covered by the City of Salford local authority, Manchester Chamber also acts as a support to Trafford and Tameside business through two separate Chamber sections. This led in the late 1980s to Manchester Chamber playing host to a number of government initiatives covering these three fringe areas plus the city core. The LEN (Network Manchester), DTI Enterprise and Education Initiative and the TEC are all based on this area. There was thus much less of an element of competition with neighbouring Chambers in these areas in Manchester than in the comparable area in the West Midlands. However, Bury, Bolton, Oldham, Rochdale and Stockport Chambers have all sought to keep themselves independent of Manchester, which is often regarded by them as a threat rather than a source of support.

Together, these examples illustrate the role that neighbouring large city Chambers of Commerce can play in providing leadership and support to organised business activity in fringe cities. The precise form of Chamber offshoot bodies and outreach depends on local circumstances and the drive and vision of the leaders of the smaller Chambers. But there is also an inherent economic logic in linking areas such as these to their local cores. The pattern of TEC boundaries which has subsequently come about reinforces this conclusion. In Manchester the history of large city Chamber support has allowed a TEC to be established covering the same four districts of Manchester, Salford, Trafford and Tameside; but the rest of the Greater Manchester TECs are as fragmented as are the Chambers. In Sandwell for example, a separate Sandwell TEC was secured, reflecting its attempt to go it alone. The fragmentation or absence of a proper set of core city-fringe links will be a major impediment to progress. However the viability of the different small area TECs and Chambers is perceived quite differently by different actors. Much depends more on historical parochialism than economic rationality, with the consequence that many problems for fringe cities remain to be solved in the future.

Persistent fragmentation

The metropolitan fringes represent one of the most important challenges to Britain's economic progress. This chapter has argued that there are seven chief constraints acting on these areas: radical underbounding; a lack of economic focus; a local resistance to integration; a fragmented and parochial local authority structure; a weak base of business leadership – organised or otherwise; a residential focus; and a strong community fragmentation. We turn in Chapter 15 to a general policy outline for these areas. Two recent developments, however, deserve concluding comment: the development of Chambers of Commerce, and TECs.

The interrelationships between business communities in the core city and fringe areas has now been recognised as a key element in building a national network of core Chambers. The Association of British Chambers of Commerce (ABCC, 1991b) and Bennett's (1991a) strategy for Chamber development are seeking to develop links between large core city Chambers and local Chambers to provide service networks and outreach for the whole of the conurbations by integrating core and fringe. In London, this is being sought by overlapping a 2-tier structure of London central (high order services) and local Chambers (lower order services). In Merseyside, Glasgow,

Edinburgh and Manchester there is an integrated structure being developed for the whole of the conurbation. In the West Midlands there are three core city foci identified for Birmingham, Coventry and Walsall-Wolverhampton; these cover the whole West Midlands as well as Warwickshire, South Staffs, Shropshire and North Worcestershire.

The area coverage of TECs initially sought to achieve the same type of core-fringe links using a different concept. At a slightly smaller scale than the core Chamber networks, it was hoped that TECs would develop around wedges of core and fringe areas. This had the advantage of linking the areas of normal labour demand and supply which are a key element in TEC's training action. In the event, the government have had to agree to a pattern of TECs in which many cover small and entirely fringe areas, few cover wedges in some sense, and no TEC satisfactorily covers a whole conurbation by an effective linkage structure. In this sense the TECs have tended to exacerbate rather than diminish the problems of local leadership in metropolitan areas by adding yet another fragmented central government initiative. We comment further on this in Chapter 15.

13. *DISPERSED INDUSTRIAL AREAS*

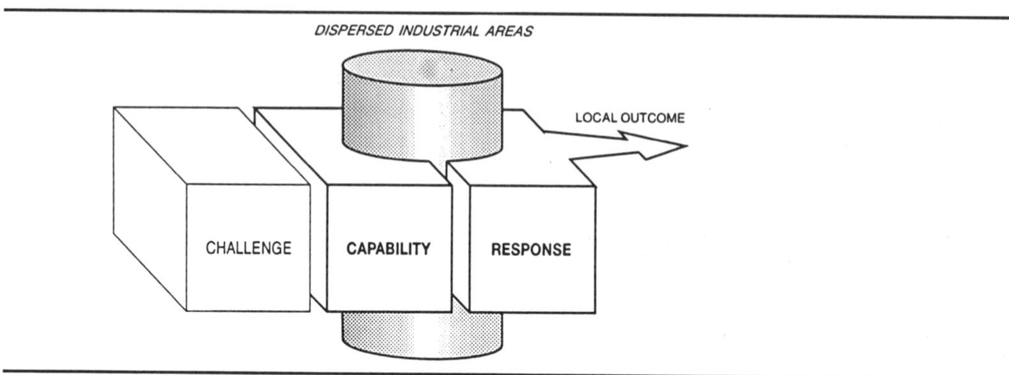

Introduction

Dispersed older industrial areas are characterised by a spread of industry over a number of small and medium-sized settlements with an absence of a single or dominant focal point. There is thus no immediate local equivalent of a core city. Leadership may be divided between a number of the more dispersed centres, or the area may look to a larger core city at a distance away. In some areas the dispersal may also look more like an extension of the fringe metropolitan areas, but is less continuously built-up, and has little, if any, leadership. The absence of local focus and the dispersal of the settlement present considerable problems for these areas. However, there is considerable diversity between dispersed areas, and recent developments have shown the possibility for them to develop a significant local capacity. They compare favourably, in general, with the attempts to build local economic partnerships in metropolitan fringe areas.

Dispersed industrial areas cover a surprisingly large part of Britain's economy, and their incidence may be increasing. There are two main types of origin. The first is the spread of small industrial towns arising from 19th and early 20th century economic development. The second is more recent and arises from the dispersal of business to rural areas as well as to older industrial areas close to, but separated from, the major cities. The second may often have a basis in high-technology. Where the second phenomenon is present two eras of development may overlap. As a result, dispersed older industrial areas have two differing characteristics – those with major economic development difficulties resulting from the continuing needs of economic restructuring, and those with more buoyant and rapidly growing economies.

Examples of the older dispersed industrial areas are Calderdale, North-East Lancashire, Durham, Gwent, Mid Glamorgan, Teesside, Fife and Lanarkshire. Approximately 14 Training and Enterprise Councils (TECs) fall into the dispersed industrial category. This accounts for 94,000 businesses, approximately 8% of the national economy. Like metropolitan fringe areas, therefore, they are an important part of the economy. Like these fringes they also suffer some considerable constraints on development. The 7 main constraints are:

- These areas are frequently "over-bounded" (Figure 10.2, q.v.) with a number of rival major settlements each having significant economic and governmental power in its own right;
- There is a lack of a single focal point, often multiple small foci, with transport links frequently carving the areas into separate corridors of development;
- Frequently there is rivalry and distrust between the dispersed settlements leading to a "we can do it alone" mentality, as well as resentment of economic relations to larger regional centres outside the area, especially London (or Cardiff/Edinburgh/Glasgow/ Belfast);
- The local authority district boundaries generally reinforce dispersal and rivalry of settlements, while non-metropolitan counties (if relevant) are normally unwilling or unable to play an effective strategic role;
- A mixture of large and small firms usually giving a fairly diversified industrial base, but rarely with obvious industrial leadership and usually a relatively weak set of Chamber organisations often focused on each dispersed centre;
- There is often a rich mix of residential and business communities of varied character offering attractive economic diversity and frequently an attractive environment and quality of life;
- Community and local networks tend to focus on individual settlements, often effectively, but lack a larger scale critical mass and wider vision.

The positive elements of these dispersed areas are strong building blocks of local networks in each settlement with a "can do" mentality and pragmatism which, if they have visionary and progressive leadership, can be a foundation on which broader networks can be based for the larger area. The negative elements arise when the strength of the local networks is purely parochial and lacks a broader vision to realise the potential for each settlement's capacity to contribute to a greater regional or area whole. An approach based on "we can go it alone in Dover" (or St Helens, or Pontypridd, or anywhere else) has the attractive features of local ambition and embodies an attempt to be independent and self-sustaining. But this approach can quite often be totally unrealistic given the scale of problems that business development requires and the levels of resources that are needed.

In this chapter we contrast examples of the positive and negative aspects of situations that are typical of the potential of these areas and the difficulties they have to address.

Positive and negative parochialism

The large number of fragmented industrial areas in Britain gives a wide scope for generalisation. In our analysis we have concentrated attention mainly on Teesside and Mid Glamorgan. But we have also been able to generalise from our analysis of *all* TECs/LECs, Chambers of Commerce and enterprise agencies for the whole country. We believe from this analysis that it is possible to identify two contrasted sets of processes at work in dispersed areas which can be characterised as positive and negative parochialism. These are shown in Figure 13.1.

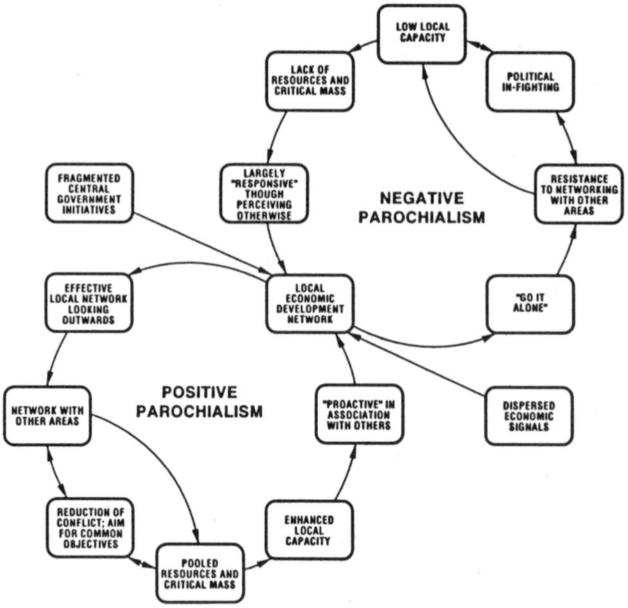

Figure 13.1 Positive and negative parochialism

In the *negative cycle* of parochialism, dispersed economic signals and fragmented central government initiatives are received and handled primarily by the individual local settlements – the local district councils, town Chamber leaders, local enterprise agencies, etc. A "go it alone" mentality is present which resists seeing local problems in a more general context. Outsiders and "newcomers" are largely kept out. As a result, opportunities to network with other areas and use incoming talent are not fully or quickly developed. There may well be political in-fighting with other areas and district councils within or between counties. Going it alone is particularly common among local politicians (particularly at district level) who have rarely been able to develop a broader vision. Chambers are small, often Chambers of Trade; if they are Chambers of Commerce, they are often non-affiliated to the Association of British Chambers of Commerce (ABCC), they have usually rarely met together, or if they meet they do little more than exchange information. Enterprise agencies are independent, mostly small and stick to their local towns. Central government initiatives usually focus on only some settlements (e.g. Urban Programme Areas (UPAs)) and not others, further increasing local differentiation.

A frequent "go it alone" approach allows only small resources to be available to tackle any problem. The result is that initiatives are generally small, localised, and tend to focus inward rather than outward. It is thus difficult to develop a critical mass of projects that can contribute to a wider and self-sustaining local capacity. Instead, local capacity relies on an individual, a leading industry, or a few individuals or sectors.

Where the locality (such as UPAs) has benefited from major central government targeting, this often further distorts local responses, frequently giving a lop-sided development to activity, rather than a broad approach, often offering the possibility for a spurious sense of local achievement to develop. This usually increases the "responsive" and dependent character of the locality, and may increase its vulnerability when central government invents a new initiative in a different field affecting a different type of area. As one leading commentator has remarked of Teesside, such economies are like a *"basket of initiatives"* that should be marked *"fragile"* for government to *"handle with care"* (Coldwell, 1989).

The *positive element* in local parochialism builds on the strength of local feeling, community loyalty, and local networks, but looks beyond the specific locality to the broader regional and larger economic questions. Community leaders following this course readily recognise the limits to their resources and seek to act with greater power and influence in their economies by gaining economies of scale through pooling resources with other areas. In the field of enterprise (Chapter 8), in particular, we have recognised the important synergies that can be used to link agencies and initiatives together. The same synergies act even more strongly between agencies in different places. Provided that a method of conflict resolution can be found that seeks to build on common objectives between places, these synergies should allow enhanced resources for everyone and an increased capacity for each settlement to be "proactive" in seeking central government or EC funds, in responding to inward investment, or stimulating business growth, education and training in its area.

The synergy concept captures the benefits of internalising cost externalities by collective action from which each area gains. Of course in the process of gaining collective benefits, each area or agent must lose a little of itself. Hence the gain of capacity is at a loss of a sense of independence. However, in the global economy of the 1990s the true capacity to be independent cannot be achieved by "go it alone" approaches in small towns which gives a spurious sense of local control that often seeks to claim local ownership for what would have happened anyway. A true local capacity must develop additional resources and additional leverage over external actors (both government and private sector) that has the ability to *affect* what would have happened anyway.

Positive parochialism is difficult to foster both because of the seeming loss of an agent's independence and because the "small-town" nature of dispersed industrial economies does not necessarily stimulate or enable local leaders to develop. Career profiles, for example, stimulate local authority officers (particularly chief executives) to move on to larger cities for enhancement of salary and status. Many smaller settlements may suffer from domination of branch plants by headquarters elsewhere that offer local business people small scope for local leadership, or a lack of permanence, as well as similar career incentives to those of local authority officers. Where there are important locally-based firms, these may also be narrow in outlook and do not necessarily perceive wider opportunities. Positive parochialism in such areas often has to draw on a few key leaders in specific sectors or locations that are then able to transmit and stimulate a wider approach across the whole area.

The older industrial areas experience dispersion across settlements whilst at the same time are having to cope with problems of economic restructuring. The experiences of economic change are often varied across the different settlements, with some areas experiencing significant growth whilst others have suffered major declines. This contrast usually also applies between sectors and neighbourhoods. There are often, therefore, differing implications for adjustment across the fields of industrial reinvestment, retraining and reorientation of infrastructure, each aspect of which requires considerable financial and leadership resources. We contrast below Teesside and Mid Glamorgan, also using examples from other areas to illustrate the greater breadth of applicability of these examples.

Teesside

Teesside has a history of association with large-scale heavy industries. Its origins lie in the steel, heavy engineering and shipbuilding industries which came to the Tees and developed during the 19th century. These industries gave rise to separate settlements at Stockton and Middlesbrough on the river and, further north, Hartlepool with its port on the North Sea. The traditional industries have suffered major decline. Major shipbuilding has now disappeared from the area, and steel production has contracted from nearly 100 blast furnaces to just 1. In place of these industries, the fortunes of Teesside have come to rely increasingly on petrochemicals, and the dominance of ICI and British Steel, which now employ in excess of 10,000 people each.

ICI first brought chemical production to the area after the First World War using local resources of salt, gypsum, anhydrite and limestone. In the post-war period, ICI developed the production of petrochemicals. This historical development of Teesside has led to a number of important features. First, reliance on a few large industries has made the area highly susceptible to the economic cycle. One commentator noted that *"every generation has experienced a period of long-term unemployment"*. At the same time, the reliance of the local labour force on a handful of businesses has led to what might be termed a culture of larger employer dependence: careers were a natural process of moving to being an employee for which, traditionally, low skills were required; this undermined entrepreneurial motivation in schools, was a stimulus to migration for others, and led to generally poor development in innovation, small businesses and self-employment.

In addition, there is a strongly developed sense of fragmentation based on identification to small individual settlements. Teesside is covered by the county of Cleveland, which is the smallest non-metropolitan county in the country (only 58,000 hectares); it has a population density approximately equal to Sheffield and is in excess of, for example, Greater Manchester. But despite this smallness and high density, major psychological barriers to the development of a local identity exist across and along the Tees valley. The creation of the County of Cleveland has had only minor impact on integration. North Yorkshire is as important a connection as Cleveland for many people south of the Tees, whilst Hartlepool remains what one interviewee called a "closed community" with most of the population living and working in the town.

Although dominated by large steel and chemical companies, a base of small and medium-sized enterprises (SMEs) has developed as product and service suppliers. These SMEs have become increasingly important in the last few years: restructuring in ICI, for example, has led to an increase in sub-contracting to smaller local employers. The relationship with these companies is not simply that of producer-customer: both ICI and British Steel have developed a tradition of allowing local firms to benefit from their training schemes and local contacts. They have acted in many ways as the key leaders in enterprise and private training development. These inter-company relationships have a longer tradition and, in some ways, offer a model for the strategic partnering we have discussed in Chapter 6.

A consequence of these features is that British Steel and ICI have traditionally been seen as the leaders of business in local initiatives. They have provided an effective lead. But, partly as a result of their dominance, there has been a *lack*, rather than a superfluity, of wider cooperative business action. The large employers have tended to *"do their own thing"*. Smaller local companies have traditionally waited on the giants for a lead. Thus the concept of a strong, broadly-based local business presence has lain dormant. Only after 1986 did the local Chamber of Commerce become an effective presence. Similarly, the development of Compact and the UDC has stimulated a broader business presence which ICI and British Steel have also done much to support.

The good track records of ICI and British Steel in public-private and strategic partnerships between businesses has been a leading UK example. ICI's record in the field of school-industry links on Teesside was described by one educationalist as "superb". They have also contributed widely to the local authority's activities, e.g. a previous chair of Cleveland County Council's education committee was training manager at British Steel. They have been strong supports of the Chamber of Commerce. But in common with other companies, ICI and British Steel have taken time and have been reluctant to develop a wider role in the local community that goes beyond their own immediate activities, of either social responsibility or mainstream training and related practice. They have been naturally reluctant to be seen to be *"taking over"*. However, in areas like Teesside where large companies dominate but also depend heavily on the local economy, and where they have an increasing need for *skilled* labour which local schools and colleges can supply, there is little choice but to provide the lead. There has also been an increasing realisation that if the skilled manpower of these large companies is not used, in part, to help the local community, no-one else has the resources or skills to provide it. Hence, ICI and BSC have found that they are in a natural position to offer leadership and to facilitate joint action with SMEs. Hence they have increasingly accepted the need to become more widely involved.

Wider involvement has, however, depended less on individual action by ICI or BSC, *qua* their firms, but more as action jointly with and through collective organisations. This has allowed them to be able to act with a broader legitimacy and to build wider networks. This overcomes the appearance of "taking over" and provides a wider base for future development. An initial stimulus was the establishment of a Local Employer Network (LEN) on Teesside. This was chiefly the result of the activity of a local Business in the Community (BiTC) group involving the large employers which came to comprise the LEN governing body. Since BiTC groups tend not to have local physical manifestations in the form of premises, which had to be found for the LEN, the Chamber was used as a host. The Chamber was also strongly represented on the LEN executive committee. This in turn required significant development of the Chamber's role, to which ICI contributed considerable staff support. This brought the Chamber and BiTC together in a concerted action. It was from this initial development that many subsequent partnership activities have sprung. Aside from hosting the LEN, the Chamber also hosted a Department of Trade and Industry Enterprise and Education Adviser (DTI EEA) and Teacher Placement Organiser (TPO), a Training Access Point (TAP) and Compact and is involved in Youth Training (YT) and Employment Training (ET). Under a series of go-ahead Presidents, and in the context of economic decline, Teesside Chamber grew rapidly at the end of the 1980s, moving to become recognised as the "employer focus for Cleveland" (Teesside TEC development bid, 1989, p. 9) and one of the most effective local Chambers in the country.

The Cleveland LEN provided the umbrella for potentially competitive business groups. It had an important unifying effect. During the late 1980s it was given responsibility for all government-funded education and training initiatives to ensure a local coherence. It was also seen as a key agent for widening the base of business involvement. The LEN, BiTC group and Chamber thus acted as a joint initiative. So successful were the developments that in February 1989 the BiTC group was incorporated along with a local CBI group as Teesside Tomorrow Ltd whose remit was to stimulate the economic regeneration of the whole area. This in turn provided a core of 5 directors who went on to become TEC Board members.

Through these developments, local business leaders have also been drawn to recognise the need for involvement with the public sector in joint action. Cleveland LEN invited the chief executive of the County Council on to its Executive Committee as the major local employer. Teesside Tomorrow sees its role very much as supplementing the role of the county and district councils and Teesside Development Corporation rather than trying to supplant them. Much of this stems from the good relationships which ICI has enjoyed with the local authorities. ICI, for example, is on the Management Committee of Cleveland Technical and Vocational Education Initiative (TVEI) and jointly owns, with the County, an Accredited Training Centre. Another nationally known project, CREATE, which encourages enterprise and skills development, involves the county, ICI, British Steel, Tioxide UK and other employers.

ICI and other large firms have, therefore, been prime movers in the stimulation and leadership of developments on Teesside. This stems from a company policy of community involvement which derives from both an enlightened self-interest and also from a desire to put back something into a community which has had to suffer economic restructuring, loss of employment and the disbenefits of hazardous and noxious industrial processes. Developing the LEN, the Chamber and the TEC have been seen as ways of broadening the base of employer participation in partnership activities. ICI has provided Chamber presidents and the chief executive of Teesside Tomorrow Ltd. Through the TEC there are *"for the first time ... people of chief executive status committed to work together as a group"* (Teesside TEC development bid, p. 10).

Teesside is a dispersed industrial area that has shown major development of initiatives and growing partnership activity since the mid-1980s. It has been able to use the benefit of its large companies to overcome the natural gaps of leadership and fragmentation that exist in dispersed industrial areas. But the wider basis of organisational support is still small. The gaps that exist are all too clear in the comments of Brian Coldwell, the first chief executive of Teesside Tomorrow Ltd and an ex-ICI personnel manager, who still believes there is a long way to go before the large employers can move from leading from the front to *"pushing from behind"*. Hence, despite the very effective development of local capacity building activities, the self-sustaining base for development in Teesside is still small, and still relies heavily on the largely "external" resources of the large companies.

Mid Glamorgan

Mid Glamorgan is a good example of how geographical fragmentation of communities can lead to functional fragmentation of business action. It is also more typical than Teesside of many areas in Britain in that the leadership of large international companies has not been so available.

Mid Glamorgan is characterised by two contrasting areas:

- The Valleys to the north whose communities grew up on the coal fields and associated steel industry;
- The coastal plain towns of Porthcawl, Maesteg and Bridgend and, further inland, Pontypridd and Llantrisant.

The economic changes of the 1980s have led to important contrasts between these two areas. The contraction of mining and the loss of steel workings has left the Valleys extremely depressed. From around 250 mining units just after the war, there were only 7 in 1990, and none by early 1991. Some parts of the valleys are now amongst the most deprived areas in the country with male unemployment of over 25%. In contrast, the economy of the south has enjoyed substantial inward investment. The post-war Treforest Industrial Estate has buoyed up the local economy by diversifying production, whilst Bridgend has been able to attract foreign firms, particularly prestigious being Sony and Ford.

These differences have accentuated traditional rivalries between the Valleys and the south. But equally important to our discussion are the traditional rivalries between the different Valley communities themselves caused by their physical separation. These differences have been embodied in the district council structure for the area which provides a separate district council for each Valley (4 in total) plus the two southern districts of Ogwr and Taff Ely. The Valleys have, for reasons of physical geography, always suffered from poor communication both with areas to the south and with one another. This has reinforced their isolation and strongly localised identity. Links with Cardiff, which one might assume to be logical, have never been strong and the Valleys have long sought to defend their separate economic viability against the threat of being swallowed up by the very different economy of Cardiff.

These features have had a major impact on the structure of local capacity building. In terms of action by the *private sector*, it had not been possible before TECs for a single business organisation to emerge to act for the whole area. It did not make sense in terms of the industrial geography of the 19th century and no leadership existed to rethink the local parochial focuses. Some highly localised employer bodies had emerged, e.g. the Association of Rhondda Industries and the Llantrisant and District Employers Association, but these were small and had narrow objectives. The nearest local Chamber was the Cardiff Chamber but this was a small and rather traditional Chamber, which was also tainted in the eyes of Valley business people by its Cardiff location.

In the absence of a strong business organisation, responsibilities became fragmented. In training the key player has arguably been the Glamorgan Counties Group Training Association which hosted the LEN and the county's DTI EEA and TPO. In enterprise, by contrast, a network of enterprise trusts and agencies emerged during the 1980s which is based upon the district and Valleys structure. With responsibilities fragmented in this way, the potential for developing a vision for the whole of Mid Glamorgan has been much reduced.

In the *public sector*, the fragmentation has made it difficult to develop a coherent strategy for the county as a whole. Loyalties remain tied to the districts, which thereby assume a greater importance than their true capacity to deliver. The sense of remoteness which many feel towards the county is reinforced by the location of County Hall in Cardiff – outside the area and in the rival centre! Indeed, many administrators, and perhaps citizens, in many ways have never accepted the split into South, Mid and West Glamorgan. Nevertheless, the county has attempted to play a wider role than the districts. Apart from being the education authority, it has a well-established role in economic development. This function dates from 1974 and consisted, by 1990, of a Business Development Unit of 15 staff. Since not all the districts have Economic Development Units (EDUs), the county has sought to play a strategic role. It is this balance between the district and county levels in a number of fields of action which has started to prove more crucial in developing a stronger local capacity.

The history of the recent emergence of a stronger local capacity in Mid Glamorgan is complex and multi-layered. For our purposes, its most important features are:

- The role of secondees (particularly from Marks and Spencer) in the development of the education-business partnership (EBP);
- The role of an enterprise agency in the EBP;
- The district basis of the EBP;
- The role of the CBI in Wales in the formation of TECs;
- Pressure from central government initiatives such as the Welsh Development Agency (WDA), Valleys Initiative, and latterly the TEC.

In Teesside the importance of large national companies has been crucial in stimulating local leadership and business capacity, particularly prior to TECs. Mid Glamorgan presents a different and more complex story. It has suffered major economic restructuring of coal and steel. But, unlike Teesside, there was not an ICI to ensure a continuation of the patterns of large company leadership. Rather, steel and coal in Mid Glamorgan moved to play a key role through their backing of a new network of enterprise agencies (through British Steel Industry Ltd and British Coal Enterprise respectively) set up in the 1980s. Two of the strongest of these are widely recognised to be the Ogwr Partnership Trust (OPT) and the enterprise agency for the Merthyr and Cynon Valleys (MADE).

It has been the enterprise agencies which have provided a basis for the development of partnership. Most importantly for us, they provide an unusual example of the involvement of an enterprise agency in education, demonstrating that they can provide suitable vehicles for business action in the absence of a Chamber of Commerce. They filled this role because they acted at the right level for the locality at the time. The major previous attempt to establish a cross-county initiative involving public-private collaboration had been the LEN. The LEN, initiated in 1988, failed to function effectively in Mid Glamorgan partly because of tensions between host and manager, but also because it was probably too ambitious at that time. In the event, effective partnership in education emerged first in Ogwr.

The Ogwr EBP emerged without county intervention. It is based on an enterprise agency and was for a long time one of the few examples of an EBP not funded by the Training Agency (TA). It has been subsequently recognised as one of the major examples of an effective EBP in Britain (see e.g. Chapter 7, and Bennett, 1992). The Ogwr EBP came about from the initiative of the Ogwr Partnership Trust, the LEA and Marks and Spencer. It is this latter involvement which is perhaps the most interesting of all for our purposes. *It is a clear example of a stimulus for partnership coming through a national company developing its own strategy at a national level, but acting as a key agent of change at a local level.* A similar pattern of experience is now affecting the Merseyside Compact, also using Marks and Spencer support, as well as other areas. In the context of a dispersed area with declining industry, OPT was able to act through an organisational structure, two of whose key backers were previously dominant large employers (British Steel and British Coal).

Marks and Spencer's role has been different to that of ICI in Teesside. Its support has been more targeted and more specific, by providing the EBP with a full-time chief executive as a secondee. The nature of Marks and Spencer's role partly derives from its structure: Wales was one of a number of places where the company might have provided support. Unlike ICI or British Steel, Marks and Spencer has a presence on a much smaller scale in almost every town. It already had links with the OPT through a secondee who ran Youth in Enterprise when in 1988 it approached the Trust with the idea of seconding a manager to run an EBP. At that time Marks and Spencer was developing its policies on both education and staff secondment and had identified

Wales as an area for involvement. Seconding a senior store manager was seen as a way of providing a worthwhile, structured mid-career break. The posting is for 2 years, long enough to be of value to the EBP, and at the end the manager returns to the company with a career enhancement in Marks and Spencer.

OPT had already provided the basis for much early experience of partnership, consisting of sponsors from both the public and private sectors and possessing a Board whose members were also drawn from the two sectors. As the Ogwr EBP got under way in 1988, it was realised by the LEA that the idea could be extended to the rest of Mid Glamorgan with Ogwr acting as a pilot for other district-level EBPs under a county-wide umbrella EBP. EBPs on a district basis made sense educationally as well: there are 42 secondary schools divided between the 6 districts, each district also housing a Further Education (FE) college. Ogwr is also the most buoyant economy where an EBP would be most likely to succeed. Partly as a result of this, it was decided that Cynon Valley, the most depressed district, would enter the EBP during 1989/90, with subsequent extension throughout Mid Glamorgan by September 1990.

The Mid Glamorgan EBP, the umbrella body, was launched in June 1989, the result of joint action by the Local Education Authority and the OPT. The launch occurred prior to working out detailed objectives and how they would be operationalised. Although Mid Glamorgan as a whole was not as advanced in its thinking on EBP as other authorities, it had at a senior level developed a vision and commitment which allowed it to move quickly. A dual reporting structure was introduced for Ogwr EBP, with the chief executive reporting to the OPT and Mid Glamorgan EBP. Funding was secured from 3-year matching grant from the DTI. The Welsh Office, when Sir Peter Walker was Secretary of State, had intervened to prevent the TA from funding any Compacts in Wales. The TA was thus restricted, partly for political reasons, and partly because of the difficulties of local businesses meeting the TA's demand for a job guarantee. The attitude in Mid Glamorgan, as in many other LEAs, was that the job guarantee was by no means central to an EBP. In the event, the Welsh Office eventually relented and Mid Glamorgan successfully bid for TA support at the end of 1989.

The development of business involvement required for an EBP subsequently made a major contribution to the development of the TEC in Mid Glamorgan. The same key individuals figured in both. The EBP slightly predated the TEC, but during the latter half of 1989 the two began to be developed together and this brought the advantage that strong links could be forged between the two. In the first phases of the TEC, a working party (one of several) was set up to examine education. It was regarded as important that the EBP did not simply become a sub-committee of the TEC since this implied a downgrading of status.

The EBP was not, of course, the sole influence on TEC development. Mid Glamorgan was affected, as was the rest of Wales, by the activities of the Welsh branch of the CBI. In the absence of a strong base of other business organisations, the CBI played a key role in Welsh TEC development. In Mid Glamorgan, the TEC interim chairman was vice-chairman of CBI Wales, so the link here was especially strong.

The relationship between the EBP and the TEC is also significant for the companies it did not include. Most important, Sony and L'Oreal, two key international companies based in the area, either would not become involved in the TEC or could not because of its requirement to have people of chief executive or MD level. From interview comments it is clear that they remain unconvinced that they have a commercial interest in sharing their considerable expertise in training and management within a UK legislative environment of business support that allows businesses to opt out and act as free riders on what they regard as forward-looking and high-investing companies. Such attitudes, if replicated in other companies, present a formidable constraint to the development of sustainable local capacity across the whole of Britain.

Mid Glamorgan thus provides an example, *par excellence*, of a fragmented industrial area. Local pride in each community is a potential force that can be enhanced to provide a strong local economic capacity. Like Teesside, external support from a major national company has been a critical ingredient in starting a process of effective capacity building. The experience so far shows many elements that encourage positive aspects of local parochialism to develop, and to support an enhanced local vision. It is accepted locally, however, that there is still a long way to go and that the TEC is only an interim, if a major, step in the development of the wider capacity required.

Lessons

The dispersed older industrial areas are places needing major economic restructuring and development. Because their focus is often on smaller towns they may be more amenable to development than other areas. They also have a tradition of industry with often a highly skilled workforce. But there are major problems of adjustment that go well beyond their local resources and local leadership capacity is often constrained. There may be important gaps, or it may be difficult for the potential leaders that do emerge for single settlements to exert a major influence over larger areas because of jealousies and negative parochialism between each settlement.

The two examples to which we have devoted chief attention, Teesside and Mid Glamorgan, both exhibit a rapid growth of a self-sustaining capacity in recent years, since about 1986 or 1987. Both have been able to look beyond local and sectoral issues to begin to develop broader agendas. This should allow both areas to reach a larger critical mass that can more profoundly affect their economies in the future.

Both Teesside and Mid Glamorgan also illustrate the important role played by large national companies in building a local capacity in dispersed old industrial areas: in Teesside, the locally-based ICI and BSC; in Mid Glamorgan, BSC and the NCB, but also Marks and Spencer with only a small local presence but stimulated by a national policy to target their social responsibility activities on selected areas needing support. The major role played by large companies is not typical of all dispersed industrial areas. Indeed the gap of such leadership may account for the greater negative parochialism in many areas. However, in Teesside and Mid Glamorgan large companies have had a very positive effect. Both areas also demonstrate the role of other wider groups of national actors, BiTC in both areas, and the CBI and Welsh Office in Mid Glamorgan. They also demonstrate the emerging synergies to be gained by combining business-led organisations with public bodies – especially with the district and county authorities, and in Teesside with the Urban Development Corporation (UDC).

In both cases external support was initially critical in developing a vision and providing the first resources and leadership base. The development vehicles that have emerged, however, are increasingly based on the emergent capacity of local actors. If still "fragile" and not yet self-sustaining, a local capacity appears to be on the right route to growth. In each case what seems to have been critical was an external agent that could seek a vehicle which could be regarded as a new and joint venture which all areas and all sectors could share. Thus, it was not in the ownership of one place or one firm. In Teesside it was the LEN and Chamber that allowed ICI and BSC to contribute, but without taking over. In Mid Glamorgan it was an enterprise agency and then an EBP which allowed Marks and Spencer and the county council to take a lead in Ogwr to provide what became a "pilot" for other areas. This model of an external stimulus catalysing a new approach to development occurs in other areas, notably the BiTC one-town partnerships in Blackburn and Calderdale.

The TECs have been able to build on these foundations. But in both of our cases the original organisations still remain – of Teesside Tomorrow and the Ogwr Partnership Trust / EBP. It remains to be seen whether the TEC can provide the new local capacity required or instead will become one further player that has to be built into the more general local capacity that is emerging. The Mid Glamorgan experience is particularly notable in this respect. Two of the key international local companies, Sony and L'Oreal, have withheld from participation in the TEC, despite extensive "courting" and governmental pressure. Their position appears to be strongly based on doubt about the TECs themselves and the general capacity of British local initiatives to provide the right environment to allow their contribution to be most positive. The dilemma that companies like Sony face in giving their committed support, even though they are best practice examples of training and community support in a more general context, is a focal point of our conclusions in Chapter 15.

14. *CENTRAL PLACES AND RURAL AREAS*

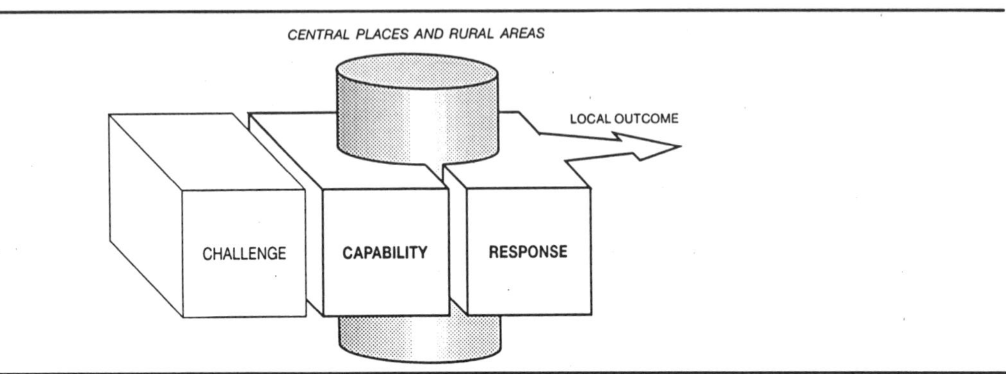

Introduction

Moving away from the large industrial core cities, their fringe metropolitan areas and the more dispersed older industrial areas brings us to most of the non-metropolitan areas of Britain. In these exist a large number of significant cities and towns, often of 100,000–250,000 population, as well as a number of smaller centres which, although less than 100,000 in population, are often significant as focuses for an area around them. These often act as important focal "central places". Many of these cities were county boroughs that existed prior to local authority reorganisation in 1974 (1976 in Scotland). They often have a strong tradition of civic leadership and independence which belies their status as a district – a status which they may resent. Indeed, proposals to give greater local government powers and status to many of these cities have been discussed by both Labour (HM Government, 1979) and Conservative governments.

Around these central place cities, often at some considerable distance away, are a variety of rural areas. Some of these represent commuter zones for the central place cities or larger metropolitan areas, whilst at the same time being rural and agricultural areas. Some are sufficiently distant to have only low levels of commuting, but may have significant elements of leisure, tourism and second homes, others are small industrial towns, and all may have significant rural and agricultural interests.

In all of these areas, there is wide variety, but there also exist some strong similarities which offer both major opportunities and constraints for the development of a local capacity:

- They are normally radically *"over-bounded"* (Figure 10.2, q.v.). Transport networks and service structures focus on the central place cities, often for historical reasons, but many rural areas are remote or quite remote from them. Since 1974 the advent of County Councils has done little to reduce this remoteness. Indeed, there is often an "accessibility gap" for the remote areas and a feeling of resentment from old county towns which now have to work as part of a larger local authority framework. Where an effort has been made to use a small old county town as an administrative base, this often leads to tension with larger cities in the area (often themselves former county boroughs), e.g. Dundee with Perth in Tayside, Southampton and Portsmouth with Winchester in Hampshire;

- There is often a high level of tension between the tiers of government – the non-metropolitan county/Scottish region and the large city districts. This affects planning, education, transport and the sense of "who is in control" (the central place city or the larger county encompassing broader interests);
- There are strong distinctions of interest between residents: city residents focus on commuting and see rural areas as a source of leisure; rural residents often resent commuting, second homes, leisure and tourist influences which unbalance their economies (particularly house prices) and undermine their rural focus;
- There are strong distinctions in the economy: city businesses tend to be larger, more outward looking and focus on services as well as manufacturing; rural businesses tend to be smaller, cater more for the local market and agriculture, and have only very localised service development;
- Business organisations, such as Chambers and enterprise agencies, largely as a result of these influences, tend to focus on the cities and often have thin membership and activities outside: many of these areas thus have a "measles" pattern of business support with small centres of activity surrounded by near-voids (see e.g. Figures 5.10 and 5.11). In rural areas, business organisations focus largely on sectors – usually agriculture through the National Farmers Union (NFU) or Council for the Protection of Rural England (CPRE). Where non-agricultural business groups exist these are often also sector specific, as in Yortek (North Yorkshire, high technology industries) or in tourism;
- There is often a strong complacency in most sectors that "everything is going all right" linked to concern by actors to retain their ownership. Hence, there is a low perceived need and relatively equivocal support for new initiatives that seek to enhance local capacity building. This partly reflects on the relatively few "traditional" economic problems: there is usually lower than average unemployment; school achievement and quality is usually very high, with high staying-on rates, etc; and these areas have often experienced some of the most rapid rates of economic growth in both the 1970s and 1980s. Often there is a feeling that "these sorts of activities need not concern us";
- However, growth of employment has often been concentrated in the central place cities and immediate surroundings leaving pressures from (a) pockets of severe deprivation in some of the most rural areas, (b) increased commuting to the cities from the rural areas and pressure for greater rural housing development, and (c) competing environmental objectives between the districts that may be industry- and growth-orientated, and the county which has often sought to constrain and divert economic growth as well as residential development thus creating some distortionary pressures on particular development sites and places. The result is often an absence of sites, inadequate and saturated infrastructure, such as roads, and increasing skill shortages because of restricted housing;
- A shifting economic scale of focus with the influence of global and European integration. This draws the cities into wider regional groupings with other central places and larger metropolitan areas which conflict with the existing counties. Effective economic promotion often requires an inter-county cooperation by local authorities which is very difficult to achieve.

The area of Britain covered by central place cities and rural areas is the largest part of the UK. It contains approximately 40% of all businesses, covering 30, or 28% of TECs/LECs, and 34 of the main Chambers of Commerce. Hence it is an important area in size and economic significance. If everything was indeed "going all right", then these areas could be left to themselves. But it has become increasingly clear in recent years that these areas have their own different, but major, barriers to economic growth that must be overcome if a broader national and local economic capacity is to be achieved.

Conflicting focuses of concern

The differing characteristics of rural areas and central place cities leads, in many cases, to a tension which has to be overcome if a proper local capacity is to be built. The differing situations are depicted in Figure 14.1.

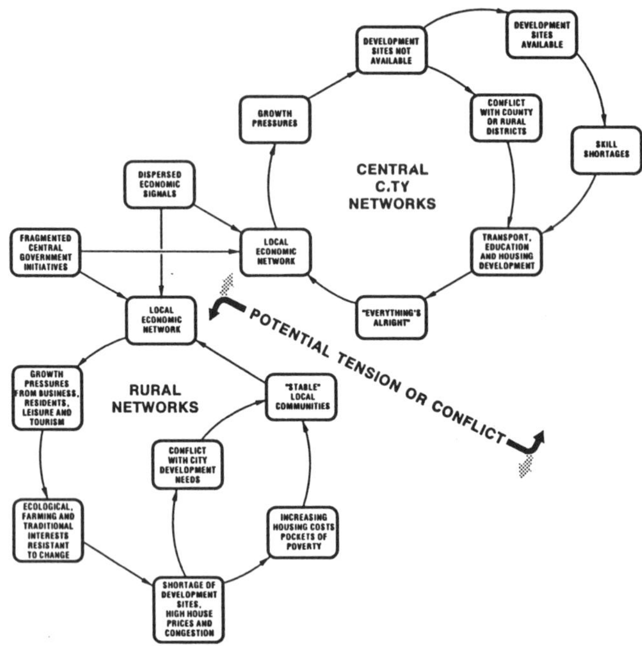

Figure 14.1 Separate networks of economic response in central place cities and rural areas, and the tension or conflict between them

In the larger *central place cities* the response to growth pressures internally or for inward investment is normally receptive: they have an active concern for employment development and usually have had a long experience in coping with industry's needs. The form of response will differ, depending upon whether development sites are readily available locally or not. In some situations space is available through restructuring older land uses: particularly in the ports in Southampton, Hull and Cardiff, or old industries such as potteries in Stoke on Trent, or jute and ports in Dundee, or chemicals in Warrington and Widnes. In many of these central place cities, however, there are few obvious sites and there are strong interests resistant to freeing green field land for development. In this case development possibilities are often modest and, if demands are met, development is often channelled into high-technology high skill and "environmentally friendly" industries. Many areas feel that they can be selective, e.g. with science park industries in Cambridge, or administration and computing in Winchester, or high technology and advanced food processing in North Yorkshire. In a number of these constrained cases, however, the development pressures are strong and there are sources of tension with rural or semi-rural areas surrounding the central city which seek to resist growth. This is evident in most non-metropolitan counties, but notable tensions are evident around Oxford, Cambridge, York, Leicester, Nottingham, and in Kent, Surrey, Hertfordshire, Warwickshire and North Cheshire. In some cases the resistance to economic growth in otherwise rural areas has been overcome by new town or expanded town status. This has often facilitated the growth of formerly small settlements, e.g. Telford, Aylesbury and Basingstoke.

Generally the central place cities have received considerable benefits from economic growth and have been able to respond to it. There is generally a positive image of these areas, a good "business climate" and a sense that "everything's going all right". If there are tensions, it is usually with adjacent districts or the county/Scottish region that want to resist development of the infrastructure and housing pressures from the crowded central places. This can create workforce shortages especially in certain skill categories.

In the more *rural areas* the response to economic growth pressures is more variable. A number of pressures are experienced, all of which appear to local people to come from outside of their area: pressures for new sites for smaller and high-technology companies, pressures for homes for commuters in the central place cities, pressures for second homes for urban dwellers, pressures for leisure and tourism from non-residents, pressures for new roads, water reservoirs or other infrastructure mainly aimed at benefiting large cities or the national economy. These areas also have had little experience of dealing with industry and have poorly developed business organisations. Their traditional business focus has been on agriculture, agriculture-related industries and local services. It is not surprising, therefore, that these areas are often resistant to change and seek to assert their own local needs over what are seen as pressures from "outsiders" – whether from businesses or residents. This resistance may occur through their local authority district, but rural areas are often able to control the county council because of the spread of counsellor constituencies which usually gives a disproportionate number of seats to rural areas.

The resistance to external pressures for economic development usually primarily affects planning by making it difficult to release new industrial land and sites for development, restricting the form of conversion of old sites, and leading to strong resistance to new housing development. Often green belt and other restrictions such as National Parks, Sites of Special Scientific Interest (SSSIs), Areas of Outstanding Natural Beauty (AONBs), etc. are used as weapons of resistance. Many county structure plans aim for "zero growth" (e.g Surrey) or "growth only for the needs of the existing population and local workforce" (e.g. Hampshire and North Yorkshire). In South-East England a frequently quoted phase is "we don't want to be like Berkshire – an urban sprawl corridor". These strategies of resistance are long-standing but have recently been recast as "green" or environmental strategies to protect heritage, landscape and a traditional agricultural environmental character.

The aim of creating a "stable" community is laudable in itself. But it creates problems for many small rural areas and "pockets" of young and older workers who cannot find jobs. And it has frequently brought these rural areas into a friction with the central place cities and the needs of the national economy. This friction can either affect the process of economic growth itself, where there may be entirely different strategies at county and district level in response to plans for particular housing or industrial development sites, or it may affect the structures and objectives of the networks of relations between actors. Many central cities sit, as the focus of generally forward-looking networks, as islands in counties or regions in which another set of networks have entirely different focuses. This gives rise to the "doughnut" phenomenon which is well recognised in Derbyshire, Nottinghamshire and Leicestershire. Similarly, national development pressures may also be resisted, e.g. as in Kent where national development requirements related to the Channel Tunnel have been only reluctantly, and partially, met.

As a result of these and other tensions a major objective has to be the development of a means to enhance the broader development capacity of these areas. The next section looks at some contrasting experiences.

Contrasted experiences

There is a great variety of experiences in central place and rural areas. We illustrate here four of the main types:

- "Over-bounded" large central places (e.g. Norwich, Leicester, Nottingham, Southampton-Portsmouth, York);
- "Over-bounded" networks of smaller central places (e.g. Cheshire, Kent, Hertfordshire, Somerset, Northumberland, Durham, Suffolk, Cumbria, Tayside);
- Radically "over-bounded" small centres in large rural areas (e.g. Dyfed, Powys, North Wales, Lincolnshire, Cornwall, Scottish Highlands, Southern Uplands);
- Isolated rural areas and island communities (e.g. Western Isles, Isle of Wight, Orkney, Shetland, Ross and Cromarty, Caithness, Argyll).

The first situation is of a large city, almost always a former county borough, in a larger county/region or rural setting. This city is large enough to form a critical mass of projects, personnel and resources for its own development. Indeed the focus and intensity of networking for the area may be strong and very effective. Particularly good examples of strong and effective networks exist in Nottingham, Southampton, Portsmouth and Norwich. But the difficulty is that these areas do not necessarily provide the broader capacity for the more rural area beyond. In this sense they need to be encouraged "to reach out" and take on a wider vision. If they are already trying to do this, they need the support, or at least acquiesence, of the larger administrative counties.

In the case of Southampton-Portsmouth there appears to be acceptance of its size and effectiveness as a development corridor where a focus can be achieved. The Chambers of Commerce, enterprise agencies and districts have recently developed close working relationships (only since 1991 in the case of the 2 main Chambers). But there is a weak structure of business support in much of the rest of Hampshire and adjacent areas. For example, whilst Southampton Chamber of Commerce has been a leader in organising a network of local Chambers stretching as far as Basingstoke, Andover and Salisbury, this network mainly focuses on information exchange and liaison rather than large-scale pooling of resources and strategy. Indeed, the local Chambers outside South Hampshire are mostly small, usually with no more than one full-time staff member. A similar pattern of concentration of activity in South Hampshire is also evident in the emerging TEC. Hampshire County Council has an environmentally-orientated low growth strategy for Hampshire. Hence, to provide a proper business support service requires a reaching out of business support bodies, which has so far not been fully achieved. This need is recognised in the ABCC development strategy (Bennett, 1991a).

In the case of Leicester and Derby a more tense situation has emerged. This is illustrated by the Compact initiative. As an Urban Programme Authority (UPA), only Derby (Conservative-controlled) was eligible for Compact status, whilst the Labour-controlled county, which is the education authority, had difficulties accepting the scheme in only part of its area. As a result, the local Compact initiative became highly politicised and Derby became the only Compact that had received TA development funding that failed to secure operational funding. Derbyshire has also proved to be fragmented for Chamber development and has two TECs. To a lesser extent similar problems confront a number of other non-metropolitan counties, e.g. Nottinghamshire, Leicestershire and Cambridgeshire where there are "doughnuts" of development with resistance to the incursion of the large cities by the rural areas. The contrast is Norfolk where, despite a Labour-controlled city of Norwich in a Conservative-controlled county, a network of services, both focused on Norwich and using Norwich as a distributional base, has emerged. A strong coherence has thus been established. For example, Norwich and Norfolk Chamber provides a travelling office as a service point for the whole county, whilst the county has closely integrated its economic development services with the districts, Chamber, enterprise agency and the TEC.

The *second* and *third* situations arise where a network of smaller central places exists in a large county/region or rural area. In this case the central place may well have a strong network of internal support, but it is usually limited in size and resources, and thus also usually in vision and capacity, either to satisfy fully its own needs or to offer support to other areas. The negative forces of parochialism may be particularly strong in these areas: as one local business leader commented, *"I can tell you that business in Widnes is nothing like that in Wigan, we have no common ground together"*. Kent's local fragmentation between 33 tiny Chambers and independent enterprise agencies has been likened by some to "feudal warfare". In contrast to the larger central places, therefore, these areas cannot normally reach a full critical mass across all activities, they do not have the resources which can easily be drawn on or adapted to the needs of other areas, and often they do not appreciate the need to look more broadly beyond their locality. A broad institutional development is thus required. Where the rural area is large and remote this problem is extreme.

For the situations in the outer south east of Britain, and in areas such as Cumbria, Cheshire, Somerset, Northumberland, Durham or Tayside much can be achieved by developing a coherent mass of support at a county/region level. Many Chambers of Commerce, TECs and county/region local authorities have been doing this. A good example is emerging in Cumbria where the county, districts, Chambers, enterprise agencies and TEC are beginning to pool resources together.

But in many areas there are considerable tensions. In the outer south east the TECs, local authorities and Chambers are in an early stage of working more closely together. There is a low perceived need for action, and many negative local parochial forces are still at work. For example, in Kent, whilst the TEC and county council are working very closely together on enterprise development, a federation of the small Kent Chambers of Commerce was formed only in 1990, Dover and some other key small Chambers are not members, and the Chamber federation has only recently developed a wider vision that goes beyond meetings and exchange of information. In Hertfordshire and Essex the overlap with London to the south, and other economies to the north is limiting action. Many of these areas, although large in both population and number of businesses, are small in relation to their interconnections in the regional economy. To the north of London, for example, the corridor of Milton Keynes (Bucks), Luton (Beds) and Watford – St Albans (Herts) is of major and growing importance, but it cuts across three counties for which there is no tradition of active joint economic development activity. A similar problem arises for the mixed small and large city corridor of Burton-on-Trent (Staffs), Derby, Nottingham, Loughborough and Leicester. For these areas the TEC boundaries have tended to ossify existing institutional boundaries. The ABCC Chambers development strategy has more fully begun to grasp the need for wider corridors of business support services, but has suffered from major resistance from some established Chamber interests.

Where the over-bounding reaches an extreme level, as in the highly dispersed rural areas of Wales, Scotland, Lincolnshire and Cornwall, the requirements for a critical mass of resources for local capacity building are even more difficult to satisfy. In both the TECs and the ABCC Chamber development strategy it has been recognised that access to business services can only be economically and effectively provided by a 2-level approach comprising a strategic body with local outreach. This is reflected in the area board sub-structures of many TECs and LECs in these areas, and the complex web of relations between small and large Chambers and other agencies being built into the ABCC development strategy.

For the *fourth* group of areas, the isolated rural communities and islands, over-bounding as such is less of an issue because even within a larger area there may be insufficient resources to meet local development needs. Their peripherality and remoteness, as such, cannot be overcome. But a local capacity can be built to the scale that is needed in these areas through a mixture of strategies: (i) strong local integration between TEC, Chamber, enterprise agency, local authority and other activity, (ii) effective networking to regional and national centres that fill local service gaps, especially for more expensive high order services (such as export advice and support, foreign business missions, data bases and research), and (iii) external support which can be increasingly sought through European Community (EC) as well as central government funds.

Overcoming complexity and complacency: Dundee and Tayside

To illustrate the intricacies of the way in which the different forces interact to produce a particular outcome, one area was the subject of much deeper analysis: Dundee in Tayside Region. This is a significant example to study, not just because of the relationships it reveals between local context and action, but also as an example of what happens when local actors fail to agree on a common framework for effective action in responding to change. It is a good example of a number of the problems we have outlined more generally in this chapter, of integrating action across policy fields and creating a lasting momentum that can sustain a continuing local capacity for economic development. The difficulties faced in Dundee are due less to the "structural" factors of geography or business character than to the "contingent" factors discussed in Chapter 10 that arise from the different objectives of different actors and their chosen courses of action. Because of this there is significant variation between the different fields of action in the experience of local capacity building.

Dundee sits on the north bank of the Tay estuary and is the main focus for economic activity in Tayside Region as well as the area in North Fife at the opposite end of the Tay Bridge (see Figure 14.2). Notwithstanding Dundee's industrial pre-eminence and status as a major central place city, there are traditional rivalries and tensions with the other parts of Tayside, particularly with Perth and Angus, both predominantly with a larger rural sector resentful of their minor role in the recently imposed regional government structure, and therefore resentful of Dundee. There has also been a lesser tension with North Fife local authorities and rival Fife Chamber. This is accentuated by Dundee being seen as traditionally "a predominantly working class city" with dominant Labour Party control within which is a significant far left element. Dundee also has limited opportunities for diversified housing and tourism, and needs major improvement of its image as an industrial city in an otherwise idyllic rural surrounding on the sea at the edge of the Scottish Highlands.

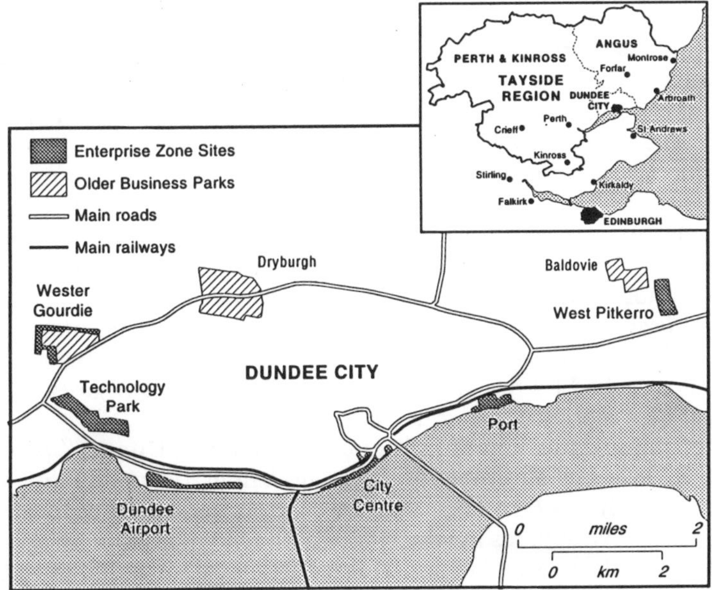

Figure 14.2 Dundee city in its regional context of Tayside

The industrial structure of Dundee has traditionally been said to focus on the "three Js" – jute, jam and journalism! – though there was also a traditional shipbuilding industry. The jute industry has undergone a major contraction in the last 20 years, declining from over 70 mills to 4. Post-war regional policy saw NCR and Timex, as well as a number of other middle-sized electrical companies, bring new industry to Dundee. High-technology industries have recently developed in the bio-technology field, drawing on expertise from the Crop Research Institute, the University and Nine Wells Medical Centre.

Despite this diversification, though, the traditional industries have offered strong constraints on the development of the area. Jute mills called for essentially unskilled labour. Like many such industries in other places, they appear to have had the influence on many families of allowing educational skills to languish. Thus although Dundee and Tayside has a generally good educational system, there are recognised problems of adult functional illiteracy which particularly affects the retraining of workers. Also, like other traditional industrial areas, low skills and large firm dominance have tended to cultivate an employee "dependency culture" and lack of individual entrepreneurial motivation. Small firm formation and entrepreneurism has been low. Where the area had opportunities, barriers have often limited their takeup. For example, the D.C. Thompson publishing group have for long resisted the use of its "*Beano*" and "*Dandy*" characters (Desperate Dan, Dennis the Menace) in marketing and product development, as well as in local heritage centres. Until recently, this was a major forgone opportunity for growth and diversification of the economy. Similarly, as in many cities and towns, local shops and hoteliers have long resisted the expansion of new shops and hotels, thus holding back the potential for growth opportunities as a major regional and retail centre. That resistance has found acquiesence in the regional authority because of the rivalry of other areas. Perth, in particular, has cast its role as the main retail and service centre, despite its small size relative to Dundee and obvious environmental constraints.

This complacency has affected other institutions. The local Chamber of Commerce in Dundee is relatively large by British standards (1,000 members). In terms of its traditional range of services it has been progressive, and it has also sought to participate in a number of initiatives such as LENs, Compact and the LEC. Yet there has been a constraint on the Chamber's perceptions and contribution. It dis-affiliated from the ABCC, and it has resisted a number of other overtures for involvement – it was described by one interviewee as "*not the greatest risk taker*". The Chamber has developed a natural and understandable resistance to initiatives that were underfunded and short term; it has argued along the lines "*why should an adaptation be made when the money will soon disappear and the external influence may soon evaporate or shift to other objectives – we will be here for the long term and will have to live with the long term effects*". This hesitancy is matched by the Tayside regional education authority which has also cast its role as at best modestly progressive.

The field of business-education links is one in which the "Dundee" problem is most evident. The late 1980s saw a number of initiatives being "dropped into" a situation in Dundee in which both the Chamber and the Region had a strong desire to control events in their respective spheres in which they both felt "everything was all right" and their own role was basically satisfactory. This led to a local view that the city was either being told what the government wanted it to do but the city could probably do better without the government, or that for Dundee to struggle to fulfil government remits for "small" sums of money was not worthwhile. This view stands in contrast to that found in other areas (notably Sheffield) where the possibilities were identified of fulfilling central government's requirements at the same time as meeting local needs. What the government's initiatives actually did in Dundee was to reveal some of the weaker parts of the foundations upon which any local capacity or partnership would have to be built. It also revealed the problems of government short-termism in contexts needing sustained action. This was especially true of Compact. Although the Dundee Compact eventually secured TA operational funding, Dundee ran into problems over who would be signatory to the contract. The TA insisted that this be a business organisation, but in Dundee it was the Region which wanted to sign and the Chamber, reluctant to take on an extra administrative burden or to conflict with the Region, agreed with this (its idea of a separate company had been rejected by the council). The ensuing conflicts with the TA delayed operational funding for a year. This episode reveals much of the approach of Dundee's local actors to outside agents and to stimuli to change.

Again, in the field of education, Tayside has a generally good reputation for its education service, and school-industry links date back some 25 years. However, as one commentator noted, the Region's approach is *"old-fashioned paternalism"* and its FE colleges are only now in the early 1990s, and with LECs, moving to a more targeted means of responding to local training needs. The education authority was also described as *"not a great risk taker"* and suffers both from a reluctance to be bound by central government schemes and strong tensions amongst its members, and between officers and members along marked political lines. As a result, it was made clear that, in education, central government schemes were either supporting what Tayside (and indeed Scottish) education was doing anyway, or, if new, would collapse when central resourcing came to an end. The potential of Dundee education has also been weakened by the need to maintain equity with the rest of Tayside. This all reinforces the traditional rivalries in the Region which are typical of many core city-rural areas.

Into this complex, and essentially complacent, web of local relationships marched the Scottish Development Agency (SDA) which established in 1982 *The Dundee Project*, a partnership between itself, Tayside Regional Council (TRC) and the City of Dundee District Council. Its aim was to regenerate Dundee and to integrate local activities in order to change the local industrial structure and employment base to industries based on new technologies.

In scope and resources, The Dundee Project has dominated the regeneration field in Dundee. Amongst other things, it developed 6 new industrial sites in the city, established a Technology Park in part based on an Enterprise Zone, and instigated *Dundee City of Discovery* as a marketing "brand" to improve the local image. Between 1982 and 1988 the three Project partners collectively invested £38m in local schemes, levering an additional £46m from the private sector (including indirect private sector investment stimulated by the Project, the private sector contribution is estimated to be £82m) (SDA, 1991, "The Dundee Project, 1982–1991: achievements and objectives").

Apart from its impact stemming from the magnitude of the resources it has been able to deploy, The Dundee Project clearly had an effect on more general local capacity building. The private sector has been increasingly involved through the Project Steering Committee and in particular through the Oil Ventures Group which seeks to promote the oil industry and which one commentator cited as "the only genuine local partnership prior to the LEC".

Like other "external" initiatives, the SDA was not initially a welcome influence in Dundee. Acquiesence in its activities was initially levered in the early 1980s by the prospect of considerable funds. The real commitment to a major change in their activities was admitted by all concerned to be small. As time progressed commitment to the Project became stronger as the results became more evident. However, the SDA met strong resistance to the initial proposals for the Waterfront Development, new road schemes and the location of the Technology Park. In this the Regional Council was normally combative and torn by its regional division of interests resistant to Dundee's progress. The District Council was more pragmatic, had a tradition of industrial estates and support, and had a better sense of what was good for Dundee, but was also constrained in vision and by infighting between members, particularly on the location of retail-related developments.

The tense experience of the SDA mirrors that arising in the replanning of many local areas. We have noted earlier the problems of small local authorities that take a purely internal view. In Dundee the local and regional structure plans had earlier called for the main new business development to be in the north-east of the city. There was district development land available, it made sense in terms of balancing internal geography (there was a need for new jobs in this part of Dundee, and it fitted with the Region's objectives to preserve green fields in the south-west of the city). However, given the general location of Dundee, the north-east part of the city was the least attractive location. The Project quickly recognised the benefits of a business park in the south-west close to the Tay Bridge, the airport and the rest of Scotland. Similarly, growth could be further stimulated by a new road to connect airport, Tay Bridge, Nine Wells Medical Centre, and the Waterfront at the centre of Dundee, giving the capacity for the whole to become a high-technology and bio-medical growth corridor well connected to the external economy. After considerable resistance from Tayside region, this plan is now being developed. Similar tensions still beset the location of the Discovery and its associated waterfront development. The Region is still attempting to show the SDA investment in a new dock facility to be "a waste of money" and wants it relocated elsewhere. The concept of partnership promulgated in The Dundee Project must, therefore, be seen as one highly levered by external forces and still subject to ongoing local battles.

The importance of levering local actors is still a key issue for the LEC which took on the SDA functions in 1991. Already in 1990 the frustration of the SDA with local actors not taking over The Dundee Project became very evident and it became clear that if the SDA withdrew, any activity that was greater than the sum of the Dundee local parts would collapse. Hence, the long-term commitment of local agents to offering a self-sustaining local capacity for Dundee was still limited. The advantages of the synergies and wider goals for each actor, beyond themselves and their immediate needs, are yet to be fully grasped. In sustaining the vision of the Dundee Project, therefore, the new Tayside LEC is crucial. But as a LEC for Tayside as a whole, it is already experiencing some of the same tensions and constraints that have held back Dundee in the past.

Lessons: need for a non-metropolitan vision

This chapter has concluded the discussion, covering Chapters 11–14, of different institutional and geographical contexts for developing local economic capacity. It has combined 2 types of areas often treated as distinct: central place cities and dispersed rural areas. But the discussion has demonstrated that each has interdependencies and that spreading a broader capacity to more rural areas will often require support from the resources, personnel and experience of the larger central places. Clearly a 2-level structure can be developed of local outreach combined with pooled central services. This approach is already being used by many TEC/LECs through their area board sub-structures. It is also part of the ABCC's national Chamber development strategy. Enterprise agencies, and local authority districts and counties/regions must also play a major role in this structure. The aim should be a local integration over coherent areas of business geography.

In arguing for this structure we have illustrated some of the major tensions that are already present. We have pointed to some successful strategies of local integration in Norfolk, Cumbria and parts of Scotland. But more remains to be done in the non-metropolitan areas in the future than in most other parts of the economy. Many have been the recipients of considerable economic growth in the 1970s and 1980s, and most have not suffered the classic problems of "inner cities" or economic restructuring on a major scale; they generally have some of the highest quality local education services, and they generally have highly desired environments. As a result, many have succumbed to the temptation of complacency.

But if Britain's economy is to develop to cope with the competitive pressures of the 1990s and beyond, outlined in Chapter 2, it is these areas more than any that must lead the way in the development of education, training, enterprise development and innovation and entrepreneurism. It is these areas upon which the main strengths of the economy now largely depend. Their adaptability and local capacity will be crucial to the whole system. We turn in the next chapter to how these, and other areas, can be helped to develop a greater capacity in the future.

PART IV

An Agenda for the 1990s

15. *TOWARDS A NATIONAL STRATEGY*

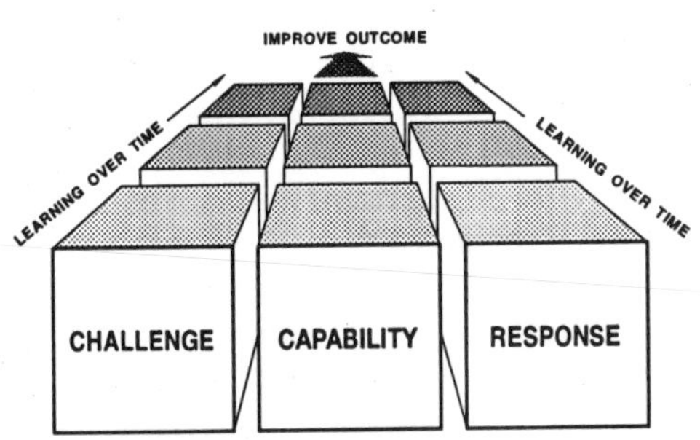

Reversing the "perverse policy syndrome"

This book has argued that many economic problems confront Britain as it approaches the 21st century. But the experience gained in recent years offers important indications of the way in which successful developments can be made to face the challenges of the future. In this concluding chapter the results of the analysis of the earlier chapters is used to suggest means of moving forward. The argument is that this process must go beyond halting experiments. Instead it must build up firm structures with a sustained commitment that allows *a national strategy* to be developed and sustained.

The concept of a national strategy builds on the key tenets of Chapter 1:

- *Doing nothing is not an option*: The analysis has evidenced a wide range of national and local gaps and concludes, with other commentators, that reversals of long-term economic decline in the 1980s have not yet produced a long-term system that will assure Britain's economic growth in the future;
- *Recovery lies in places we would often prefer to avoid*: Many aspects of Britain's systems failures require difficult problems to be tackled since large and powerful interests have been built up to avoid or limit change. Major economic advantages will be gained by releasing resources that are presently tied up in maintaining these barriers, or avoiding them;
- *Institutional development* is the key gap that faces the British economy. It is this which leads to the *perverse policy syndrome* by which additional resources applied to programmes customarily make matters only a little better, and may often make matters worse;
- Institutional development at present requires many gaps to be filled. Gaps lead to *system failures* because the needs of one sector of activity are not fully registered and responded to in other sectors. This is particularly true of education and training. These gaps are primarily in the public sector and *governmental institutions* that surround enterprise, but they also permeate business culture itself;

- Many of these gaps can be overcome only by drawing upon local institutions. They cannot rely solely on national programmes. Institutional development is simultaneously a *national and local problem,* for which local leadership and local experiences offer national lessons and solutions; the strength of the national system must derive from the strengths of its parts;
- Institutional development can be learnt. *Developing a learning process* is the most fundamental change in culture that must be sought since institutions based on this concept should have the capability not only to improve and become self-sustaining, but they should also be able to adapt and develop in the future as new needs emerge;
- But a learning process is not a purely local phenomenon. It requires government and national institutions also to change. The local learning process must be mirrored by similar patterns of response and adaptability at a national level. National bodies also need to provide a *sustained supportive environment* within which the learning processes can move progressively forward.

These tenets lead this chapter to offer the foundations upon which a national strategy should be built. The chapter assesses each key element, but to emphasise the need for "bottom-up" learning processes within a stronger sense of national economic purpose. We discuss in turn:

- Local experiences;
- Training;
- Education;
- Enterprise;
- Developing a national economic strategy.

This order of presentation is taken because the development of national strategic purpose seems most clear in the field of training; it is emerging strongly in education; and is least developed in enterprise. For each issue are discussed (i) progress so far, (ii) gaps to be filled, and (iii) priorities for the future.

Local experiences

It is people that make programmes work. Both people and programmes are founded in locations that are accessible to clients, and have sufficient critical mass to be viable. Few programmes are nationally focused in delivery, most have to work through local institutions and agents. The people who manage these local programmes are, therefore, the key agents for transmitting change and delivering enhanced capability to Britain's economy. Recognising that this "bottom up" process must complement, indeed is an *essential* ingredient of, any *national strategy* has been a key lesson of the 1980s in the search for an alternative to former "top-down" interventionism.

Because of this essential role Chapters 9 to 14 have given a large space to the analysis of local experiences. This has led to some important conclusions on the basis of a national strategy that is founded on local strengths:

- Local policies cannot create enterprise and entrepreneurism, but *local environments* have a large effect on enterprise and can be modified to encourage it;
- Some areas have considerable constraints on developing sufficient weight or leadership of economic development activity on their own; to succeed, these areas will

normally have to work with other areas and outside agents to develop their vision and obtain sufficient initial *critical mass*;

- No agents, public or private, have enough resources or vision to "go it alone" in development, most are constrained by their geographical area of coverage or by their absolute level of self-sustaining resources; *collaboration* is one way to increase the resources that can be applied to a problem. This lack of resources is particularly acute in the field of enterprise;
- Most places have a baffling array of different programmes which overlap, compete with each other and leave gaps; considerable economies of scale could be achieved, the scale of resources that can be applied to a problem can be increased, and the accessibility of the system can be enhanced if all agents are drawn together into a locally flexible *common system*; this is particularly true of enterprise activities;
- Most places still have major gaps in the relation of education and training to the needs of enterprise. Considerable enhancement of economic performance could be achieved if a stronger *coherence*, or partnership, of links between education and training and the country's economic needs was achieved; but these gaps have to be filled by local agents;
- Different places are in entirely different positions with respect to their resources, existing experience, and the requirements of their economies. For some areas developments may be easier than others because of closer "natural" lines of economic and administrative boundaries (e.g. large central cities); but for all areas a major *learning process* is required;
- Development must be built into local communities and their leaders, not imposed or "parachuted" in from outside; but this is difficult to achieve in Britain's situation of system gaps. For the immediate future, partnerships that unequally favour economic ahead of other requirements appear essential, particularly since local business leaders are usually the most isolated from other local decision makers; this requires a major programme of economic partnerships to seek the *development of community economic leadership*;
- Many complexities and difficulties at local level have derived from central government initiatives that have cut across local capability; they have also been subject to shifting priorities with political or bureaucratic fashion; what is required is a *sustained commitment to a national economic development purpose*.

The analysis concludes that a significant part of the process of learning at local level has to be built around local partnerships that bring agents together into effective economic development organisations. This learning process will differ considerably between areas. Some areas will have the advantage that local conditions reinforce one another so that the resulting momentum can be a partnership that is greater than the sum of its parts. The examples of "successful" partnerships examined in earlier chapters are characterised by these mutually reinforcing local activities. Some localities undoubtedly have more favourable local conditions than others. But every area will have some positive factors. From the assessment in Chapters 10–14 we conclude that the key to building local capacity is 2-fold: (i) to *maximise* the benefits of local *positive* conditions; and (ii) to *minimise* the effect of local *negative* conditions.

Local agents must focus on those conditions which are *changeable* and establish appropriate frameworks to neutralise the negative effects of those conditions which cannot be changed. For each local condition, the following questions ought to be asked:

- Does it have a positive or negative effect on local capacity?

- Does it need to be changed?
- Is it changeable?
- If it is not changeable itself, how can its effect be minimised?
- How does it interact with other conditions?
- Do we have any missing conditions/factors which could be introduced?

Many local conditions are not changeable in the short to medium term and must be treated as given. However, many barriers *can* be circumvented or removed through committed, decisive local action; they are questions of *will* and *organisation*. And it is these which should be focused upon. Some localities will undoubtedly have to work harder than others, but there is no reason why a successful partnership, adapted to local conditions, should not be possible in every area.

We can summarise those main conditions which present barriers or inhibitions to each of the three main agents (business, the public sector and voluntary and community groups) but which can be adapted or circumvented to bring about an increase in involvement.

In *business* it is clear that the key problem is to overcome dispersion of activity across small companies and small business communities. A key part of any solution entails the development of an effective local business support organisation. This must have sufficient critical mass to make a major impact on filling the gap in business services for micro and meso businesses. The challenges presented to large companies and particular sectors could be accommodated by an organisational framework which recognises (i) the particular contributions they can make to local partnership activities, and (ii) the benefits that they can receive by greater local purchasing and community involvement.

The problems of the governmental and *public sectors* require different efforts. The 2-tier structure of county areas is a major impediment to effective local networks. Similarly, many local authority boundaries cut across "natural" economic areas. These problems will not be easily overcome by reforms, but can be significantly reduced by greater collaboration between local authorities, as is already happening in many areas through the influence of Training and Enterprise Councils (TECs) and education-business partnerships (EBPs). The lack of capacity of local government to play a more stable and effective role in partnerships is again not easy to enhance through reforms. But major improvements would derive from an internal local government organisation that gave officers a greater degree of freedom from the negative, debilitating and handicapping effects of cumbersome committees. Though the political lines of accountability must be maintained, localities would be strengthened in their ability to build partnerships with other local actors if officers were granted greater power to deliver. This would be an important adaptation by local government to a changing environment.

Of all actors, it is the *voluntary / community organisations* which face the greatest challenges. Almost all the factors which are intrinsic to their organisation are negative influences on partnership formation. It is almost certain that most community groups will need substantial inputs of resources and considerable persuasion to secure their effective involvement in local partnerships. Spontaneous demands from community groups for inclusion in local partnerships are unlikely; they will normally need to be given a lead by other actors. Key tasks will be to stimulate voluntary organisations to play key roles; and to demonstrate to them and to the community the substantive benefits from their involvement.

Training

Our assessment of training has not dealt with the detailed requirements of the training process; rather it has analysed the institutional structures that contribute to the success or failure of *training to meet the needs of the economy*. We have argued that training has, until recently, been undervalued by business and government. It has tended to be seen by business as a "bolt-on" to fill limited gaps rather than as part of a long-term strategy; and by government there has been a tendency for it to be viewed as a political palliative to reduce unemployment. It has only recently been recognised that training performs a crucial link between people's motivations and skills and the need to enhance the competitiveness of businesses. It is this link which is one of the crucial steps in achieving a high value added economy.

Our analysis in Chapter 8 shows that much has been achieved in the later 1980s and early 1990s. It can now be argued that some of the most fundamental problems of Britain's training system are on the way to finding a solution: indeed that a proper *system* is now being developed which will be in place in the mid 1990s. The key positive developments are:

- A shift in emphasis to a culture of training within firms and an internal organisation to facilitate "learning by doing"; on-the-job training (OJT) has been enhanced both in status and level of provision in firms; and it has also become better integrated with off-the-job training;
- At the same time, college-based training and general vocational skills have been enhanced and their status increased, together with new contributions from school-based EBPs;
- A business-led structure, of TECs and Local Enterprise Companies (LECs), has been established to provide a systematic employer input to assess training demands which can provide both guidance and public money leverage on providers (in firms and among public and private providers);
- TECs and LECs have a local community as well as business representation. This might offer the chance to build genuine *social* partnerships at local level that might enhance workplace collective bargaining and encourage more effective worker-manager interactions;
- A form of dual system has been established in which employers' salary support for 16–19 trainees is supplemented by a state training credit voucher for off-the-job training;
- Vouchers have been accepted by Government as an entitlement for all 16-year olds; this cannot be as easily cut as training programmes such as the old Youth Opportunities Programme / Youth Training Scheme / Youth Training (YOPs / YTS / YT);
- The fragmentation of post-16 qualifications (the "alphabet soup") has been reduced by introducing a national system of vocational qualifications through NVQs. This has been established with content determined by industry bodies and with a commitment by government and other key agents to clear targets for high levels of achievement at NVQ level 2 – which is claimed to be roughly equivalent to the German dual system;
- A balance in NVQs has been established between core skills and specific vocational elements;
- NVQs have a clear progressive structure, balancing inclusion of almost all potential trainees at NVQ level 1, through majority participation in level 2, to high level skills at or above the German dual system standard at level 3, with the possibility of progression beyond to equivalence with degree and professional qualifications;

- Transferability of NVQ and other qualifications has been established allowing greater flexibility through credit accumulation transfer. Prior learning accreditation will facilitate recognition and enhancement of skills in the majority of the population who are already in the workforce, thus allowing a wide age spectrum to participate;
- A general national vocational qualification, GNVQ, is being established which it is hoped will have equivalence of status to "A" levels with a similar modular structure to SEAC's proposed 6 module base for "A" levels. This should allow comparability with, and transfer to, higher education through more vocational routes, as well as providing a more suitable route for wider participation in the further education of 16–19 year olds;
- These developments have been agreed with the main representative bodies of the CBI, ABCC and TUC, as well as many other bodies (see CBI, 1991a, *World Class Targets;* see also DEG, 1991 and DES / DE / WO, 1991). It is hoped, therefore, that a consensus will assure stable and progressive development over the considerable time period needed for implementation;
- The commitment of employers to training is much higher in the 1990s among major companies than up to the middle 1980s, as evidenced by the maintenance of a larger number of employer training budgets during the 1990–2 recession compared to their dramatic decline in 1981–3;
- A system of accreditation and quality control of employer-based training has been established through the Investors in People (IIP) kitemark. With money from TECs being available only to IIP accredited companies, it is expected that the spread of a training culture to smaller firms could develop rapidly. If the proposals for a training levy, from which IIP companies are exempt are implemented, then this leverage will become more compelling;
- The slow development of a trainer training route within businesses, equivalent to the German meister, is still recognised as a problem, but it is hoped that IIP and Management Charter Initiative (MCI) will allow a system to be established;
- This should lead to the development of a training culture in which firms will act as a monopoly interest that will not accept recruits who are not properly qualified or who do not enter a proper OJT programme; this in turn will lever schools, Further and Higher Education (FE and HE) institutions into change;
- Adaptability is built into the system through changes in NVQ content by industry bodies, changes in local training place supply through TEC and employer activity, and the effects of the demand mechanism offered by vouchers.

This structure has emerged since the debates of 1985–7 rejected the use of an enhanced Chamber of Commerce system that would mirror German practice. The developments certainly provide a system aiming at a world class quality standard with the potential for a stability that can be used to improve and develop it over time. This amounts to a major leap forward. The question that must be asked, however, is how far can this system be achieved. The following problems can be identified:

First and foremost is the question of stability. The system of NVQ for level 2 will not be complete before 1993, so that the first people to gain the new NVQs will not appear before 1995. The leverage of IIP on companies, therefore, cannot be properly implemented fully until 1996. IIP also only applies initially to companies over 200 employees and is extremely slow to take-up. The timetable for GNVQ is even slower. Hence, the full effect of the new system will not be evident until the end of the 1990s. This covers the life of 2 further parliaments. NCVQ and other agents hope that the consensus they have achieved will maintain the politicians' commitment. However, the consensus clearly does not involve everyone, whilst past precedent shows the dramatic effects of changes in governments and changes in ministers on programmes. The stability and strength of purpose needed to implement the system will require an alertness on the part of the key agents to keep the government on the path of progressive development. In a real sense, the need is to emulate the German or Japanese qualities – of water wearing away on rock, to solve problems by progressive development and improvements of institutions and programmes – rather than Britain's normal history of leaving difficult core problems untouched with the peripheral programmes modified by creation of new, and destruction of old, initiatives.

Second are problems associated with the TECs and LECs. Whilst business-led, there is a tension over their long-term ability to satisfy business needs[1]. This comes from 2 directions: first, there is the problem of lack of Board control over staff quality, performance and working conditions.[1] The shape and purpose of TECs is, therefore, an open question. Second, there is the issue of how representative TECs/LECs can ever be of their business communities when their Boards are appointed and there is not a network of relations with SMEs. Indeed, TECs/LECs compete with existing networks based on private sector bodies such as Chambers. It is known that the then Department of Trade and Industry (DTI) Secretary of State, Peter Lilley, raised in 1991 with his then employment opposite number, Michael Howard, the question of why the public sector initiative of TECs should be seeking to displace private sector bodies such as Chambers. A long-term tension remains which will not be fully addressed until the Chamber concept is again examined by Government with relation to TECs. The DTI proposed One-Stop Shops will only partially achieve this.

Third, trainees at present receive normal full pay despite being unqualified, relatively unproductive and occupying considerable time in training release. This contrasts with German practice in which trainees obtain allowances of DM 650 per month in Year 1 rising to approximately DM 800 per month in Year 3, equivalent to £240 to £340 in 1991. This recognises the reality that trainees contribute little to productive effort, and also represent dead-weight costs on the time of trainers and other staff until their second or third year. The proposals for national wage bargaining with respect to this group, and concepts of a national minimum wage would not help in this regard. The long-term sustainability of a training commitment by business must be in doubt if wages do not reflect either true labour product or the competitive conditions in other OECD economies.

Fourth, the commitment of government to young people's entitlement to vouchers may be limited in practice by restrictions on their value. There is a continuing conflict between the concept of entitlement, and the Treasury's view that if employers want their staff to be qualified then they should pay for them.

Fifth is the problem of diffusing the training culture down the size spectrum from the large firms, mostly signed up as CBI members, to the smaller and medium-sized businesses. The pressures of the IIP kitemark and the diminishing public money of the TECs is unlikely to lever many smaller firms unless labour supply is very tight. The alternative of the leverage of a training levy would be greater, but presents genuine difficulties for many small firms that cannot readily offer their own training tracks, or may find it inappropriate to their needs. Again there is competitive inequality compared to, say, Germany, where small firms pay only nominal registration fees (to Chambers) into the dual system. It is at this point that the gap between thinking on training and thinking on enterprise development is evident. A link between the needs of training on the one hand, and the needs of business support in a wider sense, through the stages of foundation, development and growth, on the other hand, is the key gap in smaller firms. Without a proper link to, and representation of, small business interests, TECs/LECs are handicapped compared to European Chamber systems.

Sixth, there is a major gap in the current proposals on trainer training. Whilst all the developments will stimulate the development of training management and supervision within firms, this has no proper organisational base within the present institutional network and it is not built into the system of NVQs. There is thus no equivalent of the German meister. This deficiency has also been recognised by the CBI (1992). Although there are some outstanding examples of the implementation of MCI in large companies, even the most fervent supporters of MCI recognise that it is not an adequate system for the transmission of stimuli and that it is disconnected from other developments. Most TECs are also highly critical of it, and few have been enthusiastic to adopt MCI (see Bennett *et al.*, 1993).

Seventh, the IIP quality control is itself open to a number of challenges. Whilst too early to judge fully, it is clear that the diffusion to businesses is extremely slow. Although the National Training Task Force (NTTF) and TEC Boards are concerned to specify high quality standards, there is no reason why the companies that most need to develop standards should participate.

Eighth is the problem of coverage, standards and comparability of NVQs. Whilst the long-term will undoubtedly lead to useful developments, during the whole of the 1990s there are likely to be important difficulties. For example, a wide range of highly respected and eminently useful vocational qualifications remain outside of the formal NVQ equivalence; and there is strong criticism of equivalence of standard among different NVQs, particularly between retailing, catering and clerical skills, on the one hand, and technical and engineering skills, on the other hand; and there is not yet a formal equivalence of NVQ to EC standards. These problems are capable of solution and are being worked on, but will take considerable time to overcome.

Ninth is the problem of equivalence of status. Transferability of NVQs, particularly between GNVQ and "A" levels will take a long time to establish and will need strong employer leverage if it is to overcome deep-seated parental and other prejudices against the vocational route.

Tenth is the problem of linking vocational development post-16 to a better information service to pupils in schools. The reform of the Careers Service and school-based careers guidance is still a political football; the full implementation of a national Record of Achievement is still in its infancy; and the development in schools of vocational education, business links and work experience hangs in the balance pending the evolution of the national curriculum (as discussed in Chapter 7). Section 24 of the Education Reform Act can be used as a strong lever to make NVQs and business involvement a common currency after 1993. But there has to be considerable doubt that this will be fully achieved without strong political commitment against the considerable vested interest of the traditionalists of the educational community.

This assessment is not intended to be overly negative. On the contrary, the foundations of a strong system have now been established that could allow Britain at last to achieve a world class standard in training – a goal that has eluded the country since at least the 1870s. However, it is right to identify the problems which still remain. These problems must be worn away at in a sustained and committed way for a period of at least 10 to 15 years before the attitudes of employers, employees, trainers, educationalists and parents have changed sufficiently to assure a self-sustaining momentum.

Education

The discussion of education has focused on the specific issue of *fitting education to the needs of the economy*. We are aware that, in a large, complex and frequently controversial field, this focus will appear too narrow to many. However, the key argument has been that system failure results from the institutional overdevelopment of some parts of the system at the cost of comparable underdevelopment in others. In the field of education, an imbalance of purposes has led to the underdevelopment of education's contribution to the economy. This has been a severe impediment to developing the economic potential of all the country's other systems – particularly in training, enterprise and innovation as well as enhancing personal motivation.

The analysis in Chapter 7 has demonstrated that major progress has been made in adjusting the balance of the aims of education closer to the needs of the economy. A new system has emerged from which further developments can be made in the 1990s. The key positive developments have been:

- The development of a national curriculum which will have the capacity to assure every school pupil a common core of educational experiences;
- An emphasis on the core skills of reading, writing, numeracy, science and languages – which are also major requirements of businesses;
- The implementation of a set of tests and other means of assessment to allow proper monitoring of progress of each child from the age of 7;
- The development of broader-based examinations for the 14–16 age group (GCSEs) which allow most pupils to attain a level of passes that can be used by employers;
- The development of a system of Records of Achievement for parents and employers and annual reporting to parents, that allow attainment across a broad spectrum of disciplines and skills to be recorded;
- Changes in school government to direct more attention to local school management where effectiveness can be better monitored and changes more readily made to improve performance;
- Widening of school governor membership to include stronger involvement of local businesses and parents;
- The development of work experience to the level of at least two weeks in Years 4 and 5 for *all* pupils;
- The broadening of the curriculum to include a wider set of skills through business awareness and cross curricula themes, stimulated particularly by Technical and Vocational Educational Initiative (TVEI) and Technical and Vocational Educational Extension (TVEE);
- The development of considerable experience in school-business Compacts with the development of specific targets that can be monitored and developed;
- The development of a widened Compact concept and EBPs that can stimulate a sustained and organised approach to links between business and education;
- The early beginnings of an integration between EBPs, Compacts, wider education policy and the leadership of business through TECs, Chambers of Commerce, and other business bodies.

These educational developments will be put in place and will be developed over the 1990s. They provide, as for training, a system that aims at both improved educational results and the inclusion of all students in the process of developing and monitoring attainment targets. This will allow a new balance to be achieved between academic/

traditional and vocational requirements. Thus major steps forward have been made since the initiation of the "Great Debate" in education in 1976. However, there are a number of major uncertainties about developments in the future.

First is the question of stability. As with the development of training, the lead times before new outcomes can be achieved are very long. The first students leaving school at 16 who have experienced the national curriculum throughout the system from age 7 will not be available until the year 2000. Others will experience parts of the system before that date, but many subsequent developments of the curriculum and its teaching will not have any impact on school leavers until well into the 21st Century. This covers at least the lifetime of two or three further parliaments in which there are major differences of opinion on the role of Local Education Authorities (LEAs), the relative autonomy of teachers within the curriculum, the shape of school governing bodies, the salary and employment conditions of teachers, and the extent of business involvement through TECs or other bodies.

A *second* issue is the balance of vocational and broader goals. Our analysis in Chapter 7 has argued that many developments do not need a direct business involvement, but rather depend upon enhancing schooling methods, management and finance. However, we have also argued that the experience of SCIP, TVEI, Compacts, EBPs and many business link bodies is that business links with education are still not integrated into the mainstream. As a result, they are often largely "bolt-ons" with rather narrow objectives that fail to be fully integrated within all disciplines, in all schools and at all school levels. For example, the analysis of school-business links in 1991 finds 72% of LEAs needing to develop an organised EBP across *all* schools at *all* levels for *all* disciplines[2]. The Partnership Initiative and expansion of Compacts is leading to improvement in this regard. But there is still a major problem that Compacts, EBPs and links are too marginalised from the important system development of the national curriculum. The result is a danger of fragmentation of government's educational initiatives that contributes to the overall "patchwork quilt" of central-local relations and fails to offer a proper integration of education, through the national curriculum, with the needs of the economy.

Third are a number of important technical developments that are not yet fully assured. *Work experience*, although now widely developed is not fully integrated into the classroom process and curriculum. In the 1991 assessment of EBPs only 31% of LEAs assure that work experience is used in the classroom to go beyond simple debriefing to be used as assessed work in at least one subject (Bennett, 1992). *Records of achievement* are a key part of the development of broader-based materials covering all people leaving school that can be used with employers and other outside bodies. Their guaranteed use across all LEAs is not yet resolved. This is not satisfactory as part of a comprehensive and national commitment. *School government* still leaves many gaps. The LEA control of school governors is de facto often still too strong leaving inadequate scope for local business and parental involvement. On each of these issues there is, therefore, a gap of national commitment to development of an ongoing strategy, although many improvements have been made.

The *fourth* area of concern is the relationship between education and business bodies. This overlaps with the issues of enterprise development. In general, education links with business are held back by the fragmentation and complexity of business link bodies. Development of the enterprise field would greatly facilitate EBPs and related initiatives. For the TECs, whilst LEA representatives generally serve on TEC Boards, and TECs are playing important roles in Compacts and EBPs, there has been the phased discontinuation of TVEI/TVEE and the return of many educational influences from the Department of Employment back to the DES. This all weakens the hand of TECs in relation to education and relies on the extent to which collaborative relations can be developed locally. There is a general danger that, without a major budget to influence schools, TECs can be treated by LEAs as involving inconvenient additional consultation, and are not taken seriously as local business lead bodies that can offer support to schools. This is reinforced by the fact that there is a strong tendency for schools and LEAs still to view business chiefly as a possible source of finance rather than a potential source of inputs into classroom experiences and the curriculum. Across the rest of the enterprise field *Chambers of Commerce* and *enterprise agencies* play a varied role, in some communities being the important agents to animate, sustain and nurture business links with education. They offer important opportunities to transmit links to smaller firms, but they are generally held back by resources which are even more meagre than the TECs.

As with the assessment of training, the assessment of education is not intended to be too negative. Much has been achieved in the 1980s and important building blocks are now in place that can help to assure an improved relevance of education to the needs of the economy. However, there are grave concerns arising from the lack of consensus to make success of the very considerable improvements that have been achieved. As we saw in Chapters 3 and 4, there has been a continual barrage of attacks, since the 1870s, on the problem of improving the balance of the educational curriculum towards economic objectives. The pervasive influence of the perverse policy syndrome in education means that continual reassertion will be required of the basic needs of business and the economy before a self-sustaining momentum of commitment can be assured from educationalists, parents and employers.

Enterprise

Enterprise is the most crucial building block of the national economy since it is the core of business development, income and wealth creation. As argued in Chapter 4, national economic development depends less on the special attributes of a country, as such, and most on the success of its businesses. Business success in turn, however, depends on how far the country, region or locality in which a business produces and trades has the crucial attributes that reinforce success. These key attributes are:

- *Factor conditions*, particularly capital availability, education, skills, infrastructure and motivation;
- *Demand conditions* that reinforce quality products and encourage transferability;
- *Related and supporting industries* that have international links and stimulate world standards;
- *Business strategy and structure* that stimulate progressive organisation and management within a supportive government environment.

Gaps across these attributes are argued by Porter (1990) to underpin Britain's weaknesses, particularly in the fields of human resources, motivation, supportive institutional structures and demand conditions.

Considerable developments have been achieved in the 1980s in the field of enterprise. But unlike training and education, for enterprise support it is not yet at all clear that the firm foundations have been developed of a system that will assure a stable and sustained commitment. The major developments that have occurred are:

- The initiation of a major shift of the *attitudes* and *motivation* of individuals towards the realisation that people must be responsible for their own personal development and not depend on large employers or government guarantees of full employment. This has been translated into policy through reform of the unemployment and benefits system and enhancement of the role of self-employment;
- *TECs* have been established with a prospectus that seeks to make them key business agents in the economic development of their localities. High level business leaders have emerged on TEC Boards who are engaging, many for the first time, in confronting the problem of their area's local economic development. At a programme level, TECs have begun to reorientate to local needs the national programmes of enterprise allowances, small firms service and business growth training;
- The *Chambers of Commerce* have initiated a series of major developments which for most areas are now being implemented, sometimes with the aid of minor DTI support. This involves the development of generally larger scale core Chambers with a major range of business services managed and accredited to BS 5750, a major focus on management seminars, business information, business-client links and search, and international trade, export and single market support. Their focus is predominantly on established businesses;
- *Enterprise agencies* have become more closely integrated into the national system of delivery of enterprise allowances and counselling for the self-employed. Most TECs contract with enterprise agencies and through their influence and that of BiTC, quality recognition to the IIP kitemark and BS is being developed;
- There has been growing recognition of the needs of business *R&D*, with a number of attempts to build closer links between business needs, R&D institutes and higher education.

However important these developments are in themselves, compared with the significance of the enterprise field, a major series of gaps remain. The result has been an underdeveloped national institutional environment to support business for its development needs. As the emphasis of these needs has at the same time shifted from national to more local levels, the gaps in institutional environment have become major inhibitors of enterprise development. The extensive analysis in earlier chapters has concluded that:

- There is very *uneven* development of business support services across the country, with considerable scope for *overlap, competition, gaps and confusion* in local enterprise support structures. There is no general "heavy point" for business support in local networks, and this is particularly marked in fringe metropolitan and rural areas. This has held back enterprise development and it has also contributed to the difficulties of organising a stable and committed business input into training and education;
- The TECs have been a useful innovation for the better coordination of *unemployment schemes, training, and consultancy* and advice for self-employment. However, the separation of the Employment Service from TECs into an executive agency is a major lost opportunity that would have allowed integration of counselling with DSS contact. This could have simultaneously addressed the problems of accessing information and motivation of the unemployed. As a result, the hopes of a one door system (or one-stop shop) for linking unemployment training and self-employment have been set back;
- The success of some voluntary solutions to enterprise needs through donations and sponsorship of enterprise agencies and BLTs has masked the lesson that the greatest

successes have been built on *strategic alliances* of public and private local actors with formal shared strategy and contractual relations;

- The success of programmes to stimulate self-employment and micro-businesses through public and quasi-public agencies such as TECs and enterprise agencies has left a *strategic gap* in support *for meso-businesses* (of approximately 5 to 20 or 100 employees). These have been the main area of concern of Chambers of Commerce, which have been squeezed of resources;
- There has been a fragmentation between the Department of Employment (DE) and DTI that has resulted in a harmful rivalry and a confusion of different initiatives. But this reflects a deeper uncertainty in government about the appropriate role of government's enterprise policy for established businesses. This gap, more than any other, explains the absence of a coherent enterprise strategy for the country as we move further into the 1990s;
- There are major gaps in availability of venture and other capital resources which will not be overcome until *improved support systems* are available that offer a better *capacity for risk-appraisal* that can be used by those with capital funds;
- R&D, implementation of new technology and innovation still tends to be treated by the same discounting methods used for other investments rather than as opportunities for organisational change and new product opportunities; the result is a *short-term* emphasis and a lack of leadership of change;
- There is still a deep-seated separation of pure research (largely government-funded) and applied research (largely industry-funded) resulting in gaps where new resources from either sector may often be *misapplied;*
- Labour market structures still too frequently separate employees and managers leading to pay settlements *separated from productivity* that tend to *increase unemployment and inflation* and reduce potential flexibility on both sides;
- Gaps in enterprise development reinforce, and are reinforced by, gaps in skills and motivation which depend on the general *system developments needed in education and training* discussed earlier.

Many important achievements have been made in the field of enterprise; in particular the enhancement of local institutions through the establishment of TECs and the development of Chambers of Commerce. But in the field of enterprise a major gap exists in national strategy. In the main this seems to reflect a tension in government policy. On the one hand, enhancing factor conditions, demand, and industrial structure requires mostly a hands-off policy that seeks to remove barriers to competition and factor mobility. On the other hand, many improvements of factor inputs and the development of business support organisations requires either government participation, championship or regulation. This is more than amply evidenced by the contrast of the DTI's free market championship, encouragement of private sector development of professional services and strong constraint in almost all fields of business support, with the DE's use of public money to lever change through TECs. But the problem is not simply one of different departmental styles or approaches. It is also a question of perception of what the problem is and hence how best to address it. This issue is addressed in the next section. Four major developments underpin its argument: first, increased emphasis on meso-businesses to compliment that being devoted to micro-businesses; second, to work for a fuller integration of enterprise with education and training; third, to develop government's role as champion and partner in a wider range of major business developments; and fourth, to develop a more powerful and broader-based structure of *local* business agencies.

An institutional strategy

Enhancing through government

The key basis for developing local business services has to be the activities of local agents and self-help, since economic growth depends ultimately on individual and corporate commitment, entrepreneurship and personal productive effort. But relying on self-help alone is unlikely to fill the gaps that will allow Britain to develop a new system of structures that our earlier analysis has demonstrated it so desperately needs.

The limits to self-help are drawn where voluntary networks alone are insufficient to assure the long-term sustainability of services. Networking, we have seen, is a method of linking agents and organisations. It is less satisfactory for linking together individual businesses or people. These differences arise from the constraints of externalities and multiple programmes and fields of activity. Under a voluntary system of networks the main resources that can be drawn upon to stimulate development are social responsibility, altruism, exhortation and "peer" pressure. These approaches are often expensive (particularly in time), or soon reach limits of depth or breadth of coverage. The present situation in Britain suggests that some of these limits have been reached.

The limits to voluntary networking define the point at which government action is required in order to assure a system-wide response. Government has the capacity to limit some types of behaviour, it can employ financial leverage, it can overcome thresholds and other constraints, and it can concentrate minds to adhere to a long-term strategy by supplementing and encouraging voluntary networks.

The system-wide gaps that exist in Britain's local capacity suggest that a larger vision must be developed. The issue that has to be tackled is the dilemma that *the greater the need for a market-lead, often the greater is the need to supplement the market mechanism.* For example, the greater the emphasis on market-led approaches to training, the greater is the stimulus to free riding. The greater the reliance on subscriptions to support Chambers' representation of business interests, the greater is the incentive for businesses to opt out. The greater the assertion of NVQ or equivalent skills in the workforce, the greater are the salary implications and hence the greater the stimulus to businesses to downgrade job specifications. The greater the reliance on *small* business entrepreneurism and enterprise development, the greater are the externalities to any individual business and hence the greater is the need to provide pooled services, information and strategic commitment. And so on, for other business services.

The key elements to which Government can respond are:

- Externalities – these stimulate the need to prevent free riding which usually needs legislation to overcome;
- Limits on business client ability to pay, especially for small firms – these require pooling of resources and some public core funding of agencies;
- Long time periods for development, particularly of R&D – these require start-up funds and long-term strategic commitment where government can play a role;
- The involvement of multiple producers and clients – these require a long-term organisational structure of reliable quality which is difficult by voluntary action alone;
- Lack of information on what best fits needs – this requires a business information service tightly tailored to business needs.

These developments can be achieved through developing networks, both independently and with government support. The objective of supporting network development is the establishment of a force that seeks to integrate actors into a shared vision and set of programmes that can deliver a quality local product in terms of local business support services. This should seek to provide a vehicle that allows clients to avoid having to find their way through a complex web of different agency ownership and procedures. Instead, the objective should be a networking vehicle, the elements of which are largely "invisible" to the client. In many cases this might be a "one-stop shop" such as those being developed with DTI support since 1992. More commonly a range of agents can offer an integrated system of business services.

The possible developments required are large and complex. They must provide a foundational set of policies for enterprise, and links to training and education. The detail goes beyond the remit of this book. However, the three main areas can be indicated:

i) *Overcoming training gaps*. There are three key gaps that an enhanced government role could fill: to encourage a deeper commitment of businesses to training, particularly among SMEs; to improve the incentives to the organisation of business training through NVQs and other leverage to assure a trainer-training structure equivalent to the German meister; and the development of quality controls that are more independent of civil servants.

These gaps could be overcome by government regulatory activity. Deeper commitment by businesses to training cannot be mandated and legislated in a direct sense, since only businesses can define their training requirements. But the incentives to train and enhance the skills of the existing workforce can be radically increased. In this context proposals for a training levy / tax break appear the best-founded approach. They increase incentives, but leave decisions on appropriate training within the businesses themselves.

The development of trainer training is far more problematic. But the combination of a training levy / tax break with an NVQ structure recognising trainer-training skills in the workplace would provide a structure through which these skills could be developed.

Quality controls independent of the civil service are essential to avoid political manipulation and to assure a fit to businesses needs. Whilst BS 5750 offers one strong route, it does so along a series of dimensions that are not fully designed for this type of quality assurance. It also leaves quality as a process that is judged too externally to local needs. A preferable alternative would be to form business-led, *locally* managed quality assurance bodies working to national standards. Such a local body fits with other *local* requirements, outlined below.

ii) *Overcoming education gaps*. There are two key gaps that enhanced government action could fill. First is the need to assure a long-term balance of vocational and broader educational needs. This requires further development of the national curriculum content and mode of delivery to more fully include work experience and business links. Second is the need to enhance local business inputs. This requires the further development of locally organised business bodies such as TECs and Chambers that can sustain and coordinate responses to the needs of education as well as transmitting links to a wider spectrum of firms. The two requirements come together, since businesses have no incentive to offer better organisation until there is a curriculum guarantee that their activity has a significant impact on education and is not a waste of their time.

iii) *Overcoming enterprise gaps*. The gaps here are much larger and cover the wider problem of institutional development. In the simplest terms there is (i) a gap of core and support services for meso-businesses, as opposed to micro-businesses (mostly of the self-employed); (ii) a gap in counselling (Employment Service) and support for the unemployed into employment (TECs/LECs under DE); (iii) a gap of effective applied R&D and technology transfer.

Each of these gaps covers different client requirements and often different business clients. Each requires system development. And each has a strong local basis to overcoming the gaps that are present. The discussion moves to this local basis.

Enhancing local institutions

There will always be a significant degree of fragmentation between government programmes and agencies. Local and central governmental structures and accountability preclude complete integration, and different interest groups will naturally wish to safeguard their individual domains – whether this be business, unions, local government, central government agencies, or voluntary and community bodies. Against these forces of inevitable fragmentation, therefore, is needed a *local* countervailing force that seeks to integrate agents into a shared vision and set of programmes. To overcome system gaps and failures there has to be strong integration so that business clients can find their way through the complex web of agency ownership and specific procedures; and so that the development of one field of activity fully take account of the needs of other fields.

Our analysis of system gaps and failures in Britain all suggest that the major gap that exists in Britain is not primarily programmatic – in training, enterprise or education. Although there are certainly gaps in each of these programmes, the main gap is one of *integration*. Tackling this problem can only be overcome by government integrating its programmes better between departments and levering business involvement across the board. But filling the integration gap most of all needs a new or enhanced *agent to deliver* the support services to businesses that government action would be aimed at ensuring. This agent has to be local since not only has it to manage programme delivery; it also has to be able to fit programme needs to the wider national system needs – which must be preeminently local in emphasis. The need is for a "heavy point" for business – an agent that provides a strong focus for local networks.

Such an agent cannot be the TECs or LECs in their present form. Apart from the relatively narrow focus dictated by their uncertainty of budgets, they presently lack a representational relationship to their business communities. This strongly undermines their capacity as change agents. Although business-led, they are not business-controlled in the sense of drawing from a broad representative business base. Nor have they gained full autonomy over hiring and firing staff. Also, because they have been created by government there is a danger that they become increasingly the tool of government – treated more as an adjunct to the Civil Service than as self-sustaining independent service strategists. On the other hand, the present Chambers of Commerce have a representational structure; they also have a self-sustaining base derived from businesses' desires to meet together and their willingness to pay limited subscriptions. But they mostly lack the scale of resources to be the major vehicle required. Other agents, such as enterprise agencies, are certainly important to key areas of service delivery, but tend to be too small geographically, too programme specific, and they also lack the necessary resources. As is clear from Figure 5.5, business-led bodies all generally have small resources in relation to their large geographical coverage and service remit.

To link broad geographical coverage, resources and representational structure suggests that an agent could be developed by building together the *Chamber concept* with the *TEC concept*; as well as drawing on the strengths of the other key local business organisations, particularly enterprise agencies. For Chambers and TECs this association has to be close because they cover very similar-sized territories and functions.

There has been a recent surge of interest in the concept of an agency that seeks to draw Chambers, TECs and enterprise agencies into a single system. A meeting of TECs, Chambers and enterprise agencies in September 1991 at Sunningdale produced an accord between the three bodies (see also Bennett, 1990c). Termed the "Sunningdale model" this has been very influential on thinking at the local level and on the DTI initiative to create one-stop shops. There has been a growing belief that Chambers plus TECs plus enterprise agencies could start to offer services at a level equivalent to the Chambers of Commerce in Europe. With the announcement in July 1992 by the DTI of "one stop shops" there appears also now to be a government commitment to this form of development.

There are various ways in which the Sunningdale model can be developed. Here we can only outline a brief agenda.

- Developments must be sensitive to present local capacity: sometimes the new institution will be Chamber-led, sometimes TEC-led, sometimes agency-led;
- Whatever the leadership, the ultimate target must be a *system* development bringing each agent into partnership;
- The overall objective must be quality of services, so that strong management controls and client relationships are crucial;
- A large scale agent with major capability is required, but this must be combined with a strong local outreach in all major business centres; this requires a 2-level approach as envisaged for Chambers of Commerce (q.v. Figure 6.4);
- Government must seek to deal with this agency in a sustained and committed way across its relevant departments: such an agency cannot be "owned" by one department; the local agent should be independent and not be subject to the control that TEED presently seeks to exert over TECs;
- The contracting relationship with government should be clear and limit detailed tracking of public expenditure flows to the level of the management board of the agency: there should not be the detailed scrutiny of programmes and internal procedures to which TECs are subject.

This vehicle would look like a special form of the Chambers of Commerce in Germany. But it would build on Britain's special experiences by combining the major strengths of TECs/LECs, a considerably enhanced form of Britain's present Chambers of Commerce and other local business agencies. This is not a difficult or impossible. To guarantee strong market support it must be business-led – and hence cannot be used as part of a return to tripartism. But it must have the benefit of sustained backing to overcome the constraints of the market. Most important of all, it must overcome the constraints of ownership by different local agents with different interests, particularly those which involve different government departments as funders. To use the economic theory of externalities, *de facto* government would have granted to this new vehicle a property right over local business representation, not as a public good, but as a collective good owned by local businesses. This is a classic way of dealing with market failures such as free riders. Of course, such property rights do not preclude a variety of multi-agency and multi-level structures of delivery. Indeed, the benefits of combining a new governmental approach with existing local structures would be that the strengths of existing agents could be built on, whilst developing new agents and new linkages and partnerships between agents to fill gaps and enhance the whole system.

These lines of development probably have a broad range of agreement at local level. But it would be possible to go 2 stages further – through compulsory registration and use of the non-domestic rates.

A compulsory registration system for all businesses, but with special treatment of the self-employed, would have significant benefits of providing for the first time in Britain a reliable information base on the number, character and location of businesses – a most significant resource for business policy. But the main purpose would be to allow local business agents to identify clients and to allow training policies and educational links to be more easily developed. A second step would be to levy a small fee for registration, which would then be available to the new local agent as a "subscription" for core services. This fee would be graduated by size of company, and could be zero for the self-employed and very small firms. This fee could be related to the training fee concept. Third, could be to give the local agent a "property right" in the public policy arena: to ensure that the new local agent had to be consulted in local authority, education, vocational education, training, enterprise, planning and local environmental policy decisions. Fourth, would be a major national development programme for these agents to develop a new vision, leadership, staff training and broad capacity to manage services to businesses, and raise revenue to support them.

The use of the non-domestic rates presents a further opportunity which also allows many tensions with local government to be overcome. An explicit role for the new local business agent over non-domestic rates provides a revenue source but also would allow the defects of the unified business rate system to be overcome. Since 1990 the UBR has undermined the relevance of local government consultations with businesses. The share of the rates could be used as a basis for funding the local business agent and, as a powerful independent local taxing body, would have a natural and strong relationship with local authorities. Business would be for the first time in an equal position to lobby and bargain with local government; consultation would have real meaning. Significant resources would be available to businesses to work with local government for the economic development of their area. Of course such a taxing power would require an essential representational structure to the business subjects. This again argues for the development of the Chamber concept with the additional powers of TECs/LECs. This power of local taxation of business on itself is similar to that existing in Germany and Austria. We recognise this is a radical step. But it would be most influential in bonding a partnership of government and business.

With or without the radical step of giving to the local business agent power over all or part of the non-domestic rates, the new agent, with its wider representational base and full inclusion of SMEs through registration, would also have considerable capacity to fill some of the other key gaps identified above: the support for trainer training, independent but locally-based quality controls, a broad business body to facilitate educational links, an emphasis on meso-businesses and inter-company R&D links, *as well as* the development of micro-business and self-employment. We develop these concepts further in subsequent studies (Bennett *et al.*, 1993) which detail proposals for the enhancement of TECs and the enhancement of enterprise systems drawing on the experience of Chambers of Commerce. Radical solutions are required to overcome the perverse policy syndrome: new institutions and powers to lever change require a new model. Radically developing the local institutions of TECs/LECs and Chambers of

Commerce to meet the challenges of the 21st Century we believe to be the only assured way to create a durable and self-sustaining local agent for economic development capable of responding to the changes that lie ahead.

At the time of publication of this book the DTIs proposed one-stop shop initiative is being implemented in a number of areas around the country. Under the market branding of "business bureaux" this initiative does seek the objective of drawing enterprise bodies such as TECs/LECs, Chambers and enterprise agencies together into a common body. This is an important initiative. It certainly moves in the right direction. But it is only a step on a long road. The doubts that surround it are:

- The need to ensure high quality of business services, not rush for any local solution;
- The need to ensure client-focus, not producer-focus;
- From these requirements the pre-eminent need to ensure entrepreneurial and progressive staffing. This requires a delivery outside the TEC/LEC by suitably qualified staff *with recent business experience*;
- Enough long-term and sustained resources and commitment from government to make local agents believe that change is worth participating in;
- A proper business lead, independent of TEED and government, with proper membership and other transmission mechanisms to SMEs.

The evidence so far is that the first business bureaux to go live in April 1993 will not all assure these qualities. Meanwhile our recommendations about business registration and the non-domestic rates lie on the table. The DTI initiative is an important step forward. But we conclude that there is still a long learning curve before the challenges of the 21st century will be fully met by Britain's local institutional capacity.

Footnotes: Chapter 15

1. Greater detail of these tensions is given in Bennett *et al.* (1993). There had also been political uncertainty until the 1992 General Election, with Labour's core leadership clear about the need to retain business commitment and business leadership even within a rebalanced Board; whilst their employment spokesman had suggested very different approaches (see McLeish, 1991).

2. Source: Bennett (1992), i.e. they have not gone beyond the level of a basic Compact at level 3.

APPENDIX

Methodology

This book is based on detailed original analyses of many of the key national programmes, complemented by local studies. The methodology is not made explicit at all points in the text since it is our concern both to develop the argument as clearly as possible and to integrate our new research findings with other studies. The source of information is at all times made clear in the text.

The study has gathered a mass of new national level data through a series of surveys. The most important of these national surveys were:

- Chambers of Commerce;
- Enterprise Agencies;
- Education-Business Partnerships;
- All first round Compacts;
- Local Employer Networks;
- Local Authority EDUs.

In addition the study has been informed by the results of our subsequent study of TECs and LECs which is reported in full in Bennett *et al.* (1993).

In addition to surveys a range of detailed studies and interviews with key decision-makers covered all major national agencies and actors. Some of these were covered in depth as a result of the consultancy studies listed in the acknowledgements at the start of this book. In all, over 100 interviews took place with key national or regional bodies, and many were covered several times as developments occurred.

A major aspect of the research also involved a series of waves of interviews with key agents in a group of case study areas. These formed the basis for Chapters 9 to 14, as well as other parts of the book. At least 10 interviews took place in each area, normally of at least 2 hours each. In most areas there were also follow-up interviews with other agents and subsequent updating. The first main wave of interviews took place in May – September 1988 (i.e. pre-TECs), a second wave covered May – November 1989 (i.e. early TEC development), and a third wave covered 1990 (i.e. early TEC establishment). In addition, interviews are drawn upon up to mid-1992. In all over 200 interviews were undertaken in case study areas.

It is on the basis of these many interviews that the detail and insights of this study are based. It is a unique knowledge-base, which is fully reflected in the text but unfortunately can only be occasionally explicitly acknowledged because of the confidentiality qualification we found was essential to our discussions.

The eleven main case study areas covered in depth were:

- Dundee
- Teesside
- Sheffield
- Manchester
- Salford
- Birmingham
- Sandwell
- Mid Glamorgan
- Cardiff
- East London (chiefly Newham)
- West London (chiefly Richmond-upon-Thames)

In addition over 20 other areas were covered in lesser depth in order to assess specific details and local differences, particularly in rural and central place locations.

In general the interviews covered a structured set of topics, but through an open set of questions. The main objective was to determine how programmes worked, or did not work, how local networks were organised, and how strategies were being developed. The topics usually covered three levels:

- Strategy / conception / leadership;
- Implementation / management / participation;
- Delivery mechanisms.

Within each level the questions sought to determine:

- Who is involved?
- Who is key animator and leader?
- Who is a key participant?
- Who is linked to whom?
- What is the form of relationships: co-operative, conflictual, led externally / levered, relations to targets, critical gaps and constraints, finance.

The questions were applied to each stage in each programme or initiative:

1. Initiative / conception;
2. Development of strategy / definition of objectives;
3. Finance;
4. Management and implementation;
5. Delivery;
6. Evaluation;
7. Monitoring;
8. Political aspects.

This allowed the study to concentrate on the organisational structures from which outcomes derive. It does not attempt to evaluate outcomes as such.

The actors interviewed in the eleven detailed case studies, with variations to suit the different agents in each area, were:

1. *Businesses*

- Lead local business people
- TECs: chief executive, Chair / Board member
- Chambers of Commerce: chief executive / president
- LEN: director / chair
- Enterprise agencies
- Phoenix initiative / major developers
- Technology centres

2. *Training bodies*

- TA area board / regional directors / TECs / LECs
- Managing agents (emphasising areas of innovations in training)

- WRFE colleges: principal / vice principal
- Careers service
- LMI providers

3. *Schools / LEA*
- Chief education officer (schools)
- Chief education officer (WRFE)
- Compact director / SCIP / SILO / Trident coordinator
- Careers service
- Key school or Compact school (head, careers adviser, etc.)
- Curriculum / resources planning / TVEI links / advisors
- Relations to other initiatives (e.g. housing, social care, single parents)

4. *Local authority*
- LED unit director / planning director
- Economic development agency / enterprise board
- Chief executive
- Local councillor

5. *Other*
- Key voluntary sector bodies
- Unions / trade councils
- EZ / UDC / Task Forces
- DTI EEAs, etc.
- Universities / polytechnics / research centres

REFERENCES

ABCC (1990) *Effective Business Support: A UK Strategy*, Association of British Chambers of Commerce, London.

ABCC (1991a) *Effective Business Support: A UK Strategy: Phase Two*, Association of British Chambers of Commerce, London.

ABCC (1991b) *Minimum Requirements for Chamber of Commerce Services*, Association of British Chambers of Commerce, London.

ABCC (1991c) *Proposal for the Devolution of DTI Export Services*, Association of British Chambers of Commerce, London.

ACAS (1988) *Labour Flexibility in Britain: The 1987 ACAS Survey*, Arbitration and Conciliation Advisory Service, London.

Advisory Council on Science and Technology (ACOST) (1990) *The Enterprise Challenge: Overcoming Barriers to Growth in Small Firms*, HMSO, London.

AGF (1988) *New Technology-Based Firms in Britain and Germany*, Anglo-German Foundation, London and Bonn.

Aldrich, H. and Zimmer, C. (1986) Entrepreneurship through social networks, in R. Smilor and D. Sexton (eds.) *The Art and Science of Entrepreneurship*, Ballinger, New York.

Amin, A. and Goddard, J.B. (eds.) (1986) *Technological Change, Industrial Restructuring and Regional Development*, Allen and Unwin, London.

AMRC (1988) *Management for the Future*, Ashridge Management College, Berkhamstead.

Annan, N. (1990) *Our Age: Portrait of a Generation*, Weidenfeld and Nicholson, London.

Armstrong, H.W. and Fildes, J. (1988) Industrial development initiatives in England and Wales: the role of district councils, *Progress in Planning*, 30 (2), pp. 85-156.

Arrow, K. (1973) Higher education as a filter, *Journal of Public Economics*, 2, pp. 193-216.

Ashby, P. (1991) Doing the Government a favour, *Training Tomorrow*, February, pp. 5-7.

AST (1956) *Management Succession*, Acton Society Trust, London.

Atkinson, J. (1985) The changing corporation, pp. 13-35 in D. Clutterbuck (ed.) *New Patterns of Work*, Gower, Aldershot.

Audit Commission (1985) *Obtaining Better Value from Further Education*, HMSO, London.

Audit Commission (1986) *Reports and Accounts, Year Ended 31 March 1986*, HMSO, London.

Audit Commission (1987) *The Management of London's Authorities: Preventing the Breakdown of Services*, HMSO, London.

Audit Commission (1989) *Urban Regeneration and Economic Development: The Local Government Dimension*, HMSO, London.

Audit Commission (1990) *Urban Regeneration and Economic Development: Audit Guide*, Audit Commission, London.

Aydalot, P. and Keeble, D.E. (eds.) (1988) *High Technology Industry and Innovative Environments*, Routledge and Kegan Paul, London.

Bain, J.S. (1956) *Barriers to New Competition*, Harvard University Press, Mass.

Ball, C. (1985) The triple alliance: what went wrong? what can be done?, *Oxford Review of Education*, 11, 3, pp. 227-234.

Ball, R.J. (1989) The United Kingdom economy: miracle or mirage?, *National Westminster Bank Quarterly Review*, February, pp. 43-59.

Ball, S.J. (1990) *Politics and Policy Making in Education: Explorations in Policy Sociology*, Routledge, London.

Bannock, G. (1981) *The Economics of Small Firms*, Basil Blackwell, Oxford.

Bannock, G. (1989) *Governments and Small Business*, Paul Chapman, London.

Bannock, G. (1990) *Taxation in the European Community: The Small Business Perspective*, Paul Chapman, London.

Barnes, D. *et al.* (1987) *A Second Report on the TVEI Curriculum: Courses for 14-16 Year Olds in Twenty-Six Schools*, TVEI Evaluation Report 5, The Training Agency, Employment Department, Sheffield.

Barnes, N.K. (1974) Rethinking corporate charity, *Fortune*, October, pp. 169-182.

Barnett, C. (1972) *The Collapse of British Power*, Eyre Methuen, London.

Barnett, C. (1986) *The Audit of War: The Illusion and Reality of Britain as a Great Nation*, Macmillan, London.

Baumol, W.J., Panyer, J.C. and Millig, R.D. (1982) *Contestable Markets and the Theory of Industry Structure*, Harcourt, Brace and Javonovich, New York.

Bayliss, B.T. and Butt-Philip, A.A.S. (1980) *Capital Markets and Industrial Development in Germany and France: Lessons for the UK*, Saxon House, Farnborough.

Beesley, M.E. and Hamilton, R.T. (1986) Births and deaths of manufacturing firms in the Scottish regions, *Regional Studies*, 20, pp. 281-88.

Bell, C., Homieson, C., King, K. and Raffe, D. (1988) *Liaisons Dangereuses? Education-Industry Relationships in the First Scottish TVEI Pilot Projects*, Training Agency, Sheffield.

Bennett, R.J. (1989a) *Local Economy and Employment Development Strategies: An Analysis for LEDA Areas*, Report of a study of the EC Local Employment Development Action Programme, London.

Bennett, R.J. (1989b) Business bids for a role in the Philadelphia Story, *Times Educational Supplement*, 2 June 1989, p. A13.

Bennett, R.J. (ed.) (1989c) *Territory and Administration in Europe*, Frances Pinter, London.

Bennett, R.J. (ed.) (1990a) *Decentralisation, Local Government and Markets: Towards a Post-Welfare Agenda?*, Clarendon Press, Oxford.

Bennett, R.J. (1990b) *Orientations for Local Employment Development: Capacity Building*, LRDP, London.

Bennett, R.J. (1990c) *Attaining Quality: the agenda for local business services in the 1990s*, Department of Geography Research Papers, London School of Economics.

Bennett, R.J. (1991a) *Developing a National Chamber Network*, Association of British Chambers of Commerce, London.

Bennett, R.J. (1991b) *The Development of Services by Chambers of Commerce, 1989-91*, London School of Economics.

Bennett, R.J. (1992) *Education-Business Partnerships: The Learning So Far*, Confederation of British Industry, London.

Bennett, R.J. and Fearnehough, M. (1987) The burden of the non-domestic rates on business, *Local Government Studies*, November, pp. 23-36.

Bennett, R.J. and Krebs, G. (1988) *Local Business Taxes in Britain and Germany*, Nomos, Baden-Baden.

Bennett, R.J. and Krebs, G. (1991) *Local Economic Development: Public-Private Partnership Initiatives in Britain and Germany*, Belhaven, London.

Bennett, R.J., Krebs, G. and Zimmermann, H. (eds.) (1990) *Local Economic Development in Britain and Germany*, Anglo-German Foundation, London and Bonn.

Bennett, R.J., McCoshan, A. and Sellgren, J. (1989a) *TECs and VET: The Practical Requirements: Organisation, Geography and International Comparison with the USA and Germany*, Department of Geography Research Papers, London School of Economics.

Bennett, R.J., McCoshan, A. and Sellgren, J. (1989b) *TECs and VET: Conference Papers*, Department of Geography Research Papers, London School of Economics.

Bennett, R.J., McCoshan, A. and Sellgren, J. (1989c) *The Organisation of Business/Education Links: Further Findings from the CBI Schools Questionnaire*, Department of Geography Research Papers, London School of Economics.

Bennett, R.J., McCoshan, A. and Sellgren, J. (1990a) *Local Employer Networks (LENs): Their Experience and Lessons for TECs*, Department of Geography Research Papers, London School of Economics.

Bennett, R.J., McCoshan, A. and Wicks, P. (1990b) *Partnership of Education, Business and the Community*, 2 vols, Report to London Borough of Richmond upon Thames, London School of Economics.

Bennett, R.J., McCoshan, A. and Wicks, P. (1991a) *TECs: Early Experiences: Report of an LSE Survey*, Department of Geography, London School of Economics.

Bennett, R.J., McCoshan, A. and Wicks, P. (1991b) *LECs: Early Experiences and Comparisons with TECs: Report of an LSE Survey*, Department of Geography, London School of Economics.

Bennett, R.J., Wicks, P. and McCoshan, A. (1993) *Britain's TECs and LECs*, UCL Press, London.

Bennington, J. (1985) Economic development: local economic initiatives, *Local Government Policy Making*, 12 (2), pp. 3-8.

Beyers, W.B. (1989) *The Producer Services and Economic Development in the United States: The Last Decade*, Technical Assistance and Research Division, US Department of Commerce, Economic Development Division, Washington D.C.

Binks, M. and Jennings, A. (1986) New firms as a source of industrial regeneration, pp. 3-32 in M. Scott, A. Gibb, J. Lewis and T. Faulkner (eds.) *Small Firm Growth and Development*, Gower, Aldershot.

Birch, D. (1988) *Managing Resources in Further Education: A Handbook for College Managers*, Further Education Staff College, Bristol.

Birch, D.L. (1979) *The Job Generation Process*, MIT Program on Urban and Regional Change, Cambridge, Mass.

BiTC (1986) *Enterprise Agencies, Trusts and Community Action Programmes*, Business in the Community, London.

BiTC (1987) *Guidelines for Developing and Managing Enterprise Agencies*, Business in the Community, London.

BiTC (1988) *The Future for Enterprise Agencies*, Business in the Community, London.

BiTC (1989) *A Review of the Enterprise Agency Network*, Business in the Community, London.

BiTC (1990a) *Springboard for Growth: Guidelines for Local Purchasing Initiatives for Business Support Organisations*, Business in the Community, London.

BiTC (1990b) *A Local Enterprise Agency Accreditation Charter*, Business in the Community, London.

BiTC (1991) *Quality in Business Support*, Business in the Community, London.

BiTC (undated a) *Building Partnerships with Education: Making Middle Managers More Effective*, Business in the Community, London.

BiTC (undated b) *Writing a Boardroom Policy for Partnership with Education*, Business in the Community, London.

Black, H., Malcolm, H. and Zaklukiewicz, S. (1988) *The TVEI Pilot Curriculum in Scotland*, Training Agency, Sheffield.

Blackwell, T. and Seabrook, J. (1985) *A World Still to Win: The Reconstruction of the Post-War Working Class*, Faber and Faber, London.

Blanchflower, D.G. and Meyer, B. (1990) *An Empirical Analysis of Self-Employment in Australia and the US*, Centre for Labour Economics, London School of Economics.

Blanchflower, D., Millward, N. and Oswald, A.J. (1988) *Unionisation and Employment Behaviour*, Centre for Labour Economics, London School of Economics.

Blanchflower, D. and Oswald, A.J. (1991) *Self-Employment and Mrs Thatcher's Britain*, Centre for Economic Performance Discussion Paper No. 30, London School of Economics.

Blandford, D. and Jamieson, A. (1989) *Building Partnerships with Education*, CRAC, Cambridge.

Bluestone, B. and Harrison, B. (1982) *Deindustrialisation of America*, Basic Books, New York.

Boddy, M., Lovering, J. and Bassett, K. (1986) *Sunbelt City? A Study of Economic Change in Britain's M4 Growth Corridor*, Clarendon Press, Oxford.

Bolton, J.E. Committee (1971) *Small Firms: Report of the Commission of Inquiry*, Cmnd 4811, HMSO, London.

Bongers, P. (1990) *Local Government and 1992*, Longmans, London.

Bostock, D.A. and Smith, L.J. (1990) *Human Resource Development: Education and Training Needs*, Education Support Services, Birmingham.

Breheny, M., Hall, P. and Hart, D. (1988) *Northern Lights: A Development Agenda for the North in the 1990s*, Derrick, Wade and Waters, London.

Bridgwood, A., Hinckley, S.M., Sims, D. and Storey, S.M. (1988a) *Perspectives on TVEI: Summary of Management Themes*, Training Commission, Sheffield.

Bridgwood, A., Hinckley, S.M., Sims, D. and Storey, S.M. (1988b) *Perspectives on TVEI: Evaluation Report 4*, Training Commission, Sheffield.

Brittan, S. (1978) How British is the British sickness?, *Journal of Law and Economics*, 21, pp. 245-268.

Broadfoot (1980) Assessment, curriculum and control in the changing pattern of centre-local relations, *Local Government Studies*, 6, 6, pp. 57-68.

Buckley, P.J. (1989) *The Multinational Enterprise: Theory and Applications*, Macmillan, London.

Buckley, P.J. and Casson, M. (1976) *The Future of the Multinational Enterprise*, Macmillan, London.

Burke, J. (ed.) (1990) *Competency Based Education and Training*, Falmer Press, Brighton.

Business in the Cities and Bennett, R.J. (1990) *Leadership in the Community: A Blueprint for the 1990s*, Business in the Community, London.

Cable, J. and Schwalbach, J. (1990) International comparisons of entry and exit, in P.A. Geraski and J. Schwalbach (eds.) *Entry and Market Contestibility: An International Comparison*, SSRC, Berlin.

CAF (1988) *Charity Trends*, Charities Aid Foundation, London.

Callaghan, J. (1976) Ruskin College speech, *Times Educational Supplement*, 22 October, p. 72.

Campbell, A., Sorge, A. and Warner, M. (1989) *Microelectronic Product Applications in Great Britain and West Germany: Strategies, Competence and Training*, Gower, Aldershot.

Cantor, L. (1989) *Vocational Education and Training in the Developed World: A Comparative Study*, Routledge, London.

Carr, C. (1990) *Britain's Competitiveness: The Management of the Vehicle Component Industry*, Routledge, London.

Cary, L. (1989) *The Venture Capital Report Guide to Venture Capital in the UK*, 4th edition, Pitman, London.

Cassels, J. (1990) *Britain's Real Skill Shortage: And What To Do About It*, Policy Studies Institute, London.

Casson, M.C. (1982) *The Entrepreneur*, Martin Robertson, Oxford.

Casson, M.C. (1990) *Enterprise and Competitiveness: A Systems View of International Business*, Oxford University Press, Oxford.

Cawson, A. (1985) Corporatism and local politics, pp. 127-147 in W. Grant (ed.) *The Political Economy of Corporatism*, Macmillan, London.

CBI (1988) *Building a Stronger Partnership Between Business and Secondary Education*, Report of Task force, chaired by Sir Adrian Cadbury, Confederation of British Industry, London.

CBI (1989a) *Towards a Skills Revolution*, Confederation of British Industry, London.

CBI (1989b) *Training and Enterprise Councils - The Way Forward*, Confederation of British Industry, London.

CBI (1991a) *World Class Targets: A Joint Initiative to Achieve Britain's Skills Revolution*, Confederation of British Industry, London.

CBI (1991b) *Business Success Through Competence: Investors in People*, City and Guilds, and Confederation of British Industry, London.

CBI (1992) *Focus on the First Line - the role of the supervisor*, Confederation of British Industry, London.

CBI / Manpower plc (1990) *Employment and Training*, Mercury Books, London.

CBVU (1981) *Whose Business is Business?*, Community Business Ventures Unit, Calouste Gulbenkian Foundation, London.

CCS (1986) *Company Support for Charities: Guidelines*, Council for Charitable Support, London.

CE (1991) *Europe in 1995: Economic Outlook by Sector*, Cambridge Econometrics, Cambridge.

CEC (1985) *Programme of Research and Action on the Development of the Labour Market: Local Employment Initiatives: Local Enterprise Agencies in Great Britain: A Study of Their Impact, Operational Lessons, and Policy Implications*, Commission of the European Communities, Luxembourg.

CEC (1987) *Small and Medium Sized Enterprises and Employment Creation in the EEC Countries*, Report for Commission of the European Communities DGV, Study No. 85/407, coordinated by D.J. Storey and S. Johnson, Brussels.

Cecchini, P. (1988) *The European Challenge 1992: The Benefits of a Single Market*, EC, Brussels.

CEI (1986) *Community in Business*, Centre for Employment Initiatives, London.

CEI / BiTC (1985) *The Impact of Local Enterprise Agencies in Great Britain: Operational Lessons and Policy Implications*, Centre for Employment Initiatives / Business in the Community, London.

CEN / CEA (1990) *Cleveland Education and Business Partnership: A Special Report*, Cleveland Employer Network and Cleveland Education Authority, Middlesbrough.

CEST (1991) *Attitudes to Innovation in Germany and Britain: A Comparison*, Centre for the Exploitation of Science and Technology, London.

Champion, A.G. and Townsend, A.R. (1990) *Contemporary Britain: A Geographical Perspective*, Edward Arnold, London.

Chandler, A.D. (1989) *Scale and Scope: Dynamics of Industrial Capitalism*, Harvard University Press, Mass.

Chandler, J.A. and Lawless, P. (1985) *Local Authorities and the Creation of Employment*, Gower, Aldershot.

CLES (1990) *Challenging the TECs*, Centre for Local Economic Strategies, Manchester.

Cleverdon, J. (1988) *Report on Education/Employment Links*, Industrial Society, London.

CMED (1988) *The Management Charter Initiative*, Charter for Management Education, London.

Cohen, S.S. and Zysman, J. (1987) *Manufacturing Matters: The Myth of the Post-Industrial Economy*, Basic Books, New York.

Coldwell, B. (1989) A business view from a potential TEC in Teesside, *Regional Studies*, 24, pp. 74-77.

Constable, J. and McCormick, R. (1987) *The Making of British Managers*, British Institute of Management and Confederation of British Industry, London.

Corney, M. (1991) Credits, tax and partnership, *Training Tomorrow*, October, pp. 15-16.

Cottrell, A. (1981) *What is Science Policy?*, Royal Institution, Maxwell/Pergamon, London.

Coulson, A. (1990) Evaluating local economic policy, pp. 174-194 in M. Campbell (ed.) *Local Economic Policy*, Cassell, London.

Coulson, A., Mills, L. and Young, K. (1991) *The Training Needs of Economic Development Officers*, Report, Institute of Local Government Studies, University of Birmingham.

Cowie, H. (1985) *The Phoenix Partnership: Urban Regeneration for the 21st Century*, National Council of Building Material Producers, London.

Cross, M. (1981) *New Firm Formation and Regional Development*, Gower, Aldershot.

Curran, J. (1986) *Bolton Fifteen Years On: A Review and Analysis of Small Business Research in Britain 1971-1986*, Small Business Research Trust, London.

Dahl, R.A. (1961) *Who Governs? Democracy and Power in an American City*, Yale University Press, New Haven, Conn.

Dahrendorf, R. (1990) *Reflections on the Revolutions in Europe*, Chatto and Windus, London.

Dale, R. *et al.* (1990) *The TVEI Story: Policy, Practice and Preparation for the Workforce*, Open University Press, Milton Keynes.

Daly, A. (1986) Education and productivity: a comparison of Great Britain and the United States, *British Journal of Industrial Relations*, Vol. 24, 2, pp. 251-266.

Daniel, W.W. (1987) *Industrial Relations and Technical Change*, Francis Pinter, London.

Daniels, P.W. (1986) Producer services in the UK space economy, pp. 291-321 in R. Martin and B. Rowthorn (eds.) *The Geography of Deindustrialisation*, Macmillan, London.

Davies, H. (1990) Mrs Thatcher's third term: power to the people or camouflaged centralisation?, in R.J. Bennett (ed.) *Decentralisation, Local Governments and Markets: Towards a Post-Welfare Agenda*, Clarendon Press, Oxford.

Davies, H., Campbell, J. and Barnes, J. (1986) An evaluation of local authority financial assistance to small firms, *Local Government Studies*, May/June, pp. 37-50.

Davies, H. and Powell, H. (1992) Breaking up is hard to do: the impact of client enpowerment on local services in Britain 1987-1991, in R.J. Bennett (ed.) *Decentralisation Initiatives in Local Governments and Markets*, United Nations University Press, Tokyo.

DE (1989) *Small Firms in Britain*, Department of Employment, Sheffield.

DE (1990) *Think Big ... Buy Small: Guidelines on Purchasing from Small Firms*, Department of Employment, London.

Newchurch (1990) *A Survey of Owner Managed Businesses*, Department of Employment, Newchurch and Co Ltd, London.

Deakin, N. (1987) *The Politics of Welfare*, Methuen, London.

Deakin, N. (1988) *In Search of the Postwar Consensus*, STICERD Welfare State Programme Papers 25, London School of Economics.

Deakin, N. and Wright, A. (eds.) (1990) *Consuming Public Services*, Routledge, London.

DEG (1990a) *The Partnership Handbook*, Department of Employment Group, Sheffield.

DEG (1990b) *The Partnership Primer*, Department of Employment Group, Sheffield.

DEG (1991) *A Strategy for Skills*, Guidance from the Secretary of State for Employment, London.

Deming, W.E. (1986) *Out of the Crisis*, Cambridge University Press, Cambridge.

Dennis, L.B. (1976) Charitable contributions: coming out of the corporate closet, *Vital Speeches*, 42, 19, pp. 597-602.

DES (1986) *Report by HM Inspectors on the Effects of Local Authority Expenditure Policies on Education Provision in England - 1985*, Department of Education and Science, London.

DES (1987) *NAFE in Practice*, Department of Education and Science, London.

DES (1988) *Report by HM Inspectors on the Youth Training Scheme in Further Education*, Department of Education and Science, London.

DES (1991) *TVEI - England and Wales 1983-90*, HMSO, London.

DES/DE/WO (1991) *Education and Training for the 21st Century*, 2 vols, Cmn 1536, HMSO, London.

DES / Welsh Office (1987) *Managing Colleges Efficiently*, HMSO, London.

DHS (1984) *Local Enterprise Agencies: A New and Growing Feature of the Economy*, Deloitte, Haskins and Sells, London.

DHS (1989a) *Local Authority Assistance to Growing Businesses*, Deloitte, Haskins and Sells with Business in the Community, London.

DHS (1989b) *Training in Britain: Employers' Activities*, Deloitte, Haskins and Sells / IFF Research Ltd, London.

Dicken, P. (1986) *Global Shift: Industrial Change in a Turbulent World*, Paul Chapman, London.

Dicken, P. (1988) The changing geography of Japanese foreign direct investment in manufacturing industry: a global perspective, *Environment and Planning A*, 20, pp. 633-653.

Dicken, P. (1990) European industry and global competition, pp. 37-55 in D. Pinder (ed.) *Western Europe: Challenge and Change*, Belhaven, London.

DoE (1988) *Creating Development Trusts: Good Practice in Urban Regeneration*, Department of the Environment, HMSO, London.

DoE (1989a) *New Economic Development Power for Local Authorities in England and Wales: A Consultation Paper*, Department of the Environment, London.

DoE (1989b) *Local Authorities' Interest in Companies in England and Wales: Consultation Paper in the Form of a Draft Circular*, Department of the Environment, London.
Dore, R. and Sako, M. (1989) *How the Japanese Learn to Work*, Routledge and Kegan Paul, London.
Doyle, J. and Gallagher, C.C. (1986) *The Size Distribution, Potential for Growth and Contribution to Job Generation of Firms in the UK 1982-1984*, Department of Industrial Management, University of Newcastle upon Tyne.
Drucker, P.F. (1985) *Innovation and Entrepreneurship*, Harper and Row, New York.
Drucker, P.F. (1989) *The New Realities*, Mandarin, London.
DSC (1989) *A Guide to Company Giving*, Directory of Social Change, London.
DTI (1988) *DTI - The Department of Enterprise*, Cm 278, HMSO, London.
DTI (1990a) *Electronic Components and Decade of Change: The European Market to 1995*, Department of Trade and Industry, London.
DTI (1990b) *Electronic Components and Decade of Change: An Overview of European Users' Purchasing Practices*, Department of Trade and Industry, London.
DTI (1991) *The Government's Industrial Policy*, Speech given by Peter Lilley to the Institute of Directors, 30 April, DTI, London.
van Duijn, J.J. (1983) *Interregional Models of Economic Fluctuation*, D.C. Heath, Lexington, Mass.
Elliot, J.H. (1970) *Imperial Spain 1469-1716*, Penguin, Harmondsworth.
Evans, A. (undated) TVEI extension means managed curriculum change, in *TVEI Developments 9: Extension*, The Training Agency, Sheffield.
Evans, D. and Leighton, L. (1989) Some empirical aspects of entrepreneurship, *Economic Review*, 79, pp. 519-535.
Fass, M. and Scothorne, R. (1990) *The Vital Economy: Integrating Training and Enterprise*, Abbeystrand, Edinburgh.
Fay, S. (1988) The acceptable faces of Thatcherism, *Business*, December.
FESC (1989) *A Guide to Work Based Learning Terms*, Further Education Staff College, HMSO, London.
FEU (1987) *Quality in NAFE*, Further Education Unit, DES, London.
Field, G. (1988) The focussing of LENs, *Employment Gazette*, August, pp. 448-452.
Field, R. (1990) The business role in local economic regeneration: the Sheffield story, in R.J. Bennett *et al.* (eds.) *Local Economic Development in Britain and Germany*, pp. 49-64, Anglo-German Foundation, London.
Finegold, D. and Soskice, D. (1988) The future of training in Britain: analysis and prescription, *Oxford Review of Economic Policy*, 4, 3, pp. 21-53.
Finegold, D. *et al.* (1990) *A British Baccalaureate*, Education and Training Paper No. 1, Institute for Public Policy Research, London.
Foley, P. (1991) The impact of the World Student Games on Sheffield, *Environment and Planning C: Government and Policy*, 9, pp. 65-78.
Forn, W.H. and Miller, D. (1960) *Industry, Labour and Community*, Harper and Row, New York.
Forster, N. (1983) *Chambers of Commerce: A Comparative Study of their Role in the UK and in other EEC Countries*, IAL Consultants, London.
Fosler, R.S. and Berger, R.A. (eds.) (1982) *Public-Private Partnerships in American Cities: Seven Case Studies*, Lexington Books, Lexington, Mass.
Foster, P. (1990) *Models for Partnership: A Report of a Project on the Development of Education Industry Partnerships*, Education Department, West Sussex County Council.
Franko, L.G. and Stephenson, S. (1982) The micro picture: corporate and sectoral developments, pp. 193-219 in L. Turner and N. McMullen (eds.) *The Newly Industrialising Countries: Trade and Adjustment*, Allen and Unwin, London.
Freeman, C., Patel, P. and Pavitt, K. (eds.) (1991) *Technology and the Future of Europe*, Francis Pinter, London.
Freeman, C.C., Foraro, T.J., Bloomberg, W. and Sunshine, M.M. (1963) Locating leaders in local communities: a comparison of some alternative approaches, *American Sociological Review*, 28, pp. 791-798.

Friedland, R. (1982) *Power and Crisis in the City: Corporations, Unions and Urban Policy*, Macmillan, London.

Friedman, M. (1970) *Capitalism and Freedom*, Chicago University Press, Chicago.

Fröhler, L. (1965) *Zur Abgrenzung von Handwerk und Industrie: der dynamische Handwerksbegrift in der deutschen Rechtsprechung*, Handwerksrechtinstitut, München.

Funnell, P. and Müller, D. (1991) *Vocational Education and the Challenge of Europe*, Kogan Page, London.

Gallagher, E.C. and Stewart, H. (1986) Jobs and the business life cycle in the UK, *Applied Economics*, 18, pp. 875-900.

Geroski, P.A. and Schwalbach, J. (1990) *Entry and Market Contestibility: An International Comparison*, SSRC, Berlin.

Gertler, M.S. (1988) The limits of flexibility, comments on the post-Fordist vision of productivity and its geography, *Transactions, Institute of British Geographers*, NS 13, pp. 419-432.

Gibbs, P.S. (1983) Enterprise agencies, *The Planner*, 69 (5), pp. 153-154.

Gleeson, D. (1989) *The Paradox of Training: Making Progress out of Crisis*, Open University Press, Milton Keynes.

Glennerster, H. (1985) *Paying for Welfare*, Basil Blackwell, Oxford.

Goldsmith, W. and Ritchie, B. (1987) *The New Elite: Britain's Top Executives*, Weidenfeld and Nicholson, London.

Grayson, D. (1990) *Small Business Megatrends*, Business in the Community, London.

Greenleaf, W.H. (1983a) *The British Political Tradition 1: The Rise of Collectivism*, Methuen, London.

Greenleaf, W.H. (1983b) *The British Political Tradition 2: The Ideological Heritage*, Methuen, London.

Greenleaf, W.H. (1987) *The British Political Tradition 3: A Much Governed Nation*, Methuen, London.

Gudgin, G. (1978) *Industrial Location Processes and Regional Employment Growth*, Saxon House, Farnborough.

Gulick, L.H. and Urwick, L. (1937) *Papers on the Science of Administration*, Institute of Public Administration, New York.

Gunnell, J. (1990) Enterprise Boards: An Inside View, pp. 128-155 in M. Campbell (ed.) *Local Economic Policy*, Cassell, London.

Gurr, T. and King, D. (1987) *The State and the City*, Macmillan, London.

Gyford, J. (1985) *The Politics of Local Socialism*, Allen and Unwin, London.

Hakim, C. (1987) Trends in the flexible workforce, *Department of Employment Gazette*, 95, pp. 549-560.

Hall, P. (ed.) (1986) *Technology, Innovation and Economic Policy*, Philip Allan, Oxford.

Hall, P., Breheny, M., McQuaid, R. and Hart, D. (1987) *Western Sunrise: The Genesis and the Growth of Britain's Major High-Tech Corridor*, Allen and Unwin, London.

Hall, P. and Preston, P. (1988) *The Carrier Wave: New Information Technology and the Geography of Innovation 1846-2003*, Unwin Hyman, London.

Hamilton, F.E.I. (ed.) (1976) *Contemporary Industrialisation: Spatial Analysis and Regional Development*, Longmans, London.

Hamilton, R.T. (1989) Unemployment and business formation rates: reconciling time-series and cross-section evidence, *Environment and Planning A*, 21, pp. 249-355.

Hampden-Turner, L. (1984) *Gentlemen and Tradesmen: The Value of Economic Catastrophe*, Gower, London.

Handy, C. (1985) *The Future of Work*, Penguin, London.

Handy, C. (1989) *The Age of Unreason*, Business Books, London.

Handy, C. and Aitken, R. (1986) *Understanding Schools as Organisations*, Penguin, London.

Hannah, L. (1990) *Human Capital Flows and Business Efficiency: Sense and Nonsense in the Wiener Thesis*, Centre for Economic Performance Working Paper, London School of Economics.

Harding, A. (1990) Public-private partnerships in urban regeneration, pp. 108-127 in M. Campbell (ed.) *Local Economic Policy*, Cassell, London.

Harding, A. (1991) The rise of urban growth coalitions, UK-style?, *Environment and Planning C: Government and Policy*, 9, pp. 295-318.

Hargroves, J.S. (1987) The Boston Compact: facing the challenge of school dropouts, *Education and Urban Society*, 19, pp. 303-310.

Harrison, R.T. and Mason, C.M. (1986) The regional impact of the Small Firms Loan Guarantee Scheme in the United Kingdom, *Regional Studies*, 20, pp. 535-550.

Harvey-Jones, J. (1988) *Making it Happen: Reflections on Leadership*, Collins, London.

Hawkins, K. (1985) The role of local authorities in economic development, *Local Government Studies*, 11 (3), pp. 1-7.

Hebbert, M. (1991) The borough effect in London's geography, Chapter 11, pp. 191-206 in K. Hoggart and D. Green (eds.) *London: A New Metropolitan Geography*, Edward Arnold, London.

Heller, F.A. (1973) Leadership, decision-making and contingency theory, *Industrial Relations*, 12, pp. 183-199.

Hendry, J. (1990) *Innovating for Failure: Government Policy and the Early British Computer Industry*, MIT Press, Cambridge, Mass.

Hepworth, M. (1989) *Geography of the Information Economy*, Belhaven, London.

Heuer, H. (1985) *Bald mehr als 1000 Technologiezentren*, Berichte des Deutschen Instituts für Urbanistik, 3, pp. 3-5.

Hickman, L. (ed.) (1981) *Technology and Human Affairs*, Mosby, St Louis.

Hicks, W.K. (1947) *Public Finance*, Nisbet, London.

Himmelfarb, G. (1984) *The Idea of Poverty: England in the Early Industrial Age*, Alfred Knopf, New York.

Hinckley, S.M., Pole, C.J., Sims, D. and Storey, S.M. (1987) *The TVEI Experience: A Summary*, Manpower Services Commission, Sheffield.

HM Government (1931) *Report of the Committee on Finance and Industry*, Cmnd 3897 (Macmillan Report), HMSO, London.

HM Government (1959) *Report of the Committee on the Making of the Monetary System*, Cmnd 827 (Radcliffe Report), HMSO, London.

HM Government (1979) *Organic Change in Local Government*, Cmnd 7457, HMSO, London.

HM Government (1984) *Training for Jobs*, Cmnd 9135, HMSO, London.

HM Government (1988) *Employment for the 1990s*, White Paper, Cm 540, HMSO, London.

HM Government (1992) *People, Jobs and Opportunity*, Cm 1810, HMSO, London.

HMI (1990) *The Teaching and Learning of Reading in Primary Schools*, Her Majesty's Inspectorate for Schools, London.

HMI (1991) *Report on NVQs*, Her Majesty's Inspectorate for Schools, London.

HM Treasury (1991) *Competing on Quality*, Cm 1730, HMSO, London.

HoC (1988) *The Employment Effects of Urban Development Corporations*, House of Commons Papers 327-I, Commons Employment Committee, Third Report Session 1987-88, HMSO, London.

Hoggart, R. (1971) *The Uses of Literacy: Aspects of Working Class Life, with Special Reference to Publications and Entertainments*, Chatto and Windus, London.

Holland, S. (1976) *Capital Versus the Regions*, Macmillan, London.

House of Lords (1990) *A Community Framework for R&D*, House of Lords Papers 66 (1988-90), HMSO, London.

House of Lords (1991) *Science Policy and the European Dimension*, House of Lords Papers (1990-91), HMSO, London.

Howarth, M. (1991) *Britain's Educational Reform: a comparison with Japan*, Routledge, London.

Howells, J. (1987) *Economic, Technological and Locational Trends in European Services*, Gower, Aldershot.

Howells, J. (1989) Externalisation and the formation of new industrial operations: a neglected dimension in the dynamics of industrial location, *Area*, 21, pp. 289-299.

Huppes, T. (1990) *The Western Edge: Work and Management in the Information Age*, Kluwer, Dordrecht.

ILEA (1987a) *The London Compact - East London Phase: Monitoring the School and Pupil Goals*, Paper 84, Inner London Education Authority, Research and Statistics Branch, London.

ILEA (1987b) *16-19 Participation Rates*, RS1095/86, Inner London Education Authority, Research and Statistics Branch, London.

ILEA (1987c) *Post-School Education: Labour Market Trends and Issues*, RS1140/87, Inner London Education Authority, Research and Statistics Branch, London.

Illersic, A.R. (1962) *Parliament of Commerce*, Association of British Chambers of Commerce and Newman Neame.

IMS (1986) *Changing Patterns of Work*, Institute of Manpower Studies for National Economic Development Office, London.

IPM (1981) *What Do UK Employers Look for in School Leavers?*, Institute of Personnel Management, London.

IPM (1984a) *TVEI: Recommendations for an Improved School/Work Liaison*, Institute of Personnel Management, London.

IPM (1984b) *Schools and the World of Work: What do Employers Look for in School Leavers?*, Institute of Personnel Management, London.

Johnson, C. (1982) *MITI and the Japanese Miracle: The Growth of Industrial Policy 1925-1976*, Stanford University Press, Stanford, California.

Johnson, P. (1990) *Ageing and Economic Performance*, Centre for Economic Performance Discussion Paper 34, London School of Economics.

Johnson, P.S. and Cathcart, D.G. (1979) The founders of new manufacturing firms: a note on the size of their "incubator" plants, *Journal of Industrial Economics*, 28, pp. 219-224.

Jones, D. (1985) Efficient effectiveness in colleges - a practical approach, *Coombe Lodge Report*, 18, pp. 138-150.

Jones, D. (1990) *The Machine that Changed the World*, Maxwell Macmillan, London.

JURUE (1981) *Assessing the Cost Effectiveness of Local Economic Initiatives*, Joint Unit for Research on the Urban Environment, Birmingham.

JURUE (1983) *An Evaluation of Development Commission in Selected Areas: Summary Report*, Joint Unit for Research on the Urban Environment, Birmingham.

Kanter, R.M. (1981) *The Change Masters: Corporate Entrepreneurs at Work*, Allen and Unwin, London.

Keeble, D., Bryson, J. and Wood, P.A. (1990) *Small Firms, Business Services Growth and Regional Development in the UK: Some Empirical Findings*, Working Paper No. 7, Small Business Research Centre, University of Cambridge.

Keeble, D.E. and Kelly, T. (1988) The regional distribution of NTBPFs in Britain, pp. 149-171 in AGF (eds.) *New Technology-Based Firms in Britain and Germany*, Anglo-German Foundation, London and Bonn.

Keeble, D. and Wever, E. (eds.) (1986) *New Firms and Regional Development in Europe*, Croom Helm, London.

Keep, E. and Mayhew, K. (1988) The assessment: education, training and economic performance, *Oxford Review of Economic Policy*, 4, 3, pp. i-xv.

Kellner, P. and Lord Crowther-Hunt (1980) *The Civil Servants*, Macdonald and Jane, London.

Kindleberger, C.P. (1969) *American Business Abroad*, Yale University Press, New Haven.

King, B. (1989) *Recent Developments in Education-Business Partnerships*, paper given on teachers course, Lincoln.

King, R. (1985) Corporatism and the local economy, pp. 203-228 in W. Grant (ed.) *The Political Economy of Corporatism*, Macmillan, London.

Kirby, K. (1989a) *Education-Business Partnerships: Lessons from America*, Training Agency, Sheffield.

Kirby, K. (1989b) Pick your partners, *Education*, 7 July, pp. 7-8.

Knox, J. and Ashworth, M. (1985) *An Introduction to Corporate Philanthropy*, Charities Aid Foundation and British Institute of Management, London.

Kondratieff, N.D. (1926) *The Long Wave Cycle*, (edition of 1984), Richardson and Snyder, New York.

Kornai, J. (1980) *The Economy of Shortage*, Magnetö, Budapest.

Kozmetsky, G., Gill, M. and Smilor, R. (1985) *Financing and Managing Fast-Growth Companies: The Venture Capital Process*, Lexington Books, Lexington, Mass.

Lammers, C.J. (1967) Power and participation in formal organisations, *American Journal of Sociology*, 23, pp. 201-216.

Lane, C. (1989) *Management and Labour in Europe: The Industrial Enterprise in Germany, Britain and France*, Edward Elgar, London.

Lawless, P. (1988) Enterprise Boards: evolution and critique, *Planning Outlook*, 31, pp. 13-18.

Lawton, D. (1982) *The End of the 'Secret Garden'?: A Study in the Politics of the Curriculum*, 2nd edn, Institute of Education, University of London.

Lawton, D. (1989) *Education, Culture and the National Curriculum*, Hodder and Stoughton, London.

Layard, R. and Nickell, S. (1985) The causes of British unemployment, *National Institute Economic Review*, III, pp. 62-85.

LEG (1989) *London Employers' Group Report*, Department of Employment, London.

LEL (1986) *The Regional Alternative for Jobs and Industry*, Enterprise Boards Joint Publication (LEL, GLEB, MEB, WMEB, WYEB), Lancashire Enterprise Ltd, Preston.

LEN (1987) *A Foundation for the Future*, UK Network Head Office, Sheffield.

Lever, W. and Moore, C. (1986) *The City in Transition: Policies and Agencies for the Economic Regeneration of Clydeside*, Clarendon Press, Oxford.

Linzey, E. (1990) *The Use of Procurement Strategies*, paper presented at London School of Economics seminar on Management and Leadership of Local Economies, September 1990, London.

Lloyd, P.E. and Mason, C.M. (1984) Spatial variations in new firm formation in the UK: comparative evidence, *Regional Studies*, 18, pp. 207-220.

Logan, J. and Molotch, H. (1987) *Urban Failures: The Political Economy of Place*, University of California Press, Berkeley.

Lorenz, E. (1991) *Economic Decline in Britain: The Shipbuilding Industry 1890-1970*, Clarendon Press, Oxford.

Macey, R. (1982) *Job Generation in British Manufacturing Industry: Employment Change by Size of Establishment and by Region*, Department of Industry Regional Research Series No. 4, HMSO, London.

Mackenzie, D. (1991) *Inventing Accuracy: A Historical Sociology of Nuclear Missile Guidance*, MIT Press, Cambridge, Mass.

Mackintosh, I. (1987) *Sunrise Europe*, Basil Blackwell, Oxford.

Maclure, S. (1988) *Education Re-formed: A Guide to the Education Reform Act, 1988*, Hodder and Stoughton, London.

Main, D. (1989) Training and Enterprise Councils: an agenda for action, in *TECs and VET: Regional Studies*, 24, pp. 69-71.

Malecki, E.J. and Nijkamp, P. (1988) Technology and regional development: some thoughts on policy, *Environment and Planning C: Government and Policy*, 6, pp. 383-400.

Malinvaud, E. (1977) *The Theory of Unemployment Reconsidered*, Basil Blackwell, Oxford.

Mansfield, E. (1962) Entry, Gibrats Law, innovation and growth of firms, *American Economic Review*, 52, pp. 1023-1051.

Mansfield, E. (1982) *Technology Transfer, Productivity and Economic Policy*, W.W. Norton, New York.

Marsden, C. (1991) *Education and Business: A Vision for the Partnership*, BP Education Affairs Division, London.

Marshall, N. (1985) Technological change and local economic strategy in the West Midlands, *Regional Studies*, 19, pp. 570-578.

Martin, R. (1989) The growth and geographical anatomy of venture capitalism in the United Kingdom, *Regional Studies*, 23, pp. 389-403.

Martinos, H. (1989) *The Management of Local Employment Development Strategies*, LRDP, London.

Mason, C. (1987) Venture capital in the United Kingdom: A geographical perspective, *National Westminster Quarterly Review*, May, pp. 47-59.

Mason, C. (1989) Explaining recent trends in new firm formation in the UK: some evidence from South Hampshire, *Regional Studies*, 23, pp. 331-346.

Mason, C., Harrison, J. and Harrison, R. (1988) *Closing the Equity Gap? An Assessment of the Business Expansion Scheme*, Small Business Research Trust, London.

Mason, C.M. and Harrison, R.T. (1989) Small firms policy and the 'north-south' divide in the United Kingdom: the case of the Business Expansion Scheme, *Transactions, Institute of British Geographers*, NS, 14, pp. 37-58.

Mason, C. and Harrison, R. (1991) Informal investors, *CBI Smaller Firms' Economic Report*, January, pp. 12-18, CBI, London.

Mason, C. and Harrison, R. (1992) A strategy for closing the small firms' financing gap in Britain, *Environment and Planning C: Government and Policy*.

Mawson, J. and Miller, D. (1986) Interventionist approaches to local employment and economic development: the experience of Labour local authorities, pp. 143-199 in V. Hausner (ed.) *Critical Issues in Urban Economic Development*, Vol. 1, Clarendon Press, Oxford.

McInnis, J. (1987) *Thatcherism at Work*, Open University Press, Milton Keynes.

McKean, B. and Coulson, A. (1987) Enterprise Boards and some issues raised by taking equity and loan stock in major companies, *Regional Studies*, 21, pp. 373-384.

McKeown, P. (1987) County councils and economic development in the early 1980s, *Local Government Studies*, 13 (6), pp. 37-49.

McKleish, H. (1991) Labour's approach to TECs, *Training Tomorrow*, September, pp. 5-8.

McPherson, A. and Raab, C.D. (1988) *Governing Education: A Sociology of Policy since 1945*, Edinburgh University Press, Edinburgh.

Meade, J.F. (1982) *Wage-Fixing*, Allen and Unwin, London.

Mensch, G. (1979) *Stalemate in Technology*, Ballinger, Cambridge, Mass.

Merchant, K. (1990) Only a poor cousin, *Financial Times Venture Capital Survey*, 26 November, p. 2.

Metcalf, D. (1988) *Trade Unions and Economic Performance: The British Evidence*, Centre for Urban Economics, London School of Economics.

Metcalf, H., Pearson, R. and Martin, R. (1989) *Stimulating Jobs: The Charitable Role of Companies*, Institute of Manpower Studies, University of Sussex.

Meyer-Krahmer, F. (1985) Innovation behaviour and regional indigenous potential, *Regional Studies*, 19, pp. 523-534.

Middlemas, K. (1990) *Power, Competition and the State: Vol. 1: Britain in Search of Balance 1940-61; Vol. 2: Treats to the Postwar Settlement in Britain 1961-74; Vol. 3: Power Competition and the State*, Macmillan, London.

Mills, L. and Young, K. (1986) Local authorities and economic development: a preliminary analysis, in V.A. Hausner (ed.) *Critical Issues in Urban Economic Development*, Clarendon Press, Oxford.

Minford, P. (1983) Labour market equilibrium in an open economy, *Oxford Economic Papers*, 35, pp. 207-244.

MINTEL (1990) *The Employee Report*, Mintel, London.

Monk, S. (1991) Job creation and job displacement: the impact of enterprise board investment on firms in the UK, *Regional Studies*, 25, pp. 355-362.

Monnet, J. (1978) *Memoirs*, Collins, London.

More, C. (1980) *Skills and the English Working Class, 1870-1914*, Croom Helm, London.

Morison, H. (1987) *The Regeneration of Local Economies*, Clarendon Press, Oxford.

Morita, A., Reingold, E.W. and Shimomura, M. (1987) *Made in Japan*, Collins, London.

Moyes, A. and Westhead, P. (1990) Environments for new firm formation in Great Britain, *Regional Studies*, 24, pp. 123-136.

MSC (1985) *A Challenge to Complacency: Changing Attitudes to Training*, Manpower Services Commission, and National Economic Development Office.

MSC (1988) *Compacts: Guidelines for MSC Support*, Manpower Services Commission, Sheffield.

MSC/ABCC (1986) *National Collaborative Project: Final Report*, Manpower Services Commission and Association of British Chambers of Commerce.

MSC/NEDC/BIM (1989) *The Making of Managers: A Report on Management Education, Training and Development in the USA, West Germany, France, Japan and the UK*, Manpower Services Commission, National Economic Development Council and British Institute of Management, NEDO, London.

Müller, D. and Funnell, P. (1991) *Delivering Quality in Vocational Education*, Kogan Page, London.

Murray, C. (1984) *Losing Ground: American Social Policy 1950-1980*, Basic Books, New York.

Murray, C. (1989) Underclass: a disaster in the making, *Sunday Times Magazine*, 26 November, pp. 26-45.

NAO (1991) *The Implementation and Development of the Technical and Vocational Education Initiatives*, National Audit Office, HMSO, London.

NEDC (1991) *Partners for the Long Term: Lessons from the Success of Germany and Japan*, National Economic Development Council, London.

NEDO (1986a) *External Finance for Small Firms*, National Economic Development Office, London.

NEDO (1986b) *Venture Capital in the UK and its Impact on the Small Business Sector*, National Economic Development Office, London.

NEDO (1991) *Training and Competitiveness*, National Economic Development Office, Kogan Page, London.

NEDO/MSC (1984) *Competence and Competition: Training and Education in the Federal Republic of Germany, the United States and Japan*, National Economic Development Office, London.

Network Memo (1988) *Local Employment Networks: A Review and Guide for Employers*, Issue 5 supplement, UK LEN Network Head Office, Sheffield.

NFER (1990) *Standards of Reading of Seven Year Old Children*, National Foundation for Educational Research for DES, London.

Nicholson, C. (1988) Local budgetary development, relative efficiency and local fiscal crisis, *Regional Studies*, 22, pp. 241-245.

Nickell, S., Wadhwani, S. and Wall, M. (1991) *Productivity Growth in UK Companies 1975-86*, Centre for Economic Performance, London School of Economics.

Nijkamp, P., van der Mark, R. and Alsters, T. (1988) Evaluation of regional incubator profiles for small and medium sized enterprises, *Regional Studies*, 22, pp. 95-105.

Nordlinger, E. (1981) *On the Autonomy of the Democratic State*, Harvard University Press, Cambridge, Mass.

North, J. (ed.) (1987) *The GCSE: An Examination*, Claridge Press, London.

Northcott, J., Kretsch, W., de Lestopis, B. and Rogers, P. (1985) *Micro-Electronics in Industry. An International Comparison: Britain, France and Germany*, Policy Studies Institute, London.

Norton, M. (1989) *Raising Money from Industry*, Directory of Social Change, London.

Nuttall, D., West, A, and Varlaam, A. (1991) *Pupil Goal Achievement in the Inner London Compacts 1989-1990*, LSE Centre for Educational Research, for London Education Business Partnership, London.

Oakey, R.P. (1984) *High Technology Small Firms*, St Martins Press, New York.

Oakey, R., Thwaites, A.T. and Nash, P.A. (1980) Regional distribution of innovative manufacturing establishments in Britain, *Regional Studies*, 14, pp. 235-254.

Oakley, B. and Owen, K. (1990) *Alvey: Britain's Strategic Computing Initiative*, MIT Press, Cambridge, Mass.

OECD (1985) Employment in small and large firms: where have the jobs come from? *OECD Economic Outlook*, September, pp. 64-82.

OECD (1986a) *Venture Capital: Context, Development and Policies*, Organisation for Economic Cooperation and Development, Paris.

OECD (1986b) *OECD Employment Outlook*, Organisation for Economic Cooperation and Development, Paris.

OECD (1987) *Managing and Financing Urban Services*, Organisation for Economic Cooperation and Development, Paris.

OECD (1989) *International Direct Investment and the New Economic Environment*, Organisation for Economic Cooperation and Development, Paris.

OECD (1991) *Partners in Education: The New Partnership Between Business and Schools*, Organisation for Economic Cooperation and Development, Paris.

O'Farrell, P.N. and Hitchens, D.M. (1989) The competitiveness and performance of small manufacturing firms: an analysis of matched pairs in Scotland and England, *Environment and Planning A*, 21, pp. 1241-1263.

O'Farrell, P.N. and Hitchens, D.M. (1990) Producer services and regional development: key conceptual issues of taxonomy and quality measurement, *Regional Studies*, 24, pp. 163-172.

Oliver, N. and Wilkinson, B. (1988) *The Japanisation of British Industry*, Basil Blackwell, Oxford.

Olson, M. (1982) *The Rise and Decline of Nations: Economic Growth, Stagflation and Social Rigidities*, Yale University Press, New Haven.

Oxenfeld, A.R. (1943) *New Firms and Free Enterprise*, American Council for Public Affairs, Washington D.C.

PA (1989) *Manufacturing into the 1990s*, Report by PA Consultancy Group to Department of Trade and Industry, HMSO, London.

Parkinson, M. and Judd, D. (eds.) (1990) *Leadership and Urban Regeneration*, Sage, London.

Parry, G., Moyser, G. and Day, N. (1992) *Political Participation and Democracy in Britain*, Cambridge University Press, Cambridge.

Paxman, J. (1990) *Friends in High Places: Who Runs Britain?*, Michael Joseph, London.

Peters, T. (1987) *Thriving on Chaos*, Harper and Row, London.

Peters, T. (1990) *Towards the Entrepreneurial and Empowering Organisation*, Lecture presentation, TRG/3i/The Economist, London.

Peters, T. and Waterman, R.H. (1982) *In Search of Excellence*, Harper and Row, London.

Peterson, P.E. (1981) *City Limits*, University of Chicago Press, Chicago.

Pettigrew, A. and Whipp, J. (1991) *Managing Change for Competitive Success*, Warwick Business School.

Pilkington, A. (1984) Business in the Community: where do we go from here?, *Policy Studies*, 4 (4), pp. 12-22.

Pinch, S.P., Mason, C.M. and Witt, S.J.G. (1989) Labour flexibility and industrial restructuring in the UK 'Sunbelt': the case of Southampton, *Transactions, Institute of British Geographers*, NS, 14, pp. 418-434.

Piore, M.J. and Sabel, C.F. (1984) *The Second Industrial Divide: Possibilities for Prosperity*, Basic Books, New York.

Pollert, A. (1987) The 'flexible firm': a model in search of reality (or a policy in search of a practice), *Warwick Papers in Industrial Relations*, No. 19, University of Warwick.

Porter, M.E. (1980) *Competitive Strategy: Techniques for Analysing Industries and Competitors*, Free Press, New York.

Porter, M.E. (1985) *Competitive Advantage: Creating and Sustaining Superior Performance*, Free Press, New York.

Porter, M.E. (1987) From competitive advantage to corporate strategy, *Harvard Business Review*, 4, July-August, pp. 149-160.

Porter, M.E. (1990) *The Competitive Advantage of Nations*, Macmillan, London.

Prais, S.J. (1976) *The Evolution of Giant Firms in Britain*, Cambridge University Press, Cambridge.

Prais, S.J. (1987) Education for productivity: comparisons of Japanese and English schooling and vocational preparation, *National Institute Economic Review*, February.

Pratt, G. (1990) Venture capital in the United Kingdom, *Bank of England Quarterly Review*, Vol. 30, pp. 78-83.

Premus, R. (1988) US technology policies and their regional effects, *Environment and Planning C: Government and Policy*, 6, pp. 441-448.

PW (1991) *Keys to Growth: For Owner Managers Seeking to Expand*, Price Waterhouse for the Department of Employment, London.

Rae, J. (1989) *Too Little, Too Late? The challenges that still face British education*, Collins, London.

Raffe, D. (1989) Making the gift horse jump the hurdles: the impact of the TVEI pilot on the first Scottish cohort, *British Journal of Education and Work*, 2, 3, pp. 5-15.

Rajan, A. (1990) *1992- A Zero Sum Game*, Industrial Society, London.

Ramsdale, P. and Capon, S. (1986) *Small Factories and Economic Development*, Gower, Aldershot.

Reid, R.P. (1986) *The Role of Industry in Society*, Shell lecture, Shell UK Ltd, London.

Reid, R.P. (1989) *Management Charter Initiative - The Way Ahead*, speech at CBI conference, 8 November 1989.

Rhodes, R.A.W. (1981) *Control and Power in Central-Local Relations*, Gower, Aldershot.

Rosenberg, N. and Mowery, D. (1990) *Technology in the Pursuit of Economic Growth*, Cambridge University Press, Cambridge.

Rossano, K.R. (1985) *A Partnership for Excellence: The Boston Public Schools and Boston Business Community*, Boston Chamber of Commerce, Boston, Mass.

Rothwell, R. and Zegveld, W. (1982) *Innovation and the Small and Medium Sized Firms*, Frances Pinter, London.

Rothwell, R. and Zegveld, W. (1985) *Reindustrialisation and Technology*, Longman, London.

Roussel, P., Saad, K. and Erikson, T. (1991) *Third Generation R&D*, Harvard Business School Press, Cambridge, Mass.

Rubery, J., Tarling, R. and Wilkinson, F. (1987) Flexibility, marketing and the organisation of production, *Labour and Society*, 12, pp. 131-151.

Rubinstein, W.A. (1986) Education and social origins of British elites, 1880-1970, *Past and Present*, 112, pp. 163-207.

Sadler, P. (1989) Assessment and accreditation: TVEI, CPVE and external examinations, pp. 239-255 in D. Warwick (ed.) *Linking Schools and Industry*, Basil Blackwell, Oxford.

Sampson, A. (1982) *The Changing Anatomy of Britain*, Hodder and Stoughton, London.

Sanderson, M. (1972) *The Universities and British Industry 1850-1970*, Routledge and Kegan Paul, London.

Saunders, M. and Halpin, D. (1990) The TVEI and the National Curriculum, in CSTIT, School of Education, Univeristy of Exeter, *TVEI and the National Curriculum: Proceedings of a National Conference*.

Sawyer, G.C. (1979) *Business and Society: Managing Social Impact*, Houghton Mifflin, London.

Schumpeter, J.A. (1939) *Business Cycles*, McGraw-Hill, New York.

Schumpeter, J.A. (1942) *Capitalism, Socialism and Democracy*, Harper, New York.

SCIP (undated) *SCIP: Information for Education*, School Curriculum Industry Partnership, London.

SCSST / SATRO (1988) *Review of Activities 1988*, Science and Technology Regional Organisation.

Seabrook, J. (1985) *Landscapes of Poverty*, Basil Blackwell, Oxford.

Segal, N.S. (1985) The Cambridge phenomenon, *Regional Studies*, 19, pp. 563-570.

Sellgren, J. (1987) Local economic development and local initiatives in the mid-1980s: an analysis of the Local Economic Development Information Service, *Local Government Studies*, 13/6, pp. 51-68.

Sellgren, J. (1988) Assisting local economies: an assessment of emerging patterns of local authority economic development activities, pp. 232-264 in D.C. Gibbs (ed.) *Government Policy and Industrial Change*, Croom Helm, London.

Sellgren, J. (1989) *Local Economic Development in Great Britain: An Evolving Local Government Role*, unpublished PhD, University of London.

SEPSU (1991) *The Contract Research Business in the UK*, Science and Engineering Policy Studies Unit, London.

Servan-Schreiber, J.-J (1967) *The American Challenge*, Haughton Mifflin, New York.

SI (1990) *Computer Integrated Manufacture for the Engineering Industry*, Strathclyde Institute, Glasgow.

Sims, D. (1988) School-industry links: TVEI and strategy development, in *TVEI Evaluation Report 4: Perspectives on TVEI: A Set of Papers Exploring Management Themes within TVEI*, NFER/Training Commission.

Singleton, J. (1991) *Lancashire on the Scrapheap: The Cotton Industry 1945-1970*, Oxford University Press/Pasold Research Fund, Oxford.

SQW (1985) *The Cambridge Phenomenon: The Growth of High Technology Industry in a University Town*, Segal Quince Wicksteed, Cambridge.

SQW (1988) *Encouraging Small Business Start-Up and Growth: Creating a Supportive Local Environment*, Segal Quince Wicksteed, HMSO, London.

Stahl, M. and Bounds, G. (eds.) (1991) *Competing Globally Through Customer Value*, Quorum Books, London.

Stanley, D. (1988) *Local Employer Networks Project: Directors' Report*, UK Network Head Office, Sheffield.

Stanworth, P. and Giddens, A. (1974) *Elites and Power in British Society*, Cambridge University Press, Cambridge.

Steedman, H. and Wagner, K. (1987) *Machinery, Production Organisation and Skills: Kitchen Manufacture in Britain and Germany*, Discussion Paper No. 117, NIESR, London.

Stevenson, H. (1990) *Banks and Venture Capital*, presentation at ABCC / BiTC conference, 26 March.

Stiglitz, J. (1975) The theory of screening, education and the distribution of income, *American Economic Review*, 65, pp. 283-300.

Stohr, W. (ed.) (1990) *Global Challenge and Local Response*, Mansell, London.

Storey, D.J. (1982) *Entrepreneurship and the New Firm*, Croom Helm, London.

Storey, D.J. and Johnson, S. (1987a) *Job Generation and Labour Market Change*, Macmillan, London.

Storey, D.J. and Johnson, S. (1987b) *Are Small Firms the Answer to Unemployment?*, Employment Institute, London.

Storey, S.M., Pole, C.J. and Sims, D. (1986) *The Management of TVEI*, Manpower Services Commission, Sheffield.

Stratton, C.N. (1989) TECs and PICs: the key issues which lie ahead, *Regional Studies*, 24, pp. 70-74.

Streeck, W. (1989) The territorial organisation of interests and the logics of associative action: the case of *Handwerk* organisation in West Germany, in W.D. Coleman and H.J. Jaak (eds.) *Regionalism, Business Interests and Public Policy*, Sage, London.

Sweeney, G.P. (1987) *Innovation, Entrepreneurs and Regional Development*, Francis Pinter, London.

TA (1988) *LENs: Case Studies in Five Areas*, a summary of findings from research carried out by Price Waterhouse and the Training Agency, Sheffield.

TA (1989a) *Training in Britain: A Study of Funding, Activity and Attitudes*, Training Agency, HMSO, London.

TA (1989b) *Training and Enterprise Councils: A Prospectus for the 1990s*, Training Agency, Sheffield.

TA (1989c) *Compacts: Guidelines for Applications for Development Funding*, Training Agency, Sheffield.

TA / DHS (1989) *Management Challenge for the 1990s*, Training Agency and Deloitte, Haskins and Sells, London.

Taubman, P. and Wales, T. (1973) Higher education, mental ability and screening, *Journal of Political Economy*, 81, pp. 28-53.

Taylor, F.M. (1911) *Shop Management*, Harper, London.

TC (1988) *The Compacts Development Handbook*, Training Commission, Sheffield.

Thomas, D. (1990) Reading between the lines, *Times Education Supplement*, 6 April, p. 21.

Thomas, H. (ed.) (1959) *The Establishment*, Anthony Bland, London.

Thompson, E.P. (1974) *The Making of the English Working Class*, Penguin, London.

Thompson, F.M.L. (1990) *The Cambridge Social History of Britain 1750-1950: Vol. 1: Regions and Communities; Vol. 2: People and their Environment; Vol. 3: Social Agencies and Institutions*, Cambridge University Press, Cambridge.

Thurley, K. and Wirdenius, H. (1989) *Towards a European Management*, Pitman, London.

Times Educational Supplement (1989) *Truancy*, 3 January.

Times Educational Supplement (1990a) *One in Three Confirms a Decline*, 6 July.

Times Educational Supplement (1990b) *Falls in Literacy May Soon Go Unnoticed*, 13 July.

Toffler, A. (1985) *The Adaptive Corporation*, Gower, Aldershot.

Towler, D. (1989) *The Management Education and Training Market for Small Firms: How to Make it Work Efficiently and Effectively*, unpublished MPhil thesis, University of Buckingham.

Travers, T. (1988) Local taxation and services: present and future, *Regional Studies*, 22, pp. 235-238.

Tschetter, J. (1987) Producer services industries; why are they growing so rapidly, *Monthly Labour Review*, 12, pp. 31-40.

TVEI (1988) *Profiles and Records of Achievement*, TVEI Developments 5, Training Agency, Sheffield.

TVEI (1989) *Education, Enterprise and Industry*, TVEI Developments 6, Training Agency, Sheffield.

TVEL (1990) What do employers want from education? Summary of Thames Valley Enterprise Ltd report, *Skills and Enterprise Briefing*, 3/91.

Twining, J. (1987) Updating and retraining initiatives in the UK, in J. Twining (ed.) *Vocational Education*, World Yearbook of Education 1987, Kogan Page, London.

Vazquez-Barquero, A. (1987) Local development and regional state in Spain, *Papers Regional Science Association*, 61, pp. 65-78.

Verba, S. and Vie, N. (1972) *Participation in America: Political Democracy and Social Equality*, Harper and Row, New York.

Verba, S., Vie, N.H. and Kim, J. (1978) *Participation and Political Equality: A Seven Nation Comparison*, Cambridge University Press, Cambridge.

Vittas, D. and Brown, R. (1982) *Bank Lending and Industrial Investment*, Banking Information Service, London.

Walker, D. (1983a) *Municipal Empire: The Townhalls and their Beneficiaries*, Maurice Temple Smith, Hounslow.

Walker, D. (1983b) Local interest and representation: the case of 'class' interest among Labour representatives in inner London, *Environment and Planning C: Government and Policy*, 1, pp. 342-346.

Wallace, I. (1990) *The Global Economic System*, Unwin Hyman, London.

Warwick, D. (ed.) (1989) *Linking Schools and Industry*, Blackwell, Oxford.

Webb, I. (1991) *Quest for Quality*, The Industrial Society, London.

Welton, J. and Evans, J. (1986) The development and implementation of special education policy: where did the 1981 Act fit in?, *Public Administration*, 64, pp. 209-227.

Wernet, W. (1965) *Zur Frage der Abgrenzung von Handwerk und Industrie: Die wirtschaftlichen Zusammen Länge in ihrer Bedeutung für die Beurteilung von Abgrenzungsfragen*, Handwerkswissenschaftliches Institut, Münster.

Westhead, P. (1989) A spatial analysis of new manufacturing firm formation in Wales, 1979-1983, *International Small Business Journal*, 7, pp. 44-68.

Westhead, P. and Moyes, T. (1991) *Reflections on Thatcher's Britain: Evidence from New Production Firm Registration 1980-88*, Imperial College Working Paper, London.

Wetzel, W.E. (1986) Informal risk capital: knowns and unknowns, in D.L. Sexton and R.W. Smilor (eds.) *The Art and Science of Entrepreneurship*, pp. 85-108, Ballinger, Cambridge, Mass.

Whipp, R. and Clark, P. (1986) *Innovation in the Auto Industry*, Francis Pinter, London.

Wiener, M. (1981) *English Culture and the Decline of the Industrial Spirit, 1850-1980*, Cambridge University Press, Cambridge.

Wicks, P.J. (1990) *Bureaucratic Change in Further Education*, unpublished PhD, London School of Economics, University of London.

Widdicombe, D. (1986) *The Conduct of Local Authority Business: Report of the Committee of Enquiry into the Conduct of Local Authority Business*, 1985-86, chaired by Mr. David Widdicombe QC, Cmnd 9797, HMSO, London.

Wilkie, T. (1991) *British Science and Politics since 1945*, Basil Blackwell, Oxford.

Williams, G. and Woodhall, M. (1979) *Independent Further Education*, Policy Studies Institute, Vol. 45, No. 587, London.

Wilks, S. and Wright, M. (eds.) (1987) *Comparative Government-Industry Relations: Western Europe, the United States and Japan*, Clarendon Press, Oxford.

Wilson Committee (1980) *Report of the Committee to Review the Functioning of Financial Institutions*, HMSO, London.

Wood, P.A. (1991) Flexible accumulation and the rise of business services, *Transactions, Institute of British Geographers*, NS, 16, pp. 160-172.

Worswick, G.D. (1985) *Education and Economic Performance*, Gower, Aldershot.

Wright, M., Coyne, T. and Lockley, H. (1984) Regional aspects of management buy-outs: some evidence, *Regional Studies*, 18, pp. 428-431.

Wrobel, B. (1979) *Organisation und Aufgaben kommunaler Wirtschaftsförderungs dienststellen u. -gesellschaften, Ergebnisse zweier Umfragen*, Deutsches Institut für Urbanistik, Berlin.

Young Enterprise (undated) *The Future Starts Here*, Young Enterprise, London.

Young, H. (1990) *One of Us: A Biography of Margaret Thatcher*, Macmillan, London.

Young, K. (1986) Economic development in Britain: a vacuum in central-local government relations, *Environment and Planning C: Government and Policy*, 4, pp. 439-450.

Young, M. and Willmott, P. (1957) *Family and Kinship in East London*, Routledge and Kegan Paul, London.

INDEX